Anthropological Approaches to Political Behavior

Frank McGlynn and Arthur Tuden

Editors

University of Pittsburgh Press

in cooperation with *Ethnology*

Published by the University of Pittsburgh Press, Pittsburgh, Pa.
15260
Copyright © 1991, University of Pittsburgh Press
Eurospan, London
Manufactured in the United States of America

The essays in this volume are reprinted by arrangement with the editors of *Ethnology* and have appeared in the following issues of that journal: "Ritual Resolution in Meta Legal Process," vol. 15, no. 3 (July 1976): 287–99; "The Place of the Big Man in Traditional Hagen Society in the Central Highlands of New Guinea," vol. 10, no. 2 (April 1971): 194–210; "Killers, Big Men, and Priests on Malaita: Reflections on a Melanesian Troika System," vol. 24, no. 4 (October 1985): 237–52; "All Talk and No Action? Saying and Doing in Kwanga Meetings," vol. 28, no. 2 (April 1989): 97–115; "Anuak Politics, Ecology, and the Origins of Shilluk Kingship," vol. 15, no. 2 (April 1976): 151–62; "Class, Politics, and Family Organization in San Cosme Xalostoc, Mexico" and "Strategies of Legitimation and the Aztec State," vol. 23, no. 4 (October 1984): 289–300, 301–14; "The Structure of Violence Among the Swat Pukhtun," vol. 20, no. 2 (April 1981): 147–56; "The Oaxacan Village President as Political Middleman," vol. 12, no. 4 (October 1973): 419–27; "Patronage and Community-Nation Relationships in Central Italy," 172–89; "Egalitarianism in an Autocratic Village in Israel," vol. 8, no. 1 (January 1969): 54–75; "Conflicting Political Models in a Swiss Commune," vol. 22, no. 1 (January 1983): 17–26; "Popular Devotions, Power, and Religious Regimes in Catholic Dutch Brabant," vol. 24, no. 3 (July 1985): 215–27; "From Cannibal Raid to Copra Kompani: Changing Patterns of Koriki Politics," 309–31; "Reciprocal Influence of Traditional and Democratic Leadership Roles on Ponape," vol. 8, no. 3 (July 1969): 278–91; "The Effects of Writing on the Cuna Political System," vol. 18, no. 1 (January 1979): 1–16.

Library of Congress Cataloging-in-Publication Data

Anthropological approaches to political behavior / Frank McGlynn,
Arthur Tuden, editors.
    p. cm.
    Includes bibliographical references.
    ISBN 0-8229-1162-0. — ISBN 0-8229-6094-X (pbk.)
    1. Political anthropology. 2. Power (Social sciences)
I. McGlynn, Frank (Frank S.) II. Tuden, Arthur.
GN492.A59   1991
306.2—dc20   90-50916
                                               CIP

A CIP catalogue record for this book is available from the British Library.

To Barbara, Sean, and Erin
with warm gratitude

Contents

Preface

THE FOLLOWING chapters and articles are in response to the class-room experience and were selected on the basis of the judgment of faculty, graduate students, and undergraduates. The articles highlight theoretical concerns in the field of political anthropology as initially published in the journal *Ethnology* and were accepted for publication in this volume based on student comments.

The introduction is an overview and discusses how the study of power is indeed the concern of political anthropology. We present the historical intellectual traditions in political anthropology and indicate the consistency as well as change in these concerns. We try to place current works within the framework of critical but constantly revised theoretical problems.

Further discussion focuses on the universal components of political action and some tentative comparative generalizations which draw on earlier studies and more recent fieldwork.

This book is not intended for the anthropologist alone. Presently a new view of political behavior is necessary. The professional researcher has been interested for far too long in problems and questions that are of concern only to a limited number of other like-minded scholars.

This book springs from twenty-five years of teaching courses in political anthropology to both undergraduates and graduate students. In the last five years, teaching in general has been difficult; teaching political anthropology has been even more strenuous. In the sixties, student interest in politics was unusually heightened. Concern over political activity made teaching a raucous, stimulating, and exciting activity, but in the seventies student behavior radically shifted. Student involvement in academic interests was not diminished, and concern for grades and completion of a degree was a major motivation. However, the obvious disinterest and disdain of political analysis was obvious. The general mood was illustrated by a cool apathy concerning the operation of politics, and students typically responded by almost completely withdrawing from engagement with the political process. Students and, if one interprets the precipitous voting decline in the United States, the general public appears indifferent or avoids politics.

This abdication of the political process and of interest in politics generally resulted in a view of society in which the political institution was missing. The reasons for this behavior were many, and the end result was disturbing. Political behavior, broadly defined, is the most consistent method of organizing people for group goals—to ignore it is to become unable to implement social change or adapt to a changing environment.

Hopefully, there are indications that this intellectual posture is changing. When we presented a version of this text to three undergraduate classes, the students were neither deeply involved nor passive. Their reaction seemed to be a selective interest in political materials. Some sections—primarily conflict, leadership, authority patterns, and ideology—aroused informed discussions, and there was a submerged awareness of how these universal components might affect their lives.

Acknowledgments

A WORK which clearly rests on earlier studies owes a debt to many individuals. We would like to acknowledge our thanks to the earlier scholars who initiated analyses of political behavior. To the editors of *Ethnology,* Professors L. Plotnicov and R. Scaglione, who carefully sifted through manuscripts, we pay our respects. But mostly we thank the undergraduate students of the University of Pittsburgh at Greensburg who took such interest and concern in evaluating and criticizing articles and their drafts: Joseph Ayes, David Barlock, Stephen Bottom, Brian Cassidy, James Christafano, Diane Chuboy, Mark Ciocco, Don Czekaj, Michael DeLuca, Sherry Dohey, Karen Findle, Robert Frye, George Grab, Evan Harr, Judith Harris, Walter Hough, Barry James, Roger Kral, Michael Kurela, William Lavelle, Kenneth Lipyance, Anthony Lollo, Scott Maust, Kelly Miller, Shawn Nedley, Neal Paulsen, Jill Pozzuto, Michael Rasco, Anna Ripple, Kassie Santos, Timothy Segina, Christopher Skatell, Mark Stewart, Frances Tartal, Tina Tlumac, William Uschock, David Voit, Joy Walmsley, Lee Walsh, Frank Winn, David Wolk, Rosemarie Wolford, and Linda Yeager.

To the graduate students of the Department of Anthropology and GSPIA who kept us aware of different levels of analysis and teaching: H. J. Freij, M. R. McDonald, N. Pant, Bruce Roberts, A. F. Saifuddin.

Special thanks to Gerry Enlow for rendering the final draft into clearer expositions. Obviously, however, the responsibility for the articles rests on the authors.

As several contributors have changed their institutional affiliations since their articles were first published in *Ethnology,* they and their current institutions or addresses are listed below:

Richard G. Dillon, Hobart and William Smith Colleges
Ernest Brandewie, 2604 Marine Street, South Bend, IN 46614
Roger M. Keesing, Australian National University
Karen J. Brison, East-West Center, University of Hawaii
L. Lewis Wall, Ahmadu Bello University, Nigeria

Donald V. Kurtz, University of Wisconsin-Milwaukee
Charles Lindholm, Boston University
Richard Miller, private enterprise
Phillip A. Dennis, Texas Tech University
Sydel F. Silverman, Wenner Gren Foundation
Harvey E. Goldberg, The Hebrew University
Daniela Weinberg, University of Nebraska
Mart Bax, Free University of Amsterdam
Robert F. Maher (deceased)
Daniel T. Hughes, Ohio State University
James Howe, Massachusetts Institute of Technology

*Anthropological
Approaches
to Political
Behavior*

Introduction

Anthropology and the Study of Power

P OWER IS IMMANENT in human affairs; by definition, human beings are political animals. Power in this sense cannot be reduced to a single social or political instance by either external or internal criteria. Whether or not the social grouping under scrutiny is collectively aggregated by conditions of gender, age, kinship, class, or hierarchy, power is present. In the most basic sense, power is what the political scientist Harold Lasswell defined as political: who gets what and how. Or, as the anthropologist Edmund Leach provocatively noted, all social and cultural change is a quest for power.

It is not our intention to foist a residual definition upon the already overloaded shoulders of humanity that is at once everything or nothing, but we do wish to emphasize that whatever we are as a species is necessarily manifested through the social and cultural experience of power. Power is not a domain but one of the essential forms and conditions of human relations. In addition to the fact that power is intrinsic to all social relations where asymmetry is present we wish to establish that the domain of power as studied by political anthropologists is inclusive at the societal level. Political anthropology is concerned with power in the socio-cultural context.

The relations of power need to be comprehended first at the level of the society under scrutiny. The initial question to be asked is, "What are the strategies or scarce resources within a culture that give definition and focus to Lasswell's aphorism and Leach's dictum?" Power will exist in differing realms within a culture as those realms express themselves as arenas for the expression of socially activated relations of power. In that sense, and taking our own society as an example, we recognize that the home, workplace, or leisure site are all settings for the active relations of power. However, the only manner in which we can fully comprehend and analyze the complexities of power is by locating where the material, psychological, and social dimensions of political power are ultimately

3

and socially situated and whether and in what manner these dimensions reproduce themselves at home or work or play.

In its broadest sense, the study of power by anthropologists and other social scientists requires investigators to keep in mind constantly the inclusive nature of power in any society. The principal subject of political anthropology should be to examine the domains and hierarchies of power within any society whether that society conforms to one of the myriad social classifications of band, tribe, or state. Only then can the investigator analyze the intrasocietal aspects of power relations and finally, and most importantly, account for the dynamics of change that is synonymous with the concept of power itself. In other words, we must confront the political with a key question of anthropological science; namely, what are the universal properties and processes of societal power and what accounts for their variations?

In this regard, we do not maintain that there should be any qualitative distinction shown between political scientist and political anthropologist at the level of theory. We recognize that an anthropologist's perspective and contribution to the understanding of things political have been derived from the discipline's research into non-Western cultures, the political anthropologist's pioneering of micro-political studies, and the anthropologist's comparative and universalizing tendencies. This is not to say that these concerns are not evidenced within some perspectives of political science just as anthropologists have contributed to the "machinery of government" studies associated with political science. But political anthropologists are less likely to limit their assessment to overt manifestations of the political such as the state or government which in many cases, as we shall see, are neither universal nor coterminous with the domain of societal power where states do exist. For it is not only the overt political institutions which manifest social power, but the latent as well. Anthropology demands that the intrinsic consensual and conflicted merging of the private and public spheres of power are where the institutional and behavioral aspects of power achieve their transformations, and this is foremost an issue of group social relations rather than merely formal political institutions.

The rest of this introduction will seek to delimit the various contributions of political anthropology to the study of power. Our appraisal will be presented from a narrative of the history of the subdiscipline by considering the work of anthropologists whose research is the indispensable heritage of our discipline. Their works—however archaic the data or misplaced the precision of their theory—remain very much the living corpus of theoretical questions and data interpretation without which no inventory or advance in social science is possible.

This exposition is organized by the major theoretical constructs which dominated a particular period of political anthropologists' research history and will focus particularly on the manner in which various periods defined and dealt with the nature of social power. We will discuss certain works of those periods to place them within the theoretical currents of their time and to situate those parts which still endure. The works selected for discussion are meant to be merely representative, not complete or even necessarily prime examples. We are attempting to piece together a quilt which will hopefully show off to best advantage the web of patterns which make up political anthropology's contributions to the understanding of social power.

Beginnings

Since anthropology is a relative newcomer to the rapidly changing social sciences and political anthropology an even more recent development (Tuden, 1959), many of the theoretical problems and approaches have their roots in other disciplines. Anthropology owes an intellectual debt to earlier writers for structuring—albeit in a gross manner—some of the perennial problems still being analyzed today. Historically, anthropologists have contributed rich ethnographic materials bearing on the problems of state formation, political change, and the structure of conflict.

The historical perspectives gained by analyzing theoretical trends is illusionary. Although science is purportively accumulative and findings should build upon each other to some degree of closure, it appears more likely that in political anthropology, as in other social sciences, this does not occur. Rather, what appears to emerge from any study of historical development are radical shifts in researchers' interests and theories. In political anthropology a theoretical school may dominate the field for a period of time; then, another theoretical insight emerges which supplants the previous work. Merging or cross-fertilization of ideas and work from earlier concerns rarely occurs. Some studies may introduce different concepts and problems, but the building upon research rarely culminates in an answer or resolution of the earlier inquiries.

In reviewing the materials, there does appear to be a gradual sophistication in methodology and a presentation of more complex and richer ethnographic materials, but the theoretical development does not accompany this refinement. Some of the studies in the past which, in their time, provoked intense debate and filled the journals with counterarguments have drifted into the dust bin of history and left little if any impact upon present-day studies. Some fortunate studies may be read by a diligent graduate student, but it seems as if the social sciences have no collective sense of history. Fads and fashions are the rule.

In this introduction, the various interests of past researchers will be discussed, not only to document what has been done in the past, but to try to indicate which of those themes and concerns have historical value, have been continuously followed, and have left some impact upon present research. These concerns will then be compared with contemporary articles.

In reviewing the earliest anthropological studies that deal with political behavior, one should be aware that there were not a large number of anthropologists per se; most were general specialists. No specialization existed, so there were actually fewer problems than those that might exist today, such as when a linguist has difficulty exchanging information with an archaeologist. The entire field was more interrelated and exchanges between anthropologists were common. As a consequence, we cannot talk about individuals who specialized in political anthropology as an exclusive interest. To complicate the situation, most anthropologists who dealt with political materials used them to validate or support major theoretical concerns of the total field at the time. Political research was dominated by other interests and the political materials were incidental to proving or refuting a theoretical orientation.

Early political studies must be viewed with the concerns of anthropologists in the 1920s in mind: the political implications of state formation and interaction between societies. Interestingly enough, after an intervening period of fifty years, this topic has reemerged as a concern of anthropologists working with political problems.

The first area, state formation, considered the evolution of society and the political system that is labeled a state. The aim of these studies was to validate an evolutionary system by indicating stages or causes for the evolution of the state. Earlier researchers ignored or did not have available the rich complex data from a wide range of societies that we have today; thus, in the earliest period, anthropological interest in political systems was initially cast in terms of the classical evolutionary approach, which exerted a profound influence on all early anthropological research.

Sir Henry Maine and L. H. Morgan were the most prominent and influential proponents of the evolutionary approach (Maine, 1861; Morgan, 1877). A fundamental postulate guided and inspired their studies. In 1861, Maine proposed a basic principle underlying and structuring political activity:

> The history of political ideas begins, in fact [and] with the assumption that kinship in blood is the sole possible ground of community in political func-

tions; nor is there any of those supervisions of feelings which we term emphatically revolutions, so startling and so complete the change which is accomplished when some other principals—such as that, for instance, of local continuity—established itself for the first time as the basis of common political activity. (p. 129)

The dichotomy between political behavior based on kinship and that on territory was linked to an evolutionary process; political behavior and organization that were dependent on kinship ties were held to have preceded political systems based on local continuity: "The set of political ideas . . . which being those of ourselves, our contemporaries, and in great measure of our ancestors, rather obscure our perception of the older theory which they vanquished and dethroned" (p. 132).

Sixteen years after Maine proposed his fundamental distinction between political organizations based on kinship ties and those based on territorial ties, Morgan (1877) injected a third factor—property. His conclusion, an elaborate architectonic plan of the worldwide evolution of political systems, depicted two broad levels. On a temporal plane, political behavior appeared to be based on a relationship of the individual with the members of his kinship unit. Morgan called these kinship units "societies." Later, with political allegiance transferred to a township and the people adhered to demarcated borders and property, a society developed which ultimately progressed to political behavior structured on a territorial basis: this was the *civitas*.

> It may be here premised that all forms of government are reducible to two general plans, using the word plan in its scientific sense. The first, in order of time, is founded upon persons, and upon relations purely personal, and may be distinguished as a society. The gens is the unit of organization; giving as the successive stages or integration, in the archaic period, the gens, phratry, the tribe, and confederacy of tribes, which constituted a people or nation. The second is founded upon territory, and upon property, and may be distinguished as a state. The township or ward, circumscribed by meters and bounds, with the property it contains, is the basis or unit of the latter and political society is the result. Political society is organized upon territorial areas and deals with property as well as persons through the territorial relations. (p. 7)

Morgan further embellished these two categories with specific organizational characteristics of leadership and law-enforcing agencies. According to the scheme, the simplest form had a more direct and personal relationship; political organizations closer to the "elementary forms" were composed of consanguineal groups headed by a chief of their own election. Later the political leaders, maintained by their kinsmen, formed a council of chiefs. During this period, the kinship bodies or *gentes* retained the rights, privileges, and obligations conferred and imposed upon its members; they were autonomous. These rights and political activities, or *"jus genticium,"* comprised the laws of the kinship bodies. The political leadership positions were nonhereditary; leaders were elected and could be deposed by peers of the gens. The dominant political agency was the council, the instrument of authority in the kinship organization. "The council was the greatest feature of ancient society . . . it was the instrument of government . . . as well as the supreme authority over the gens, the tribe as well as the confederacy" (Morgan, 1877, p. 85).

Morgan's work scantily treated the dynamic aspects of political institutions. There was no discussion of factors leading to the transformation nor, as Kurtz discusses in "Legitimation and the Aztec State," how a state maintains or expands itself because of the internal dynamics inherent in this particular political structure. At a future period, according to Morgan, the society fissioned either as a result of natural increase or because of other factors not listed. These sections of society again subdivided and in time reunited into two or more phratries. Eventually a tribe emerged with all its members speaking a mutually related dialect and recognizing common descent. Thus for Morgan (1877) the development of leadership and political institutions consisted of a series of progressive steps: "Out of the necessities of mankind for the organization of society came the gens; out of the gens came the chief, and the tribe with its council of chiefs; out of the tribe came the segmentation of the group of tribes, afterwards re-united in a confederacy, and finally consolidated by coalescence into a nation" (p. 321). These stages were assumed to be universal and provided an understanding of the rate and state of political development in a given society.

With time, most anthropologists came to reject Morgan's logical, deductive, developmental sequence. The criticisms directed against the classical evolutionary anthropologists applied also to Morgan's examination of political systems. First, his method was deductive in the sense that it was supported solely by an indiscriminate application of ethnographic data wrenched from their proper historical and temporal context; that is, by the use of the classical or comparative method. The specific stages of the universal development of political structures and leadership—from a gens to a tribe with chief and council proceeding to a confederacy and eventually culminating in the birth of a nation—have never been documented in any one society, let alone in a number of them.

Another criticism, and the more pertinent one, is simply that ethnological data refute the scheme. Scholars, notably Lowie (1927), attacked the foundation of the theory that societies were based solely on kinship affiliation and territorial ties. On the basis of the ethnographic data, Lowie demonstrated that while kinship relations predominate in some societies which fit Morgan's gentile society, a territorial basis also operated. Others have substantiated this point. Schapera (1956) indicated that even the smallest societies inducted individuals into their membership who were linked by nonkinship ties. Societies have a territorial basis, and local territorial ties and kinship ties must coexist among all people. One set of political obligations usually involves kinship relations; a second level of relationships, based upon territorial bonds, coexists with these.

Field evidence clearly demonstrates, moreover, that in societies that fall into the category of states, kinship units are an important component in the total cultural pattern. "Consanguineal kin groups," using Morgan's terms, are retained and function in societies which he would classify as states. In nonliterate societies, the neatly arrayed dichotomy of the kinship society versus the territorial society is spurious. Various associations such as men's clubs, age classes, and secret organizations function politically and somewhat independently of kinship regulations. The two types of societies, one based on kinship and the other on territorial bonds, thus present a false polarity and do injustice to ethnographic data.

The question of the relative importance of the existence, in a political system, of kinship relations and those which are dependent on nonkinship ties continues to be examined. The questions concerning the components of political systems' cultural patterns and the effect of such kinship structures in the total culture pattern, as the extended family group, lineages, and segmentary corporate bodies, as opposed to associations and administrative units of nonkinship controls in political systems, still have not been adequately answered. Further, the complexity of the cultural patterns as they emerge in leadership roles, sanctions, and authority patterns within statelike contexts or within a kinship society still draws the attention of present-day students. These problems, however, must be attacked with an awareness of the complexity and variety of cultures instead of limiting research to simplified static classifications based on two or three types of social groupings. By way of a century-long critique of Morgan's data and model, one can see what enduring legacies are there. Once this evolutionary/functional menu of evolutionary change has been rejected, there still remains the importance in Morgan's attempt "to introduce a definite order into the history of primitive man," as recognized by Engels (1884). Although Morgan's concept of power, like his view of progress, remained simplistically wedded to a one-dimensional view of expanding and contracting social power, he nonetheless had identified—however inconsistently and problematically—a key variable in the dynamics of power relations and changing political institutions: property. He had also permanently introduced into anthropology a dichotomous view of the political in human societies; namely, the secular and qualitative distinctions between power as experienced in primitive societies and state societies and the rupture between private and public spheres of power at a parallel level.

The period prior to 1940 was largely preoccupied with a series of amendments or resolutions amounting to outright rejection of any evolutionary processual intersocietal dynamics of change. There was a period of specified neglect of political questions and theories, except at the most reductionist level of definitions and cultural particularism and relativism. Then in 1940, quite characteristically, there occurred one of those rare but dramatic events in any discipline from which all of that subject's vitality and urgency seems to derive.

The Emergence of
Political Anthropology and Structural Functionalism

According to G. Balandier (1967), the true origin of political anthropology may be successfully derived from the publication of *African Political Systems*, by Fortes and Evans-Pritchard.

Beginning in 1940, as a result of the crystallization of a theoretical trend, the study of political anthropology received an infusion of energy. The publication of *African Political Systems* (Fortes and Evans-Pritchard, 1940) set a tone and direction that dominated anthropologists' comparative study of political behavior for the next twenty years, influencing students and anthropologists alike. A steady stream of publications and research resulted from the original study. This study of political behavior was guided by a structural-functional orientation derived from Durkheim (1895) and Radcliffe-Brown (1946). The research posited a particular range of objectives, interests, and methods which were clearly enunciated by the social anthropologists.

Reasons for the success of this approach are not too difficult to understand. *African Political Systems* was the first work that focused on political behavior, a core concern—politics—that many of the other studies did not have. During the 1940s the study of anthropology and anthropologists themselves were being influenced by drastic changes that swept many nonwestern areas. These political changes directed intellectual interests toward research in political behavior. Another factor influencing the direction of social science, especially anthropology, was the vacuum of theoretical interests which existed. The demise of evolutionism, acculturation, and diffusion left the field ripe for a new approach. The sophistication of a structural-functional approach appeared to be far superior to earlier comparative approaches. A further attraction was the rich, detailed ethnographic material presented in the work. Many of the earlier studies did not rely upon material collected first-hand by trained anthropologists. *African Political Systems* represented years of field research and the material covered only one ethnographic area.

These studies generally tended to ignore historical depth and formulated static classifications so that primary concern was with synchronic studies of political structures and the taxonomic classification of political systems on the basis of social relationships. This approach ignored the concepts of culture and cultural change and resulted in such statements as: "The comparative study of political systems has to be on an abstract plane where social processes are stripped of their cultural idiom . . . and the structures laid bare. Their goals are to note structural units which exercise political functions and their interrelationships with other social units. . . . We speak for all social anthropologists when we say that a scientific study of political institutions must be inductive and comparative, and aim solely at establishing and explaining the uniformities found among them and their interdependence with other features of social organization" (p. 3).

A structural analysis applied to kinship units, a major concern of social anthropology, has been relatively successful, but a structural emphasis applied to political systems has not afforded commensurate rewards. The definition of political organization advanced by Evans-Pritchard and Fortes (1940) as: "those structures or relationships which maintain or establish social order within a territorial framework, by the organized exercise or coercive authority through the use, or the possibility of the use of physical force" (p. xiv), does not isolate elements of political systems comparable to those defining types of kinship systems. However, with this approach the authors advanced a tentative threefold classification.

One type referred to societies which have centralized authority, administrative hierarchies, clearly defined judicial institutions, class structures, and territorial delineated political behavior. In essence, the administrative structure contains the political structure and thus possesses a "government" resembling states familiar to the European investigator.

The second category of political structures lacks centralized authority, administrative machinery or courts with power to hand down judgments, or, as it was phrased, "is a stateless society." In these societies, the lineages serve as the framework of the political unit so that political behavior is inextricably linked with and encompassed by the kinship system.

A third group, unfortunately only briefly discussed and not ethnologically represented in *African Political Systems,* depicts the extremely small societies in which the political unit embraces a group of people all united by kinship bonds, such as a band or roving extended family on the order of Bushmen, Andamese, and Pygmy groups.

The proposed classification closely approximates the dichotomy drawn between stateless and state societies by earlier writers, its basic criterion being the importance of kinship and nonkinship bonds in controling disruptive behavior in a society. In Africa, however, this first type does not appear as frequently as do some of the other kinds of statelike political systems, particularly those which combine a kinship structure within an administrative framework. In the well-organized states of the Alur, Busoga, Ngoni, Yoruba, and Ashanti, for example, lineages serve as important factors in maintaining cohesion and regulating administration. The two basic principles of authority, and kinship and kingship are both crucial for an understanding of political behavior in these societies. A new model suggested itself to reclassify political systems into those that utilize kinship units as checks or balances while operating in conjunction with administrative units, as differentiated from those employing primarily administrative organization. In those terms, the kinship administrative political systems have been labeled a segmentary state while the administrative system is called the unitary state. Here we follow a familiar course wherein the broadening of a classification leads inevitably to still other classes, resulting in an unmanageable framework as still more divisions begin to appear.

Thus Brown (1951), on the basis of West African material alone, carries the process further when she suggests that, in some centralized societies, associations and not kinship or administrative organizations are the instruments of political control. This study adds another type not included in the original classification.

Similar criticisms have been raised about the category of political systems based on kinship structures which lack a clearly recognizable administrative organization, primarily on the grounds that varieties or types of kinship-based political systems which are not included in the original suggestion are not taken into account. The organization of such kinship units displays great variations. East African material indicates that the age-sets play an important role in political behavior in these societies, perhaps more important than the kinship units (Gulliver, 1963). Leach's Assam data (1954) includes a kinship society which is hierarchical and class-based, with slave classes as an important ingredient. All these features fall outside the major classifications of state, lineage, and kinship political systems.

Still other criticisms levied against the original aim of the social an-

thropologists go further than disputes about possible variants of the three
basic types of political systems. The aim of the social anthropologists, the
classification of political systems on the basis of social units alone, has
been directly attacked. Lloyd (1954) suggests that, for an understanding
of political behavior, a study of structural components is not enough and
holds that classification of types cannot be regarded as a primary end of
research since other factors and more generalized concepts such as authority, the formation of decision-making bodies, and the basis of authority and leadership also figure prominently. In actuality, even where similar
structures occur, the form of political behavior may be quite different.
For instance, the Yoruba chieftaincies differed in the composition of councils and the way the authority was defined by the councils, although the
structural factors were similar.

Perhaps these criticisms explain why later research by social anthropologists moved away from attempts to classify political systems to aim at
analyzing general problems of political behavior. One emerging interest
was in investigating the degree of stability of political systems, as is seen
in the works of Leach (1956). Fallers (1963) reviewed the problem of
stability and integration but refocused interest in types of social units in
terms of type of patterns of authority. His hypothesis suggests that a
political system that incorporates two competing principles of organization, namely kinship and bureaucracy, is unstable.

Aside from these technical criticisms of omission, this approach promulgated orientations that ignored or made it impossible to investigate
critical problems of political behavior. The theoretical stance acted as a
barrier to many realistic aspects of political change. The structural definition of politics acted as hermetically-sealed phenomena which gave pre-
eminence to permanent social groupings. The types of social groupings
were implicitly considered to be well defined, critical, and resistant to
political changes. This view presented an ahistorical perspective or ignored outside events as triggering changes or intimately involved in the
political process. For example, even though they analyzed African societies during a period of enormous political change, resulting from colonial domination, and past momentous events such as the African slave
trade, no mention is made nor attention given to this external turmoil as a
cause for change. In some cases, an awesome unreality pervaded the
studies.

A more pervasive effect of this classic work is the orientation of its
research to weld the political system with social groupings, leading to a
view of political behavior as unidirectional. That the political system aids
implicitly political behavior is merely a reflex of a limited number of
social grouping combinations. Political research also ignored how poli-

tics affects the hierarchy and power of social groups. This one-sided role of politics appeared to have inevitably resulted in the major theme of the classical structural functional approach—a classificatory thrust. Most of the subsequent work was devoted to filling out charts on the possible types of political systems that were extant. Soon a proliferation of typologies of political systems in Africa and elsewhere was part of the anthropological tradition (Middleton and Tait, 1958; Vansina, 1962). This move to classify the total society and to suggest what type of political behavior was associated with the societal component, as we have suggested, led to an ossification of political analysis. It stressed the equilibrium of a society and unknowingly invited a stable view of society and the political system and prevented change. It also ignored the frequent appearance of political action as leading to rapid and drastic change.

What has been suggested about the structural-functional orientation of political analysis by anthropologists is not simple to explain. The unconscious bias of the times possibly prevented a clearer picture of the political process or rapid change. It is more likely, however, that the earlier structural training and transference of stable family and kinship structures was difficult to avoid. Whatever the reasons, the earlier works' success and concerns soon were overshadowed and the problems were transformed by subsequent research by anthropologists who broke away from the major theoretical framework of the earlier British social anthropologists.

Questions were also raised concerning the validity and effectiveness of a major theoretical framework for social and cultural anthropology as a whole. This question was transfered to the study of political aspects of society; however, the major question was not raised directly. Is there any possibility of studying political activity without constructing a separate theory for politics? In anthropology political analysis was an adjunct to a core theory, and some of the distinctive aspects of political behavior were subsumed under a larger rubric. Even though we have listed some of the shortcomings of the earlier orientation, a large number of studies that focused on political behavior were to come and enlarge the area of analysis.

If the earlier classificatory aims of the social anthropologists have not been too successful, subsidiary rewards emerged. Another problem under examination is the role of kinship systems as they bear on possible centralization of authority. This hypothesis essentially suggests that the presence of a lineage system affects the growth of centralized leadership and that an inverse relationship exists between the articulation and importance of lineages and the centralized authority's degree of specialization. A strong clan system, other things being equal, is correlated with a weak political system. This generalization was first suggested by Eggan (1966).

The stress on internal control has furnished a wealth of detailed studies of law. Other generalizations differing from the original static approach have been promulgated. Fortes and Evans-Pritchard (1948) links regicide and divine kingship in African societies to the segmentary structure of the society. "Divine kingship is an institution typical of, although doubtless not restricted to, societies with pronounced lineage systems in which the political segments are parts of a loosely organized structure without government function" (p. 3). Nadel (1942) states that Nupe kingship is linked in so many ways with religious usages and forms of religious symbolism that the kings invariably become instruments of political solidarity since rites and beliefs are focused upon the person of the king. The religious beliefs and practices supply the spiritual sanctions of chieftainship and authority in general. Gluckman (1963) states that periodic rebellions are necessary and inevitable if society is to exist. "They affirmed allegiance to the kinship and the royal title to kingship ... civil wars preserved the unity of the system." Fortes (1953), analyzing unilinear descent groups, offers the proposition that "the political structures of these societies were always unstable and this was due in considerable degree to the internal rivalries arising out of the division between lineages." Cunnison (1951) establishes a tentative relationship between myth and the degree of centralization of a political system. Barnes (1954) deals with a warlike, expanding society and its implication for political control.

As more and more information was forthcoming, the objectives of anthropological study were broadened. There is a more generalized approach to the more inclusive, wider-ranging aspects of change and stability, and even the inclusion of nonkinship aspects is noted. Such questions dealing with the localization of authority, changing political systems, roles of leadership, and religious sanctions of leadership were investigated. However, among social anthropologists who were committed to synchronic structural studies, the research emphasis has continued to ignore the questions of historical depth and of culture patterning and change.

Except for the earlier studies, an ahistorical approach prevailed, for no consistent attempts were made to study the processes of change by observing the working of a political system with a historical perspective. This neglect of the historical method has had an obvious effect on the methodology and has influenced the research on political systems. The lack of a historical dimension, by necessity, rules out studies of change and focuses on synchronic studies or typologies of political systems.

Indeed, the work by anthropologists abounds in types of political systems but neglects possible avenues leading to change and the mechanisms involved in change.

A second facet of the studies is the neglect of political behavior per se. The work that has been carried on deals with societies and not with components or features of a political institution. The majority of the studies attempt to relate societies to political institutions and do not begin with political institutions. This approach results in studies in which typologies of societies are constructed and then political behavior and political variation are seemingly associated with societal types.

The types or characteristics of social units within a society inescapably affect political behavior. But the earlier emphasis upon narrowly defined social groups, primarily in types of kinship grouping, did not appear to lead to meaningful insights. An emphasis upon relating the type of society to political behavior also appeared to have been too gross a variable. Some of the articles in this publication, however, still rely upon a structural-functional approach—but with great differences. Miller's article, "San Cosme Xalostoc, Mexico," can be labeled structural-functional because it analyzes the relationship between class, family, and politics. But he looks at a particular social context to show the interplay between variation and change rather than stressing the stable aspects of these groups.

This same orientation emerges when we investigate the type of social controls operating in different societies. We in the modern states tend to emphasize the importance of coercive social controls. The state bureaucracies, police courts and prisons emerge as critical institutions to control and curb deviant behavior. Most of the societies anthropologists work with are familiar with violence as the ultimate curb, but the literature indicates that most of human history did not stress coercion as a key factor in organizing a safe society. Gossip, joking, and the withdrawal of economic rewards appear to be much more usual than brute force in regulating human history (Colson, 1974; Gluckman, 1965).

To illustrate this point further, Schneider's (1957) study of incest on Yap is an excellent example. As an anthropologist, he looks at how societies control disruptive behavior. On Yap there are no centralized political forces nor permanent coercive bodies. The major social units are kinship groups. Schneider points out that every society tries to protect its most critical institutions from conflict. To maintain the solidarity of the kinship group, incest regulations apply. When a member of the kin group breaks this critical rule he or she will be punished. He then relates the religious institution to the political process. On Yap deviators will be punished by supernatural sanctions. Those who have broken the incest regulations will be punished by ancestral spirits. His reasoning is that, because it is difficult to punish individual members in a family, punishment would threaten the well-being of the group. The religious institution plays a direct political function. Schneider thus documents a typical anthropological approach to politics. He incorporates material not usually considered by political scientists and portrays a holistic picture of how politics is studied in a total social context.

As we commented earlier, the 1950s heralded a shift in the questions raised about political behavior and resulted in a gradual moving away from the more rigid view of politics. There was no clear, direct repudiation of the earlier works, but studies were published which obviously were concerned with a different range of problems. Some of the works are hybrid publications; they straddle two traditions in an uncomfortable fashion— one gradually out of favor and another not yet sharply delineated.

The Processual Approach

Leach (1954) stated that all social and cultural change springs from people searching for power. This sweeping statement represents an orientation that many political scientists would reject or ignore, but it is typical of the approach that many anthropologists have adopted. Politics is not a neutral force obeying laws of its own. Anthropologists see political behavior as an interlocking network of individuals using power for specific ends. *Politics is a constant struggle of individuals who have banded together and use tactics and strategies to achieve group goals.* As such, anthropologists tend to stress conflict in their research rather than politics as a consensus mechanism. Political activity can be viewed cross-culturally as those kinds of actions that reflect groups struggling to control what they culturally define as valuable in a particular society.

In the more recent anthropological studies of politics there is a heavy emphasis toward a conflict orientation. The political processes are individuals' activities which control or allocate scarce resources in the society. Their search is aimed at the repetitive patterns that occur in all societies. When are the groups in opposition? What signals a confrontation? What are the similar practices that groups use to gain a victory? How is the struggle ended? What are the goals that are achieved? The political areas and accompanying conflicts are omnipresent.

In this sense, political behavior emerges whenever there are groups in opposition. Wherever there are scarce resources there will be a struggle over the control or the allocation of these defined resources. Bailey (1969, 1977) writes about this political process in many different contexts—on college faculties to boards of trustees in banks.

What we suggest indicates that anthropologists see politics and political behavior emerging wherever there are humans organized in groups. Political scientists would stress the political behavior in a context of elected officials with official posts. Anthropologists have a tendency to stress the activity of humans struggling for their own needs and not societal goals. The context of political behavior for most anthropologists is not played out against a large network such as a society, but rather in smaller, more intimate groups or restricted networks. Anthropologists tend to miniaturize the scope of political activities; political scientists paint a larger scale.

Inevitably, most anthropologists are drawn to a perhaps disturbing conclusion, that when humans organize for political struggles, they are not concerned about the large social unit but act to maximize the advantages for the group they most closely identify with and belong to. In smaller-scale societies, individuals tend to maximize the family, lineage, or the clan (Colson, 1974). If this were translated to larger-scale societies, individuals operate to increase the advantages of their caste or class group but with less frequency. Political scientists would stress the larger social unit and their benefits to the total society. Their predilection is to overlook loyalties on the primary level and emphasize the larger social framework. We are not implying that in political behavior individuals solely act out their own individual interests, but we are saying that individuals do not consistently engage in political behavior for the largest social unit with which they can identify. Loyalties are a human quality, but group loyalties and actions are of a more fundamental group nature.

Individuals tend to react politically when their social ties are intensified, carry the most effect and, therefore, have the highest returns. This criteria usually does not apply to large, removed social groups.

The Alur: A Study in Processes and Types of Domination (Southall, 1953) grappled with an old problem and introduced a fresh perspective. This analysis of an East African society focuses on the spread of a centralized political system. The work points out the influence that neighboring groups have on each other politically in a historical perspective. The less centralized societies "borrow" leaders from a centralized society to produce ethnically diverse groups with similarity of leadership. Southall also attempts to rectify the earlier typological approach by indicating that there is a variety of types of states within the African continent, some not included in the earlier work *African Political Systems* (1940). The material indicates there is a wider range of types of states and stresses no sharp distinctions between state societies and those that contain large kinship units. The Alur can be defined as a state, but also lineages or kinship groups play a critical role in the allocation of leadership. The Alur have bureaucratic organization, and lineages function in many areas of life. This work, while still adhering to a typological approach, begins to inject into the literature a concern for historical change, the impact of groups upon each other, and also raises questions about defining a political and classifying system in terms of the types of social units in the society.

Shortly after, and again from the East African region, another study that deviated from the earlier conceptual frame was published. *Bantu Bureaucracy* (Fallers, 1963) introduces a focus of political change and raises a variety of new problems in political anthropology. Combining a typological approach with a theoretical discussion of change, Fallers analyzes the Busoga of East Africa to evaluate whether or not the political structure is critical in selecting out directions of change.

The Busoga society contains both a bureaucracy and a lineage system. As formulated by Fallers, there are two incompatible, contradictory demands upon the members of the society. They are caught within a social network that stresses formal regulations to get the job done and the embracing, encompassing kinship obligations. These competing demands place stress upon individuals. When the British colonists encountered the Busoga, the choice was to move in the direction of British political structure—an impartial, formal, bureaucratic model. In this study, emphasis is placed upon the obligations of the kinship system and the needs of the bureaucratic for leaders to maintain their positions and to enforce regulations. Individuals will tend to move out of stressful situations by choosing options to remove the stress. Therefore, they will seek cultural and organizational alternatives. Political change, then, from this ethnographic work, will be based upon the vulnerability of and tensions within the structure. Fallers's work on the total society was later followed by a study of the role of chiefs in Busoga society to indicate the number of stresses this particular political role generates.

This anthropological study was the forerunner of modernizations or developmental analyses of the 1960s. While the approach has been criticized (Bennet; Tuden, 1969), at a minimum it turned the attention of anthropologists to stress within the political area. Previous studies emphasized the almost idyllic nature of the system and the harmonious function of society. It also introduced the effect of colonialism and usurpation of political power of Europeans in nonwestern areas. Most anthropologists had assiduously avoided the question of the role of intruders in nonwestern societies; they were describing closed systems while the world was rapidly changing. Anthropologists only much later raised the question of the political impact on colonial countries (Asad, 1973). With this study one can also see the beginning of attention being paid to political roles. The study of a chief starts to devote attention to clearly political matters and not solely on the total society.

These trends of devoting specific interest to political aspects of a society and relationships between societies mark a significant shift from earlier studies. The tendency to direct research within a common anthropological framework and incorporate political research has had a unifying effect upon anthropological research but also delayed developing political anthropology as a distinctive field. The focus of most work until 1966 was an uneasy combination of a general anthropological research and utilization of political studies to document its utility. For example, Evans-Pritchard's study of the Nuer (1940) combined a general social structural approach and political generalization. The portrayal of the Nuer was as a segmentary society with kinship groups combining and forming alliances based upon genealogical distance. Warfare and conflict is tied primarily to types of social units without describing in detail the basis of these units other than on kinship principles. Very little mention of uneven distribution of economic resources or competitive strategies was made. One is forced to conclude that analyzing political behavior from most of the previous theoretical vantage points of theories in anthropology has led to a deemphasis of political behavior or an avoidance of some initial variables underlying politics.

During the 1960s the traditional anthropological approaches appeared to be waning in popularity or in credibility. Questions of allocation of power, political change, leadership, and competition over economic resources were being researched. One of the last attempts to combine some of the earlier approaches, a typological approach plus social groupings, is Leach's (1954) study, *The Political System of Highland Burma*. Although Leach stresses a typology of political systems, his overall approach represents a mixture of the old and the new. He essentially suggests a typology of two political types: one centralized, autocratic, and powerful; the second decentralized, not powerful, and based upon kinship ties. However, Leach suggests that political groupings vary over time. He introduces the concept of a type expanding and changing over time but within a limited parameter of change. The decentralized system, due to the manipulations and actions of a leader, accumulates power, and the political behavior changes from one based upon kinship egalitarian controls to one in which the kinship bonds are overridden by social and political distance.

The Kachin society as portrayed by Leach (1954) was basically a kinship society with egalitarian political patterns. The ancestral spirits were open to all kin members, and economic ties were basically reciprocal—individuals did not control the surplus with asymmetrical political patterns. A kin head gradually accumulated economic and religious power, one supplementing another. The kinship ties became weaker and gradually a degree of stratification emerged. However, this system never developed into a centralized or permanent hierarchical position. The political power then evolved and the kinship system re-emerged. Political patterns in the process of development and individuals making choices which lead to the accumulation of power and centralization of control over other individuals are described here for the first time.

A hereditary system in which a limited number of people in the society control trade and other economic assets exists side by side with the egalitarian systems that fluctuate between equal access to power and a limited degree of control. The hereditary system is part of a ruling class which dominates over other members of the society. This type of political system is more permanent in its structure and allocation of political power, and there is no mention of phases or shifts in the power relationships between people in that society. The degree of inequality between segments of the population is consistent and accepted.

The contract between two systems is not detailed, but in broad general outlines we see a relatively unstable set of political relations vulnerable to manipulation by individuals as opposed to a stable series of political transactions between unequals. One can clearly deduce from the material how religious or ideological factors helped political relations and how economic controls either assured political supremacy and/or aided in bringing about changes in the political sphere of behavior.

Leach's (1954) work documents that political patterns are vulnerable to change and that the role of individuals seeking more power take tortuous turns. It raises the question of whether or not we can justifiably utilize the concept of a political system with its connotation of stability and set patterns that we can anticipate will continue to reoccur.

A final study, which marks the sharpest distinction with the earlier tradition of structure and political behavior, is F. Barth's (1959) study, *Political Leadership Among the Swat Pathans*. There is no attempt to classify the type of political system or to look at the structured components of the society. Classification is ignored in favor of a focus on the actions of leaders and the leaders themselves. For the first time, the preoccupation of the anthropologist is with political behavior and not with attempts to relate political behavior to types of kinship units.

The study of the Swat Pathans describes two categories of leaders in the society: the Khans and the Saints. The Khans are leaders who are in a constant struggle to collect followers, adding to their strength in competition with other Khans. In essence, the Khans are secular leaders. They have a basis of power by virtue of their reputations and resources. These leaders are typically aggressive, combative men. They have followers who need support to protect them from other Khans. As Barth (1959) suggests, the struggle is over scarce resources in the society—primarily land, gold, and women. Each leader is constantly in search of more resources in order to assure his followers that they will not lose what they have.

Barth's description of the machinations and constant struggles of the Swat Pathans evokes a nightmare picture of perpetual conflict. The secular leaders, the Khans, organize for aggression against other similar leaders. Initially one of his followers will attempt to usurp land from a neighbor who is not a member of his political solidarity unit. If the other leader does not resist, more and more land is appropriated until one leader and his followers have economically and politically decimated a competitor. The picture of politics among the Swat Pathans is perhaps overdrawn. The constant struggles to defeat another competitor, we are sure, does occur, but there must be alliances and periods of peaceful interaction. However, the ethnographic material presented by Barth does, for the first time, indicate intricate and involved planning by leaders. It moves the study of politics to a completely different level. Now politics is a struggle for resources within a society, and we begin to see the vague outlines of politics as a rough-and-tumble game that involves not maintaining peace and serenity but an activity which generates conflict. Political behavior originally was defined as maintaining peace. We now observe the converse—individuals and their followers employ tactics to obtain resources and defeat others.

Among the Swat Pathans, as we mentioned earlier, there were two categories of leaders: the Khans, a source of conflict; and the Saints, individuals whose function was to maintain the struggle within bounds and to not destroy the fabric of society. The Saints, in opposition to the aggressive Khans, are individuals whose authority and power rests on their nonaggressive behavior and their known reputation for neutrality and learning. The material suggests that, in every society, political action generates competition, no matter what the cultural definition of resources in that society might be.

Politics is a struggle, but in societies other political roles emerge that are designed to ameliorate, regulate, or dampen the struggles. These leaders do not have followers who engage in conflict; rather, their power depends upon ideological grounds of restricting struggles and maintaining a degree of tranquility in society. Among the Swat Pathans, when the struggle between two Khans has reached an impasse and there does not appear to be a quick victory or resolution in the near future, the Khans turn to the Saints for aid in reducing the conflict. The Saints have access to supernatural powers, and if the Khans reject their resolution, purportedly the Saints can curse the combatants. From the description, it also appears that, on rare occasions, the Saints' followers will resort to physical force to enforce peace. The description of the struggles among the Pathans is reminiscent of the role of the leopard chief among the Nuer. Here we again have politics on two different poles; kinship leaders struggle against one another. Segments of a society are organized around principles of organization and compete with similar groups for gain. The leopard chief is one who does not have access to secular power—that is, men, guns, and economic resources—but his authority depends on religious or ideological groups to maintain some degree of peace within the society.

Among the Swat Pathans, these two types of leaders complement each other. The Khans represent the expanding leadership whose power ultimately comes from conflict and their ability to accumulate followers for physical combat. The Saints represent the structure of society whose authority is derived from the ability to restore peace in the society.

The articles by Brandewie, "Big Man of New Guinea," and Keesing, "Killers, Big Men, and Priests on Malaita," indicate refinements and complexities in Barth's initial study of leadership. Brandewie documents how Big Man accumulates economic power initially by a kin position and enhances and increases his position by shrewd economic activities. Keesing's article stresses the varieties of leadership in a society and how they can shift from one category to another—as if a Khan in a career pattern ended up as a Saint.

In 1960, political anthropology was transformed. The interests of an earlier generation of scholars were dropped, and a different emphasis emerged as being central to research. The genesis of the approach is difficult to locate with exactness, but the contributions of the social anthropologists from Manchester—Bailey, Epstein, Turner, and Gluckman—are obvious. The thrust of their work is radically distinct from earlier studies. No longer is structure or function the key interest, and typologies are ignored. The definition of what is political behavior or activity moves into a different area while the underlying assumptions of politics move to a different context.

The key terms employed in the processual research design reveal its assumptions and direction. A highly structured system of political behavior is no longer stressed; instead, the term "political arena" defines a view of political behavior. Politics is basically a struggle between contestants, and the attempt to impose a rigid frame on the political struggle is not a major concern. The emphasis in the research is on analyzing and describing the universal aspects of the struggle between individuals and groups who are competing for socially defined prizes. Therefore, the researcher gives attention to those factors that outline political struggle. Research has shifted from the types of groups that compose a society or group to focus on the universal processes involved in a political struggle (Swartz, Turner, and Tuden, 1966). From this theoretical vantage point, politics is a constant struggle between groups in a society. The assumption behind the collection of data is that, in every collectivity, the political process operates in a similar fashion. Bailey's work comparing political tactics in tribal structures, English cabinet activities, and college faculties accurately portrays the universality and commonality of political behavior.

This processual approach also depicts political activity as a constant preoccupation of the combatants. Political activity in this theoretical view is unconsciously portrayed as a neverending struggle in human societies. The major elements in the political process are phases of a struggle between groups over items that are deemed valuable within a society. The first appearance of this research approach appeared in 1966 in an edited work by Swartz, Turner, and Tuden, entitled *Political Anthropology*. In a simplified presentation, the introduction outlined some of the significant differences between approaches to political behavior.

New terminology plus a new approach was crystalized in the work. First, the emphasis was upon politics; it did not focus on leadership as Barth did, nor upon the type of society, as in the earlier structural approach of the British school. The aim was to document the process of political behavior, those reoccurring aspects of actions made by participants in the struggle between groups. The work assumed that the political struggle is repetitive, and inevitable events emerge in any societal context. That is, if groups are in competition, regardless of the cultural context, actions will be taken that will materialize in any human group. The political process is conceived to be made up of a universally limited number of choices for humans to decide upon, and that the political process is, in broad terms, similar in all cultural contexts. The objective was to outline the choices that emerged. Because of the ambitious aims of the research, the outline of the political process was by necessity abstract and not at all precise in its description.

While the authors did not present a clear definition of *process,* what emerged from their writing was a complex series of choices that individuals might make to achieve their political goals. Process is viewed as a complex, intricate, but flexible set of actions by actors choosing action out of a range of possibilities that they conceive to be leading to objectives. The political process is an individual who is not alone but represents group interests and chooses alternative ways of acting to compete with another group for resources. The political process can include members of a lineage competing within their own lineage for a political post or, in a more complex society, a representative of a class competing for societal resources against another class group. The process becomes political when the member struggles over a societal resource or prize. Without belaboring the distinction between what is political or not political behavior in this theoretical context, one can simply state that a fight between a husband a wife over the allocation of household finances is not a political event, but if, in a societal context of a lineage system or an extended family where the family also plays a political role in the society, this fight over household finances might possibly be a political struggle. If, however, individuals represent large units within the society and competition exists over societal resources, the conflict is a part of the political process. The distinction between political and other aspects of the operation of human behavior is not necessarily drawn by the particular groups involved but by its effect upon the dimension of drawing in other members of society.

This way of viewing political behavior required new terminology and a conceptual framework, one that we suggested earlier was intricate but flexible. The political process is repetitive and assumes a limited number of options for successful competition but, with the complexity of political behavior, there is another caveat. In some cases, the group's process is such that unsuccessful choices are made. An outline of the process of politics with its complexity implies that the repetitive appearance of actions not only leads to success but that the individuals who are involved in the political struggle have made a serious judgmental error in their choices of actions. This factor makes the validation or falsification of the approach to political behavior different than any other area of scientific research. It injects into the study of political behavior a dimension of efficiency in human behavior.

Another implication of this approach is a subtle but critical question of human nature, or a definition of the quality of human living. If we conceive of political behavior as competition and struggle as a constant, this approach to the study of societies can leave the impression of constant struggle, competition, dirty tactics and a view of human behavior tinged with deep cynicism about the actions and motives of individuals. To further complicate matters, the intensity of political action fluctuates over time. There are periods when political behavior or the number of individuals involved in the process is intense. There are other times when individuals or groups do not enter into the contest, or else there is no contest. The explanation for the variation in the intensity and frequency of political behavior also partially explains potential misunderstandings or misinterpretations of the nature of human behavior. Human behavior is not constantly political. Individuals do not enter the political process with any innate drive, nor can one make unqualified statements about the quality of life. Politics, as we suggested earlier, can be viewed as resulting from other factors in society. Political behavior is an epiphenomena. Politics intensifies or increases its scope because it can potentially resolve problems that emerge in other areas of life. If there are questions about allocations of resources in a society, tensions occur. Individuals will gravitate to the political process to resolve their problems from another area. The quality of life in other areas determines the nature and dimension of the political process.

The description of the political process view of political behavior required a new vocabulary. Most of the terms conveyed an overall impression of a specific viewpoint of politics. The viewpoint is one of struggle, competition, action, movement, punishment, and coercion. The conceptual framework of this political approach is still more literary than precise. In any description of politics as a process over time, certain terms have gained currency and usage.

First, political behavior is not anchored to any one specific area of a society. The political struggle is not restricted to one social unit, nor is it contained in a particular group. To convey this dimension of politics, the term political *arena* is employed. The implication is that a struggle will develop, but it can and usually will spread to other groups within the society. The term *arena* justifiably replaces *political system*. Earlier views of politics implied a restricted or tightly organized series of isolated groups or societies. In the present discussion, political processes are only limited by the choices made by the participants. A struggle can emerge, and the participants will orchestrate and involve other members who enter the fray. The analogy to political processes is an unrestricted field of action only limited by the resolution of the struggle. However, most political struggles spread and incorporate other groupings over time. One example from the United States was the community school board control in New York City, which was initiated by community members against the New York School Board. Before there was a resolution, both contestants involved many more groups, ranging from unions to political parties to nationwide foundations. In another context, Kopytoff's work in Central Africa indicates that individuals will escalate the contest when they sense that they are not winning their goals. There appears to be a tendency for political struggle to widen until most of the original causes and participants are swamped by the events.

As mentioned earlier, political processes can be idealized or isolated into a series of phases of the entire struggle. But one must be extremely careful to realize that, in the normal flow of events in a political struggle, it is difficult to realistically expect that all political struggles will follow the idealized or predictable categories.

In any human context, the norm is a relative lack of overt conflict over goals or resources. Even though human history is punctuated by periods of repressive violence and horrendous bloodshed, and these actions are so noticeable that they appear to dominate history, most human societies are tranquil. This is not to ignore the seething tensions in human relations that go unperceived. During periods of no overt conflict, potential disagreements between groups begin to be perceived. In an analysis of political behavior, the authors of *Political Anthropology* attempt to systematically categorize the political process; that is, how groups seek to achieve their goals (Swartz, Turner, and Tuden, 1966, pp. 32–39). Political analysis does not attempt to list goals, but abstractly describes the actions taken by groups to achieve them.

Once a potential conflict is perceived, political opponents mobilize their political capital or resources. During this period, alliances can be formed, foot soldiers assembled, and attempts made to undermine the potential opponents. In the articles in this volume dealing with the political process, Keesing, Stewart, and Lindholm describe three different cultural contexts where conflict emerges over different goals. When leaders believe that the opportunity is at hand, peace is breached by a drastic event—the notification to society of open conflict. Once the society is aware of the crisis, it attempts to stifle or prevent continued violence through recognized leaders, middlemen, or religious figures who fear the consequences of the violence. Dillon's essay, "Ritual Regulation in Meta' Legal Process," describes how, in many nonwestern societies, ritual plays a key role in resolving or stopping conflict. Kurtz's "Strategies of Legitimation and the Aztec State" can be interpreted to indicate that, when the social contact of violence is a state, the ritual resolutions diminish.

If the conflict at this stage is not stopped, the next phase of the political process is in changing the power relationships within the social context. This aspect of the political process has been least studied. Brandewie's essay, "Big Man of New Guinea," indicates that the purpose of Big Men is to achieve a higher status. This charge inevitably realigns traditional groups, restructures the allocation of resources, and creates new and sometimes radically different cultural values.

Peace is inevitably restored in human societies. There are mechanisms—ritual, social, or political—that allow for peaceful relations to be reestablished, albeit with a changed social order and the potential for the conflict to reemerge at a later date when one of the opponents judges the time to be appropriate.

This description of the political process can be applied to a wide variety of contexts, not merely between classes or kin groups within societies. Bailey (1988, 1977) and his students effectively applied this description of political process to a wide variety of contexts—board rooms of corporations, faculties in universities, and in small villages. The cultural arena in which the struggles operate obviously influence the type of social breech which declares the conflict, the tactics used in the social conflict, and the mechanisms that restore harmony. Each social context produces variations in playing out the conflict and the restoration of relative tranquility.

The strengths and limitations of the processual approach are evident in Bailey's attempt to identify those universals of political behavior which are found everywhere regardless of social structure or cultural constructs. According to Bailey, there are general principles of political tactics which are implicit in all political systems. These are the pragmatic rules which politicians play to win. Such rules are never to be confused with the normative, ideological rules; that is, the anthropological "proper" rules of the game. These normative rules provide the cultural contexts of politics, but power and the spoils which are its prizes are awarded to those who win them and that winning is never clean, honest, or public. If, in Bailey's scenario, any politician kept to the normative rules of what a political contest should be, the consequences would be personally disastrous and considered a betrayal to his followers. Manipulation, cheating, and corruption wins the spoils.

The implications of this perspective are far-reaching. First, we have here the clearest signpost of the distance traveled from functionalism through the processual approach. Bailey has defined politics as necessarily contained and opposed by the moral versus the transactional. Never again can anthropology assume a single reality between the constitutional, the right way, the formal, structural rules and the realities of power. This dynamic of power is the processual approach's greatest contribution to the study of political behavior, but it also suggests its limitations as exemplified by its practitioners. For an approach that emphasizes dynamics, their view of process, paradoxically, is a hermetically sealed event. The arenas in which power is examined remains, for the most part, devoid of any external reflections on the determinations of power itself. Issues of class, race, ethnicity, gender, or even national politics rarely enter the discussion of strategy and spoils. For an approach to politics which stresses spoils, it is oddly devoid of the material and historical context which define those contested resources. A view of politics which stresses gamesmanship and corruption without cultural contexts and historical placement comes perilously close to being an ideological concomitant of the very theories of function and consensus to which the processual approach was purportedly opposed.

Culture and Politics

Another area where comparative materials from the anthropological literature sheds light on the operation of human societies and political control is the symbolic area. Some have stated that perhaps this is the most crucial area for anthropologists to investigate (Cohen, 1974). In every society, the relationship between leader and led is couched in partially mystical and partially highly symbolic terms. For people to obey and become co-opted in a potentially punitive relationship, symbols aid in obfuscating and masking the political reality.

In the 1970s, and heavily influenced by the processual schools, another focus of political anthropology emerged in the literature (Cohen, 1974). Interest centered on the "dense" aspects of culture—religion, ritual, values, and symbols—in human societies.

These areas of behavior, especially rituals and symbols, were not viewed for their intrinsic content or the functions they played in evoking emotions but were focused upon because they clearly displayed and defined the power relations in society.

Cohen and Middleton (1967) and Asad (1973) argue forcibly that rituals and symbols are part of the grist of social anthropology and, therefore, become part of the political power of social groups and individuals within society. The symbols and rituals, because of their ranking within society and their emotional effect upon individuals, are a critical element in the power distribution within human societies. One article in this collection, "Regimes in Catholic Dutch Brabant," by Mart Bax, documents how pilgrimages and processions document the power hierarchy within a Dutch community.

Rituals and symbols can not only be analyzed as an index of power relations, but they also enter into the political process as resources in conflict. Those individuals or groups that control and regulate the rituals and accompanying symbols reap political benefits. As Cohen (1976) stated, relations of political and economic power "are objectified, developed, maintained, expressed or camouflaged by means of symbolic forms or patterns of symbolic action."

Cohen's study (1981) documents how an African elite add to the economic power by manipulating rituals and symbols. One has to only remember the United States presidential election of 1988 to grasp the importance of symbols in a political struggle. Both candidates tried to appropriate the American flag and the Pledge of Allegiance as a critical resource for their respective parties.

The control of rituals, in the widest sense, is a human resource. The performance requires human personnel, and these individuals usually are the cadre of the basic support group in any conflict. The ritual and symbolic always become intertwined with fundamental economic resources. Although Bax's article does not discuss the resources collected during the performances, we are not aware of many societies that do not ritually and symbolically support the collection and distribution of resources.

We have briefly discussed the use of symbols as an index of political inequality and their use in political arenas. Another utilization of ideology and symbols is found in the Janus aspect of ideology, that is, its power lies in blunting the reality of subordination and in the acceptance of hegemony.

Symbolic ritual behavior may seem to be paradoxical. The control of ritual by a social class, group, or faction demonstrates and cements a power relationship. However, the use of symbols which contain elements of a larger group context or values of a community may obfuscate or obscure the power relationship. Studies of political conflict indicate that the values of symbol, contained within rituals, are critical for cohesion of a wider network (Gluckman, 1963; Evans-Pritchard, 1949).

Anthropologists usually base their generalizations on material from smaller societies, but the same patterns prevail in more complex societies, such as the state in all of its variations. Donald Kurtz, "Strategies of Legitimation and the Aztec State," and Mart Bax, "Religious Regimes in Catholic Dutch Brabant," demonstrate how the control and manipulations of these symbols operate in a state on a micro level. In smaller societies, the varieties of competing groups and the variations in rituals are perhaps less limited but operate effectively in political dramas and conflicts.

The Problem of Leaders

When anthropologists perform fieldwork studying political activity, they tend to work on a micro level, stressing the smaller networks in which individuals act. This attitude and type of work presents problems. In complex societies, the different levels in the society are sometimes ignored. The field techniques that the anthropologist employs lead to an incomplete picture of how political changes occur. For example, a study of a small town in Mexico for the purpose of understanding how political processes operate may be incomplete unless one has some indication of how the major political parties whose concerns are national and international have an impact upon the town. An anthropologist can understand those actions which are primarily regulated by the people in the town, but if larger political bodies impinge upon the town, the anthropologist is usually incapable of analyzing these actions or may ignore them. The micro view alone usually presents an incomplete picture.

Political behavior has a structure; this structure contains invariant features which are necessary in carrying out political activities. Political actions are based upon a culturally defined concept of *authority*. To carry out political actions, people must perceive others as being able to command and utilize power in an effective manner.

An anthropologist documents the varieties of concepts of authority or power that exist in different societies. All societies do not view power and authority in exactly the same fashion; some societies, such as the western ones, generally see authority and power as useful and desirable. Miller's study of the Fox Indians (1955) finds that these Indians regard power as dangerous and avoid it. How individuals react to their leaders may depend upon their definition of power and authority. Many disposed or lower-class individuals in the United States distrust authority and try to avoid those in society who exercise it. They have learned that trouble seems to result in their interaction with these individuals. Any understanding of the operation of political systems should start with the society's definition of and viewpoints on authority.

Secondly, every political system has individuals who exercise *leadership*. One critical comparative question is why these leaders are selected. Every group has regulations and patterns of leadership selection, and no society leaves leadership recruitment to chance. In some societies, leaders are selected from a particular family group, and thus the leadership recruitment is from a very small portion of the total society. In a limited number of cases, a leader is selected from an even smaller potential range of possibilities—they have come from the offspring of brothers and sisters. In a class society, leaders generally are recruited from only certain classes; rarely are lower-class leaders selected. In addition to the group orientation to leadership selection, all societies have other criteria they demand from their leaders. Age and gender enter into the mixture, but some societies, in a limited number of cases, are not concerned with the gender factor. The majority of class societies, however, tend to stress the gender factor and, therefore, mostly males are recruited for leadership posts.

A very small number of societies primarily recruit women for leadership positions. As we have suggested, politics is not an isolated institution but is heavily influenced by other institutions in the society. Political rules are affected by other domains. Where women are selected for leadership posts, it is usually implied that group recruitment is important and women from a particular family may be selected. Group membership overrides gender.

We have represented political anthropology as portrayed on different stages and have stressed that in most cases anthropologists are comfortable with material of a micro level, but a large number of studies also suggests that a very general type of comparative study can be generated by anthropologists. The comparative study, however, by the nature of the materials, is of a very general nature and cannot adequately discuss some of the finer techniques of political infighting. A number of excellent case studies exist (see Bailey), and this type of comparative study explores broad universal features of every political action or political control within a restricted social unit.

For political activity to be carried out, some rationale for constructing a leader-led relationship has to be developed. Fundamentally, a society must have in its cultural repertoire some expectations of how to interact with a leader, some grasp of what the leader can and cannot do. There are great variations between societies, as we will indicate later in the work, that make a difference in how authority relationships are organized.

Political Economy and Marxism

Rarely, as we have seen, do new social science concerns or theories arrive in a single dramatic moment. However, the timing of such arrivals are often unannounced and carried by historical currents of the moment. Although the prevailing paradigm of structural functionalism and processual analysis coexisted uneasily with perspectives emphasizing historicity, evolutionism, and levels of social analysis the social and cultural changes of the sixties and seventies accelerated the demands for theory which would encompass change, comparison, and contradiction. Power in all of its manifestations became a central and overt concern of varieties of anthropological discourse.

A key factor in the analysis of social being is obviously the political. Some anthropologists argue that too much emphasis is given to the political, and that what passes as political explains either too much or too little at the expense of economic, cultural, or social factors. However appropriate those criticisms may be, the need to elaborate a comprehensive anthropological approach to the crucial political sphere is not diminished. As we have already shown, the anthropological views on political behavior and institutions are eclectic and varied. There does appear to be a theoretical construct which may allow us to formulate a fairly systematic, coherent, and methodologically powerful view of the relationship between politics and society—political economy, for example, and especially its Marxist variants.

There are several important dimensions to this approach. First, a traditional emphasis in anthropology, however breached in practice, is holism. Holism accepts that, however anthropology's subject matter (economics,

culture, religion, kinship, politics) may be separated for analytic purposes, the various branches actually form a social totality. Political economy, for example, accepts this holism by reflecting a social process in
which political, economic, and cultural factors are inevitably and inextricably enmeshed.

The political economy approach makes it possible to transcend
structural/functionalism and processual models by reformulating the
problematic of power and by redefining the basic focus of interest. The
focus would be reinterpreted from the context of a specific ethnographic
analysis of individual political systems or from the universalist approach
to political behavior. Political economy has redefined interest in power
along several new axes: the analysis of the unit of study not as a political
system but as a social formation; the analysis of the corresponding concept of the mode of production rather than of political processes; and the
coexistence and articulation of various modes of production. Together
with a renewed interest in social stratification or the unequal accumulation of power in the types of societies anthropologists have studied, there
is a new emphasis on the processes and social relations of production as
well as those of authority or adjudication and a concern with social
dynamics and history. All of this has two immediate consequences for the
political realm. First, there is a shift in the emphasis on method from the
traditional concern with micro-level participant observation to include
the methods of the historian, economist, sociologist, and political scientist. The political economist is aware of the layering of power which
cannot be accurately measured or accounted for at the micro level because of the evolution of the state. Therefore, the new emphasis requires
interdisciplinary links from which the conventional disciplinary boundaries may appear arbitrary and irrelevant at best or an ideological obfusca-
tion of political meaning at worst.

The approach of political economy has certain affinities with the
anthropological idea of holism. The idea of totality is of great significance
to anthropologists since the unit of analysis as an integrated whole is not
split arbitrarily into disciplinary or institutional subdivisions (such as the
political system). Subsequent analysis must take into account the concrete socio-historical nexus in which the political behavior is situated. As
an idea, totality (as in *Political Economy)* is powerfully attractive, but
the Marxist anthropologist might well ask how one might operationalize
this idea.

Without showing distinctions between those ideas found in Marx and
those which claim inspiration from him, an inventory of key concepts are
in order. The definitions of these concepts are taken from Jonathan Friedman (1975).

Mode of production: the specific manner in which the means needed to provide maintenance are produced; for example, feudalism, slavery, capitalism.

1. *Societal formation:* the actual empirical instance of a mode of production such as in France, Athens, or the United States are examples of feudalistic, enslaving, and capitalistic modes of production, respectively.

   a. *Forces of production* refers to the relations between the producer, the means of production, or the production process.

   b. *Social relations of production* refers to the relations between the producer, the means of production, and the control mechanisms which dominate production and the producers.

   c. *Superstructure.* The above two modes of production factors may be conceived metaphorically as the base or infrastructure of a social formation upon which lies the existence and form of dominant institutions, including the political plus social consciousness.

2. *Model of social reproduction.* If the above factors of a mode of production constitute a structure, its construction is by varying degrees unstable and shifting. In any social formation the combination of historically received conditions, the maturing and developing factors within the forces and relations of production, and the external factors operate variously to either constrain, strengthen, and/or transform the social formations' structured means of reproduction. The articulation of these factors represent the dynamic model of social reproduction.

This model questions and tests the applicability of Marxist ideas to nonwestern society. Historical materialism either explains all societies or none. The analytic problems that Marxist anthropology confronts within the debates on modes of production are appropriation of surplus product, fetishism, labor, theories of value, relation between base and superstructure, and the reanalysis of the origins of the state, Asiatic mode of production, primitive communism, and slavery, to name a few. Decisive issues which are only implied—such as uneven development and gender—can be added to the classically received problems.

The use of a Marxist analysis in the study of societies is advantageous because the type of reality chosen to function as a starting point for social analysis (whether it be political, economic, or familial) should end up revealing power relations and the different modalities whereby they function. The analysis of ideology, power, and conflict, however, present the complexities of Marxist anthropology.

Ideology has usually been identified with the study of belief systems in anthropology, leading to a total lack of discrimination in the belief systems' social basis and history. The varieties of beliefs—religion, witch-craft, political theories, fetishization of kinship, and commodities—map out the roles we play in social reproduction concerning family, knowl-edge, and wealth, which, in turn, define our life chances. Ideology con-structs the forms of subjects and their historical objects (domination) by providing the supports of social relations and inserting people into the structures of the social formation. The very separation of the ideological from the political allows ideology to perform a role in securing social reproduction and domination. In sum, the state, or the lineage, is not the reality that stands behind the mask of political practice. The state is itself a mask which prevents our seeing political practice as it is. The relation-ship between a kinship system and a kinship idea or a state system and a state idea and other forms of social power should be central concerns of political analysis, and such concerns direct our attention to the everyday practice of politics. Thus, the basis of politics is in the interplay between systems and ideas in which interconnections between life circumstances and subjectivity and, therefore, between the strategies of domination and the patterns of hegemony, are accomplished. In the context of experi-ence, the activity itself has significance. Here then is the basis of politics. The difficulty inherent in an ideological approach lies in the question concerning the types of politics that are possible when the actions and wishes of its recipients are not reduced to a choice between either action or complacency. Through ideology, collective action and individual needs are bound together.

The processual approach realized that normative rules and their sym-bols are vague and manipulable. Symbols are, therefore, as Abner Cohen (1979) states, "bivocal"; they express the human condition in a charged ideological sense and, therefore, express relations of power. This is clearly shown in the recent work of Maurice Godelier (1988). Godelier posits that, in a societal analysis, it is wrong for anthropologists to sepa-rate relations of production from superstructure. Class and power are inseparable from ideology because culture is itself a code extending from language to material symbols through which hierarchy, gender relations, and so on, reproduce themselves both in ideal and real realities. The study of political economy finds that the cultural domain is inseparable from power and its transformations.

Maurice Godelier (1988) has contributed significantly to the study of ideology from a Marxist perspective. His difficulty lies with one of the classic issues in political economy and political anthropology—namely, the relationship between cultural ideas and political practice or, in tradi-tional Marxist terminology, the interpenetration of base and superstructure. For instance, in Australian aboriginal society all social relations are embedded in a kinship group. In other words, kinship functions as a relation of production. However, among aborigines kinship constructs do not reflect actual kinship relations. Instead, kinship determines which ties are operative for filiation. This theory raises a few questions: does kinship, then, have primacy in the daily politics of aboriginal life? Or does religion dominate in Sumerian society because peasants gave their labor and product surplus to the temples of the city-state? Or were all relations in Ancient Greece—including the role of slavery—determined by political constitutional ideas because civic politics, which determined access to the land and citizenship itself, dominated?

Godelier's exploratory solution to these problems was to consider the meaning of the apparent primacy of religion, kinship, or politics in these three modes of production. Godelier looked to the interaction of ideas and relations of production in the manner in which ideas of kinship in an aboriginal social formation functioned both in the direct appropriation of nature by kinship constituted groups and as an ideology of nature and social relations. The ideas of Sumerian theocracy, in turn, functioned to expropriate the peasant's product and provided a cosmological and unified ideology of power and hierarchy. In the case of Ancient Greece, citizenship in the polis was inseparable from the democratic constitution's clear connection between the ideas of freedom and the civil status of slaves in the slave mode of production.

Michael Taussig (1980) examines the way in which an ideology of resistance that reflects an opposition to the hierarchical and dominating ideology of church and state may arise and reproduce itself. In *The Devil and Commodity Fetishism in Latin America* (1980), Taussig traces alternative religious beliefs to Spanish Catholicism with its local reworking that arose among Columbian blacks under slavery, peasantry, and, finally, proletarian plantation working conditions. Taussig argues that Spanish Catholicism provided an ideological resistance for the blacks during the various regimes of political economy in the last two hundred years. Under the current regime, according to Taussig, the plantation workers make contracts with the devil to increase wages and productivity. Taussig examines the manner in which money enters into the folk beliefs of the field workers in otherwise Catholic ritual settings. The peasants, in effect, attempt to transfer blessings from the intended souls into hard currency, thereby objectifying the needs and neglects of their lives in exchange for the wages that hold them in thrall and which they desperately need to increase. Although Taussig offers a sophisticated report and analysis of these African-Latin beliefs, it is difficult, as the above example indicates, to accept his contention that these beliefs are in opposition rather than

an instance of interpenetration, in Godelier's sense, between the hege-
monic beliefs and practices of the powerful and their distortion as lived
ideology by the powerless.

The question of ideology is, therefore, inextricably linked to the issue
of power—an issue with which Marxist anthropology has just begun to
grapple. The analysis of ideology shows that social formation and political
conventions are embedded in the social relations of production. Whether
the accumulation of power in a social formation centers on gender, seniority, rank, status, or the articulations between them, ideology qualifies
the uses of power from a domination mediated by exploitation.

One of the most successful studies to treat the issue of ideology and
power is June Nash's *We Eat the Mines and They Eat Us* (1979). Nash's
work is concerned with the miners in Bolivia of mixed Aymara and
Ladino background who speak Spanish and seem to have adopted the
norms of Ladino culture. The miners consider their work prestigious
and important for social mobility. Nash makes an important contribution
to the comparative treatment of power relations by focusing on class
formation and community solidarity, thus giving political anthropology a
special relevance for class analysis. The mine workers and their families
are better informed of world events than U.S. workers, and they clearly
articulate the nature of capitalist exploitation. So why is there a lack of
effective revolutionary militancy? According to Nash, the miners and
their community may adapt fluid social ties, cocoa chewing, and com-
mercialization as aspects of their exploitative living and working conditions, but their identity has reinforced the idea of a sense of "self as
members of a community," which is forged by a class consciousness
opposed to the mine operations, the military, and the government. The
life style, conditions, and ideologies of the miners are not only the locus
of their resistance to the power structure but also the setting of their
domination.

Rarely has a scholar been able to weave a multilayered analysis of
individuals, communities, and regions as has Sidney Mintz (1990). Although his studies are multifaceted and broad, the best sample of his
work is *Caribbean Transformation,* a collection of some of his early
essays. Three sections—"Slavery, Forced Labor and The Plantation System," "Caribbean Peasantries," and "Caribbean Nationhood"—constitute
clues to Mintz's approach to political economy. His work is historical in a
sense in that it attempts to place the local community into a context of
global processes and situates both the receiver and responder of these
processes in time. Local and regional practices and institutions are seen
as creative as well as imposed responses to the power of economic
enterprises, state agencies and empires. These essays show that an ap-

proach from political economy alone can situate the subject matter of anthropology in its fully local and global settings.

Conflict is the third modality of analysis for a Marxist informed research of politics. For Marx, human objectification takes place through definite forms of social relations, which can be grouped into historical stages. Each has its own particular form of domination, which Marx broadly defined as the control of one group over the production and reproduction of another. These social inequalities provide the laws for the historical transformations in the social relations of production. Domination, exploitation, repression, and resistance are the objectives that capture the emphasis and practice of political conflict situated in relation to production.

Eric Wolf's *Peasant Wars of the Twentieth Century* (1969) is an important contribution to the study of political conflict in the twentieth century. Wolf examines six major revolutions of this century in which peasant participation has proven decisive: Mexico, the Soviet Union, China, Vietnam, Algeria, and Cuba. Wolf sets out to determine the processes of peasant rebellion and its place within revolutionary events and transformations and in doing so focuses on class analysis within the peasant community as well as between the rural population and the elites. He considers the roles within a rural class conflict of landlords, rich peasants, middle peasants, poor peasants, and the rural proletariat not only in terms of land ownership but also in the relations of production.

Wolf maintains that the poor peasants and proletariat constitute the revolutionary mass but, due to their economic dependence, require other class segments to initiate the revolutionary movement. According to Wolf, the middle peasants, with their initial victories over the elite, broke the controls over the poor peasants and propelled them into revolutionary action. "Ultimately, the decisive factor in making a peasant rebellion possible lies in the relation of the peasantry to the field of power which surrounds it. A rebellion cannot start from a situation of complete impotence" (p. 240). The peasants had to have had an organizational vehicle with which to marshal their forces and struggle for power. Wolf sets out important variables in the class struggles of the countryside: the degrees culture of solidarity in the peasant community, the strength of the administrative and repressive apparatus of the state, and the relative autonomy of the peasants from direct control of the landlord class.

One of Marx's central contributions to social science is his classification of societies according to relations of production. His classification cannot be reduced to economic foundations because the relations of production by definition include politics and ideology. His judgments and analysis obviously must stand on their own merits, but it is clear that much of what passes as political anthropology is decidedly pre-Marxist in its grasp of social theory. An encounter with the diverse and contradictory examples of Marxism should bring the discipline of anthropology—and not just the artificial consideration of an unhistorical and one-dimensional political anthropology—back to the total unity of theory and practice that is anthropology's strongest and best conceit.

The perspective of political economy, especially its Marxist variant, can be witnessed by the various contributions that we have lumped under this category. We must note that the various authors and works that we mention are not necessarily committed to political economy, nor would they necessarily recognize the categorization of political economy for their work. We have, however, chosen to interpret their contributions within the context of political economy.

The literature of political economy signifies the return of anthropology to questions of change and comparisons in short; history itself as patterns and processes. These issues need not concern themselves with the distant past alone. In fact, history is inevitably concerned with the contemporary—how we have arrived here and how we cope with the present. Unlike the processual approach, political economy stresses that whether the level of research is the small-scale community, the nation, or global processes, certain fundamental research configurations are defined by asking variations of the following questions: What large-scale processes is it necessary to understand in order to account for change? (As we have seen, the mode of production provides a partial model for this answer.) How are systemic, large-scale changes reflected at the micro level or relations of production? What is the role of comparison in understanding political behavior? The answer to these questions should validate the value of political economy.

Anthropologists have made signal contributions to the above issues, but of particular note is the degree to which these issues have become increasingly interdisciplinary in their approaches and concerns. Many current studies within the anthropology of political economy are products of dialogue with scholarly practitioners who formally are characterized as economists, historians, political scientists, and sociologists. The works of Amin, Braudel, Frank, Wallerstein, Anderson, Skocpol, Hobsbawm, Williams, and Brenner, are mined by anthropologists with the same ease as the aforementioned may find reference to anthropologists such as Sahlins, Roseberry, Wolf, Mintz, Leacock, Terray, Rey, Meillousoux, and Geertz. The most striking synthesis and pathbreaking work within anthropology proper, and which represents this new eclectic representation of political economy, is found in Eric Wolf's *Europe and the People Without History* (1982). No further work on the subject of political anthropology can proceed without this benchmark study, which defines the elements of class, race, and ethnicity as the fundamentals of the anthropological subject. Wolf's study and other related works call for nothing less than a rereading and reanalysis of the traditional corpus of ethnography and in turn direct our attention again to those received problems of the past such as the nature of the state and its origins.

The one concern of political anthropology which has provided a torrent of theoretical currents and interests has been the study and analysis of the origins of social stratification and the state. The origins of the state and social hierarchy also inevitably create dialogue and collaboration between archaeology and social anthropology. We have already taken note of the perspectives on the state and social stratification formed in the very foundation of the field of anthropology itself. The reader may trace this study under its various guises through Morgan and Maine to today's research.

Perhaps the study of state formation, like no other issue in political anthropology, reveals the preconceptions of the scholar or researcher. Terms such as *complex* or *civilized* in anthropological or ethnological terms reveal a particularly static view of social process. The state viewed in this manner rejects the world historic moment of time. According to Engels (1881), the "state is a product of society at a certain stage of development . . . a power seemingly standing above a society in its ability to arbitrate conflict and maintain order among the citizens inhabiting a certain territory." The state, then, has not existed from all eternity. There have been societies that have had no idea of the state and state power. At a certain stage of economic development, the state became a necessity with the split of society into classes. The state as a "public power," then, which maintains itself by taxing its citizens is, as a rule, the state of the most powerful, economically dominant class which, through the medium of the state, becomes also the politically dominant class. This conceptualization of the state is a direct rebuttal to Radcliffe-Brown's (1946) contention in his introduction to *African Political Systems* that the idea of the state should be eliminated from political analysis. Engels's position is also opposed to attempts to categorize the state by its reputed functional problems, functional subsystem, political culture, and style. This reductionism means that all real world state systems are "functional" and all structures are mixed. Such fuzzy conceptions have no need for the state—the state has not been explained but, rather, explained away.

Although not all political anthropologists would totally accept Engels's definition of the state, all would accept that the study of the state is primarily an examination of the distribution of power and social inequality.

If one accepts the view that the state developed as an instrument for the protection of class relations and an instrument of domination by an economically powerful class, then a model of social stratification that encompasses the forms of "domination" and surplus appropriation is required. This in turn belies any anthropological reference to simple functions of the state and, rather, demands a complex interweaving of levels of combined processes of the state that reflect the constant struggle of domination versus resistance. This connection should be not only between classes and class factions, but between the state and its bureaucracy, which has its own degree of autonomy to protect.

Christine Ward Gailey, *From Kinship to Kingship* (1987), examines the effect and processes of state formation and class stratification by emphasizing changes in gender relations, roles, and ideology as reflected in the changes and contradictions in the forces and relation of production. Gailey examines changes in women's status over three hundred years in the Polynesian kingdom of Tonga. This study has implications not only for the study of the evolution of the state but also for the effects of colonialism on indigenous systems of social order. Gailey describes a process in which class and state formation affect the gender stratification of men and women. The multiple roles of women in autonomous kin-based communities such as Tonga cannot be tolerated by the rising hierarchies and civil authorities. As wives, sisters, traders and producers of mats—the markers of status and kin ties—it was essential that women were subordinated both reproductively and productively to class formation and emerging state institutions. This remarkable book, via ethnohistory, returns to the issues of inequality and exploitation as first raised by Engels.

Political anthropology should provide important contributions to the issues of race and gender. Racism in its boundary-marking and castelike social oppression is a particularly virulent outcome of Western expansion in the world today. To paraphrase W.E.B. Du Bois (1969), race and the race question remains a global issue of paramount importance for the twenty-first century. Anthropology has been able to extricate the cultural symbolization of racism from its social moorings, but it has not been able to move them alone. Studies by Mintz, Wolf, Hannerz, Williams, Bolland, Abrahams, Herskovitz, and others have made significant contributions to the analysis of racism. But the synthesis of what Cohen (1974) or Godelier (1988) recognize as that bivocal of the ideal and real in racism as it reproduces itself in the social practice of power is yet to be comparatively and theoretically studied and given due importance within political anthropology.

The saliency and urgency of gender analysis shares many of the same flaws as race. However, the crucial difference is that the last several years have witnessed a proliferation of both ethnographic and theoretical concerns with gender studies. Probably no single issue of power has transformed the way we think of traditional anthropological subject matter, such as kinship and the family, and made them inseparable from the social analysis of power than gender studies. The necessarily forceful pioneering work of feminist anthropologists has contributed to making the half of humanity otherwise ignored in the discourses of power physical, vocal, and active. Gender studies have helped to liberate the full meaning of stratification from its sexist, racist, and class bias. As with racism and class, the current issues of gender relations often reflect the traditional disputes between cultural and social explanations of the human condition. Neo-Marxists have found that the explanations of gender hierarchy and power are apparent in a dynamic interplay between class and gender cultural constructs and specific conditions of stratification.

Political anthropology always reflects the occurrence of opinions, however veiled, of power relations. In the 1990s, pervasive changes require a coherent perspective so that we may order what we think we know, examine what we need to learn, and signal those events which are, as yet, unanticipated so that they may be understood. Political economy—itself no solvent—goes beyond political anthropology with its quest to combine and recombine the elements of power in a manner that recognizes and accepts the constant dynamics of all social life.

BIBLIOGRAPHY

Asad, Talal. *Anthropology and the Colonial Encounter.* Ithaca, 1973.
Bailey, Frederick G. *Humbuggery and Manipulation: The Art of Leadership.* Ithaca, 1988.
———. *Morality and Expediency.* Oxford, 1977.
Balandier, Georges. *Political Anthropology.* New York, 1970.
Barnes, John. *Politics in a Changing Society.* Manchester, 1954.
Barth, Frederick. *Political Leadership Among the Swat Pathans.* London, 1959.
Bourdieu, Pierre. *Outline of a Theory of Practice.* Cambridge, 1977.
Brown, Paula. "Patterns of Authority in West Africa." *Africa* 21 (1951), 261–95.
Cohen, Abner. *Two-Dimensional Man.* London, 1974.
———. "Political Symbolism." *Annual Review of Anthropology* 8 (1979), 87–113.
Cunnison, Ian. *History of the Luapuin.* Manchester, 1951.
Donham, Donald. *History, Power, Ideology: Central Issues in Marxism and Anthropology.* Cambridge, 1990.
Du Bois, W.E.B. *The Souls of Black Folk.* New York, 1969.
Durkheim, Emile. *The Rules of Sociological Method.* Paris, 1895.
Eggan, Fred. *The American Indian.* Chicago, 1966.

Engels, Frederick. *The Origins of the Family, Private Property, and the State.* New York, 1881.

Evans-Pritchard, E. E. *The Nuer.* Oxford, 1940.

———. *The Sanusi of Cyrenaica.* Oxford, 1949.

Fallers, Lloyd. *Bantu Bureaucracy.* London, 1963.

Fortes, M., and E. E. Evans-Pritchard. *African Political Systems.* Oxford, 1940.

Fortes, Meyer. "The Structure of Unilineal Descent Groups." *American Anthropologist* 55 (1953), 117–41.

Fried, Morton. *The Evolution of Political Society.* New York, 1967.

Friedman, Jonathan. "Tribes, States, and Transformations." In *Marxist Analyses and Social Anthropology,* ed. Maurice Bloch. London, 1975.

Gailey, C. W. *From Kinship to Kingship.* Austin, Texas, 1987.

Gledhill, J., B. Bender, and M. Larsen, eds. *State and Society.* London, 1988.

Gluckman, Max. *Order and Rebellion in Tribal Africa.* London, 1963.

———. *Political Law and Ritual in Tribal Society.* Oxford, 1965.

Godelier, Maurice. *The Mental and the Material.* London, 1988.

———. *Perspectives in Marxist Anthropology.* Cambridge, 1977.

Gulliver, Phillip. *Social Control in an African Society.* London, 1963.

Leach, Edmond. *Political Systems of Highland Burma.* Boston, 1954.

Lloyd, Peter. "The Traditional Political System of the Yoruba." *Southwestern Journal of Anthropology* 10 (1954), 366–84.

Lowie, Robert. *The Origin of the State.* New York, 1927.

Maine, Henry. *Ancient Law.* London, 1887.

Middleton, John, and David Tait, eds. *Tribes Without Rulers.* London, 1958.

Miller, D., M. Rowlands, and C. Tilley, eds. *Domination and Resistance.* London, 1989.

Miller, Walter. "Two Concepts of Authority." *American Anthropologist* 57 (1955), 271–89.

Mintz, Sidney. *Caribbean Transformations.* Ann Arbor, 1990.

Morgan, Lewis Henry. *Ancient Society.* New York, 1877.

Nadel, Seigfried. *A Black Byzantium.* Oxford, 1942.

Nash, June. *We Eat the Mines and the Mines Eat Us.* New York, 1979.

Radcliffe-Brown, A. R. "Introduction." In *African Political Systems,* ed. M. Fortes and E. E. Evans-Pritchard. London, 1946.

———. *Structure and Function in Primitive Society.* London, 1952.

Schapera, Isaac. *Government and Politics in Tribal Societies.* London, 1956.

Schneider, David. "Political Organization, Supernatural Sanctions and the Punishment of Incest of Yap." *American Anthropologist* 59 (1957), 791–800.

Scott, James. *Domination and the Arts of Resistance.* New Haven, 1990.

Southall, Aiden. *Alur Society.* Cambridge, 1953.

Swartz, Marc, Victor Turner, and Arthur Tuden. *Political Anthropology.* Chicago, 1966.

Taussig, M. *The Devil and Commodity Fetishism in Latin America.* Chapel Hill, 1980.

✓Tuden, Arthur. "Trends in Political Anthropology." *Proceedings of the American Philosophical Society* 113 (1969), 336–40.

Upham, Steadman. *The Evolution of Political Systems*. Cambridge, 1990.

Vansina, Jan. "A Comparison of African Kingdoms." *Africa* 32 (1962), 324–35.

Vincent, Joan. *Anthropology and Politics*. Tucson, 1990.

Wolf, Eric. *Europe and the People Without History*. Berkeley and Los Angeles, 1982.

———. *Peasant Wars of the Twentieth Century*. New York, 1969.

Worsley, Peter. *The Trumpet Shall Sound*. London, 1957.

Ritual Resolution in Meta' Legal Process

Richard G. Dillon

The regulation of conflict in societies varies greatly and depends upon the social and cultural variables in the society. In complex industrial societies coercion is consistently employed, usually indicating social distance between members of the societies. In societies where the stratification is not as well developed, other techniques to regulate and adjudicate conflict appear more frequently. Among the Meta', religious-supernatural factors play a critical role in resolving conflict. Social pressures and supernatural punishment facilitate the resolution of conflict. One can speculate that perhaps the ethno-historical record does not reveal the complexity of the social context, and that other factors—such as human manipulation—also played a role.

In this case, we see how the corporate kin group is considered inviolate, and that within this group four criteria of power receive magical expression: authority, age, wealth, and sex. Dillon's analysis of ritual resolution shows how ritual mediates between the politico-rural domain and the domestic kinship domain or between the power of kin segments and the real-life situations of the members of kin segments.

SPECIALISTS IN CONFLICT resolution by ritual means, such as the much discussed Nuer Leopard-Skin Chief, have long been familiar in the anthropological literature (Evans-Pritchard 1940, 1956; Howell 1954), and a number of studies have shown how disputes may be resolved by linking social conflict and supernatural danger (Fortes 1940, 1945; Harper 1957; Huber 1959; Llewellyn and Hoebel 1941; Schneider 1957;

Winans and Edgerton 1964). However, relatively little progress has been made in understanding ritual conflict resolution as a legal phenomenon. Specialists in the anthropology of law have rarely integrated it into their discussions of the variability of human legal systems (Nader 1969; Nader and Yngvesson 1973; Pospisil 1971). Moreover, those scholars now writing on ritual conflict resolution generally stress the symbolism and ritual involved while de-emphasizing conflict resolution itself (Douglas 1966; Lienhardt 1961; Turner 1968, 1969). As a result the debate continues as to how ritual conflict resolution really worked in classic examples such as the settlement of homicide cases by the Leopard-Skin Chief (Beidelman 1971; Greuel 1971; Haight 1972), and many important questions regarding the role of ritual resolution procedures in human legal systems remain unanswered.

The purpose of this paper is to define those factors that are essential to the operation of ritual conflict resolution as a legal process. Data from Meta' society in the United Republic of Cameroon will be used to illustrate three distinct kinds of cases in which this approach to legal problem solving was employed in pre-colonial times.[1] The focus is on the immediate pre-colonial period (ca. 1900), as it was at this time that the Meta' relied on ritual resolution most extensively.[2] As will be seen, the relationships of the disputants and the issues at stake may have varied from case to case, but common factors underlay the working of ritual conflict resolution in every instance. Specifically, ritual resolution is shown to have operated as a process of psycho-social intimidation.

Meta' Society

In the immediate pre-colonial period, the Meta' (also known as Menemo) were a group of about 15,000 living on the southwestern edge of the Bamenda plateau in what is now the United Republic of Cameroon. The settlement pattern was predominantly one of dispersed homesteads or compounds. In the absence of centralized government, it was mainly common language and a strong sentiment of shared descent that united the Meta' people. Internally, Meta' society was divided into both patrilineal descent groups and villages. Localized patrilineages of ten to forty households regulated the inheritance of farmland as well as the distribution of bridewealth valuables, and most lineages asserted ties of clanship with comparable groups in other parts of Meta' territory. However, there was no inclusive genealogy that structured the relationships of all patrilineal groups within the society.

Villages were groups of several hundred inhabitants in which several unrelated lineages were normally co-resident. Village-level leadership was provided by a set of lineage-head/councillors known as *meukum si* ("notables") who protected the village from hostile supernatural influences and resolved many inter-lineage disputes. One of their number, the *fɔn* had a preeminent and chieflike role.

Meta' economy in pre-colonial times was based on a bush fallow system of cultivation, the major crops being yams, maize, groundnuts, plantains, and palm oil. Bridewealth, payable in goats, brass bracelets, palm oil, cloth, and other commodities was substantial, and marriage quite late for males other than those succeeding to a compound headship. Although the Meta' were not active long distance traders like some of their highlands neighbors (Chilver 1961; Warnier 1975), important trade routes did pass through several Meta' markets (Dillon 1973a, 1973b).

Conflict in pre-colonial Meta' focused mainly on rights over persons, property, and essential resources. The theft of goats—the principal component of bridewealth payments—posed a serious problem, as did disputes over the ownership of farmland and groves of raffia and oil palms. In addition, inter-lineage conflict frequently arose because of the failure to refund bridewealth in cases of divorce.

The Meta' system of law and conflict resolution provided a range of alternatives for handling such problems. Although uncentralized at the societal level, this system was capable of resolving conflicts between even the most widely separated Meta' villages. In some instances, dispute settlement depended on the use of coercive force, as when one lineage seized a hostage from another to insure the return of a runaway wife. Just as frequently, however, the Meta' approach to legal problem solving was subtle and indirect. Numerous procedures for resolving disputes without confrontation were available, the processes of ritual resolution to be discussed here providing but one example.

Concepts of Supernatural Power and Danger

Beliefs about supernatural power and danger laid the foundations for ritual conflict resolution in Meta' and must therefore be outlined before the discussion of ritual resolution itself can begin. One of the most important such beliefs was the idea of *ndɔn*. Briefly, *ndɔn* was a state of supernatural danger or susceptibility to supernaturally caused misfortune. Often translated as "bad luck" by English speaking Meta', *ndɔn* could be manifested in illness, poverty, death, the barrenness of women, and countless other misfortunes.

Several characteristic *ndɔn* situations can be distinguished, and describing two of these affords a convenient entry into Meta' conceptions of supernatural danger. The first type of *ndɔn* typically occurred when important moral rules had been violated within the kin group or community. For example, if a man fought with an agnate, committed adultery with the wife of a fellow clansman, or failed to pay bridewealth promised to an affine, he might suffer *ndɔn*. Usurping the political position of another, such as a chief or a lineage head, could also lead to *ndɔn*.

In cases such as these, it was first and foremost the speech of the offended party that was believed to cause *ndɔn*. His complaint was described as an *njɔm* ("statement of correct words"), a term applied to supernaturally powerful speech in many other contexts. The potency of the *njɔm* was thought to depend on several factors, including the truthfulness of the statement, the seriousness of the offense, the volume of the complaint, and the status of the complainer. A wholly truthful complaint repeated by many persons besides the injured party was believed almost certain to cause *ndɔn,* and complaints by lineage heads and village notables were thought to be more effective than those of ordinary persons.

It should also be noted that God was thought to have an important role in the genesis of *ndɔn*. The Meta' believed in a single Creator Spirit called Ŋwiə and saw themselves as being in a close relationship with this deity. In the view of many, it was actually Ŋwiə who heard the complaint of the injured party after a supernaturally dangerous offense and decided whether to punish the offender with *ndɔn*. Both the will of God and the word of man were thus important in the causation of *ndɔn*.

In situations where supernatural danger resulted from the complaints of an injured party, a remedy was usually sought in a negation or reversal of the *ndɔn*-causing speech. In some cases, the offender simply took steps to satisfy the offended party so that he would cease to complain, while in other instances either the offended party or his lineage head was asked to perform a ritual blessing the offender. As a general rule, one attempted to cut off *ndɔn* at its source by satisfying the person capable of speaking the strongest *njɔm* in the case.

A second type of *ndɔn* occurred in what are best described as situations of ritual pollution. Certain unusual or unnatural events were interpreted as evidence of *ndɔn*. These included death by lightning, death by falling from a tree, suicide, the death of a pregnant woman, the burning of a hut, a fight in which calabashes of wine are broken, acts of symbolic aggression such as throwing a spear at an enemy's roof, and many others. Although Meta' informants did not speculate freely on the causality of *ndɔn* in cases such as these, they treated each event as a serious manifestation of *ndɔn* that could lead to additional suffering if proper rituals were not performed.

Treatment for polluting *ndɔn* involved the intervention of an hereditary specialist (*weut ətu əʃay'i*). Each such specialist had the exclusive power to remove the *ndɔn* associated with specific unnatural events whenever they occurred within his territory, a monopoly that was itself sanctioned by *ndɔn*. Should anyone fail to summon the specialist after one of the aforementioned manifestations of *ndɔn*, that person ran the risk of suffering additional *ndɔn* from having violated his rights. The procedures by which ritual specialists ended states of polluting *ndɔn* usually entailed the removal of objects identified with the supernatural danger. For example, the *ndɔn* of suicide was removed when a specialist carried off the corpse for burial. Since these procedures were themselves considered to be supernaturally dangerous, specialists were normally well paid for their services.[3]

Finally, it should be stressed that *ndɔn* in all forms was believed to be contagious. The *ndɔn* resulting from a moral infraction was thought likely to spread from the offender himself to related persons, and in cases of polluting *ndɔn*, supernatural danger was often seen as something rather like a contagious disease. If one suicide or death by lightning went ritually untreated, another was believed likely to occur in the same compound or locality.

Varieties of Ritual Conflict Resolution in Meta'

The supernatural concepts outlined above were closely interwoven with the legal institutions of the Meta' and made possible the ritual resolution of numerous conflicts. The characteristics of Meta' ritual resolution can be simply stated: according to the usual process, one disputant performed an act that was believed to threaten him, and/or other parties, with *ndɔn*. This threat of supernatural danger then came to serve as a spur to the resolution of the conflict. Some party other than the offender always had a monopoly over the power to end *ndɔn* in the case and typically used this as the basis for extracting fines or fees from the disputants. Furthermore, in all varieties of ritual resolution, the monopoly of the resolution agent provided a source of leverage that could be used to press for the settlement of the dispute itself.

In the remaining part of this paper, I shall describe the typical sequence of events in three kinds of cases in which variant forms of ritual conflict resolution were characteristically employed in pre-colonial Meta' society. First, the treatment of homicide will be considered as an illustration of immediate ritual conflict resolution used to resolve a dangerous situation. Second, cases involving "acts of symbolic aggression" will be discussed in order to demonstrate how disputants sometimes deliberately induced the ritual resolution process to stimulate settlement of a chronic conflict. Finally, the way in which sickness and other signs of *ndɔn* were used to encourage men to atone for past offenses against their affines will be considered as an instance of delayed ritual resolution. In addition to illuminating common factors underlying the working of ritual conflict resolution in all cases, these examples will be useful in conveying some sense of the wide variety of situations in which this approach to dispute settlement was applied within the pre-colonial Meta' legal system.

Immediate Ritual Resolution in Homicide Cases

In certain disputes that occurred in pre-colonial Meta' society, a single significant act, performed in the course of the conflict, was seen as creating an imminent and terrible threat of *ndɔn*, and the ritual resolution process was immediately begun in order to relieve what was perceived as an already dangerous situation. Homicide occasioned this type of ritual resolution as did violent physical fighting with a clansman; betraying an agnate to slave catchers, thieves, or murderers; and clan incest or adultery with a fellow clansman's wife. In all such cases, the fear that the *ndɔn* caused by the supernaturally dangerous act would spread to the kinsmen of the offender was great.

Here, the treatment of homicide cases will provide the main example of immediate ritual resolution. In pre-colonial times, the resolution of homicide cases was a lengthy process involving the co-ordinated action of numerous ritual specialists and other conflict resolution agents. Whenever one Meta' person killed another—whether deliberately or accidentally, and regardless of whether the killer and victim were kin—the first reaction of those nearby was to raid the compound of the murderer, destroying crops and seizing valuable possessions. This despoiling of the killer's compound, referred to as *nayi* or *ɔkwatreu*, was joined in by relatives of the victim and bystanders alike. Although partly an act of revenge by the victim's kin (especially his own agnates), it also represented the first reaction of a mob, enraged that one Meta' man had shed the blood of another. This heinous offense was seen as a threat to the entire community, and the killer was usually forced to hide until the wrath of the crowd had subsided.

Once the initial uproar was over, the process of ritually resolving the homicide case began. Any killing, deliberate or accidental, was believed to threaten the killer himself, his agnates, and even unrelated parties with *ndɔn*. First, the act of homicide was in itself considered to be polluting and dangerous. Like the various unnatural events mentioned earlier, homicide was thought to create a severe state of contagious *ndɔn* in the place where it occurred, a form of *ndɔn* that might affect anyone in the immediate locality. Second, homicide was also viewed as a moral violation of an extreme sort, one that could cause personal *ndɔn* affliction for the killer.

He was seen as "carrying" (*bɛ'ɛ*) a heavy load of *ndɔn* on his head, and as in many other cases of *ndɔn* produced by moral infractions, the supernatural danger here was believed to be capable of spreading from the killer to his agnates.

The ritual resolution process in homicide cases included measures designed to remove all these dangers of *ndɔn*. The first step was the burial of the corpse that had come to symbolize the polluting *ndɔn* of homicide. This was normally effected by an hereditary specialist in the village concerned who was summoned by the owner of the compound in which the killing had occurred and paid by him to remove the corpse and the *ndɔn* from his place. After receiving a goat and other valuables, the specialist constructed a bamboo litter and began to depart with the victim. However, this was not the end of his extortion, for en route to the burial site he and his assistant normally stopped to rest at each compound they passed, and before leaving, they demanded a fowl from the people of that compound, "in order to buy their footsteps away from the place." If any compound owner refused, the specialists simply departed, leaving their litter with the corpse and its horrible load of *ndɔn* to the miserly compound head.

In the next phase of the resolution process, the murderer and his close agnates made substantial payments to the notables of the village in which the killing had occurred. These fines typically included amounts such as seven goats, together with several dozen brass bracelets, and large numbers of fowl. The payments, which sometimes took several months to complete, were necessary to satisfy the local authorities before they would consider the case closed and permit it to pass to the ultimate homicide specialist. In general, the village leaders were in a good position to enforce their prerogatives at this point in the case. They were considered to be capable of speaking the strongest *njɔm* or ritual statement concerning any serious conflict in the village, and accordingly, if they declared the matter of homicide unfinished, the killer was thought likely to continue suffering *ndɔn,* regardless of what other steps he might take.

It should be emphasized here that the payments to the village leaders were seen as fines rather than compensation and that the agnates and other kin of the murdered man normally received no part of them. Although Meta' lineages often acted as strong corporate units in defending their members' interests in other kinds of disputes, they were not entitled to kill the person who had murdered one of their number, since a revenge killing would be construed as a separate case of homicide. They were likewise unable to press for compensation. On the other hand, the killer's agnates did generally make substantial contributions to the fines paid by him to the village notables. They did so in part because the *ndɔn* of homicide was believed likely to spread to other members of the killer's lineage, perhaps causing the entire group to die out, if the ritual resolution process was not satisfactorily completed.

In the final phase of ritual resolution, the murderer was obliged to present a goat and a slave to Chief Tabi of Zang Tabi village, the ultimate specialist for all cases of homicide occurring in Meta' territory, in order that Tabi might finally "remove all the *ndɔn* from his head." However, this last step in the resolution of the case was frequently delayed for several months while members of the killer's lineage tried to assemble sufficient wealth to acquire the slave. Throughout this period, the killer was required to let his hair grow without cutting it to symbolize his disgrace and the threat of *ndɔn* that hung about him.

Once the slave had been acquired, the murderer could travel to Zang Tabi for the final expiation of his offense. But here again his task was complicated, this time by the fact that there existed certain intermediaries in different parts of Meta' with the function of "showing the road to Zang" to murderers. Naturally, the intermediaries had to be paid for their services, and one could not bypass them without incurring their anger and that of the homicide specialist himself. Attempting to do so would only result in still greater fines and possibly additional *ndɔn* from having violated the rights of the intermediaries.

After the killer had satisfied all the intermediaries, he was taken, with the slave whom he would present to the specialist tied to one arm and a goat tied to the other, to the residence of Tabi. The latter then took the killer into his sacrificial hut where he performed a series of rites designed to cleanse him of the *ndɔn* associated with his offense. In addition to giving him food and water from a special cup, Tabi shaved the murderer's head in order to symbolize the end to his disgrace and the removal of the threat of *ndɔn*. He also spoke an *njɔm* to the effect that the case had been properly settled, and sacrificed the goat which the killer had brought. Finally, he poured water on the ground outside the sacrificial hut to the accompaniment of a second *njɔm*. These last two acts served to establish a barrier against anyone who might try to reopen the case or cause *ndɔn* by saying that it had not been properly finished.

The ritual outlined above completed the formal expiation for the offense of homicide. Afterwards, the slave brought by the killer was kept as a retainer by Tabi. He could not be sold by the specialist since he represented the replacement of the Meta' person who had originally been killed. The murderer himself was free to return to society as a normal member and suffered under no formal liabilities.

The preceding description of pre-colonial procedures for resolving homicide cases provides a clear example of immediate ritual conflict resolution, and illustrates several features that were characteristic of the approach. First, it is apparent that ritual resolution in cases like this was at least as much a process of deflecting and defusing conflict as one of resolving it in a literal sense. Any killing, even an accidental one, presented a situation with a great potential for explosive violence. The public was outraged and perhaps fearful that the *ndɔn* stemming from it might spread. It gave vent to such feelings in the institution of *əkwatreu,* the customary raiding of the murderer's compound. The agnates of the victim were also understandably ready for revenge, and in some cases they took advantage of *əkwatreu* to attack the killer's lineage.

It is in this context of a potentially explosive situation that the complex process of ritually resolving homicide cases must be seen. The redefinition of the conflict in supernatural terms transformed this situation completely. Suddenly, the focus was shifted to the terrible *ndɔn* that threatened the killer, his agnates, and anyone else who might be marginally involved in the case. Simultaneously, the problem of satisfying the requirements of numerous ritual specialists, each with the power of blocking the settlement of the case, came to the fore. In this phase, the murderer and his kinsmen were ground down by incessant threats of *ndɔn* and demands for additional payments, much to the satisfaction of the friends and kinsmen of the victim and the general public. The potential for violence and feuding between the kin of the victim and those of the killer was thus deflected as the case entered the ritual resolution process, and in part this may have been due to the intricacy and demanding character of the resolution process itself.

At this point, the question of the killer's motivation to comply with the complex and costly ritual resolution procedures naturally arises since their ability to deflect violence and prevent feuding depended on such compliance. The answer to this question might be sought in a generalized fear of *ndɔn* on the part of the killer. However, numerous case histories of various disputes involving *ndɔn* suggest that the killer's fear of supernatural danger by itself would not have been a sufficient motivation (Dillon 1973a: 197–200). What factors might then have induced the murderer's co-operation in ritual resolution?

One likely answer is apparent if we consider the character of the ritual resolution process just described. In it, the general tendency was to focus a strong network of social pressure on the murderer and his kin group. After a supernaturally dangerous offense had occurred, a number of new parties entered the dispute, each having a somewhat different motivation for seeing it settled according to the correct procedure. The various ritual specialists, ranging from the corpse removal agent to the ultimate homicide specialist, naturally wanted to profit from the performance of their exclusive roles. The village notables shared this motivation, while at the same time having a general interest in curtailing *ndɔn*, disorder, and conflict in their village. Finally, the agnates of the killer wanted to see the case settled so that the contagious *ndɔn* would not spread to them and possibly wipe out their lineage.

The redefinition of an offense like homicide in supernatural terms thus established a network of parties interested in settlement of the dispute and capable of exerting different pressures for compliance on the killer. It was very likely this mobilization of social pressure that made the ritual resolution of homicide a workable procedure and enabled it to defuse explosive cases. Finally, it should be noted that all of these consequences flowed naturally from the Meta' concept of *ndɔn*. Ritual specialists were able to pressure the murderer because they held exclusive rights to remove certain varieties of *ndɔn* and because their prerogatives as ritual resolution agents were in turn supernaturally sanctioned. The village notables were in a similar situation, and the agnates of the killer, who were generally in a good position to press for his compliance, were strongly motivated to intervene in the case because of the contagious character of *ndɔn*.

Deliberately Induced Ritual Resolution in Cases of Symbolic Aggression

In a second variety of ritual conflict resolution, actions believed to induce a state of *ndɔn* were deliberately performed to stimulate the resolution of a chronic dispute. Included in this category were cases in which one disputant threatened another by performing an " 'act of symbolic aggression," cases in which oath-taking procedures were employed to resolve conflicts of testimony, and cases of malicious rumor in which the ritual specialty of *mbaŋ mania* was used to curtail dangerous talk by threatening those who helped to spread the rumor with *ndɔn* (Dillon 1973a: 417–422).

In this section, I will illustrate deliberately induced ritual resolution by describing the sequence of events in cases involving acts of symbolic aggression. These acts included the throwing of a spear into an opponent's roof, the slashing of a plantain stalk in the yard of his compound, and even the commission of suicide by hanging one's self from a tree in the opponent's yard. All were believed to carry the threat of *ndɔn* to the person who was their target, and they were performed to bring pressure to bear on an intractable fellow disputant or in some cases to obtain revenge.[4] They often occurred in disputes involving long unpaid debts. For example, in a case of divorce where there had been prolonged failure to refund the bridewealth, the woman's first husband could resort to an act of symbolic aggression as a final warning. This action might be taken in either the ex-father-in-law's compound or that of the new husband, depending on who was responsible for the non-refund of bridewealth. Most commonly, the father-in-law was the target.

When the first husband slashed a plantain stalk in his father-in-law's compound, he was conveying a dire message to the man: "If I had not cut the plantain, I might have cut you instead." But in addition to serving as a warning, such an act was thought to create a severe state of *ndɔn* in the compound where it occurred. The severed plantain stalk (or spear in the roof, or man hanging from the tree) remained as a highly visible reminder that the offender and all other residents of the compound were likely to suffer *ndɔn* if preventive measures were not taken.

The purpose of performing an act of symbolic aggression was to set in motion a complex but effective process of ritual conflict resolution. This process had two principal components. One was the intervention of the local political authorities and an attempt by them to resolve the issues entailed in the dispute. Whenever an act of symbolic aggression was performed, the notables of the village in which it had occurred were informed so that they might come to judge the underlying dispute that had led to such a dire event. This contrasted with their usual role. Ordinarily, inter-lineage disputes over bridewealth debts, divorce, and similar issues were seen as private matters in which the village leaders had no authority to interfere. However, the performance of an act of symbolic aggression in the context of such a dispute made their intervention obligatory and also legitimized their imposing fines on the disputants. In making this point, some informants drew an analogy with the present-day court system, characterizing the act of symbolic aggression as a kind of indirect "summons" through which a deserted husband or other hapless creditor could insure a proper hearing of his case.

The second important aspect of the ritual resolution process in cases involving symbolic aggression was the intervention of a ritual specialist. In all such cases, summoning the appropriate specialist became mandatory. Should he fail to come, it was believed that people in the compound where the act of symbolic aggression had occurred would surely begin to sicken and die. It was the role of the specialist to remove the tangible evidence of the symbolic attack (e.g., the slashed plantain stalk or the spear) from the compound, thereby removing the threat of *ndɔn* as well. For this work he received one or more goats along with other valuables and palm wine. In describing this aspect of the resolution process, informants often emphasized the way in which ritual specialists used their monopoly over the power to remove *ndɔn* to extract ever-increasing payments from the afflicted. Sometimes, the basis for determining fees itself facilitated this. In cases where a spear had been thrown into the

roof, for example, part of the specialist's fee consisted of one brass brace-
let for every rung of the ladder that he climbed to retrieve the weapon,
and specialists are said to have often used ladders with very closely
spaced rungs in order to receive the highest possible fee.

In most accounts, the combined intervention of the village authorities
and the ritual specialist was portrayed as leading to a just and binding
settlement of the dispute that had occasioned a hostile symbolic attack.
Normally, the person who had been the object of the attack bore the
major burden of paying fines and ritual specialist's fees. Since acts of
symbolic aggression were not performed lightly, he was most likely to be
at fault. Furthermore, he was usually the party with the strongest motivation for removing *ndɔn* from his compound. It was only if a runaway wife
returned so that the erstwhile disputants became in-laws once again, or if
the party who had performed the act of symbolic aggression had completely lacked justification that the attacker himself would be likely to
pay fines to the village notables or ritual specialist's fees.

We have so far discussed cases involving acts of symbolic aggression
as an illustration of deliberately induced ritual conflict resolution. Are
any insights into how and why this process worked suggested by the
foregoing description? First, it should be noted that in disputes like these
the main obstacle to resolution was typically a reluctant debtor, such as a
father-in-law who refused to refund bridewealth. The key to the resolution of the case thus lay in obtaining the compliance of the uncooperative
disputant. There are several ways in which an act of symbolic aggression
and the resolution process that followed it could be seen as contributing
to this goal. One possible motive for the offender's compliance lay in the
threat of more direct aggression implied by symbolic attack. Although the
importance of the warning aspect is difficult to estimate, several case
histories suggested that it was sometimes an important factor. Another
possible explanation for the reluctant disputant's co-operation rests on
the nature of the ritual resolution process itself. Just as in homicide cases,
the result of a supernaturally dangerous act in cases involving symbolic
aggression was a transformation of the social structure of the conflict
situation. Before the symbolic attack, the dispute represented an unbalanced dyadic structure. There were two principal parties involved in the
case, the debtor and the creditor, and only one of these had a strong
motive for seeing it properly settled. The act of symbolic aggression and
the subsequent reinterpretation of the dispute in supernatural terms
transformed this situation on two levels. First it altered the dyadic character of the dispute by introducing several additional parties, including
the hereditary ritual specialist and the notables of the village concerned.
At the same time, however, it established a whole new structure of the

interdependent motivations among the parties involved in the dispute and its resolution. While the debtor might now be moved to compromise because he was threatened with imminent *ndɔn* and a possible direct attack, the ritual specialist and the village notables were spurred on by self-interest, since they stood to profit from their roles as conflict resolution agents. The notables also had a general interest in controlling supernaturally dangerous conflict in their village. Finally, the relatives of the debtor were worried that his *ndɔn* might spread to them. Thus, just as in homicide cases, the commission of a supernaturally dangerous action in cases involving symbolic aggression helped to establish a new network of relationships and motivations that facilitated the co-operation of all parties in the resolution of the dispute. Here, however, ritual conflict resolution was used to break the deadlock in a chronic conflict and turn the tables on the recalcitrant offender rather than to relieve an explosive situation such as that posed by homicide.

Delayed Ritual Resolution in Disputes Between Affines

In the final type of ritual conflict resolution to be considered, the resolution typically commenced only after the offender had begun to suffer from *ndɔn*. Delayed ritual resolution was in fact often a rather opportunistic process of waiting for a person to suffer *ndɔn* and then taking advantage of his condition to press for the settlement of previous disputes in which he or his kinsmen had been involved.

In practice, delayed ritual resolution was employed in a variety of cases. The following were among the most frequently committed *ndɔn*-producing offenses that could result in delayed ritual resolution: disobeying the testament of a dying father, failure to satisfy an affine's legitimate claims for bridewealth, secretly betraying a kinsman to outsiders, unjustifiably seizing the land of another person, and usurping the exclusive political rights of another. Here, a common type of dispute between affines will be used to illustrate the approach.

According to Meta' custom, numerous rights of the members of a wife-giving lineage were sanctioned by *ndɔn*. These included the right of the men of the bride's lineage to shares of the bridewealth given by her husband and also their right to receive periodic gifts and services from the son-in-law throughout his wife's lifetime. For example, if there was a death in the father-in-law's compound, the son-in-law was required to bring a party of dancers to the funeral and feast them at his own expense. He was also frequently obliged to supply a goat and a quantity of palm wine to help defray the heavy expenses of mourning.

Since many of a man's obligations toward his wife's agnates were *ndɔn*-sanctioned in this way, *ndɔn* caused by the complaints of a dissatisfied affine was a constant threat. According to Meta' belief, this kind of *ndɔn* usually struck the wife and children of the errant son-in-law rather than the man himself. In some cases the wife became ill or barren, while in others the children of the union began to sicken and die. Whenever such calamities struck, it was the responsibility of the husband or father to visit a diviner in order to ascertain the cause. If the diviner indicated dissatisfaction by the wife's father or one of his lineage mates as the root of the problem, the stage was then set for delayed ritual resolution, and the members of the woman's natal lineage were in a good position to use *ndɔn* as a lever in pressing for the redress of any past grievances. When the son-in-law came to request that they perform rituals blessing his wife and children, they took advantage of the situation to indicate to him the precise nature of their complaints. If a failure to pay bridewealth was involved, some money would have to be handed over, and firm arrangements made concerning the payment of the rest. Once such steps had been taken and *ndɔn* had been cut off at its source, the father of the woman or the head of her natal lineage then spoke an *njɔm* to the effect that all *ndɔn* from the case should be ended and replaced by good luck and prosperity. In some cases a goat or a fowl, provided by the son-in-law, was also sacrificed and shared among the members of the wife's lineage as a sign of reconciliation and an indication that the prior state of supernatural danger was completely ended.

The preceding scenario for the resolution of a dispute between affines highlights several factors that were essential to the operation of delayed ritual conflict resolution. The fact that *ndɔn* was not merely threatened but manifest was often important in such cases. The son-in-law was motivated to comply with the demands of his affines to end actual suffering in his household. In addition, the belief in the contagious nature of *ndɔn* seems to have been critical in these cases. When one child died from *ndɔn,* it was thought that another would soon follow, if steps were not taken to head off supernatural danger at its source. However, delayed ritual resolution, like all forms of ritual conflict resolution practiced in Meta', also tended to encourage the offender's compliance by implicating additional parties with their own motives for settling the dispute. When children began dying, for example, the mother often pressured her husband to set aside material considerations and satisfy all demands made by her agnates in order to save the children. Any co-wives in the compound would support her at this point, fearing that their own children might next be sacrificed to the compound head's greed. On the other hand, if a married woman was suffering *ndɔn* because an agnate had not received bridewealth, her father often goaded her husband to pay the debt in order to save his daughter's life.

Although the foregoing example has suggested that delayed ritual resolution sometimes provided an effective means of dispute settlement, it must be borne in mind that it was a more random and opportunistic approach than the other forms of ritual conflict resolution. Because this process depended on signs of *ndɔn* being actually manifest, disputants could not rely on it for the redress of their grievances within a reasonable period of time. Still delayed ritual resolution did have important uses in the Meta' legal system, since it often served to maintain the long-term balance of kinship obligations and to reaffirm the authority of senior persons in the kinship sphere. Not only did fathers-in-law enforce their prerogatives through this process. Lineage heads used the sanction of *ndɔn* and the process of delayed ritual resolution to reassert their authority over junior members of the lineage from time to time and to obtain redress for offenses committed by them in the past.

Ritual Conflict Resolution as a Legal Process

In this paper, I have analyzed the ritual resolution process in three kinds of dispute in pre-colonial Meta' society. In addition to demonstrating the versatility of the ritual approach to legal problem solving, this analysis has suggested some important insights into its operation. Most significantly, it has been shown that ritual conflict resolution characteristically served to focus a network of social and psychological pressure on the offender. Unique factors, such as the attribution of actual illness to the action of *ndɔn* in instances of delayed ritual resolution or the implicit threat of a direct attack that lay behind an act of symbolic aggression, may have increased the effectiveness of this process in some cases. However, in each of the examples considered, ritual conflict resolution was shown to have worked in essentially the same way. Typically, the redefinition of a dispute in supernatural terms set in motion a complex social process that encouraged conflict resolution by involving additional parties in the case and focusing diffuse pressure for compliance on the guilty party. Ritual resolution was thus a rather economical approach to social control that worked by enhancing the offender's intrinsic motivation for co-operation, and the analysis given here points to a process of psycho-social intimidation as the basis of ritual conflict resolution.

NOTES

1. The data presented in this paper were obtained in fieldwork carried out in Meta' between January 1970 and July 1971 that was supported by a National

Institutes of Health fellowship (1F01MH1246601) and field research training grant (1T01MH1202401). Thanks are due to Igor Kopytoff, Robert M. Netting, John Swetnam, Jane Schneider, Shirley Lindenbaum, John Kelly, and Joyce Dillon for reading and commenting on earlier drafts of this article. I would also like to thank Jean-Pierre Warnier for raising several important questions regarding the interpretation of Meta' supernatural beliefs.

2. The picture of ritual conflict resolution presented here rests on both ethnohistorical and ethnographic evidence. While the testimonies of elderly informants supplied most of the information about legal procedures that were suppressed during the colonial period (e.g., the ritual resolution of homicides and "symbolic aggression" cases), the forms of ritual resolution still practiced at the time of fieldwork (e.g., "delayed ritual resolution" in disputes between affines) were studied through both ethnographic and ethnohistoric work. See Dillon (1973a: 30–44) for a discussion of the methodology used in this study.

3. It should not be assumed that all ritual specialist roles were prestigious. Some, like the specialty of removing a corpse after a suicide or murder, were regarded as demeaning.

4. Suicide of course differed from the other acts of symbolic aggression in that it entailed the death of the perpetrator. However, it was sometimes performed to give *ndɔn* to a fellow disputant in cases where the suicide felt that the person who was the target of his act had already brought about the irreparable ruin of his life. On occasion, suicide was also merely attempted to intimidate a fellow disputant.

BIBLIOGRAPHY

Beidelman, T. O. 1971. Nuer Priests and Prophets: Charisma, Authority, and Power among the Nuer. The Translation of Culture: Essays to E. E. Evans-Pritchard, ed. T. O. Beidelman, pp. 375–415. London.

Chilver, E. M. 1961. Nineteenth Century Trade in the Bamenda Grassfelds, Southern Cameroons. Afrika und Ubersee 45: 233–258.

Dillon, R. G. 1975a. Ideology, Process, and Change in Pre-Colonial Meta' Political Organization. Ph.D. dissertation, University of Pennsylvania.

———. 1975b. Notes on the Pre-Colonial History and Ethnography of the Meta'. Paper read at the Conference on Cameroonian History, Centre National de la Recherche Scientifique, Paris.

Douglas, M. 1966. Purity and Danger: An Analysis of Concepts of Pollution and Taboo. New York.

Evans-Pritchard, E. E. 1940. The Nuer: A Description of the Modes of Livelihood and Political Institutions of a Nilotic People. Oxford.

———. 1956. Nuer Religion. Oxford.

Fortes, M. 1940. The Political System of the Tallensi of the Northern Territories of the Gold Coast. African Political Systems, ed. M. Fortes and E. E. Evans-Pritchard. London.

———. 1945. The Dynamics of Clanship Among the Tallensi. London.

Greuel, P. J. 1971. The Leopard-Skin Chief. An Examination of Political Power among the Nuer. American Anthropologist 73: 1115–1120.

Haight, B. 1972. A Note on the Leopard-Skin Chief. American Anthropologist 74: 1313–1318.

Harper, E. B. 1957. Hoylu: A Belief Relating Justice and the Supernatural. American Anthropologist 59: 801–816.

Howell, P. P. 1954. A Manual of Nuer Law. London.

Huber, H. 1959. Ritual Oaths as Instruments of Coercion and Self-Defence among the Adangme of Ghana. Africa 29: 41–49.

Lienhardt, G. 1961. Divinity and Experience: The Religion of the Dinka. London.

Llewellyn, K. N., and E. A. Hoebel. 1941. The Cheyenne Way. Norman.

Nader, L. 1969. Law in Culture and Society. Chicago.

Nader, L., and B. Yngvesson. 1973. The Ethnography of Law and its Consequences. Handbook of Social and Cultural Anthropology, ed. J. Honigmann, pp. 883–921. Chicago.

Pospisil, L. 1971. Anthropology of Law: A Comparative Theory of Law. New York.

Shneider, D. M. 1957. Political Organization, Supernatural Sanctions, and Punishment for Incest on Yap. American Anthropologist 59: 791–800.

Turner, V. W. 1968. The Drums of Affliction. Oxford.

———. 1969. The Ritual Process: Structure and Anti-Structure. Chicago.

Winans, E. V., and R. B. Edgerton. 1964. Hehe Magical Justice. American Anthropologist 66: 745–746.

Warnier, J. P. 1975. Pre-Colonial Mankon: The Development of a Cameroon Chiefdom in its Regional Setting. Ph.D. dissertation, University of Pennsylvania.

The Place of the Big Man in Traditional Hagen Society in the Central Highlands of New Guinea[1]

Ernest Brandewie

The "big man" is a leadership position that arises from a particular ethnographic context. The post reflects general aspects of leadership within a kinship, nonhierarchical framework. The leader cannot command or exert undue control over his followers, and the ties that bind the leader to his followers are based primarily on kinship. The unusual aspect of the big man position is the flexibility and potential for growth in his following. No one is born into the position; the leader must demonstrate that he is capable of satisfying the cultural and social requirements of the post. He must be able to control land and the individuals that work on or produce from the land. The leader must be able to demonstrate generosity by distributing goods, and he must command rhetorical skills. As Brandewie's article suggests, these leadership attributes are limited and do not appear to be adaptable within a state context. Changes in New Guinea leadership are yet to unfold; and how the concept of the big man fits into the new state context is problematic.

The big man must be able to amass a store of power, which in a kinship society means matrimonial ties, dependents, and the availability of social and material resources to support them. His status is maintained by his ability to mobilize a following of kith and kin. On the local level, he must express the solidarity of the corporate territorial group and yet he must extend his networks to supralocal alliances.

MELANESIA IS CHARACTERIZED by a system of relationships referred to as the "big man" complex. This pidgin-English expression is applied to the leader of a group who is endowed with certain capabilities and skills which enable him to be effective in attaining important group goals. His success is rewarded with enhanced prestige, legitimation of his authority, and further power within his group. The big man helps integrate the group by serving as its representative, thereby giving it a common focus with which to identify itself. Through their leaders, groups also relate themselves to other groups and leaders.

There is an extensive literature dealing with the Melanesian "big man" and his position in society. However, this article is restricted to the Central Highlands of New Guinea. For this area, some studies have dealt with the big man from the perspective of exchange and economics. Strathern (1969) has contrasted production and finance as two ways of distinguishing groups throughout the Highlands of New Guinea. Those groups which stress financial means of accumulating exchange items, i.e., obtaining shells and pigs by means of judicious borrowing and credit, are also characterized by more emphasis on the big man.

Closely connected with the economic position of the big man in his society is his political role (Bulmer 1960; Finney 1969). Some authors (e.g., Watson 1967; Salisbury 1964) have described the big man as a despot, even before the arrival of the Australians with their policy of gradual contact and pacification. Others (e.g., Brown 1963; Reay 1964) have indicated that despots arose in the Central Highlands through Australian influence or at least the presence of the Australians influenced traditional politics.

This difference of interpretation can be resolved in several ways. Salisbury makes a distinction between the real leaders, who were despots even before the Australians came, and the lower-level leaders, who were more dependent on public opinion and backing for their position. These latter had to be responsive to their followers' needs and could not run the risk of being despots, although they might use the Australian presence to become despotic. However, in one place in his discussion of pre-contact despots Salisbury (1964: 228) seems to contradict himself:

> This evidence indicates that, although "public opinion" did temper indigenous despotism, sufficient leeway existed for leaders to be extremely arbitrary and dominant in their relations with nominal supporters. Arbitrariness was not merely passively accepted but was connived in by supporters, provided that it meant material profits from thefts or other aggression against both group members and outsiders. Only rarely did people feel it was worth trying to oppose a despot; when it was possible to do stand in most New Guinea societies there is sufficient flexibility to permit this— people preferred to join a despot.

Another way of resolving this difference of opinion is simply to acknowledge differences between groups. In spite of many common features, groups in New Guinea sometimes differ significantly. This has been brought out in the areas of male-female relationships (Meggitt 1964), in the emphasis placed on the principle of agnation (Meggitt 1965), in types of housing arrangements and the techniques of gardening (Read 1954), and in the variations between groups in their relative reliance on production or on finance for their exchange items (A. Strathern 1969). Highlands groups also vary in the amount of authority they give to their big man and the degree of arbitrariness they will tolerate, in other words, in the extent to which individuals are willing to give up their autonomy.

It is to this last question that the following description of the big man's traditional position in one Highlands society is addressed. The same topic was discussed by A. Strathern (1966). The field work on which his article was based was done in the same language group as the present author's study. His article, therefore, should be read in connection with this one. He, too, was concerned with pre-contact despotism in the Mt. Hagen area and came to the same conclusion as this study, namely, that one can hardly speak of despotism when considering traditional leadership among the Hageners. His primary concerns, however, are the rise of big men and the controls they bring to bear on their followers. The present paper deals more with the characteristics of the big man and the controls which followers exercise vis-à-vis their leader. Since shell exchanges are still the most important way of becoming a big man in the traditional sense I shall describe in some detail their mechanics.

Identification of the Big Man

The Kumdi-Engamoi, whose big men are the source of the following data, are a group of 700 people who live on the slopes of Mt. Hagen, twenty miles north of the town of Mt. Hagen. They are part of a larger group known variously as Mbowamp, Medlpa, or Hageners. The main published sources describing these people are Vicedom and Tischner (1943–1948), Strauss and Tischner (1 962), A. Strathern (1966, 1968, 1969), and M. Strathern (1968). They all give accounts of the big man, although sometimes from a restricted point of view, as, for example, religion in the case of Strauss.

The big man's role in society is a very pervasive one, yet difficult to characterize in clear, unambiguous terms. In some cases informants are definite: "So-and-so is a big man." At other times they are doubtful, or they state a man's position relative to that of another person. The response may also depend on the lineage affiliation of the informant. Maip of lineage X is a big man for an informant from lineage X, but someone from another lineage may call him a "rubbish man," the precise opposite.

Indeed, at times of competition, even a commonly accepted big man may be called by this epithet.

The Kumdi-Engamoi are divided into subgroups, which resemble lineages. These are culturally defined as patrilineal. They have specific names and function as units especially for weddings, funerals, and exchanges. Each lineage group usually has a ceremonial plaza, and the members often cooperate in such tasks as housebuilding and gardening. Genealogical connections are traceable, and kinship terms are used within the group. It may also be a ceremonial unit for solemn exchange purposes or other religious rituals.

At this point it seems appropriate to give a brief and simplified synopsis of the social morphology of Mbowamp society. All the people belong to named groups, which might be called tribes. One of these is the Kumdi, who number about 5,500. The members of a tribe have a vague sense of being somehow related, although kinship terms are not extended to all members. The tribe is not exogamous, and it rarely acts as a ceremonial unit. The Kumdi are divided into three groups which can be called clans, the Oglaka, Komonika, and Witika. Kinship terms are extended to the members of a clan, and it is exogamous, but precise genealogical connections cannot be traced. The Komonika clan, to which the Engamoi belong, number about 3,000.

Clans are further divided into named units, which we simply call "groups" (cf. Table 1). These groups are symbolically important; for instance, they are usually the first way of identifying and naming a person. There should be no fighting within the group. Such groups, of which the Engamoi constitute an example, are further divided into smaller groups resembling lineages. These are named, and genealogical connections are traceable within them. The lineage, or lineage group, is multifunctional and, more important for our purposes, has at least one recognizable big man. In any discussion of the big man complex, the lineage is by far the most important social group to consider.

If such a lineage group has more than one big man, this can indicate an incipient split. Or it may merely imply a division of labor, according to which one member is a big man because he knows many ritual prayers, another is such because he speaks well, especially on formal occasions when a special kind of chanting speech is required (A. Strathern 1969), while a third may be a big man because he has made many exchanges. This last is the most important criterion of a big man. Every lineage head is a big man, but not every big man is a lineage head or representative.

The expression "big man" is translated in various ways, the most common of which is *wua nuim,* meaning "great-important-wealthy man." An equivalent is *wua ou,* literally "big (large) man." A woman may be

TABLE 1
Exchanges and Kinship Categories

Kinship Category	Kinship Classification	No. of Exchanges
Brothers	Real	34
	Classifactory	
	Same lineage	51
	Same group	38
	Same clan	17
	WZH	15
	MZS	11
	Unspecified	15
TOTAL		181
Brothers-in-law	Real	
	ZH	35
	WB	42
	Classifactory	37
	Unspecified	16
TOTAL		130
Cross Relatives	Real	
	MB-ZS	24
	FZS-MBS	13
	Classifactory	64
TOTAL		101
Father and Son	Real	1
	Classifactory	49
TOTAL		50
Father- and Son-in-law	Real	12
	Classifactory	12
TOTAL		24
Unspecified in general		17
GRAND TOTAL		503

called an *amp nuim;* she is one who knows how to raise many pigs, who is strong and has many children. If any of her children are *nuim* in turn, then she is doubly *nuim*. According to Strauss, this expression also has many strong religious overtones.

The opposite of a *wua nuim* is a *wua korupa* or "rubbish man." To intensify this term, one speaks of a *wua korupa køp*. The word *køp* means "dry." The whole expression, however, was also translated by informants as "one who is bent over and looking," i.e., one who is always asking for things. In any case, he is a man who does not engage in many exchanges, or when he does is primarily concerned with his own benefit. He is not generous or magnanimous, nor does he make a return gift when it is required. His daughter will marry early because he cannot wait to acquire the bridewealth of shells and pigs. At times of ceremonial shell exchanges and pig killings his contribution is niggardly.

Other related expressions, such as *wua mumuk* and *wua peng,* which Strauss also discusses, though known to the Engamoi, are not very extensively used. *Mumuk* refers to fastening something together at the top. Stalks of sugar cane which at a certain stage of growth are tied together at the top are called *mumuk rui.* A *wua mumuk* similarly ties his group together. Engamoi informants claimed that this expression was introduced by the Lutherans. The term *wua peng* literally "man head," also refers to a big man according to Strauss. Among the Kumdi Engamoi, however, the expression is used for an exchange ceremony which is a payment for the death of an ally or for a death brought about in a fight with a related group. Another expression, discussed at some length by Vicedom, is *pukl wua* (*pukl* means "base, as of a tree, or foundation"). However, it is used primarily for a man who is considered a founding father of a lineage group and thus refers first and foremost to an ancestor. Though it may be used also of a *wua nuim,* this is only in so far as he is or may become such a founding father (Vicedom 1953–58: ii, 58; for other expressions see A. Strathern 1966: 357).

Mbowamp Values and the Big Man

The general social climate of Mbowamp living predetermines to a large degree the sort of person a big man must be, as well as the activities open to him. The maintenance of good relations with others is highly valued by the Mbowamp, even though there is a strong drive towards individualism and independence. A father can always exert his authority over his son, but the son can leave his father's place to live with his mother's brother, where he will be given garden ground. A big man can lay down the law to the members of his group, but they can flout his authority with impunity, especially if they are already married and established in life. They can attach themselves to another big man, or go their own way. All men are considered equal and autonomous. This is the climate in which the big man must operate.

Salisbury (1962: 38) sums up the situation for the Siane, and what he says can be applied directly to the Mbowamp:

> Underlying all the relationships is the Siane ideology of the autonomy and assumed equality of all people. Of their own volition individuals carry out the tasks they wish to perform, settle disputes when they wish to, argue about (and agree) upon every decision that a group makes. No one has

authority over anyone else (except, perhaps, inside the lineage), unless
those powers are delegated on an ad hoc basis through individual
choice. . . . No group admits the superiority of any other, unless it be a
group of a larger order. When groups come together they have temporary
representatives. The system works through many intricate mechanisms, but
chiefly because, coupled with their fierce individualism people seek to remain on good terms with as many others as possible.

The relationship that exists between the individual and his group is
very important to understand. It directly affects the position of the big
man in this culture, the influence he can exert for change, and how as
representative of his group he binds various other groups together in his
own person.

The value which seems to mediate among the Mbowamp between
these two foci—the individual on the one hand and the group on the
other, individualism and group conformity, aggressiveness and submis-
sion to the dictates and norms of the group—is hinted at by Salisbury in
the passage cited above. This is the value placed on social harmony, social
order, and friendly interaction. People should get along together; if they
cannot, they move away and apart, taking with them their grievances and
dissensions, so that harmony may once again prevail.

The group emphasis is repeatedly instilled into the Mbowamp through
various institutions which have developed in their society. In their exchanges, marriages, funerals, and dances, and during illness as well, emphasis is continually placed on the importance of people living in harmony and
getting along together, even though it is accompanied by the ideal of
besting others and thereby putting oneself in the best possible light and
bringing prestige to one's own group. Through illness much of the religious life of the people is concerned with social harmony and with controlling the impulses of individualism when it conflicts with the requirements
of social living (Brandewie 1968; A. Strathern 1969: 548; M. Strathern
1968: 562).

Land Rights and the Big Man

In the domestic sphere a big man must provide first and foremost for his
own wife or wives and children. Like every other adult male, he has his
own land which enables him to do this. Although land is almost invariably
spoken of by the people as if it were the exclusive property of the big
man, this definitely is not so.

The amount of land one has depends on the number of one's wives
and children. Gardens and garden plots are distributed to the wives and
daughters. The sons of a particular wife inherit their mother's as well as

their sisters' gardens. These are cared for by their wives. If redistribution, which appears to be infrequent, is necessary, or if new gardens are made, the head of the individual family does the apportioning. However, if the entire lineage group cooperates on a large garden, as is often the case with sweet potato gardens, its big man, in consultation with his lineage mates, distributes the proper sections to the other male household heads, who reapportion their plots to the women dependent upon them.

If men are generally considered equal, they are especially equal when there is a question of land rights. If a lineage group wishes to sell some land, for instance to the mission for a school or church, all adult men of the group must give their permission, even though the land "belongs" to a particular person. For purposes of alienation, land is lineage property; as regards usufruct there is individual ownership.

Usufruct rights shift rather freely within the lineage group owing to the differential growth of families. The big man may take a lead in this reapportionment, although all are consulted. This is how one informant described the process of land use and distribution:

> The father divides out his land, but he divides it to all. If in his own lifetime he did not give it to all—for example one child was too young or for some other reason he neglected to give anything to this particular child—then this task falls on the number one brother who provides for his younger brother. No one is left without land or is disinherited. If the father divides four pieces of ground out to four sons, then they in turn work these and redivide them among themselves, working them together to the advantage of all. The brothers then divide their own piece of ground to their children. If the father was not too provident, or did not foresee the large progeny he would have and so did not lay claim to much garden land, but only to enough as he foresaw he could use, then there might be a shortage eventually, as is now the case with Romakl [the big man of the Kopalige lineage group, about whom we will speak more later]. In this case another lineage group, which had plenty of land, might give a little to the group which had too little. This would only be done after much talk and discussion, and quite rarely. After all, these people had to be sure to provide for their own children, didn't they? This happened with a small piece of land which Tai's group [the Popage lineage] held. They gave it to Romakl. No one is disinherited. The land goes to all, and then is redivided as need arises by the number one brother. If the number one brother is fairly incompetent, and the number two brother is talented and has ability, then he gradually takes the task away from number one, who does not or is not supposed to mind. Number two has received his father's gift for speech and working out these things, for dealing with kinas [shells], making exchanges, and the like.

The equitable distribution of land and gardens is very important, and, as is evident from the above, the big man is very much involved in the process. It affects inheritance later on. If a woman is slighted in this respect, there is much ill feeling, anger, and resentment. A big man cannot be the cause of such resentment very often without losing the support of his immediate family and consequently running the risk of losing his position.

Distribution and the Big Man

A very important function of the big man is the fair distribution of food and exchange objects among the members of the lineage group he represents. This, perhaps more than anything else, gives him his influence and his power to exert authority in his circle of relatives and dependents.

Sharing and distributing are concomitants of every ceremony. Whenever pigs are killed the pork is distributed and shared, and it is the responsibility of the big man to make sure that all of his dependents get their share, however small. The pork is distributed ritualistically, beginning with the women and children. The distributor holds out a small piece of meat, and then chants the lineage or locality affiliation and name of the recipient, who stands up and receives the piece. Everybody is called up in this manner except for very small infants, still at the breast, in whose case it is taken for granted that the mother will give them some of her meat.

If anyone is left out in this distribution, he is very angry. Eating pork goes beyond merely savoring a delectable bit of food. It has many connotations and overtones, such as harmony, reconciliation, good will, and unity among the group eating together. If a person who has been slighted gets sick, his illness is likely to be blamed on the fact that he did not get his share of pork at the distribution. The sharing of pork is carried even further by the recipients. They share their meat with their neighbors who sit next to them. Each person cuts off a bit of his own portion and gives it to the other. The alleged reason for this is that it enables everybody to get part of different kinds of meat, e.g., lean and fat.

A big man is also responsible for distributing the shells, pigs, and money which accrue to the group as a result of some exchange. In doing so, he takes into account the desires and complaints of his group. Although resources are limited on such occasions, he must nevertheless satisfy all legitimate claimants, even at his own expense. If he cannot, or does not, this can mean one of two things. Either he is not doing what he should, in which case he will lose his effective position, or the group is becoming too large and is no longer viable for distribution purposes. In the latter case the group is likely to split soon into smaller groups, which will be publicly recognized at the next exchange of shells.

An Example of Conflict

Usually such a group split is gradual. Conflict builds up until the split finally becomes definite and obvious. There are altercations, quarrels, and harsh words until one party ultimately removes permanently to land where they have already been building gardens and thereby starts a new lineage group. One example of such a conflict which almost led to a fission will be described. The account gives insight into the nature of the relationship between a big man and his brothers and other dependents.

In July, 1968, angry words were exchanged between Romakl and Ketigla, two brothers who belonged to the Kopalige lineage group. (There were two other brothers, Opa, who was not home at the time of the quarrel, and Raima, the youngest). In addition to being the big man of his own lineage group, Romakl was well known as a big man in other groups as far away as Mt. Hagen. Indeed, he was known as *"Kumdi Romakl,"* being thus identified with all of the Kumdi. Of course, he had no effective authority over the Kumdi as a whole (who number about 5,000 people), nor over their exogamous subgroup, the Komonika (about 1,500 population), nor even over the Engamoi, a subdivision of the latter (700 people). His authority extended only to his lineage, the Kopalige, with 55 members, and even here he sometimes exercised it with difficulty.

Despite Romakl's importance and his close identification with the Kumdi-Komonika-Engamoi, it is interesting to note that his lineage group was an assimilated one. Romakl's father's mother had married a Kopalige man and had gone to live with him according to the prevailing rule of virilocal residence, but because of war she returned with her husband to live with her brother. Eventually, through her son (Romakl's father), she gave rise to the present-day Kopalige lineage. This lineage grew rapidly, not least of all because Romakl had nine wives (four were still living with him in 1968). Since land was scarce at his place, gardens were made on vacant land about two miles to the north, and some of the sons moved there on a permanent basis. Ketigla and his brother Raima also spent much time at these new sites and built women's houses there.

At this time the Engamoi, and therefore also the Kopalige, were preparing to kill pigs for a spirit ceremony. Three of Romakl's sons, Mak, Kewa, and Kombangom (the informant who described the incident), went to the home of Mak's wife, who had left him, to pick up the shells that were being returned. They stayed overnight at a pig house of their Uncle Opa. Here Ketigla saw the shells. Taking a liking to three of them, he wrapped each with a cordyline leaf, thus marking them as his own. After his departure Mak and Kewa decided to hide these three shells, partly as a joke on Ketigla, partly because they wanted to save them for another purpose. Later the same evening, when Ketigla came to look at his shells, he discovered that the three were missing, and he became increasingly angry when Kewa and Mak claimed they did not know what had happened. Had Kewa or Mak admitted that they had laid the shells aside for a future purpose, to buy another wife for Mak, all talk and discussion would have ended then and there. But they did not do so.

The next morning Ketigla saw Romakl sitting outside his house and in his anger began to berate his brother for bearing such rubbish children as Kewa and Mak. At this Romakl also grew angry, because he had nothing to do with the whole affair, and the following exchange took place:

Romakl: You are a rubbish man. You don't cook pig. You don't talk straight [referring partly to Ketigla's habit of stuttering and partly to his inability to make a public speech]. I am here [I remain, I perdure]; you don't.

Ketigla: You know how to do it. You're a big man. You know how to do it if we two stay around. Then you can be a big man. If our mother had borne only one or two sons, then you wouldn't be able to do what you have [i.e., by way of exchanges of shells and pigs]. But we are four brothers, and therefore you are able.

Romakl: You're like a small boy. You must keep looking to me; I will show you what to do; you just watch and look. You're not strong; you're like a little baby.

Ketigla: Your women-folk have received much. I got nothing. The one or two shells I did get, I returned. Your fellows over there took them all and carried them off. You are a humbug [deceitful]. Sure, you have had many wives, but if I had that many, I also would have had lots of children.

Romakl: Ah, you are no better than an outhouse [a disgusting, obnoxious place to the Mbowamp]. You have as much sense as a baby. I stand alone. People come to me, look up to me, ask me when the pigs are going to be cooked, when the ceremony is to be held.

Ketigla: Brother of mine, your talk now is just too much. I'm giving you up. Your word drives me away.

It got worse and worse. Then both began to brood. Kewa threw it up to Ketigla that his son worked for the European in town and ate his leftovers, and that his son did not stay home to help his father the way he himself did.

About this time Raima returned home from visiting his wife's people, and Ketigla talked to him about the whole business. Raima stood up for Ketigla against Romakl and his sons. The two said they would break up the group and go elsewhere for their spirit ceremony. As Kombangom, the informant, put it in pidgin English, *Em i-laik brukim lain* ("He will surely split the lineage group").

Ketigla and Romakl got into another argument, and finally held a court case to settle it. It was decided by members of the local government council that Kewa and Mak should each pay two dollars to Ketigla. At this point Romakl got up and asked why Ketigla should be the only one to receive something; he also had been badly insulted, even though he knew nothing at all about what had happened. He said he was going home stating that he would "cook his pigs outside," by which he meant that he would not cook his pigs inside the spirit-place during the ceremony, that he would not participate in it. This, of course, got everybody excited, and Raima and Ketigla went to Romakl's house to ask him why he would do this. They "cried," i.e., talked in a loud voice.

Later that afternoon Raima, Kewa, and Mak could be seen walking to their distant gardens together. They were no longer angry with each other. Raima said he had not given Romakl anything; after all, it was Romakl and Ketigla, not he, who had quarreled. Ketigla was supposed to give Romakl something, for the best way to soothe anger is to give something "to make the belly good." This is intended as the beginning of an exchange. Actually Ketigla did not give anything immediately, and later Romakl referred to him as *korupa*. Everything was over, except for lingering "bel-hot" between Romakl and Ketigla.

From this angry exchange we note that a big man is such only because of his support. If this is withdrawn, he becomes a rubbish man. There is constant tension between the individual and his rights and the group and its demands. The individual gives up his own rights only to the degree needed to attain goals. The more intimate the group and the more the individual is identified with it, the more ready he is to subordinate his own will to that of the group. His prestige and the prestige of his group are then one and the same thing; his own fame merges with the fame of his big man, who speaks in the collective singular. "I am a big man," he says, "and I made so many exchanges, gave away so many shells, killed so many people in battle," and everyone listening to him realizes full well that he also means, "My group made so-and-so many exchanges and gave away so many shells at the last *wua peng* exchange."

The main reference of the angry words was to pigs and shells, and what emerged from the exchange was the dependence of the big man on his relatives. It is incumbent upon him to maintain his position by the force of his personality, by his ability to persuade, by dealing justly with others, by recognizing all as individuals and persons to be respected, and by keeping his followers generally satisfied. These abilities increase his power. When Romakl threatened to cook his pigs outside, the rest of the lineage group became concerned. When Raima and Ketigla threatened to do the same, there was little response.

The argument did not lead to a split. The Kopalige lineage group did not divide into two at this time, despite the fact that conditions for such a split were ripening. The group is expanding; already it occupies two areas, separated from each other by two miles. Other big men are available in Raima, in Kewa, and in others of Romakl's real or classificatory sons. Moreover, Romakl is getting old. He has given up much of his position already, and will gradually give up more and more of his authority. The Kopalige lineage group was to play a leading role in the coming spirit ceremony, and they wanted to make as impressive a display as possible. Romakl, moreover, is still the best known big man of all the Engamoi. He had to participate in the ceremony if it were to succeed at all. This helped keep the group from splitting, even though a ceremony is a good time to demonstrate publicly a fission (or, for that matter, a fusion), as one group goes its own way, gets its own incantation man, and kills its own pigs in its own place, in opposition to the main group from which it is separating.

What almost happened among the Kopalige exemplifies what Langness (1965: 181) writes about New Guinea segmentation in opposition to Barnes' (1962) notion of catastrophic segmentation:

> Segmentation seems to follow leadership. . . . The antecedent conditions of segmentation probably have to do with the optimum size of groups exploiting land with horticultural techniques, the number of people who can effectively work communally at certain tasks, or the optimum number of persons who can organize themselves following relatively informal patterns of leadership. When a group gets so large that it cannot organize itself effectively for the necessary tasks of living, it must split, with some members following one big man and some another.

From this it follows that there are as many big men as there are recognizable viable social groups. A *wua nuim* will be in charge of each such group for the purposes for which it is mobilized, including social groups above the lineage level.

The Big Man as Politician and Administrator

Basically the Mbowamp apply a consensus democracy to their organizational problems. When a case or decision is being discussed, anyone who has a concern in it has the right to get up and speak. In such matters, however, the *wua nuim* has the most prominent position.

A very important characteristic of the big man is his ability to speak well and forcefully. A person may have most of the other characteristics of a big man, but if he cannot speak well he will not become very well known or become a really important man. The Mbowamp always look for excuses to speak, and any occasion calls for speeches. These are answered by others for hours on end, with the people sitting around and listening with half an ear. One must, of course, have something to say. Therefore with an ability to speak well, which includes speaking clearly and loudly since meetings are held in the open air, goes an ability to make decisions and judgments which will be acceptable to the audience. This requires an insight into the temper of the group concerned in the activity under discussion. The decision which the important man makes usually reflects this general temper of the audience. He sums up a consensus rather than announcing a decision on his own. Consequently the really important men often wait till the very end to make their speeches and voice their own opinions.

The Case for Despotism

It is a well known fact, amply attested in the literature, that there are many leaders, big men, bosbois, or councillors who lord it over others, bending them to their will and forcing them to do what the leaders want. This is especially true if the bosboi or councillor is dealing with people other than his own lineage group. Furthermore, this arbitrary authority is usually backed by the greater authority of the *kiap* (government officer), i.e., the Australian government in general. There is always the threat of jail hanging over the heads of the people if they do not listen to the councillor, or at least so they themselves think. This gives the high-handed a power which they have never had before, and, given the constant struggle for position and prestige, they tend to use it to the full and therefore also to abuse it, especially at the expense of people outside of their own immediate group. Before the Australians arrived, the ultimate appeal was an appeal to arms and warfare, and for this every big man needed the whole-hearted backing of his group. Hence he could not afford to tread on the rights of others unless he knew beforehand that his action would be approved by his own group; and he could not infringe on the rights of his own group in an arbitrary manner because he needed them for so many other things as well as military support.

There is much competition for the position of big man since everybody would like to become one: and no one wants to be known as a rubbish man. It therefore takes much time to attain the position in the first place, and much effort and energy to maintain it. Only when a man becomes *wua anda*—an old man—does he willingly give up his position as a big man and become content to sit by the fire and eat sweet potato, as the people themselves describe this condition. Old people in this culture, in other words, are not the effective leaders; they are respected, but they are no longer considered capable of the work of a big man—making exchanges, looking after the group, and so on. Otherwise, between two men there is always the possibility of conflict for the title of big man. Frequent attempts are made to increase the limits of one's authority so as to enjoy more prestige, or to perform a larger exchange in order to show up one's rival. Such competition serves effectively as a check on the absolute or arbitrary exercise of power, but it also wastes time which might be better spent in effective administration.

One result of this competitive struggle is that the influence of a big man is usually restricted to a small group, normally his immediate relatives. If a man has had many wives and children, he is more likely to be a *wua nuim,* because he will automatically have a larger group who listen to his advice. A big man must know his constituency, prove himself to them, and listen to their opinions, even if they are his close relatives. He must respect them as individuals and as people with a right to their own view of things. He must pay attention to their views or convince them somehow that their approach is inadequate in the matter under question. This also accords with the basic philosophy of personality which characterizes the people. Every individual, even a small child, is basically independent and cannot be compelled against his will to surrender any of his autonomy. A big man cannot force anybody in his group to follow his decisions. He must therefore be very personal in his approach to others if he wishes to retain his position.

Such circumstances, as was clear in the cited quarrel between Romakl and Ketigla, readily leads to fragmentation into small groups. If a big man makes a decision which many disagree with, they can always break off to form another group of their own. A potential new *wua nuim* always stands ready in the wings.

The Big Man: An Achieved Position

A big man is normally in his thirties or forties, for by this time he will have had time to prove his ability to make exchanges. Also he will have been able to acquire more than one wife, which is always an asset in making an important man. However, these criteria of age, sex, and multiple marital status are not absolute because the position of big man is primarily an achieved position. Anybody can become a big man in his group if he works hard enough at it and has the requisite skills.

A son does not necessarily follow in his father's footsteps, although the son of a big man has an obvious advantage over the son of a rubbish man. He has often accompanied his father, has observed his techniques of speaking, has become acquainted with his father's exchange partners, and has been absorbed into the wide relationships which his father established in his climb to the top. Even so, the son must give evidence of the possession of qualities befitting a big man or he can not hope to become the representative of his group. A traditional big man did not enjoy authority over his group because of birth or election to the position but because he had striven for it and proved himself. As a result, the more capable men generally come to the fore as big men.

Exchange and the Big Man

The term *wua nuim* refers to a person who is wealthy in terms of pigs, shells, and possibly land. This does not imply that he has many possessions here and now. On the basis of wealth which can be displayed at any given moment, he does not differ much from a rubbish man. His housing, way of life, clothing, and food do not set him apart from the rest of his group. In these respects he differs little from the most inconsequential of his fellow citizens, despite the ideology stating that he "eats pork every day" (A. Strathern 1966: 359). A *wua nuim* is wealthy in the sense that he has participated in many exchanges and consequently has much credit outstanding. When he wants to inaugurate an exchange, he has access through relatives and other contacts to the necessary shells and pigs.

The one visible and obvious sign of his wealth and position is the length of the *omak* which hangs from his neck and is displayed prominently on his chest. This consists of small bamboo rods which are strung together in step-like fashion. An *omak* with 50 rods reaches approximately to the navel. For each individual rod which is added to this collection the wearer proclaims publicly that he has given someone at least eight shells in a *moka*, a term meaning "exchange." A big man is therefore identified first and foremost by the number of exchanges he has conducted.

Of the various kinds of exchanges, the most important is the *kin moka*, which consists of an exchange of gold-lip shells. It can be of two kinds: a private exchange, which may take place at any time—"in the sun" as the people say—and at a public exchange, which is intended to be as elaborate, public, and prestigious as possible. For this reason, the Mbowamp try to combine as many exchanges as possible on one occasion. Some of the shells distributed, for example, may be a return for a death compensation; others may be an initiatory gift which calls for a special return later; others may be constituent elements of a particular spirit-ceremony being celebrated; and still others may form parts of marriage payments. For this reason, when a large ceremony or exchange is in the offing, marriages are more numerous than usual.

The following is a simple version of a shell exchange. Someone, a relative in the vast majority of the cases and probably a brother or brother-in-law (see Table 1), gives another person (for example, Romakl) three shells and one pig to initiate a *moka*. One of the shells is called *por,* the other two *pol pek;* the pig is called *kia kung* (*kia* being synonynous with *omak* in this context). These gifts do not, however, entitle the initiator to add a bar to his *omak*. In return, Romakl gives the initiator shells as equivalent as possible in every respect—two for the *pol pek,* one for the *por,* and four for the pig—and then adds one more shell to make a total of eight. This last shell "buys the *omak*" and entitles Romakl to put another rod to his strand. He may not return any of the shells he has received but only different ones.

If Romakl wants to be known as a big man, and wishes to spread his reputation far and wide, he adds two extra shells, making ten altogether. Then in a public exchange he runs along the line of shells he is distributing, leaps up in front of the recipient, and proclaims as he lands on both feet, *na wua nuin* ("I am a big man").

To engage in many such exchanges implies several things. It means that the person must have a large number of relatives whom he can control and influence to the extent that they help him accumulate the requisite shells for display and exchange. It probably also means that he has more than one wife and several sets of brothers-in-law. Brothers-in-law are useful both as exchange partners and as sources of shells when he needs them. This is clearly reflected in the rules of exogamy of the Mbowamp. A man may not marry two sisters, nor may two men from the same lineage group marry women from the same lineage group. This would mean a duplication of brothers-in-law, a most undesirable situation which is symbolically expressed in terms of eating one's own pork. If a group is killing pigs, a male member gives some pork to his wife, who presents it to her brother. He in turn gives some of it to his wife, who presents it to her brother. The latter is of the same lineage group as the original donor and this is not acceptable.

Brothers frequently exchange shells. Usually this is in preparation for a larger public display when the entire lineage group gives shells to another lineage group of their clan, or the entire clan gives shells to another clan in the manner described by A. Strathern (1969).

The different categories of exchange partners are shown in Table 1, which tabulates the shell exchanges of eighteen Engamoi big men.

As can be inferred from Table 1, a big man must clearly be able to influence his own agnatic group and others who are dependent on him if he wishes to make any kind of impressive display of shells. This is even more striking if we consider the set of relationships involved in a typical *moka* as described so well by Strauss and Tischner (1962).

A big man, moreover, is quick to return an exchange. The saying is that if A gives to B in the morning, B will return in the afternoon. This is not done in actual fact; indeed, it is not even the ideal to return an exchange so quickly. A big man wants to keep an exchange relationship going, and one way of doing this is to delay making the return. What the expression really means is that B will surely live up to his obligations.

The Big Man as Ritual and War Leader

Success in exchange implies that the big man also has strong ritual power; he can "pull" many shells by means of his spells (*mon*) and ritual paraphernalia. He need not be a ritual expert in every area of life where incantations are performed. Many men know the common incantations to make pigs grow fat and strong, or to ensure that taro will be firm. Since, however, the big man is thought of as the one who looks after his group, it is incumbent upon him to call in a ritual expert in serious cases, e.g., when a lineage member is sick. Certain people, of both sexes but more often men, have a reputation for being able to counteract a specific illness. Ketigla, the brother of Romakl, had the ability to cure the illness which develops when a woman gives a man food during her menstrual period and, even more important, he could make the proper incantation for a man who had had intercourse with a woman who was menstruating. The fact that he had the skill and ritual to render harmless the effects of such exposure gave Ketigla importance and prestige, so that he was called a *wua nuim*. However, he was not a big man in the sense that he represented his group in any way.

Very similar is the big man's role in warfare. A man who is a renowned warrior, like the ritual expert, is called a *wua nuim,* but he is not necessarily one who looks after the lineage group in other matters or performs many exchanges. Indeed, a big man like Romakl is not expected to take part in warfare, for he would be the special target of the enemy; he therefore stays behind when there is a question of fighting.

These are the major characteristics of the *wua nuim.* They form a constellation. Where one aspect is weak, another may be emphasized in compensation. A man with only one wife may stress his speaking skill. One with a limited number of relatives may emphasize ritual ability. A deficiency in the number of exchanges one has made can be offset only with great difficulty, but the ability to sum up consensus and thus to render an acceptable judgment in court cases can help a man to become a *wua nuim.* Also, any kind of influence is capable of being gradually generalized. If a man is a *wua nuim* because of his ritual skill, his chances of being consulted on an impending series of exchanges are improved. If he speaks well and clearly, he is likely to represent his group and serve as its spokesman at weddings, funerals, or exchanges.

The amount of compensation which is possible has limits, to be sure, but an aggressive man will test them to the utmost in his ambition to be a leader, because this position brings the prestige, the influence, the wealth, the pride of place, and the attention which he finds so gratifying.

Legitimation of the Big Man

What legitimizes the position and authority of the big man is certainly not his birth nor any other ascribed characteristics. It is, first of all, his own abilities that legitimize his position, and second, the successes that make him an acceptable leader. In the eyes of the Mbowamp, however, ability and success are not necessarily directly connected. Another variable, that of power (*rondukl*), seems to intervene. That a person is in contact with power is most obvious from his success, and it is especially from this contact his legitimization as a big man flows.

If a man cannot achieve the position of an important man, he need not feel anxious about it, and as a matter of fact very few become bitter over their failure. The Mbowamp do not employ every means and technique to achieve a position which is not meant for them. In other words, they submit to the seeming inequalities of their social system, simply because they lack the requisite power. This is not their fault, and they need not feel inferior or guilty. The "little people" or "rubbish men" realize full well that their big men are dependent to a large degree upon them and upon their cooperation. They themselves are, in a sense, the source of their power. Some lack the talent to become important men; others do not wish to expend the effort required; still others have tried and failed. All can fall back on the ideology of power to salve their wounded pride.

A big man does not maintain his position indefinitely once he has achieved it. He must continue to produce results to prove that he is still in contact with power. As he grows old, the number of his exchanges decreases, he speaks publicly less frequently, and others rise in his place to represent the group in free-for-all discussion. Such a peaceful relaxation of position is most evident when the successor is a real brother or son of the big man who is stepping down. If it is someone else, e.g., classificatory brother or son, who is rising to prominence, there is more likelihood of a separation into two groups, especially if the basic requirements of population size and resources adequate to insure the viability and structural integrity of the newly developing group are also satisfied.

Conclusion

The foregoing description of the traditional big man among the Mbowamp, specifically among the Kumdi-Engamoi, seeks to shed light on the problem of traditional despotism as discussed by Brown (1963), Salisbury (1964), Watson (1967), and A. Strathern (1966), and in so doing it confirms and supplements the conclusions of Strathern.

The traditional system of leadership and administration in the Hagen area has been very effective, given the values and the goals the people have set for themselves. The political philosophy of the Mbowamp has been that of consensus democracy. The people themselves, with and through their *wua nuim,* have decided their goals and how these were to be achieved. The big man, in his turn, had to adopt a personalistic philosophy and deal individually and on a person-to-person basis with those whom he represented. Because of this, the size of the group he represented was small, and outside of it his influence was limited. Consequently, the big man thinks first and foremost of his own lineage group.

These values and conceptions of leadership have obvious implications for the future. New Guinea is striding rapidly into the modern world, with all its complexities and strains. However well the traditional consensus democracy of the New Guinea Highlands worked in the past, it will not suffice for them as they take their place in the community of nations. Their leaders must learn to think beyond the bounds of their lineage group, and the people must be educated to follow duly chosen leaders who do not belong to their own group.

NOTE

1. The author gratefully acknowledges the aid of the Bollingen Foundation which helped support the first field trip (1963–1965) and the Penrose Fund of the American Philosophical Society for helping finance a brief restudy in 1968.

BIBLIOGRAPHY

Barnes, J. A. 1962. Africa, Models in the New Guinea Highlands. Man 62: 5–9.
Brandewie, E. 1966. An Internal Analysis of the Kinship System of the Mbowamp

of the Central Highlands of New Guinea. Unpublished Ph.D. dissertation, University of Chicago. 1968.

——. New Guinea Sickness and Values: Their Discovery and Integration. Dr. H. Otley Beyer: Dean of Philippine Anthropology (A Commemorative Issue), ed. R. Rahmann and G. Ang, pp. 101–122. San Carlos Publications, Cebu City.

Brown, P. 1963. From Anarchy to Satrapy. American Anthropologist 65: 1–15.

Bulmer, R. N. H. 1960. Political Aspects of the Moka Exchange System. Oceania 31: 1–13.

Finney, B. R. 1968. Bigfellow Man Belong Business in New Guinea. Ethnology 7: 394–410.

Langness, L. L. 1964. Some Problems in the Conceptualization of Highlands Social Structures. New Guinea: The Central Highlands, ed. J. B. Watson, pp. 162–182. American Anthropologist 66: iv, pt. 2 (Special Publication).

Lepervanche, M. de. 1967–1968. Descent, Residence, and Leadership in the New Guinea Highlands. Oceania 38: 134–158, 163–189.

Meggitt, M. J. 1964. Male-Female Relationships in the Highlands of Australian New Guinea. New Guinea: The Central Highlands, ed. J. B. Watson, pp. 204–224. American Anthropologist 66: iv, pt. 2 (Special Publication).

——. 1965. The Lineage System of the Mae-Enga. Edinburgh.

——. 1967. The Pattern of Leadership among the Mae-Enga of New Guinea. Anthropological Forum 2:20–35.

Read, K. E. 1954. Cultures of the Central Highlands. Southwestern Journal of Anthropology 10: 1–43.

Reay, M. 1964. Present-Day Politics in the New Guinea Highlands. New Guinea: The Central Highlands, ed. J. B. Watson, pp. 240–256. American Anthropologist 66: iv, pt. 2 (Special Publication).

Salisbury, R. F. 1962. From Stone to Steel. London.

——. 1964. Despotism and Australian Administration in the New Guinea Highlands. New Guinea: The Central Highlands, ed. J. B. Watson, pp. 225–239. American Anthropologist 66: iv, pt. 2 (Special Publication).

Strathern, A. 1966. Despots and Directors in the New Guinea Highlands. Man 1: 356–367.

——. 1968. Sickness and Frustrations: Variations in Two New Guinea Highlands Societies. Mankind 6: 545–551.

——. 1969. Finance and Production: Two Strategies in New Guinea Highlands Exchange Systems. Oceania 40: 42–67.

Strathern, M. 1968. Popokl: The Question of Morality. Mankind 6: 553–562.

Strauss, H., and H. Tischner. 1962. Die Mi Kultur der Hagenberg Stamme im Ostlichen Zentral-Neuguinea. Hamburg.

Vicedom, G. F., and H. Tischner. 1943–48. Die Mbowamp: die Kultur der Hagenberg Stamme in Ostlichen Zentral-Neuguinea. 3v. Hamburg.

Watson, J. B. 1967. Tairora: The Politics of Despotism in a Small Society. Anthropological Forum 2: 53–104.

Killers, Big Men, and Priests on Malaita: Reflections on a Melanesian Troika System[1]

Roger M. Keesing

*Many of the terms employed by social science researchers are impre-
cisely defined, and the term* leader *does violence to the complexities
of the variations and subtleties involved. As Keesing documents, in
Melanesia the traditional term* leader *focused on only one type of
leader that functioned in that ethnographic area. He describes the
different categories of leadership and how each differs in its activities and bases of power and authority. Keesing adds a critical historical dimension by describing how one individual over time can shift
from one type of leader and progress into a different category.*

*If we recognize that there will be a whole range of local conditions
and differing contexts of group interactions in kinship societies, it is
inevitable that differing criteria of status and leadership will emerge
in time and space. Keesing suggests some of the kinds of processes
from which formal and informal leadership may derive in acephalous
societies.*

ONE OF THE unfortunate distortions created by the elevation of the
Big Man as anthropology's stereotyped Melanesian political leader has
been a deflection of attention from warrior-leaders, who in many parts of
precolonial Melanesia had power and prestige greater than or coordinate
with that of entrepreneurial leaders. Big Men have held center stage in
the period of ethnographic observation partly because men whose prominence was achieved in warfare and feuding have been forcibly removed
from the stage by pacification.

The role men given to violence and destruction played, and the understanding of such men in folk psychology, will be examined for a part of

seaboard Melanesia (Malaita, Solomon Islands) where a complementarity between warriors and peace-keeping entrepreneurial leaders was institutionalized. On Malaita three leadership roles were clearly distinguished: a priest, who maintained relations between a kin group and its ancestors; a Big Man, in the anthropologist's sense; and a war-leader/bounty-hunter. Drawing in particular on evidence from the Kwaio of central Malaita, I examine these three leadership roles both at the level of ideal and practice; and I examine notions of folk psychology that underlie them. Whereas some Malaita peoples to the northwest and southeast seem to have more neatly and directly institutionalized these as complementary leadership positions, their separation in practice among the Kwaio was considerably less neat than the "troika"[2] idealization would suggest and that too has interesting implications in terms of folk psychology. Despite the flexibility of actual practice, I will suggest that a distinction between positive powers of peace and stability ("living") and negative powers of violence and destruction ("killing"/"destruction") runs deep in Kwaio culture.

Leadership on Malaita

Throughout Malaita the religious officiant or priest of a kin group (northern Malaita *fataabu* "speak sacred") enacted a clearly distinguished role; and throughout Malaita the type-role of warrior-champion/bounty hunter (northern Malaita *ngwane ramo*) was recognized. Secular leadership roles showed greater ethnographic variation, in that two principles— hereditary title of a senior agnate and achieved status as a Big Man—were intertwined or complementary. Finally, in both northern and southern Malaita there were ideas of a kind of paramount chiefly title, based on hereditary entitlement but achieved only when a leader of extraordinary gifts managed in his career to create a measure of unity among usually autonomous descent-based local groups.

The existence of hereditary titleholders we can legitimately call "chiefs" runs counter to the Big Man stereotype, but we now know that chiefdoms were widely distributed in Melanesia (Douglas 1979; Chowning 1979; Hau'ofa 1971). Indeed it now seems very likely that the Oceanic Austronesian-speaking peoples who colonized seaboard Melanesia had hereditary chiefs of the Western Polynesian type, and that the Big Man systems of the ethnographic present reflect political devolution in the last two millennia as regional trade systems disintegrated (Pawley 1981, 1982; Friedman 1981). Hence we should be neither surprised to find hereditary chiefly authority in the southeastern Solomons nor surprised to find such systems in communities that have maritime orientations that allow the possibility of monopolistic control over resources, trade and exchange. On Malaita chiefly title is found in clearest form in Small Malaita and southeastern 'Are'are, where *araha* exercise hereditary authority; chiefs (with rather lesser powers) also were found among the Lau speakers of the northwestern lagoons. In adjoining hill areas there are echoes of such ideas of hereditary rights based on seniority in the male line. My focus will be on the peoples of the mountainous interior of Malaita proper, where achieved secular leadership is of primary importance.

For the To'abaita of northwestern Malaita, Hogbin (1939:62–63) aptly describes the *ngwane inoto,* "man of importance," who helped to give rise to the Big Man stereotype:

> In north Malaita ... there is no recognized supreme ruler over even a small territorial group, and the individuals who command the respect of their fellows have no permanent legal claims to obedience, but rather obtain by the distribution of their wealth the cooperation necessary for the enterprises they initiate. ... Although the heir to an old leader has an initial advantage over possible rivals, any ambitious young man can supplant him if he works hard, distributes sufficient wealth, and wins the respect and approval of his relatives through superior personal qualifications. ... Practically every district has [a] ... *ngwane inoto,* though their wealth varies considerably according to the number of persons in the group and whether or not they have any serious rivals. ... In populous districts although the title is as a rule given to only one man, there is always a couple more with almost equal prestige.

Hogbin (1939:91) also noted the past importance of warriors in To'abaita:

> When it had been agreed that a dead man was to be avenged the slaying was usually carried out by a raiding party acting under the order of an experienced killer (*ngwane-ramo,* literally, "man of strength"), who had been asked to take the leadership either by the closest relatives or else by the *ngwane-inoto* of the group. In some districts there were several killers, each one of whom was capable of organizing such a raid, but where no such leader was available locally the dead man's relatives put a price on the sorcerer's head. Attracted by the prospect of this reward, and also of acquiring glory, some killer from another place then went and dispatched him by stealth.

Of the prestige formerly held by such warrior-leaders, Hogbin (1939) describes "the honour ... of [a] district, and how it has been exalted by the bloody deeds of those who are now regarded as famous warriors."

Hogbin devotes less attention to the third leadership role, that of priest. He (1939:106) notes that

Each cemetery has its own priest who has to give his approval before any offering can be made to the spirit of the persons being buried there. The office is held by hereditary right, being transmitted from father to son, but is by no means a full-time job and apart from his special position at ceremonies the priest lives the life of an ordinary man. Several in fact are *ngwane-inoto*.

For the nearby Baegu, Ross (1973, 1978) gives a picture generally similar, but complicated by the two-strandedness of secular leadership I have noted. In Baegu, a dialect closely related to To'abaita, the term cognate with *ngwane inoto* labels a hereditary senior steward of lineage land:

> The *wane initoo* ... are the hereditary, titular landowners. ... A *wane initoo* is respected as the most important member of his clan, and his opinions carry great weight. He is the symbol of the land and of his clan or lineage segment. The office of *wane initoo* is strictly hereditary with succession based on primogeniture and seniority according to birth order of siblings. ... *Wane initoo* bear themselves with the quiet, aloof dignity of those who expect deference as their birthright. (Ross 1978:12).

Ross goes on to characterize other *wane ba'ita* ("big men," the generic term for all leaders) who achieve renown and power by feastgiving and effective leadership in the manner described by Hogbin for To'abaita leaders. He (1978:13) refers to these as "de facto Big Men," noting that they "are usually gregarious, aggressive men of action." However, the conceptual and actual line between hereditary lineage head and feastgiving leader is blurred:

> Because of genealogical position their direct descent from the ancestors, and their titular role in granting permission for land use, *wane initoo* are inherently already in a strategically valuable position and can easily turn this favorable sociocentric status into a means of attaining economic and executive power. The Baegu recognize intuitively the dynamics of leadership and the status potential involved, and they sometimes by metaphor call other (non-hereditary) important men *wane initoo*, too (Ross 1973:189).

The Baegu warrior leaders, *wane ramo*, closely fit the patterns described by Hogbin (1973:190) for To'abaita. "*Wane ramo* ... appear to have been combination military-commanders-policemen-bounty hunters. *Ramo* were chosen ... by consensus ... on the basis of their physical strength, aggressive temperament, and military skill."

Elsewhere Ross (1978:13) states that "*ramo* was supposed to be an inheritable title, but non-bellicose sons could easily lose the distinction, while aggressive rivals could attain and defend the position.... Only the toughest, strongest, most wary, most dominating, and most awe-inspiring succeeded and survived."

Ross (1973:190) comments that "in the days before the British ... put an end to institutionalized feuding, many neighborhood communities (but by no means all) had a war leader (*wane ramo*)." Priests are again clearly distinguished.

> The *wane nifoa,* meaning "man who offers prayers," is a priest of the ancestral spirit cult.... Ideally a priest's eldest son should succeed to the priesthood upon his father's death. However, knowledge and demeanor are more significant than genealogical criteria, and priesthoods usually pass to the best qualified of the potential heirs. (Ross 1978:13)

Ross (1973:190) comments that "Hogbin, writing about the Toabaita [*sic*], says that the priest and the *wane inoto* roles were sometimes combined in the same person. My impression is that usually they are not."

Ross (1973:55) briefly and anecdotally characterizes the folk-psychological models and personality types associated with the Baegu leadership roles:

> Big Men ... are ambitious people who want to dominate. They are hospitable and generous to a fault, ... outgoing: loving activity, definitely extroverted, and addicted to display. These leaders as dominant persons can be highly charismatic.
> Priests tend to be more stable. Quiet, dignified, even-tempered, and knowledgeable, they are almost scholarly in comportment.
> War leaders ... no longer exist, but people still recognize the personality type. These men are wilder; have quick tempers, and are said to be immune to pain or fatigue and to show no fear of danger.... Physically, war leaders tend to be domineering mesomorphs.

Ross (1978:14) notes Baegu ideas about how in theory both ritual and secular leaders could emerge who linked autonomous local descent-based groups together into overarching regional systems:

> An exceptionally powerful pagan priest ... was able to make sacrifices at several shrines.... He was said to be a priest for ... "everybody" in a district or clan. Presumably he was a chief priest, sacrificing to a higher order of clan ancestral spirit.... The *wane taloa,* whose title means "man of renown or fame," was a Big Man whose prestige extended beyond his own district and clan, and whose right to prestige was certified by formal investiture by a chief priest.... Finally, the title of *wane 'aofia* ... belonged to the most prestigious man of all.... None of these, bigger than today's Big Men, exist except in memory or myth.

For the Fataleka immediately to the south of Baegu we have an account by Russell (1950:5–7) that gives a generally similar picture, including the blurring of ascribed and achieved secular "bigness:"

> The *nwane inoto* was the secular chief of each clan and . . . held hereditary office in the male line. Part of his duties was the provision of pigs to propitiate the *akalo* [ancestral ghosts] and in previous days to celebrate success in war. His gardens were therefore extensive and display of wealth enhanced his prestige. The more lavish his sacrifices, the more important he tended to be in the community. . . .
>
> The *fatambu,* sometimes referred to as *nwane foa,* is the priest who propitiates the ancestral spirits of the lineage or clan. Succession to the office of *fatambu* is hereditary, and the eldest son normally succeeds his father. . . .
>
> The *nwane ramo* . . . lowest leader in precedence in the clan hegemony . . . was the skilled leader in fighting chosen for ability and, although choice was confined to certain clans, succession was not usually hereditary. Sometimes at the age of twelve a boy would be set apart. "He is not the same. He will be a *ramo.*"

Russell (1950:7–8) noted that the ritually and genealogically senior of the Baegu "clans," Rakwane, could provide two further categories of leader. The priest of Rakwane could, if his son "displayed sufficient promise, if the economy of Fataleka would support the ceremonies, and if the time were auspicious proclaim his son *aofia,* thus promoting him from religious to the highest secular office in Fataleka." By being so "promoted," the *aofia* was presented with wealth and accorded great formal respect and substantial power. In a further ceremony, he could be further "promoted" to the status of *taniota,* in which capacity he "was the keystone of the society, converting it from a number of similar units into a composite structure" (1950:8). He was accorded great respect and honor, as "the man of peace" who symbolized political and ritual unity. According to Russell (1950:10), "He had the power of decision for all the Fataleka people and was the intermediary between them and other peoples. . . . His authority was absolute within the system of clans and his edicts were obeyed as if they were indeed sanctioned by the *akalo* to whom they felt indebted for his leadership."

But it is not at all clear whether this idealized office was filled regularly in practice. As Ross (1973:202) says of a similar great leader (*'aofia* or *wane saungia*) in Baegu, "there is no way to tell if [he] is myth or reality."

The intertwining of the ideas of hereditary title and entrepreneurial achievement in defining secular leadership is clarified if we examine the Lau of the lagoons adjacent to Baegu. Ivens (1930) describes the Lau chiefs and their powers in terms that are quite clear, even allowing for an earlier bias toward finding "chiefs":

> The Lau chiefs are chiefs by virtue of their birth, and not because of any prowess which they may manifest, or any wealth which they may amass, or any spiritual power which may manifest itself in them. Their functions are distinct from those of the priests, who are of the same lineage with them.... The phrase, *fisi kwau* (top branches)... is used of chiefs.... Little actual government, as we understand the term, was exercised by them in the past.
>
> The chiefs in Lau are ... responsible for the carrying out of the big feasts, and these feasts are the most important things that occur in the social life of the communities as a whole. The fishing grounds are all the property of chiefs, as also are the fishing-nets.
>
> The chiefs are the wealthy members of the community. In Lau they amass money through their ownership of the fishing-nets.
>
> The eldest son of a chief is his father's successor. . . .

Ivens (1930:90) also provides clarification of the source and nature of the concept of an overarching secular-religious leader:

> An instance of the general peaceable character of the Lau peoples is afforded by the appointment of one of the chiefs to be *aofia*. The word in itself denotes quietness.... In Tolo [i.e., Baegu, Fataleka, Baelelea] the word *Aofia* denotes a big chief, and carries no reference to any quality of peacefulness of disposition as it does in Lau. The *lau Aofia* was a man of chiefly rank, an actual chief at the time of his appointment, or the son of a chief, who was formally dedicated to be the embodiment in himself of peace. The person chosen must be one who is known to be of quiet .disposition. . . .
>
> The motive underlying the appointment of an *Aofia* was that there should be present among the Lau peoples one whose influence was exercised to keep the peace. The succession does not appear to have been maintained regularly, but at least four men have occupied the position.

Ivens (1930:199) goes on to describe the Lau priests, *hataabu,* and warrior leaders, *ramo.* The latter "might be either chiefs or commoners, who had acquired a reputation for personal prowess. In the old days, before the coming of white men, the fighting-men were not usually of chiefly rank."

For the Kwara'ae of central Malaita the past is very difficult to reconstruct. Burt (1982:395) writes of

> the pagan priests whom Kwara'ae declare to have been their only leaders in precolonial times. . . . Such formal roles did not themselves confer political leadership and authority which, in the past, was achieved ... through

the deployment of wealth, as in other societies of northern Malaita. Kwara'ae are reluctant to identify any Christians as important men (*wane inato'a*) in these terms today.

The term *aofia* has been applied in some contexts to neotraditionalist "Paramount Chiefs" in resurgent Maasina Rule *kastom* activities; the ideologue of the movement, Wadili, notes that this title was held by "a big man" of his lineage "about twelve generations ago," but Burt (1982:399) comments that *aofia* is "otherwise not in common use in Kwara'ae." From early accounts it is clear that Kwara'ae speakers, too, had *wane ramo* as bounty-hunting warrior leaders. A similar pattern, as in Lau modified by chiefly title, prevailed at the southern end of Malaita proper, among 'Are'are speakers, and on Small Mala. For our purposes, however, the northern groups provide sufficient evidence of the three-stranded system of leadership.

My own data on the Kwalo allow me to go rather further. I can not only more clearly assess relations between ideal model and practice, on the basis of more than four years of fieldwork over a twenty years span and unusually rich longitudinal data, but can more clearly show the articulation between a system of leadership and the folk-psychological conceptions that underlie and rationalize it.

Kwaio Leadership Roles and Folk Psychology

I have elsewhere described Kwaio blood feuding, the *lamo* (=*ramo*), entrepreneurial leadership, and ritual officiants in some detail (Keesing 1978, 1982; Keesing and Corris 1980); the autobiographical account by 'Elota, leading feastgiver of modern times (Keesing 1978), adds further substance. Here I condense some elements of the account, concentrating on folk-psychological models underlying leadership roles and some complexities in the institutionalization of what in theory are supposed to be three separate and to substantial degree mutually incompatible leadership roles.

A word first about the evidence. Like all ethnographers of Malaita I find it extremely difficult, on the basis of retrospective normative accounts and epic tales of violent ancestral deeds, to assess the actual scale and frequency of blood feuding, the states of confrontation and defensive isolation precipitated by killings, and the periodic large scale engagements one might rather dubiously class as true warfare. This is particularly difficult insofar as even those observers who described Malaita prior to pacification did so (with few exceptions such as explorers themselves subjected to attack) in a period when fighting had been substantially changed by the introduction of firearms (mainly "Sniders," old muskets converted to breech-loading).

Kwaio conceptualizations of their own political system, as elsewhere on Malaita, are also distorted by ideas about chiefs and "lines" (Keesing 1968) that were formulated during Maasina Rule but themselves reflected misunderstandings by the British of how "the natives" were (or ought to have been) organized. For the Kwaio there is also a special set of problems deriving from the 1927 assassination of District Officer Bell and the massacre of his entourage, and the drastic punitive expedition and mass arrests that followed. In the Kwaio interior, the leaders of an entire generation—warriors, secular leaders, even aged priests—were mainly wiped out. Those who were thrown into the breach to replace them were successors chosen of necessity from the survivors; and even the styles of leadership in the aftermath of the post-massacre were shaped by the heavy punitive hand of British colonialism. While this undoubtedly distorts my data from the 1960s and 70s, the drastic punitive expedition had a curious reverse benefit: I was able to reconstruct in great detail settlement patterns, descent group structure, and leadership as of October, 1927, when the Kwaio were forced to flee for their lives, in one direction or the other (Keesing and Corris 1980). I have remarkably detailed data on Kwaio social structure on the eve of forced pacification, and before the drastic disruption of late 1927.

First of all the Kwaio linguistic labels for the three prototypical leadership types need to be examined. For the religious officiant of a descent group Kwaio most often use *wane naa ba'e,* "man of the shrine," although the north Malaita *fataabu* is also in use. The descent group's priest is the man who *tania,* "holds," its shrine. For a feastgiving and stability-maintaining leader like 'Elota, Kwaio use *wane ba'ita,* "big man," or, mainly in contexts of neo-Maasina Rule leadership, the southern-derived term *alafa* ("chief"). Like northern Malaita peoples the Kwaio had ideas of a secular leader whose political sway would be exercised across a broad region; but for these anarchically inclined and fiercely egalitarian hillbillies, this was a unity probably never achieved (the usual label for such a leader, *alafa ni gela,* "Gela Chief," belies its alien origin).[3] For a warrior leader/bounty-hunter, Kwaio use *lamo,* or *wane lamo.* In the Malaita languages *ramo* and its cognates (*Kwaio lamo,* 'Are'are *namo*) is canonically a stative, "(be) strong," so that in conjunction with the noun for man (*ngwane, wane, mwane*) it labelled a "strong man." However, in some of the languages, and anthropological parlance, *ramo* has come to be used as a noun. For such a warrior Kwaio also used *wane kwa'i,* "killer," although the latter could be used of any successful warrior, whereas *wane lamo* was used for killers of special power and renown.

In sociological terms, only the "priest" occupied a position every descent group had to fill. A "big man" is "big" only in relative terms, and some descent groups had no prominent secular leader. Kwaio descent groups are tiny; even before the depredations of the 1927 punitive expedition they were very small (three-twenty adult men). A group in which a strong feastgiving leader had emerged acted with greater unity, at more intensified levels of production and exchange activity, than a group without such a leader. But a set of men none of whom was a prominent leader and feastgiver could act together and singly to stage mortuary feasts and organize bridewealth exchanges when the occasion arose. Every competent adult Kwaio man has sponsored some mortuary feasts, if only minor ones, himself.

So the *wane ba'ita* was "big" as a matter of degree; and in no sense was the Big Man a leadership position within the descent group, at least among the Kwaio. Even where in modern neo-Maasina Rule contexts Kwaio try to organize themselves periodically into neat arrays of "lines," each with its "chief" (*alafa* or *sifi*), the neatness is very messy in relation to actual descent group structure, as well as narrowly contextual (Keesing 1968). Rather than being a position that had to be filled, the *wane ba'ita* was a path to be followed, an idealized role to be emulated, as far as one's talents, energies, ambitions, resources, and social circumstances allowed.

So, too, the *wane lamo* in no sense occupied a position within a Kwaio descent group. As will be seen, such a man was believed to have special ancestrally conferred powers. But his *lamo*-ness was a matter of degree and context. While everyone agreed that a small array of feared bounty hunters of the 1920s were *lamo*—Basiana, Tagailarno, Maenaafo'oa, Fuufu'e—there were many men, warriors of lesser fame and power, who in some contexts would be classed as *wane lamo*. I have pointed out (Keesing and Corris 1980; Keesing 1978) that being a *wane lamo* was like being a Fast Gun in Hollywood's Old West, a distinction one was happy to forego in the presence of A Faster Gun.

If the idealized triumvirate of descent group leaders had a fairly neat correspondence with social reality in some parts of northern Malaita, this correspondence was much less neat for the Kwaio. I have touched so far on one aspect of the "messiness:" the fact that neither *wane ba'ita* nor *wane lamo* was a position that a descent group had to fill, a type of leadership represented in every group. A second form of "messiness," which has to do with the separation and mutual incompatibility of priestly, warrior, and entrepreneurial roles, can only be understood in the light of folk-psychological models of violence and peacefulness and cultural conceptions of destruction and stability; and in the light of the paths leading to "careers" as warrior, feastgiver, and priest.

Folk-Psychological Models: Violence and Stability

There is, Kwaio surmise, a natural basis for the different cultural paths followed by infant boys and infant girls toward an adulthood in which they enact complementary roles. These differences, as expressed in adult-hood, are summed up by Boori'au, a respected older woman:

> Women's minds (*manatalaga*) are one way, men's minds are another. . . .
> A woman thinks only about getting married, about her work—nothing else. . . . But men are different. They are given to being aggressive (*ngeengee'a*): they kill, they steal, they seduce. They aren't peaceful (*nabe*). Women aren't that way, given to killing rage, to destroying things. Some women are responsible (*manata'a*), others aren't—that's all. But a woman and her brother won't be the same. We have two different tempera-ments (*manata'anga*), not just one. Even a man who is good natured and fun loving will turn around and kill his sister or his wife if some cause arises.

Individual men are viewed as differing widely in personality, manifest-ing innate proclivities they displayed from infancy onward. Some are *nabe* "gentle, peaceful," in contrast to those who are *fata'a* or *ila'a*, "quarrelsome" and *ogaria'a* "anger-prone." The latter are, as young men or even as boys, likely to get into trouble from cursing or defying their elders. This axis, of peaceful, placid nature or volatile, aggressive nature, cuts diagonally across the axis of ideal leadership types. Placidity by itself is not a desirable masculine characteristic; as Boori'au's observations indicate, it is a stereotypically feminine orientation except insofar as peacefulness is combined with other personality characteristics (women, too, command special admiration only when their gentleness is com-bined with strength, energy, and ambitious industriousness).

Nor is aggressiveness by itself particularly positively valued. I have seen a particularly feisty boy of eight or ten, given to brutalizing his age-mates, spoken of with a half-admiring *lamo te'e lau* "he'll grow up to be a *lamo*" (lit. "a *lamo* will eventuate"). But Kwaio recognized that a boy or young man whose aggressiveness was not constrained was likely to be killed for his curses or defiance before he could embark on a successful "career" as warrior. The example of Wa'enilamo (Keesing 1978:57–60), who courted and eventually met death for his brash bravado, is well remembered. To put things succinctly, a nasty kid could meet an early death at the hands of his nasty elders. A case in point was Naiofi, who as a young boy of ten incurred the annoyance of his father's brother's son, the feared *lamo* Tagailamo, and then had the poor judgment to defecate in the shrine during a sacrifice. Tagailamo killed him on the spot, ostensibly for his "purification" but in reality to collect himself a blood-bounty an enemy had put up for his, Tagailamo's, death, or that of a close relative. It was not a world where defying or cursing one's elders increased one's life chances.

Folk conceptualizations of anger and its socially appropriate expression bear clarification. Kwaio describe anger in conventional metaphors centered on the belly. Anger is *ogarianga,* "belly badness"; one's belly is "hot," "red," or "bad." Such a state is contextually appropriate when honor demands—when one's person, ancestors, reputation, property, or that of one's group, the sexual purity of wife, sister or daughter, is invaded or impugned. In the face of such invasion a man should be angry and strong (*tegela*), not afraid (*ma'u,* reflex of Oceanic mataku). Stylized threat behavior of a raised arm or weapon, fierce stare and stamped heel is expected; and a man should be prepared to back his threats to the death, unflinchingly, if honor demands and if one is not placated (*fa'abaole'aa,* "to make the belly good") by compensation in shell valuables and/or pigs appropriate to the offense.

For a man to be angry or placid is not, then, valued in and of itself. What is important is the contextually appropriate display of anger and bravery, to the death if need be; and the appropriate observations of deference to seniors and ancestors, and respect to women. Being *nabe,* "placid, peaceful," is a virtue for a man in some contexts (particularly if he is known to have the physical strength and resources to respond aggressively and chooses forbearance); but to be *nabe* when honor demands aggressiveness and anger is a matter of shame, not pride. In the old days that alternative, too, could lead to premature death.

Yet Kwaio knew, in the days of blood feuding, and perceive today, that male aggressiveness and angry posturing can easily escalate into violence. 'Elota's account of his role as peacemaker gives particularly vivid examples (Keesing 1978, Chap. 16). It is here that a secular leader could play a key part in maintaining peace—along with feastgiving, a main way in which a *wane ba'ita* could express his "bigness." Such a leader, Kwaio say, *fa'angadoa,* "steers," his group: he maintains stability as a steersman steadies his canoe on its course (here *ngado,* prefixed with the Kwaio reflex of the common Oceanic causative, is "be stable, be steady"). If he is as "big" as 'Elota was, he maintains such stability beyond the limits of his own group.

The qualities of personality that give a man such powers of leadership are characterized in terms of thoughtfulness, seriousness, stability. He is *manata'a,* "responsible," "reflective," and *to'ofunga'a,* "serious" (in other linguistic contexts this describes qualities of being "real," "fundamental" or "true"). He is *nabe,* but only contextually, and backed by strength: calm as sheltered waters are calm, amidst waves of mounting confrontation; reflective while others are consumed by anger.

A *wane ba'ita* expressed his strength, power, and energies in the quest for prestige (*talo'a,* "renown"), through mobilizing valuables in mortuary feasts and bridewealth prestations (Keesing 1978, Chapters 3, 18). Kwaio admiration for the entrepreneurial ability of the successful feastgiver is colored with ambivalence, both of jealousy and trepidation. To be the target of a big man's largesse is to be challenged, potentially shamed; the aggression expressed in feasting prestations, the pride manifest in self-deprecatory conventional speeches (Keesing 1978:4), lies close to the surface. It is the "strength" (*tegelangaa*) of such deeds that gives teeth to the moral authority and peace-keeping interventions of a leader like 'Elota.

It is this aggressive entrepreneurship by the *wane ba'ita* that distinguishes him from the idealized model of a "priest." The latter is, prototypically, a man who is similarly knowledgeable, serious, and responsible; but whose concerns lie with the sacred rather than the quest for prestige. He is ideally *nabe* in his abstention from pursuits either of feasting or fighting, his preparedness to go into liminal isolation on behalf of the group, to abstain from sex or special foods when ritual duties demand. Since the group's relations with ancestors depend on his correct recitation of ancestral names and magical spells and punctiliously correct performance of complex rites, he must be *manata'a* "reflective," as well as *sua'ola'a* "knowledgeable" (lit. "able to name correctly" but nowadays used also for educated). Above all he must abstain from killing. A killing is an offense against the ancestors of the victim, which must be compensated before proper living can be restored. Because of the wide tracing of connection to a cluster of ancient ancestors, a priest and his group and his victim would be likely to have ancestors in common. The cautionary tale of Lalaimae, priest of Kwaina'afi'a, who brought ruin on his group by participating in a killing and denying doing so by taking an oath invoking his ancestral oven stones (Keesing 1978, Chap. 12), is well remembered.

Both folk-psychological theory and practice are predicated on individual diversity. The *wane lamo* will serve to illustrate. Just as the Fast Guns of the old (Hollywood) West—Jesse James, the Daltons et al.—were recognized as unique in style, volatility, hot—or coolheadedness, so the *lamo* were unique figures. The warrior leaders, although they had in common the (ancestrally conferred and personality-derived) courage, ability, and aggressiveness to kill, ranged from the most prestigious fighting leader in the days before firearms, who led his men into assaults on enemy positions carrying a giant shield and warding off arrows and spears, to the *lamo logo* (lit., "*lamo* of darkness"), whose aggressiveness and lust to kill was so beyond social control that he lived in a cave and ate his victims raw. It is perhaps more than an accident of homonymy that *talo* denotes both "war shield" and "renown." Such a leader, fearless in leading the attack, was guiding and maintaining the order and resolve of his warriors by direction and example. Like the peace-keeper he *fa'angadoa,* "maintained the stability of," his group—but in the face of enemy fire. It is in such respects that our understanding of the Malaita *ramo* as (often cowardly and excessively greedy) assassins and bounty hunters who killed helpless victims by shooting them at point-blank range (Keesing and Corris 1980:17–25, 83–90; Keesing 1978:53–62) apparently reflects changes during the nineteenth century Labor Trade. What seems to have been a code of honor of sorts had been swept aside for greed, pursued in the name of virtue (Keesing and Corris 1980). At least we must remember that Kwaio folk psychology recognized in the stylized aggression, bravery and cold-bloodedness of the *lamo* diversely individual expressions of bravery, violence and volatility, the social and the antisocial. In this connection, a confrontation between two of the most feared *lamo* of the first decades of this century, Basiana (who killed District Officer Bell) and Maenaafo'oa, as described by Basiana's son, bears note (Keesing and Corris 1980:85–86). Maenaafo'oa climbed a feasting platform and spoke to the crowd boasting of the 30 men he had killed [an exaggeration], the 30 pigs he had stolen [perhaps an understatement], and the 30 wives he had seduced [questionable]. Basiana had called out, "You're not a *lamo,* you're no good! You break the very rules we kill people for breaking!," and proclaimed his own monogamous virtue (although he had a particularly bloodthirsty career). The *lamo,* then—at least in self conception—could either be a tough guy above the law or a sort of moral executioner. Kwaio recognized, in the category *lamo 'afu,* "complete *lamo,*" that a man who was a (socially responsible) warrior leader could also be the peacekeeper and feastgiver of his group.

Paths to "Careers"

Although Kwaio recognize predilections of personality as natural (and like most ultimate matters leave them unexplained [see Keesing 1982]), the development and fulfillment of such predilections is seen as shaped by social experience, ancestral influence, life circumstance, and choice. A boy whose feisty nature was the bane of his playmates could have become a *lamo* or a young victim of his own impetuousness and bad temper. To become a *lamo* he needed, in addition to tutelage by warrior elders and a goodly measure of luck in surviving early confrontations, specific ancestral powers. Particular ancestors propitiated by some groups (Keesing 1982) conveyed powers to kill (and as we will see, to steal, seduce, destroy). A boy from one of these groups in whom qualities of violent aggression and bravery were seen, who was *lamo'a*, would be inculcated with special magical knowledge, invested with special powers, subjected to special ordeals. There were several complexes of magic and methods of passing it on, but recurrent themes emerge. One is a fruit called *kailamo* (which one might loosely gloss as "aggression food"), which was eaten by or pressed on the body of a young man to whom powers to become *wane lamo* were being passed. Another theme is anality. The *kailamo* was in one procedure placed in the anus of the *lamo* who was passing on his powers, and bitten by the novice. This and other rites for the transmission of powers as *lamo* were carried out in the men's latrine—on the one hand isolated from women, and on the other, drawing a symbolic contrast between men's excretory (and other) isolation as compartmentalizing their power, and women's as compartmentalizing the dangers of their bodily substances.

A "career" as *lamo* was thus contingent not simply on personality, physical strength and ability, and a measure of luck in initial combat; a reputation once established could be maintained by less risky acts of violence. It was contingent on being born into a group with ancestral powers of war, the right magic, and the right tutors, warriors of the parental generation.

Since each group required a priest, the path to this leadership status was seemingly less restricted. And indeed, a young man who displayed the requisite interest in ritual procedure and genealogies would be likely to be enlisted by a priest as one of his helpers. However, prior to the disasters of 1927 priestly duties tended to be passed down from an incumbent to a son (or sometimes a younger brother). In any case, there were few benefits in terms of prestige or material advantage in being a priest, and considerable disadvantages: the dangers of immediate contact with ancestors and their powers, burdens of special taboos, and the deprivations entailed by liminal isolation, as well as the heavy responsibilities of acquiring and maintaining knowledge of ritual, magic and genealogies and passing them safely on to a successor. In theory a successor was chosen by divination after death of the priest. In practice the successor to an old priest had usually long been prepared to assume these duties. The difficulties of maintaining continuity in the contemporary period must largely be consequences of the disaster of 1927 and of widespread Christianization, which has left many shrines without surviving pagan agnates.

However one aspect of succession to priestly duties bears note, prior to the discussion of a further lack of fit between ideal "triumvirate" model and sociological reality. A priest carried on his duties, assisted as necessary by younger helpers, until he was very old, even senile. Gooboo of Ga'enaafou was well into his 80s when he died in 1964 (Keesing 1978), and Si'owane of 'Ai'eda died at 94. A priest's successor was often not a young man but a man in his 50s or 60s who had assisted in sacrifices and rituals for many years. Such a successor might satisfy the requirements not only of knowledge but of abstention from killing (and when necessary sex) not because he was a gentle man of saintly virtues but because by late 50s or 60s he had retired from a career as killer and plunderer, or a career of secular feastgiving. The idealized "triumvirate" model ignores the importance of the life cycle in defining a man's orientation: retired killer may become saintly priest and/or doting grandfather.

The path to secular leadership as *wane ba'ita* was less directly constrained by access to warlike ancestors and their powers than the path to *lamo*-hood. Most descent groups include among their remote ancestors sources of power such as Amadia, conveying means to attract wealth, grow taro, raise pigs, and hence accrue prestige through feastgiving. Since the valuables left by the death of a prominent man will be consumed in honoring his death, since his networks of investment and obligation are mainly erased and some of his outstanding obligations passed down to his heirs, the son of a Kwaio Big Man gets at best a limited head start on his fellows. It helps to be an oldest son, it helps to be born a member of a group of reasonable size; it helps to have close kin who know powerful magic and have wide social networks. But as 'Elota's account shows, it takes special gifts, special energies and ambitions, and a special penchant for taking risks and keeping track of and manipulating investments to rise to secular prominence as feastgiver. To succeed as peace-keeper, steersman of one's group, requires skills of persuasion, rhetorical powers, a presence to which others will defer: decision-making in the Kwaio mountains is always consensual, never authoritarian. While men may defer in the short run to a fiery orator such as Folofo'u, a contemporary demagogue of anticolonialism, in fear of his dramatic curses rather than his powers of calm persuasion, in the long run it is the latter to which others defer.

Stability and Destruction as Cultural Foci

Before turning to assess the fit of the troika model of north Malaita leadership to Kwaio social organization "on the ground," we need to examine two complementary themes in Kwaio culture, which underlie the conceptual separation between *wane ba'ita* and *wane lamo*.

Kwaio distinguish two overarching categories of magico-ritual powers, underlying two major directions in which men direct their efforts. One is broadly categorized as *to'orungaa*, "living." The powers for "living" are conceived in terms of several major complexes. One complex comprises powers for stable living (good health, freedom from internal quarrels, freedom from outside depredation, and avoidance of major transgressions of category boundaries through pollution). A second comprises powers to attract wealth (hence powers of feastgiving and other prestations as means to *talo'a*, renown"). A third comprises powers of productivity (taro and yam production, pig raising). For each—stability-maintenance, wealth-attraction, and productivity—a descent group has special complexes of magic and calls on particular ancestors. However these creative complexes of magic-ritual, such as those focused on *mamu*, the attraction of wealth (Keesing 1982), tend to be broadly shared by different kin groups, hence societal and open in orientation rather than local and closed. The symbols deployed in ritual and magic emphasize stability (burying stones, planting cordyline or other cultigens, maintaining metaphoric mantles of protection), attraction (the magical scent of Evodia), vegetative propagation, greenness, growth.

Using such powers a descent group seeks to maintain its internal cohesion, preserve its external boundaries through peace and prestige-building exchange, and maintain the relations with ancestors on which stability, prosperity, and life itself depend. It is, of course, precisely in these creative realms that the *wane ba'ita* exerts his influence and deploys his powers—dependent on the priest to mediate on his behalf with the ancestral members of the group and the remote, ancient ancestors that are the ultimate sources of power.

The complement, the antithesis, of this set of powers comprises the set of powers of *ngada'olanga*, "destruction" (lit., "thing-destroying"). The vandalistic label is apt. These powers include not only the war magic needed to kill, and also escape retribution, but powers to steal pigs and valuables, powers to seduce other groups' women with impunity, and to destroy things as the mood suits.

Pig theft deserves special mention, because it so clearly exemplifies the contradiction between positive and destructive pursuits and the deep ambivalence Kwalo feel about destruction. Most enterprising young men try their hand at stealing pigs—initially usually small ones, and as in 'Elota's case (Keesing 1978, Chap. 5) stolen from kin and neighbors who would berate but not kill a young thief if he were discovered. Many go on, as 'Elota did, to steal pigs far and near, and become skilled in the game of evasion and subterfuge that gives pig theft such satisfactions. Successful pig theft brings great prestige to individuals and groups that steal. The powerful ancestors of such a group not only support theft but crave stolen pigs whose owners had consecrated them to their ancestors. A photograph (Keesing 1978:80) shows Alefo of Ngudu wearing the chain of woven loops, each signifying a pig successfully stolen, which is part of the mantle of prestige he and his warrior brothers have passed on; it is publicly worn, leaving the former owners of long vanished pigs to wonder which loop they might have contributed. When the thief is discovered, or suspected—and as one might guess Kwaio are expert trackers, and patrol their *keufa,* "pig rooting grounds," carefully—the costs can be high. Once discovered, the thief is forced to pay compensation substantially exceeding the value of the pig, or if it was consecrated, to replace it and pay heavy damages for "purification." With the high costs in mind, a thief often tethers a pig he has stolen in a remote spot for days, so he can return it alive if need be, and cut his losses; even so, he must compensate the pig for its suffering by paying the owner handsomely. The costs can be high for a suspected thief who chooses to deny his guilt, and his group. He may be forced to take an oath of denial, cursing all the sacred oven stones of his group's ancestors, with the destructive force of the curse contingent on his having really stolen the pig (Keesing 1979:81–83). Finally, the pig owner is likely to have kept some remnant of the pig—a bristle, a piece of ear or tail—on which he can perform all sorts of contagious black magic to wreak vengeance on an unknown thief.

From the perspective of the owner, raising a pig or fattening it for his feast, the animal represents a very real embodiment of human labor, a link to ancestors, a symbol of productive effort, a pet raised from infancy. To have one's pig stolen is an outrage against all that is creative in Kwaio life. The irony, of course, is that the owner may go out and steal someone else's pig, and certainly he had done so as a teenager.

The same deep ambivalence, the same sense of perceived virtue and self-righteousness on the part of the victim of destruction and wicked pleasure on the part of the agent, at once social and antisocial, characterize other modes of destruction. Killings may have in theory been legitimate acts of punishment or vengeance, but were often acts of homicide either randomly (though strategically) directed or taken against some innocent victim as substitute for the perpetrator of another homicide. "War spirits," *adalonimae,* sometimes demanded a victim—any victim— in purification; some were believed to have abandoned their own descendants as too peaceful, and enlisted a more bloodthirsty set of adopted descendants. Killing, especially when it enabled the killers to collect blood money and pigs in a chilling rite of mock-combat from a group seeking vengeance for a slain relative, was a means to renown as well as wealth. More than half a century after pacification, older Kwaio remain suspended in deep ambivalence over the great value and high human cost of homicide. So too with seduction and the destruction of property: the former a source of forbidden and envied pleasures in a sexually repressive society (at risk of life) and at the same time an invasion of the jural rights of another set of men.

The ancestors who conveyed bowers of destruction, saw themselves as lusting for blood, pigs, havoc, were invoked as well to protect their agents from discovery and/or retribution. Powers to kill, steal, seduce, or destroy even conferred on the descendants freedom from usual ancestral prohibitions: thief or Don Juan could slip into a clearing through the menstrual area, protected from pollution by powerful magic. The powers conferred on a young man that allowed him to kill and lead as *lamo,* to ward off arrows or bullets, were quintessential powers of *ngada'olanga.* With these powers he could face danger fearlessly; in the face of them, others would flee, give way, or stand only at their peril. Kwaio folk-psychology regarding natural propensities for aggression require as a complement to these propensities this panoply of ancestrally conferred powers.

Priests, Big Men, and *Lamo* in Kwaio Social Structure

We now return to the question of how the idealized separation and complementarity of priests, big men, and *lamo,* as underlain by folk-psychological models and cultural themes of stability and destruction, were actually manifest in Kwaio social structure.

One salient departure from the idealized north Malaita model of a triumvirate of descent group leaders was that, until pacification, particular descent groups tended to be committed either to stability and high productivity or to violence and depredation. These were by no means mutually exclusive: even those groups with the most warlike ancestors, committed most strongly to killing and depredation, depended on taro and yams as staple subsistence crops, raised pigs, gave feasts, paid bride-wealth. And conversely, even groups such as 'Elota's Ga'enaafou people killed when the occasion demanded, stole pigs and valuables. But the major focus of group effort and ritual, at least for men, was likely to be on one side of the "living" vs. "destruction" divide. In those violent days, a group that killed was likely to have to retire hastily to a fortified sanctuary, leaving gardens and pigs unprotected, or to disperse and take refuge individually with cognates and affines. Neither the concentrations of male labor on a sustained basis to produce large surpluses nor the stability to orchestrate pig breeding cycles for planned feastgiving were feasible. On the other side, a group committed to the path of peace, prosperity and prestige through sustained cycles of intensified production could not risk adventuring. Their strength and security lay in their ability to amass large arrays of valuables and pigs as blood money (*sikwa*) that would drive others of more violent bent to seek vengeance relentlessly on their behalf.

So the groups with the strongest feastgiving and peace-keeping leaders, men like 'Elota who in personality and orientation most clearly exemplified the prototypical *wane ba'ita,* were precisely those groups least likely to have a feared *lamo* at the center. Conversely, those groups (like 'Ai'eda, Ngudu and Furi'ilai, which plotted and led the Bell massacre) most directly committed to the path of destruction were those most likely to have feared *lamo*—men like Basiana, Maenaafo'oa, Tagailamo, Fuufrn'e—at their cores. Such *lamo,* although violent, had their own charisma as leaders; and the 1927 residential data show that they, like leaders in the Big Man mold such as 'Elota's father, had attracted clusters of cognates, affines, remnants of disposed groups as supporters dependent on their power, patronage and protection. However violent and aggressive to outsiders when the occasion arose, they must have been effective internally in keeping the peace and mobilizing followers. "Mad dogs," if such there were, were certainly marginalized if they could not be killed.

This bridge between Big Man-ship and *lamo*-ship in turn brings another into view. For the *lamo* who killed to collect blood bounties commanded resources, in shell valuables and pigs, that could be deployed in mortuary feasts, chain feasts (Keesing 1978), bridewealth and other arenas where Big Men operate. It seems likely that murder for profit escalated in the period of the Labor Trade: there is no way to be sure. Steel tools may have contributed indirectly, in partly freeing men from subsistence labor. Some of the most feared Kwaio *lamo* of the 1920s, notably Tagailamo and Maenaafo'oa, were also feastgivers of renown who used their access to blood bounties as a substitute for intensified production of taro and digs. However clear the separation in theory between the personality and role of *lamo* and Big Man, Kwaio leaders effectively used the instruments of wealth and power that came to hand to gain prestige and secure and maintain obligated followers. Murder for profit and feasting for prestige were in reality closely linked.

Finally, the separation of priests must be examined. I have noted that a priest, although according to ideals of folk-psychology a gentle type of spiritual bent, could in reality be a retired killer or feastgiving entrepreneur. Thus 'Ulasia (=l'elamo) of Ngudu, an old blind priest in his eighties when I knew him, was a repository of genealogical knowledge and ancestral lore. Yet unlike his slightly younger neighbor Kakale, priest of Gwagwa'emanu, who was a gentle and saintly character, 'Ulasia had been one of the most feared warriors of his age, as second brother of the *lamo* Maenaafo'oa. The emergence of venerated old priests out of fierce warriors, in the course of the life cycle, and yet the intimate part played by such priests in the ritual preparations for war, is one of the patterns that emerges in close study of the 1927 Bell assassination, its antecedents and aftermath. Two aging men insulted and assaulted by Bell's police two years before the massacre provided a focus of Kwaio resentment both because they together shared sacred duties as priests and because two decades earlier they had been famed *lamo*. When the police arrested en masse the men of the interior kin groups involved in the massacre, those arrested included several highly venerated old priests whose "guilt" lay in having sacrificed pigs to the war spirits before the attack; when these old men died when a dysentery epidemic swept the prison, the British authorities discounted "Black Hole of Tulagi" charges in the Australian press on grounds that many of the victims were "weak old men" in poor health. This pattern of ancient ex-warriors acting as priests seems to go back further than the 1920s: at the turn of the century the *lamo* Bibiasi fought off an attack and killed a rival *lamo*; but meanwhile one of the attackers struck down Bibiasi's aged father, praying behind the men's house for help for his son (Keesing 1978:58).

Conclusions

For Kwaio society, at least, there was no neat division of leadership roles such that, as is asserted in the ideal northern Malaita model, each descent group had three institutionalized leaders, the priest, the big man, and the *ramo*. Yet the separation of big man and *lamo* as contrasting type-figures rests solidly on folk-psychological theories of personality attributes, on conceptions of ancestors and their powers, and on the distinction between living and destruction as cultural themes and complexes of ancestrally-conferred powers. I have suggested why particular descent groups tended to produce leaders approximating to one ideal type or the other but also, why the two avenues to and arenas for secular power were interconnected.

The priest, as third figure in the idealized triumvirate, differs from the other two in that he genuinely occupied a position that had to be filled. Yet although ideally the priest is a man suited by temperament to the sacred duties, liminal isolation and peaceful orientation required of him, I have illustrated how these could be reached via a life cycle which, at an earlier stage, had seen a man as warrior-killer or entrepreneurial leader. Indeed in modern times the oldest of a set of brothers or senior active member of his group, such as Maakona of Talanilau or 'Alabai of To'ofe, could comfortably act both as priest and as leader in feastgiving and peace-keeping.

Perhaps, in some of the dialect groups of northern Malaita, the idealized troika pattern was more directly translated into social structural operation. In areas long Christianized and concentrated on the coast, the kind of detailed evidence available for the Kwaio may be beyond reach. But we may surmise that, whatever flexibilities and complexities intervened between idealized model and actual practice, these idealizations were, as in Kwaio, grounded in folk theories of the aggressive/violent and peaceful/stable facets of personality, and in complementary cultural themes of stability/creativity and violence/destruction.

NOTES

1. An earlier version of this paper was presented in a symposium on "Gentleness and Violence in the Pacific" at the American Anthropological Association annual meetings in Denver, November, 1984. I am indebted to Catherine Lutz, who organized the session, and to my fellow contributors, particularly Geoffrey White, for helpful suggestions. The comments of David Gegeo, an anthropologically trained speaker of Kwara'ae, were also particularly helpful.

2. The reference to a "troika" system may be obscure to younger readers who do not remember the brief period when the Soviet Union was supposed to be led by a triumvirate of leaders, who likened themselves to a Russian three-horse sled-pulling team (such a sled is a *troika*).

3. Gela (Nggela) is a cluster of islands between Malaita and Guadalcanal.

BIBLIOGRAPHY

Burt, B. 1982. *Kastom,* Christianity, and the First Ancestor of the Kwara'ae of Malaita. Reinventing Traditional Culture: The Politics of *Kastom* in Island Malanesia, eds. R. M. Keesing and R. Tokinson, Mankind (special issue) 13(4):374–399.

Chowning, A. 1979. Leadership in Malanesia. Journal of Pacific History 14:66–84.

Douglas, B. 1979. Rank, Power, Authority: A Reassessment of Traditional Leadership in South Pacific Societies. Journal of Pacific History 14:2–27.

Friedman, J. 1981. Notes on Structure and History in Oceania. Folk 23:275–295.

Hau'ofa, E. 1971. Mekeo Chieftainship. Journal of the Polynesian Society 80: 152–169.

Hogbin, H. I. 1939. Experiments in Civilization. London.

Ivens, W. G. 1930. The Island Builders of the Pacific. London.

Keesing, R. M. 1968. Chiefs in a Chiefless Society: The Ideology of Modern Kwaio Politics. Oceania 38:276–280.

———. 1978. 'Elota's Story: The Life and Times of a Solomon Islands Big Man. St. Lucia.

———. 1982. Kwaio Religion: The Living and the Dead in a Solomon Island Society. New York.

Keesing, R. M., and P. Corris. 1980. Lightning Meets the West Wind: The Malaita Massacre. Melbourne.

Pawley, A. 1981. Melanesian Diversity and Polynesian Homogeneity: A Unified Explanation for Language. Studies in Pacific Languages and Cultures in Honour of Bruce Biggs, eds. J. Hollyman and A. Pawley, pp. 269–309. Auckland.

———. 1982. Rubbish-man Commoner, Big Man Chief? Linguistic Evidence for Hereditary Chieftainship in Proto-Oceanic Society. Oceanic Studies: Essays in Honour of Aarne A. Koskinen, ed. J. Siikala, pp. 33–52. Helsinki.

Ross, H. 1973. Baegu: Social and Ecological Organization in Malaita, Solomon Islands. Urbana.

———. 1978. Leadership Styles and Strategies in a Traditional Malanesian Society. Rank and Status in Polynesia and Melanesia, ed. J. Guiart, pp. 11–22. Paris.

Russell, T. 1950. The Fataleka of Malaita. Oceania 21:1–13.

All Talk and No Action?
Saying and Doing in Kwanga Meetings

Karen J. Brison

౸

Brison treats the condition of public power in a kinship society where routine, ritual, and authoritarian action is minimized, leading to inchoate decisions and inconclusive actions. A leader or elder must balance many households and kin factions, each of which are aligned with cross-cutting interests and oppositions. The quarrels Brison records revolve around subtle issues of kinship and marriage. Leaders in their context must tread a delicate balance between respect and reputation on the one hand and personal ambition and a following on the other. The aggressive accumulation of command by a leader would threaten an end to the tenuous balance in the social structure. Conciliation and exchange provides the temper of public politics. Each challenge to this egalitarian order must be met by a kind of political gymnastics where balance is maintained through indirection and equivocation. If this balancing act of co-operation and exchange does not manifest itself in a special kind of neutrality, the kinship order may fracture through fission, feud, or warfare.

THERE IS A small but growing literature in anthropology about political language (e.g., Bailey 1983; Bloch 1975; Brenneis and Myers 1984; Paine 1981). Significantly, several recent contributions to this field have been made by scholars not primarily concerned with sociolinguistic issues. Rather, it has been increasingly recognized that in many societies politics tends to be "all talk and no action" (Myers quoted in Atkinson 1984:35) and that, therefore, to understand politics we must understand what talking accomplishes. This seems to be particularly true in acephalous,

106

egalitarian societies and also many communities with headmen who have limited power.

Long public meetings are held to discuss issues of community concern and much time and energy are devoted to these events. But in many cases either no decision is reached in meetings or a decision is made but later ignored and seemingly forgotten. Atkinson (1984:35), for example, notes of the Wana of Central Sulawesi, Indonesia: "Time and again in my fieldwork among the Wana I was personally distressed as well as analytically perplexed when after engaging in weighty discussion of vexing problems my companions would later 'fail' to act on what I took to be their resolve." Similar remarks about long meetings which either do not reach decisions or do not enforce them are made by Myers and Brenneis (1984:3), Myers (1986), Counts and Counts (1974:121), Gewertz (1977), Lederman (1984:85), Rosaldo (1973, 1984), White and Watson-Gegeo (1990:8), and Young (1971:145, 1974) for the Pacific region. Statements by Richards (1971) and Kuper (1971) about council meetings in Africa, as well as Turton (quoted in Irvine 1979) on the Mursi, and Keenan (1974, 1975) and Bloch (1971) on the Merina of Madagascar indicate that this pattern is not confined to the South Pacific.

Scholars have suggested several functions of long meetings. Simply constructing an official version of a conflict may prevent partisan gossip from distorting and aggravating the problem, particularly if this version is created with an eye toward soothing ruffled feathers by distributing blame equally on both sides rather than adhering strictly to the truth (Brenneis 1984). Airing grievances may also have a therapeutic effect (White and Watson-Gegeo 1990) and can bring satisfaction by shaming the culprit (Young 1971; 1974). Furthermore, public discussions provide a forum where people can persuade others through skillful oratory (Rosaldo 1973; Strathern 1975), and display their right to be "considered wise" (Myers and Brenneis 1984; Scaglion 1983). Oratorical displays also allow participants to "score points off one another" (Bailey 1965) and thus establish their relative rank (Bloch 1971).

Long, frequent, and inconclusive meetings have also been linked to "egalitarian" political structures (see, for instance, Myers and Brenneis 1984) where it is difficult to implement decisions since there are few means of forcing those who do not agree to comply. Furthermore, those who claim superiority by trying to enforce a decision, or even by suggesting one, run the risk of offending others and may fall victim to malicious gossip, social exclusion, or sorcery attacks (Brenneis 1984:73; Keenan 1974:129). So people are reluctant to assume leadership roles (see also Bailey 1971; Frankenberg 1957; Hutson 1971). The result is a prolonged process of negotiation in often inconclusive meetings. The association between egalitarian political structures and long inconclusive meetings, however, is problematic since similar meetings are also found in some hierarchical societies where presumably there are fewer difficulties in implementing decisions.[1]

Working among the Kwanga of the East Sepik Province, Papua New Guinea,[2] persuaded me that long discussions provided an indirect, but nonetheless effective, way of addressing conflicts, crises, and other matters requiring communal decisions in a society where more direct strategies were seldom successful and could even be dangerous. Meetings did seem to be adapted to conditions which made assertive leadership difficult. But Kwanga society is in many ways not egalitarian, as male cult initiates and lineage headmen have authority over others and have superior powers in the form of hunting and gardening magic and access to sorcerers to bolster this authority. Analysis of Kwanga meetings, therefore, will both involve finding out what they accomplish and why they take the form that they do; what it is that inhibits effective leadership there and how do meetings avoid these problems.

This will lead to a more general re-examination of the concept of egalitarianism, particularly as it applies to Melanesia. Melanesian societies are often described this way but the concept remains ambiguous. Sahlins (1963) points to a lack of hereditary ascription but Douglas (1979) finds that this exists in many Melanesian groups. Sahlins also argues that Melanesian communities lack "offices" of legitimate authority with associated sanctions, and that this checks the extent to which leadership can be consolidated over time and space. But it is clear that such offices do exist in at least some areas. For instance, male cult initiates in the Sepik possess hunting, gardening, and war magic necessary to the well-being of the community and are thought to sanction threats to their authority through sorcery (Tuzin 1974, 1976). Similar institutions exist in Vanuatu (Allen 1981). Likewise, in many areas lineage seniors inherit magic to control the weather, hunting, and harvests and can use their powers both to benefit the community and to sanction misbehavior (Young 1971, 1983; Chowning 1979).

Alternatively, egalitarianism is sometimes construed as a belief that none should command or rise above others in achievement. Forge (1970:270) argues that Melanesian societies are "aggressively egalitarian" and lack a concept of "legitimate political power, of rightful hierarchy" (Forge 1972:527). Young (1971) similarly describes a vigilant jealousy among Goodenough islanders who avoid displays of superior achievement and prowess for fear of sorcery attacks. But the Abelam villagers described by Forge (1970:269) recognize the role of leaders in defending the community from outside attack and take pride in their achievements, and this recognition of the benefits of superior power is also found among Goodenough islanders who acknowledge the authority of magicians (Young 1983) and among Arapesh people who believe that the power of male cult initiates is necessary for communal prosperity and survival (Tuzin 1976).

Nonetheless, there are indications that leadership is hazardous in Melanesian communities with hereditary rank and offices of authority. Young (1983), for instance, paints a vivid portrait of a Goodenough Island village, where headmen possessing sorcery powers and magic to control weather and harvests are often blamed for natural disasters, and one man who imprudently encouraged such attributions was attacked and almost killed. Possession of superior powers, particularly magical ones, seems to invite suspicion that they are being misused. In fact, Hau'ofa (1981) argues that the Mekeo extend a pervasive dualistic view of the world to leaders, suspecting that those with weapons useful for preserving communal well-being also use their knowledge to pursue selfish goals and attack fellow villagers. I will argue that this dualistic view of power is not confined to the Mekeo but instead is quite common in Melanesian societies and that the egalitarianism or "ambivalence" about power (Hau'ofa 1981) much noted by ethnographers of Melanesian societies (e.g., Read 1959; White 1978) with headmen and other offices of authority often consists of a suspicion that authority and power are being misused to achieve purely personal and petty ends rather than an absence of these things or a belief that leaders are not valuable and superior power, achievement, and authority are not justified. Suspicion undermines support and can even signal danger for strong leaders and this makes assertive individual initiative difficult. I will trace this pattern to particular conditions of small, relatively isolated, communities and argue that meetings are part of a system which discourages disruptive action and allows individuals to influence events in relatively cost-free ways.

The Kwanga

The Kwanga are a group of horticulturalists residing in the foothills of the Torricelli mountain range. Between September 1984 and October 1986, I lived and worked in the village of Inakor (population 400) and also collected information in the neighboring village of Asanakor (population 310).

The Kwanga held long meetings to discuss what seemed to the outside observer even the most trivial and domestic issues. Every Monday they assembled to talk about disputes, sorcery accusations, the sighting of sorcerers, proposed marriages, and a range of other issues. But they seldom came to a decision, and even when they did, these decisions were often not implemented.

Community discussions were also held after all deaths (except those of very young children whose deaths are considered natural) to investigate the cause. Funeral meetings were no less drawn out and inconclusive than other kinds. The entire day after the burial was spent in joint discussion between the village of the deceased and its neighbor (that is, when someone died in Inakor, Asanakor would take part and vice versa); on the next day, a second day-long discussion was held among the members of the village of the deceased. These first meetings produced specific theories about the death which were investigated in subsequent meetings. Often suspects from nonparticipant villages would be identified and members of these villages invited to discuss these theories.

Theoretically, people can die from accident or illness, but almost invariably people concluded that a death was an obvious instance of sorcery. The meeting then weighed the evidence to identify the sorcerer responsible and the person who hired him.[3] They looked for the quarrels in which the deceased had been involved to discover who had a motive for killing him. Other sorts of evidence were provided by signs given by the corpse, by suspicious statements made by the deceased before he died or by other people, by recent sightings of sorcerers, and so on. The discussions usually identified the guilty person or persons, and threatened to take them to court and send them to jail (currently the most frequent course of action threatened) or to resort to outright violence if another murder was committed. More subtle forms of retaliation included counter-sorcery and, what was probably the most common traditional action, forcing the accused hirer to give a large food prestation to the suspected sorcerer. This gift was believed to "close the road" of the sorcerer and prevent him from striking again in the same village or lineage.[4] It was generally not given to a specific sorcerer but to all the sorcerers in the area or in a particular village. Thus, the specific sorcerer felt to be responsible was not identified.

In fact, however, these things were seldom done. Most often, a few months after the meeting, local gossip would have assigned responsibility for the death to a different person. Indeed, people themselves stated as a general principle that the true cause of death seldom came to light until some years afterwards. An interview with a middle-aged man about the deaths and funeral discussions he had witnessed during his life confirmed that what finally emerged as the cause of death was seldom that assigned in the funeral discussions.

I will examine two cases to determine what is accomplished by funeral discussions and other community meetings, and to illustrate how meetings allow people to influence events while avoiding the potential hazards of leadership.

The Deaths of Naifuku and Ambusuroho

In October 1984, two brothers from the village of Asanakor, Naifuku and Ambusuroho, died on the same night. They had been sick for less than a week. The deaths shocked the residents of Inakor and Asanakor. The two men were in the prime of life (in their late thirties or early forties), a time when it is generally considered that the body is too strong to be killed by illness or accident. Furthermore, in living memory two full brothers had never died on the same night. Both of these facts led to the immediate conclusion that not only had there been foul play but the culprit must have been an uncommonly abhorrent character to have killed two full brothers at the same time. For all these reasons, an unusually large number of meetings were held weekly for months to discuss the deaths, and the case was actually taken to court.

Early accusations were focused on two suspects: Abel, a man from a neighboring village, Ta'uanangas; and Jeremiah, an Asanakor man married to the sister of Naifuku and Ambusuroho. Abel had a long-standing land dispute with the two brothers, and there was much discussion of the history of this conflict. Much was made, in early meetings, of how one of the brothers, Naifuku, had allegedly said in his dying breath that he had been "shot by a bamboo from Pilimbi," the piece of land over which he and Abel had disputed. This was considered a veiled reference to Abel's guilt. Several people also pointed out that lately many birds had been heard flying to Asanakor from the direction of Ta'uanangas. Sorcerers making their rounds are believed to emit a characteristic bird cry, and after a death the recent activities of birds at night always feature in the discussion.

Jeremiah, too, was discussed in early meetings. Jeremiah and his wife, Naomi, had a stormy marriage. Jeremiah was noted for his violent temper, and he frequently beat his wife and accused her of laziness. He claimed that he had been forced to marry her and had never liked her. Naomi had often run away from Jeremiah and taken refuge with her two brothers, Naifuku and Ambusuroho. Jeremiah alternately accused the brothers of trying to keep Naomi away from her husband and of trying to prevent a divorce. The affair reached village court several times. The general consensus among the villagers was that Jeremiah was unreasonably brutal with his wife and that he was wrong in trying to "hook" his two brothers-in-law into his own marital squabbles. Naifuku and Ambusuroho, people said, had no desire to interfere in the marriage of Jeremiah and Naomi; it was Jeremiah and Naomi, herself, who were always trying to involve her brothers. A recent violent eruption in this long-standing conflict between Jeremiah and his brothers-in-law made him a prime suspect in their deaths.

In the early funeral meetings, person after person got up and commented on the violent quarrel between Jeremiah and Naifuku and Ambusuroho. The consensus seemed to be that Jeremiah and Abel (who were distantly related to each other) had conspired to kill the two brothers. In sleuth style, people sought to prove that Jeremiah and Abel had met on several occasions, implying that the two had ample opportunity to hatch their plot. For instance, Adam, a classificatory brother of Naifuku and Ambusuroho, questioned Jeremiah and Abel about a time when Abel had visited a kinsmen in Asanakor and allegedly sat and talked with Jeremiah. The two men finally admitted that they did have a conversation on this occasion but denied that they talked about Naifuku and Ambusuroho. Adam commented, "Yesterday I made this point and you guys said no [that they did not meet on the occasion in question]. Now I ask you again and you say yes, you did talk. This is wrong. What you talked about, I don't know. Now I will ask for witnesses: Who saw them sitting [together]?" The implication of Adam's remarks was made explicit by another man, Ronald: "Why did you two meet? Yesterday you said you didn't talk that day. You said he was lying. Now you have changed. We are not happy about this. You are trying to cover something up."

At the end of the day, an Inakor man summarized what had been the general theme of the day's discussions, that Abel and Jeremiah conspired to kill the two brothers. Ronald, the village magistrate, concluded, "If you want to meet tomorrow, you can. But don't discuss this anymore. Just sit and tell stories of things the two men did when they were alive. This will go to the law now." Ronald, in short, was trying to end discussion of the deaths, claiming that Jeremiah and Abel were guilty and would be taken to court. He was supported by fellow villagers who spoke of the hazards of endless discussion and recommended that Ronald take immediate action against the suspects.

Despite these closing words and the seeming consensus and certainty displayed at the first discussion, in the following weeks new theories about the deaths proliferated and were the subject of many meetings. Most of these theories were quickly rejected. Furthermore, in these meetings the theory about Abel's involvement was pronounced untrue. Months after the death, in February of 1985, rumors began to circulate that it was not Jeremiah who had killed the two brothers, but Adam, one of their classificatory brothers,. He had allegedly hired a sorcerer from the neighboring Bumbita Arapesh-language group to kill the two men over a land dispute. These theories were reviewed in an informal court hearing involving Bumbita Arapesh magistrates. Led by Ronald, the Inakor magistrate (who was also married to Adam's daughter), the Bumbita magistrates quickly rejected these new theories as foundationless rumor and affirmed that, indeed, Jeremiah must have killed the two brothers. When Jeremiah tried to protest, saying that there was no better evidence against him than against the Bumbita sorcerer, he was summarily silenced by Ronald and the Bumbita magistrates.[5] A few months later, Jeremiah was officially convicted in the village court of killing Naifuku and Ambusuroho and told to pay compensation to the widows of the two men amounting to two pigs and 800 kina cash (a huge amount in an area where average annual income from coffee sales is about 150 kina per family).

No sooner had this decision been made than new rumors began to circulate in Asanakor. Gossips claimed that Adam and his son-in-law, Ronald, had conspired with Obadiah, an Asanakor sorcerer, to kill Naifuku and Ambusuroho. I later found out that the new rumors had started with an Asanakor man, Sam. Sam saw Obadiah making a fire to cook a yam even though his wife was already cooking food at another fire. Sam concluded that Obadiah was following female avoidance rules associated with building the necessary magical "heat" to practice sorcery. Obadiah, however, was Sam's sister's husband so Sam kept quiet except that he told the two Asanakor court officials, Andrew and Bruce, what he had seen. When Naifuku and Ambusuroho died some weeks later, the three men quickly concluded that Obadiah must have been responsible. But they continued to hide what they knew, and Sam even made an impassioned speech at an early funeral meeting accusing Jeremiah of the crime. Later, however, Bruce told his classificatory father, Ezra, what he knew; Ezra, in turn, spread the rumor of Obadiah's involvement to the rest of the community and, as the new rumors spread, Adam and Ronald were also implicated. People were particularly suspicious of Ronald, given the active role he had taken in attempting to stop discussion and have Jeremiah convicted of the crime; people suspected that Ronald was trying to blame Jeremiah to cover up his own guilt.

When Ronald heard of the new rumors, he quickly reassembled the magistrates for a court hearing. He said the new rumors would not be investigated in their own right; instead, the person who was the source of them must be found and charged with illegally gossiping about a case already resolved in court. Ronald accused Jeremiah of starting the rumors and the Bumbita magistrates supported Ronald in his attempts to fine Jeremiah. It was late in the day, however, and it was decided to rest for the night and reconvene the hearing in the morning. The next morning the tone of the hearings had changed. It was clear that some Asanakor men had talked to the Bumbita magistrates during the night and persuaded them to investigate the rumors. Ronald was told to step down from hearing the case since he was implicated. Sam opened the discussion with a long account of the various signs which indicated that an Asanakor sorcerer had been involved in killing Naifuku and Ambusuroho. Interestingly, one of these signs was a new interpretation of Naifuku's dying words about Pilimbi.[6] Originally thought to refer to Abel, these words were now thought to refer to an incident involving Obadiah which had occurred at the same place, Pilimbi. Also significant was the fact that Sam did not mention the incident which had originally led him to conclude that Obadiah was guilty, nor did he directly accuse Obadiah, but rather argued that it was an Asanakor sorcerer who had killed the two brothers.

After hours of discussion, the magistrates asked Deborah, the wife of Naifuku, to come forward and tell them who she wanted to be charged with killing Naifuku and Ambusuroho. She said that she felt that Obadiah, Adam, and Jeremiah, should all be charged. The magistrates rejected Adam, saying that there was no real proof against him, but said that Jeremiah and Obadiah should pay compensation to the widows. Since, however, there were no witnesses to the alleged killing, the magistrates continued, no one could really know who did it, so the whole community should aid Obadiah and Jeremiah in giving compensation to the widows.

This last discussion occurred in July 1985. When I left the field in October 1986, no compensation had been paid to the widows. Indeed, Deborah had been forced to leave Naifuku's hamlet to live with her brothers because Naifuku's patrilineage was angry with her for having accused two of their number, Adam and Obadiah. I asked Andrew, an Asanakor court official, if any action would be taken against Jeremiah and Obadiah. He replied that he was uncertain what should be done as he felt that higher courts would not support the village court decision if it were appealed, since the hearing had not been properly conducted. There was, therefore, nothing the village court could do to force Obadiah and Jeremiah to pay their fines. Moreover, Andrew was doubtful whether the charges against Obadiah and Jeremiah were justified. He commented, "Yes, me too, I think about this a lot. We men of the earth can't know the truth. Only God knows. Yes, I too think that this charge wasn't right. We didn't actually see them do anything." But he went on to say that perhaps the charge against Jeremiah was justified just because of his fight with his brothers-in-law. Andrew added,

> Jeremiah carried the blame because he fought with his two brothers-in-law for a long time. So when he wanted to [defend himself in court] the magis-

trates shut him up and said he was a troublemaker. You fought like that and they died so you can carry the blame... that's the way of the village: They look at the fights the dead person had and they accuse the person who fought with him. Sometimes it's true and sometimes it isn't. They just carry the blame because of the fight. If I don't fight with you then when you die I won't carry the blame.

Jeremiah also had much to say about the case. He was firmly convinced that he had been framed by the real murderer. Jeremiah claimed that the murderer had waited until his fight with Naifuku and Ambusuroho had reached a peak of violence and then killed the two brothers, realizing that everyone would blame Jeremiah. I asked him about the strong accusations made against him during the early funeral discussions and he replied,

Jeremiah: They were trying to find out. When they are trying to find out what happened then they speak forcefully like that.

Q: Did they believe it was true?

Jeremiah: Some of them believed it. The children will think that it is true but all the really big men will say we are just guessing... It's like this, they have heard with their ears but they really seen this man killing this other man. They don't really know so they will speak angrily and they will watch you. If it's true then you will tremble. If it's not true then you will just sit there and you won't tremble. They are evaluating you: The big men and the law men will evaluate your thoughts. They will watch your body and your talk. If they accuse you and accuse you and you hold firm then they will say: "What is this man here?" They will accuse you and accuse you and say: "If he really did it he will shake." If they accuse you and accuse you and you don't shake, they will say: "I guess not," and then they will talk calmly.

Q: When the Bumbita court officials came down and accused you of killing Naifuku and Ambusuroho did they really think you had done it?

Jeremiah: Like I said before, they knew who did it. They were clear.... In the beginning, all the big men know. Because some man has told them somewhere. For instance, if Richard [a local sorcerer] came and killed me, later he would tell you. They do it like that and they know but then when the meeting comes up they won't tell. They will just lie. They will know but they will accuse some other man. This time they accused me; they were tricking but the real thing was there. If you hear who killed my child, you won't come and tell me at first. If you do a spear will go through you. They will wait until the talk is old.... They will accuse lots of men so the discussions will have to go on and on. Then after a few years the truth will come out. So you saw how all these different points came up in the funeral discussions. Not you: It is us black skins who do it this way. We are different.

Analysis of the Case

After the two brothers died, many meetings were held but little was apparently accomplished. Many suspects were questioned and accused; court hearings were held and, after months of debate, two men were charged but when they did not pay their fines nothing was done. The difficulties which plagued the affair seemed to stem from the fact that it was very hard to find the truth. Signs, such as the bird calls from Ta'uanangas and Naifuku's dying words about Pilimbi, were ambiguous and could be interpreted in various ways. Compounding these problems was a distrust of peoples' motives in discussions. Jeremiah suspected that people were lying, hiding what they knew, and making false accusations in public meetings and his suspicions were widely shared and were thought to apply to funeral discussions more generally. It is believed that directly after a death the murderer will tell others of his deed, who will not reveal what they know in public discussions. Instead, they make accusations they know to be false in order to cover up the truth, fearing retaliation from the sorcerer or from the family of the victim.[7] Others will be genuinely ignorant and will make strong accusations in order to test the reaction of the suspect. The guilty person will "shake" or reply angrily, while the innocent will present a calm, reasoned, defense. Since people may be using any of these several strategies, speeches made in funeral meetings cannot be taken at face value and the ordinary person will be more confused than enlightened by them. Furthermore, when Sam accused Jeremiah in a meeting, but privately thought Obadiah to be responsible, his behavior confirmed these suspicions, suggesting that the local beliefs are not entirely delusional. Given this ambiguity, it is not surprising that Andrew concluded that ordinary mortals could not know the truth, as did the magistrates at the final hearing. Doubt stemming from lack of evidence and suspicion of deceit seemed to prevent action against the culprits.

The local people, in fact, frequently complain about the way talk goes on and on and ultimately creates such confusion that nothing can be done; nonetheless, funeral discussions are not without result. Many theories are examined during the course of discussions. Apparently trivial words and deeds, such as the meeting between Abel and Jeremiah and their subsequent denial that it took place, become signs of darker acts and intentions. This process has many benefits. First, meetings are seldom successful in proving guilt but are somewhat more effective in exonerating suspects. People are able to defend themselves against suspicions and can convincingly, if not conclusively, argue that they are innocent, particularly if they present themselves well, avoiding angry outbursts or brooding silences and making well-reasoned statements. In fact, many people seem more concerned with proving their own innocence than with establishing the truth in funeral discussions, which is not surprising since anyone suspected of sorcery fears counter-sorcery.

Second, accusations themselves have results even if these are not conclusively proven. Andrew maintained that Jeremiah deserved to be accused even if he were innocent because he was a troublemaker and Sam later echoed this view. Fear of being accused of sorcery discourages people from fighting with others even when they feel they are in the right. My neighbor, for instance, frequently chastised his classificatory son for fighting with other families, even when he was in the right, saying that fights led to sorcery accusations, and, indeed, the son's name was frequently raised in funeral discussions. Sorcery accusations are both unpleasant and can lead to fears of counter-sorcery.

Third, many of the theories raised suggest that the victim was killed because he was a troublemaker or violated male cult rules. Sorcerers sometimes strike out of petty grievances, as in the case of Naifuku and Ambusuroho, but in many instances, sorcerers are believed to kill people who steal, commit adultery, or generally make trouble (Tuzin 1974, 1976). Community leaders often made speeches at funerals suggesting that sorcery would stop if people behaved themselves and followed the law. Sorcery was even called "the police force of the ancestors." Thus, the theories presented in funeral discussions also discourage disruptive action by raising the specter of punishment through sorcery.

The fact that people are never sure what really happened also has benefits. The local people acknowledge the role of confusion created by funeral discussions in preventing destructive action. They say that the truth must be kept from the family of the victim until a few years after the death when feelings have cooled to prevent violence. Moreover, often the victim is eventually seen to have been killed for legitimate reasons, making retaliation inappropriate (Tuzin 1974). The family, however, would be too overcome by emotion to realize this immediately after the death. Thus, paradoxically, a process which on the surface seems to aim to label and punish a culprit, in fact prevents this from occurring. Confusion and doubt dampen the destructive potential of death to lead to violence, feuding, or community fission.

The process of sifting the evidence in meetings also contributes to the prestige of individual men and to the status of initiated men as a group. People present evidence and hint at greater knowledge and it is by no means disadvantageous to gain the reputation of having knowledge about the activities of sorcerers. Forge (1970), for example, writing of the neighboring language group, the Abelam, states that those aspiring to community leadership must claim knowledge of, and the ability to control, the activities of sorcerers. Because sorcery is the major coercive sanction in Abelam (and Kwanga) society, only those who demonstrate the ability to control it are considered powerful and able to lead the group. The massive confusion created by funeral discussions reinforces the conclusion that only big men possess the knowledge and wisdom to understand and control sorcery, as is evident in Jeremiah's comment that ordinary people will believe the lies in meetings but only big men know what is really going on. Furthermore, not only do particular individuals have the reputation of being able to control sorcerers, but initiated men as a group are closely associated with the institution of sorcery. Only initiated men, it is believed, hire sorcerers. I collected information on some 40 deaths, and in none of the cases was a woman or an uninitiated man implicated. This clearly gives initiated men a reputation for being powerful which bolsters their authority. Moreover, association with sorcery is not unambiguously illegitimate since sorcery is viewed as a "police force" punishing violation of social norms and male cult rules.[8] Conversely, where sorcery is seen to strike for illegitimate reasons, as in the case of Naifuku and Ambusuroho, it is advantageous for initiated men to publicly condemn those who, like Jeremiah, use sorcery to act on petty grievances. The accuser appears as a defender of law and order. Extensive discussions also allow big men to display oratorical skill. In fact, Scaglion (1983) argues that big men among the Abelam often prolong discussions of conflict in order to maximize the prestige they gain in their role as mediators. In short, the process of public discussion of cause of death acts in indirect ways to discourage disruptive action and to enhance the prestige of initiated men. Even when theories are eventually rejected, the community is warned that disruptive behavior is sanctioned by the sorcerer.

Unlike more direct strategies, the results are relatively cost free. Sam avoided accusing Obadiah in a direct public manner, instead making veiled allusions to the possible complicity of an Asanakor sorcerer in the final court hearing and disseminating his most damning evidence (the incident of Obadiah cooking his own yam) through gossip. In this way, he was able to preserve a proper face of goodwill toward his sister's husband (Obadiah) and, at the same time, bring about a conviction. Public sentiment against Obadiah was mobilized through innuendo and rumor so that by the time an accusation was made it came from the whole village. Sam's role was not obvious, and he suffered no reprisals. On the other hand, those who attempted to convict and punish suspects or made public and unambiguous accusations fell victim to retaliatory measures. Adam and Ronald, for instance, tried to prosecute Jeremiah and ended up being accused of the murder. Ronald's frequent attempts to stop discussion and convict Jeremiah, in fact, were seen as proof of his own guilt: he was trying to frame Jeremiah to cover up his own complicity. Similarly, when Deborah requested that Obadiah and Jeremiah be charged at the final court hearing, this not only brought her no benefit as the fines were never paid but actually harmed her when the outraged family of the men expelled her from their hamlet. Direct action is apparently both difficult (if not impossible) to carry out, as any action produces opposition, and can bring undesirable repercussions.

Social Conditions

Funeral meetings and the process of interpreting cause of death form a system of indirect action well suited to an environment where direct individual initiative is at best unsuccessful and, at worst, dangerous. Assertive action brings suspicion and the possibility of covert reprisals. Why is this so?

Among the Kwanga, community leadership is in the hands of a group of initiates of the highest grade of the male cult. These men control magic necessary to produce successful harvests, to catch game, and for success in warfare. They are also thought to control the actions of sorcerers. Initiated men have authority over others. But amongst themselves attempts to command others are resented. Just as uninitiated men and women must fear sorcery if they challenge the authority of initiated men, so the deaths of initiates are often attributed to sorcery sanctioning claims to superiority and disregard of others' opinions. Decisions on matters of communal concern should be a result of careful consultation and discussion. Individual initiative which seems to ignore the opinions of others as, for instance, when Ronald attempted to stifle discussion of the deaths and convict Jeremiah, invites retaliation or at least withdrawal of support (see also Read 1959).

A similar effect is produced by the division of the community into many sub-groups (ritual and geographically based moieties, and patrilineal totemic groups) each of which jealously guards its autonomy and resents outside interference. Furthermore, relations between groups tend to be rivalrous and mildly antagonistic. Thus any action tends to produce an automatic resistance as support groups coalesce to defend against outside interference. Jeremiah, for instance, told me that everybody had been against him after the death of Naifuku and Ambusuroho, but that a small group of close kinsmen and affines had gathered to protect him saying, "Everybody is against him, we will stay and cover him up. Whatever he has done, we must protect him." Similarly, Adam's accusations in funeral discussions produced resentful counteraccusations from the families of the accused. Again, individual initiative is discouraged by the automatic opposition which it tends to produce.

The funeral meeting, by providing a forum where accusations are made and interpretations are put forward, allows people to address a crisis situation, death, which had great disruptive potential (in many societies, for instance, death can lead to retaliatory murder), in a way which entails little individual and social cost. By casting accusations in veiled form or disseminating them through gossip networks, as Sam did, people can avoid reprisals. Furthermore, the general confusion created by beliefs that evidence is ambiguous and speeches in meetings are misleading, prevents punitive action both against the accused sorcerer and those who make accusations. At the same time, troublemakers are sanctioned when they become the object of sorcery suspicions, and people are warned that wrongdoing can be punished by sorcery.

I will now examine another sort of meeting, a community discussion to consider an unusual surfeit of rain, and show that many of the same processes are at work.

A Discussion of Rain

The discussion of rain occurred in a weekly community meeting. An unusual amount of rain for several weeks was preventing people from burning brush off new garden plots and also from drying coffee beans in the sun, of particular concern because of record high coffee prices. People thought that one of the two village rain magicians must be making the rain and wanted to find the reason. The topic was introduced by the village Councillor,[9] Gwarambu, who thought he was suspected of soliciting the services of his sister's husband, Benjamin, a rain maker. Gwarambu had the reputation of being an avid gardener who always had his next year's gardens cleared, burned, and planted well before everyone else. As well, he was said to have little interest in coffee gardening. For both these reasons, the current rain was desirable for him and he felt that others must suspect him of creating it. Another man, Bwalaka, had criticized Gwarambu for his "backwardness" and lack of interest in cash cropping and Gwarambu angrily responded to this remark in the meeting.

The topic of rain was taken up eagerly. There seemed to be a general feeling that Benjamin was responsible but there was some debate about his motive. Benjamin was a sorcerer as well as a rain magician who, due to communal pressure, had converted to Christianity the previous year and claimed to have given up sorcery. But people had little faith in these assertions and continued to accuse him of killing people. In fact, when Benjamin had recently attended a Christian revival meeting in a neighboring village there had been a rumor that he was carrying a sorcery implement in his string bag and some women were reputed to have secretly searched his bag for it. Several people suggested that Benjamin was angry about this incident, which was part of a general pattern of mistreatment of Benjamin by the Christians, and was wreaking his vengeance in the form of rain. Several Christians, however, claimed that these rumors were complete fabrications. It was true that a woman had looked into Benjamin's string bag but she was only checking to see if he had any food. Benjamin, himself, after denying knowledge of the incident, launched into a tirade against the entire community for refusing to believe that he had given up sorcery.

These denials started an attempt to find the source of the rumor. Apparently a young Asanakor man on his way to the revival meeting had been bitten on the arm by a centipede and mistook the bite for a sorcery attack, thus starting the search for the implement. But several Christian women denied that they had even heard about the centipede bite. Someone else claimed to have heard Mary, a Christian woman, predict that someone would die at the revival meeting but she answered that she had only said that the village was in a generally sinful state and this could easily result in a death. After much shouting back and forth of accusations between Christians and "heathens," Gwarambu interrupted and introduced a new topic.

Analysis

The discussion of rain was similar to the funeral discussions of Naifuku and Ambusuroho in several ways. First, neither led to any obvious corrective action. Jeremiah and Obadiah were charged but not compelled to pay their fines; the discussion of rain apparently attempted to find the person responsible for the rain and either placate or punish him (it is not clear which) but failed to do so. Second, just as rumor and doubt prevented action against Jeremiah and Obadiah in the end, so it was apparently impossible to sort through the ambiguities and denials to find out who made the rain and why. But, third, in both cases interpretations were discussed involving elaborate construction of theories from apparently trivial incidents such as the meeting between Abel and Jeremiah and the centipede bite. None of the theories could be conclusively proven. People knew that such circumstantial evidence was inconclusive and did not warrant punitive measures. But the process of constructing these theories in public had benefits. The discussion of rain, like the funeral meetings, allowed various people to deny their guilt. The Councillor, for example, went to some length to prove that he was not responsible for the rain. In fact, attempts to disprove charges took up at least as much time in meetings as efforts to find out what did happen. Furthermore, the public discussion of the event had a punitive effect in its own right. Benjamin was publicly embarrassed (as evidenced by his agitated reaction to the charges), in itself a disincentive to future rain making, and he was also informed that if he was responsible the community was on to him. This is important because, as the first case indicated, people know that visible maneuvers can bring retaliation. Thus if the culprit is unmasked he will know that he will be held responsible for future disasters, could be punished, and so will stop. In short, like the funeral discussions, the meetings about the rain acted in indirect ways to discourage actions detrimental to the community without placing the burden of corrective action on the shoulders of any one person who could be vulnerable to retaliation.

Magical Powers, Meetings, and Leadership

The two cases share another common feature: they both deal with allegations concerning the use of magical powers; in the first, sorcery, in the second, rain magic. This is not unusual as almost any conflict or issue among the Kwanga at least implicitly involves the fear of covert magical reprisals. Divorce, adultery, land disputes, and other disputes all bring with them the fear that someone will be dissatisfied and hire a sorcerer or will punish the community with rain or drought. This is a fear which permeates Kwanga life and most discussions at least implicitly address such possibilities. Thus, any issue involves an attempt to find out who might be using magical powers and, conversely, many people trying to deny that they are doing so. Interpretation of seemingly trivial statements and actions which might indicate concealed malice and intent to harm, therefore, become an important focus of discussion.

I have argued that meetings allow an indirect way of addressing problems in an environment where individual assertive action is inadvisable and seldom successful. Meetings also arise from another characteristic of Kwanga society which makes it typically Melanesian; that is, the importance of supernatural powers for leadership. Where supernatural powers are tools for leaders, then the process of interpretation in public discussions becomes important in two ways. First, claims to supernatural powers, and the authority these entail, only become effective if people indicate that it is their powers (rather than nature or someone else's magic) which are at work in particular situations and for particular reasons. Sorcery, for instance, can only sanction violations of male cult rules if people hint that they caused a certain death because a rule was broken. The efficacy of magical powers rests on advancing interpretations of real events. Second, and conversely, people have to deny that they caused things such as natural disasters or droughts when blame could lead to personal harm. Young (1983) shows how leaders claiming supernatural powers can become scapegoats and may even come to physical harm, and this process is also a familiar one to the Kwanga where sorcerers are sometimes killed if they gain a reputation for murdering their fellow villagers too frequently and without good cause. Thus meetings perform a second important role of allowing people to deny complicity in events.

Melanesian "Egalitarianism"

I raised in the introduction the question of what constituted the egalitarian ethos of Melanesian societies with headmen or other positions of authority. We have seen that among the Kwanga initiated men possess power and authority over the uninitiated but risk covert attack if they disregard each other's wishes. Furthermore, the division of the community into semiautonomous moieties and lineages means that any action tends to produce an automatic opposition.

But another force discouraging assertive action is evident; i.e., a prevalent suspicion of the motives of leaders. In the first case, people asked Ronald to prosecute Abel and Jeremiah. But when he did so he was suspected of abusing his authority as magistrate to stifle discussion and conceal his own guilt. In the second case, the village Councillor and sorcerer/rain magician were similarly accused of abusing their powers for personal benefit (the Councillor), or to satisfy personal grudges (Benjamin), to the detriment of the community. The potential benefits of the authority of the magistrate (punishing culprits), and the power of the sorcerer (sanctioning misbehavior), were recognized but the individuals occupying these roles were suspected of abusing their powers to pursue personal ends. Why is this so?

The suspicions about leaders seem to be part of a more general pattern of distrust of others (Schwartz 1973). Apparently trivial incidents such as the search of Benjamin's string bag and Abel's casual conversation with Jeremiah lead to suspicions of deeper and darker deeds. Most obviously, the suspicion that people are covertly attacking others stems from the fact that this is sometimes true. Sam, for instance, launches a hidden campaign against his brother-in-law, Obadiah. In fact, a feedback process is evident. Social conditions, including the fact that others will almost surely suspect one's motives, discourage visible action. But the more people act in secretive ways, the more they are suspected of hidden malice. Secrecy breeds suspicion which in turn breeds secrecy.

I have traced covert maneuvering to an acephalous power structure and the division of the community into moieties and lineages. But these patterns are also created by the very nature of a small, close-knit, relatively isolated, community. Kwanga villages are largely endogamous (75 per cent of Inakor marriages were between fellow villagers) and are cross-cut by dense webs of kin ties. Ethnographers of such small, close-knit, communities have often noted how they discourage active leadership (Bailey 1971; Frankenberg 1957), and the direct expression of anger (White and Watson-Gegeo 1990; Hau'ofa 1981) since even trivial quarrels draw in wide networks of related people and lead to wide repercussions. Furthermore, such communities breed gossip because people share many common acquaintances whom they can talk about (Merry 1984), and this gossip can have serious consequences since people are dependent on each other for companionship and economic aid. The role of gossip as an informal sanction has long been recognized (e.g., Gluckman 1963), but Merry (1984:272) argues that the power of gossip is greatest when people are dependent on each other and are consequently reluctant to give offense. Malicious gossip is, therefore, an object of concern and people go to great lengths to avoid it. Gossip, then, is another factor which discourages assertive action. In short, small communities discourage public action and encourage covert measures. But these secret deeds create suspicions which in turn increase the costs of active leadership.

These patterns are common in many Melanesian societies and are perhaps what evoke the label, egalitarian. There are people with "offices" of authority and superior powers, and by recognizing the potential benefits of these powers, people confer legitimacy on their leaders. But those with special powers are often suspected of abusing them. Hau'ofa (1981), for instance, says that sorcerers (who inherit their position) among the Mekeo are seen as performing a useful function in sanctioning wrongdoing (at the request of chiefs) and protecting the community. But they are also suspected of ensorcelling for money or to satisfy purely personal grievances. The most powerful are also the most dangerous. Young (1983) describes a similar process in the Goodenough Islands. I have argued that the suspicions against leaders are part of a more general pattern of distrust characteristic of small communities everywhere. Melanesian egalitarianism is not always a matter of a relative lack of "offices," hereditary ascription, or the notion that no man should be better than his fellows but is also a product of the conditions in small, close-knit villages. Offices of authority exist in many areas and, further-more, their value is recognized, but there is always a suspicion that leaders may abuse their powers for selfish reasons and this undermines their support and their ability to organize communal ventures.

Ambivalence about power is probably a universal phenomenon but the peoples' dependence on each other in small isolated communities, and their inability to seek outside sources of aid and companionship, make them more reluctant to ignore the suspicion and backbiting than they would be in larger, more impersonal, environments (Merry 1984). Moreover, suspicions about the motives of leaders are intensified by the tendencies of such small environments to generate malicious gossip and encourage covert maneuvering.

Long public debates are part of a process which allows people to shape events and enhance their own reputation while steering clear of these hazards. Problems are addressed in indirect and ambiguous ways so that no one can be held responsible.

Meetings, Egalitarianism, and Melanesian Leaders

Kwanga meetings involve the construction of elaborate theories based on circumstantial and trivial evidence. Apparently innocuous words and ac-tions become the basis for heated accusations but corrective action sel-dom follows. I have argued that this behavior is well adapted to the conditions of one acephalous Melanesian society where assertive individ-ual actions almost inevitably bring reaction and resistance. Meetings al-low people to defend themselves against accusations and to warn others that covert attacks will bring reprisals. They discourage disruptive behav-ior and increase the prestige of initiated men by hinting that they control supernatural powers and use them to sanction wrongdoing. But there is never any conclusive evidence and doubt prevents reprisals against sor-cerers, rain magicians, and those who claim to control their actions.

Many ethnographers have noted the close connection between poli-tics and dispute resolution in Melanesian societies (Epstein 1974:26; Lawrence 1971:6; Morauta 1974:22; Scaglion 1983; A. Strathern 1971; M. Strathern 1974). Those aspiring to leadership must demonstrate ability to mediate local and extralocal disputes, and mediators are as concerned with enhancing their own reputations as with resolving quarrels. In fact, mediators' concern with their own reputations may alter the style of conflict resolution procedures. Scaglion (1983) suggests that Abelam big men encourage extensive discussions which often range far from the dispute under consideration. This allows big men to draw attention to their own oratorical skills, and resolutions achieved through such procedures are often perceived to be more satisfactory and enduring by every-one involved. My analysis of Kwanga meetings has also suggested that extensive discussions allow people to win prestige and influence events in relatively cost free ways. As well, they address problematic situations in a way which is less disruptive, and more likely to restore harmony, than a narrower discussion resulting in corrective action would. "Saying" al-lows individuals to display wisdom; it also discourages disruptive action. "Doing," on the other hand, can lead to reprisals, suspicions, and accusa-tions, and can also have widespread repercussions, such as feuds, which are detrimental to the community as a whole.

Long, frequent, and apparently inconclusive meetings have been traced to egalitarian social structures (Myers and Brenneis 1984). But they are also found in communities with offices of leadership and other forms of rank. This is because conditions inherent in small, isolated, close-knit, communities make assertive action difficult even for those with acknowledged power and authority. There are good reasons, then, why talk is a preferred form of action under these conditions.

NOTES

1. Bailey (1965) describes inconclusive meetings in Indian villages with castes. Richards (1971) describes similar meetings in Bemba villages which have headmen.

2. Research in Papua New Guinea was funded by a National Science Founda-tion Grant. F. G. Bailey, Stephen Leavitt, Fitz Poole, Donald Tuzin, and Geoffrey White all assisted me at various stages of my research and writing of this paper. Theodore Schwartz and the other participants in the University of California, San Diego Melanesian Seminar commented on an earlier draft. I also thank Lekutombwai, Patrick, "Bruce," "Andrew," and "Sam," and other residents of Inakor and Asanakor who helped me gather information. The names in the cases have been changed to protect villagers from possible repercussions.

3. Most villages had a few sorcerers who had been selected by the commu-nity to undergo training paid for by the collectivity. Sorcerers were desirable for protection against other villages and to sanction wrongdoing within the village but it was also felt that they could get out of hand and kill for malicious and personal reasons. It was well known who the sorcerers in an area were but not so clear which of them had acted on any particular occasion and for what reasons.

4. People believed that if sorcerers were not adequately paid for murders they would continue to kill people from the same village or lineage. A large payment would stop them from doing this.

5. Ronald and the Bumbita magistrates were officials in the village court system. A group of neighboring villages comprise a "court area" and meet every

two weeks to hear cases. Inakor and Asanakor were part of the "Kwanga Two" court area and this village court had four magistrates, two "peace officers," and a court clerk. Village courts may impose court fines or compensation payments and can send people to jail for failing to pay such fines.

6. Sam recounted an incident in which Naifuku had found a pig snared in a trap he had set at Pilimbi. But when he turned to ask his son for his rifle the pig escaped and ran away. This was seen as evidence that the animal was really a sorcerer in disguise lying in wait for Naifuku and that, furthermore, he must have been a local man since he had understood when Naifuku spoke in Kwanga, not Pidgin English.

7. The family will suspect that anyone who knows the identity of the murderer was involved in the murder or at least had foreknowledge of the attack and could have warned the victim.

8. Tuzin (1974) comments on the role of sorcery in bolstering the authority of initiated men among the neighboring Ilahita Arapesh. This use of sorcery is thought by the local people to be legitimate.

9. Councillors (Pidgin English: *Kaunsil*) are elected officials who attend monthly district council meetings. They are responsible for reporting the proceedings of these meetings to their constituents, for assigning community labor on Mondays, a day set aside for government service, and holding mediation sessions to deal with local disputes.

BIBLIOGRAPHY

Allen, M. R. 1881. Innovation, Inversion and Revolution as Political Tactics in West Aoba. Vanuatu: Politics, Economics and Ritual In Island Melanesia, ed. M. R. Allen, pp. 105–134. San Francisco.

Atkinson, J. M. 1984. "Wrapped Words:" Poetry and Politics among the Wana of Central Sulawesi. Dangerous Words: Language and Politics in the Pacific, eds. D. L. Brenneis and F. R. Myers, pp. 33–68. New York and London.

Bailey, F. G. 1965. Decisions by Consensus in Councils and Committees. Political Systems and the Distribution of Power, ed. M. Banton, pp. 1–20. New York.

———. 1971. Gifts and Poison. Gifts and Poisons, ed. F. G. Bailey, pp. 1–25. Oxford.

———. 1983. The Tactical Uses of Passion: An Essay on Power, Reason, and Reality. Ithaca and London.

Bloch, M. 1971. Decision Making in Councils Among the Merina of Madagascar. Councils in Action, eds. A. Richards and A. Kuper, pp. 29–62. Cambridge.

———. 1975. Introduction. Political Language and Oratory in Traditional Society, ed. M. Bloch, pp. 1–28. London, New York, and San Francisco.

Brenneis, D. L. 1984. Straight Talk and Sweet Talk: Political Discourse in an Occasionally Egalitarian Community. Dangerous Words, ed. D. L. Brenneis and F. R. Myers, pp. 69–84. New York and London.

Brenneis, D. L., and F. R. Myers, eds. 1984. Dangerous Words. Language and Politics in the Pacific. New York and London.

Chowning, A. 1979. Leadership In Melanesia. Journal of Pacific History 14:66–84.

Counts, D., and D. Counts. 1974. The Kaliai Lupunga: Disputing in the Public Forum. Contention and Dispute: Aspects of Law and Social Control in Melanesia, ed. A. L. Epstein, pp. 113–151. Canberra.

Douglas, B. 1979. Rank, Power, Authority: A Reassessment of Traditional Leadership in South Pacific Societies. Journal of Pacific History 14:2–27.

Epstein, A. L. 1974. Introduction. Contention and Dispute, ed. A. L. Epstein, pp. 1–39. Canberra.

Forge, A. 1970. Prestige, Influence, and Sorcery: A New Guinea Example. Witchcraft, Confession and Accusations, ed. M. Douglas, pp. 257–275. Toronto.

———. 1972. The Golden Fleece. Man 7:527–40.

Frankenberg, R. 1957. A Village on the Border. Manchester.

Gewertz, D. 1977. "On Whom Depends the Action of the Elements:" Debating Among the Chambri People of Papua New Guinea. Journal of the Polynesian Society 86:339–353.

Gluckman, M. 1963. Gossip and Scandal. Current Anthropology 4:307–316.

Hau'ofa, E. 1981. Mekeo: Inequality and Ambivalence in a Village Society. Canberra.

Hutson, S. 1971. Social Ranking in a French Alpine Community. Gifts and Poisons, ed. F. G. Bailey, pp. 41–68. Oxford.

Irvine, J. 1979. Formality and Informality in Communicative Events. American Anthropologist 81:773–790.

Keenan, E. 1974. Norm-Makers, Norm-Breakers: Uses of Speech by Men and Women in a Malagasy Community. Explorations in the Ethnography of Speaking, eds. R. Bauman and J. Sherzer, pp. 125–143. Cambridge.

———. 1975. A Sliding Sense of Obligatoriness: The Polystructure of Malagasy Oratory. Political Language and Oratory in Traditional Society, ed. M. Bloch, pp. 93–112. London, New York, and San Francisco.

Kuper, A. 1971. The Kgalagari Lekgota. Councils in Action, ed. A. Richards and A. Kuper, pp. 80–99. Cambridge.

Lawrence, P. 1971. Introduction. Politics in New Guinea, ed. R. M. Berndt and P. Lawrence, pp. 1–34. Perth.

Lederman, R. 1984. Who Speaks Here?: Formality and the Politics of Gender in Mendi, Highlands Papua New Guinea. Dangerous Words, ed. D. L. Brenneis and F. R. Myers, pp. 85–107. New York and London.

Merry, S. E. 1984. Rethinking Gossip and Scandal. Toward a General Theory of Social Control. Volume One: Fundamentals, ed. D. Black, pp. 271–302. New York.

Morauta, L. 1974. Beyond the Village: Local Politics in Madang, Papua New Guinea. New York.

Myers, F. R. 1986. Reflections on a Meeting: Structure, Language, and the Polity in a Small-Scale Society. American Ethnologist 13:430–447.

Myers, F. R., and D. L. Brenneis. 1984. Introduction: Language and Politics in the Pacific, ed. D. L. Brenneis and F. R. Myers, pp. 1–30. New York and London.

Paine, R. 1981. Politically Speaking: Cross-Cultural Studies of Rhetoric. Philadelphia.

Read, K. 1959. Leadership and Consensus in a New Guinea Society. American Anthropologist 61:425–436.

Richards, A. 1971. The Council System of the Bemba. Councils in Action, ed. A. Richards and A. Kuper, pp. 100–129. Cambridge.

Rosaldo, M. Z. 1973. I Have Nothing to Hide: The Language of Ilongot Oratory. Language in Society 2:193–223. 1984. Words that are Moving: The Social Meanings of Ilongot Verbal Arts. Dangerous Words, ed. D. L. Brenneis and F. R. Myers, pp. 131–160. New York and London.

Sahlins, M. 1963. Poor Man, Rich Man, Big-Man, Chief: Political Types in Polynesia and Melanesia. Comparative Studies in Sociology and History 5:282–303.

Scaglion, R. 1983. The Effects of Mediation Styles on Successful Dispute Resolution: The Abelam Case. Windsor Yearbook of Access to Justice, Vol. 3, pp. 256–269.

Schwartz, T. 1973. Cult and Context: The Paranoid Ethos in Melanesia. Ethos 1:153–174.

Strathern, A. J. 1971. The Rope of Moka. Cambridge.

———. 1975. Veiled Speech in Mount Hagen. Political Language and Oratory in Traditional Society, ed. M. Bloch, pp. 185–203. London, New York, and San Francisco.

Strathern, M. 1974. Managing Information: The Problems of a Dispute Settler (Mount Hagen). Contention and Dispute, ed. A. L. Epstein, pp. 271–316. Canberra.

Tuzin, D. F. 1974. Social Control and the Tambaran in the Sepik. Contention and Dispute, ed. A. L. Epstein, pp. 317–344. Canberra.

———. 1976. The Ilahita Arapesh: Unity in Duality. Berkeley.

White, G. 1978. Ambiguity and Ambivalence in A'ara Personality Descriptors. American Ethnologist 5:334–360.

White, G., and K. Watson-Gegeo. 1990. Disentangling Discourse. Disentangling: Conflict Discourse in Pacific Societies, ed. K. Watson-Gegeo and G. White. Stanford.

Young, M. 1971. Fighting With Food: Leadership, Values and Social Control in a Massim Society. Cambridge.

———. 1974. Private Sanctions and Public Ideology: Some Aspects of Self-Help in Kalauna, Goodenough Island. Contention and Dispute, ed. A. L. Epstein, pp. 40–66. Canberra.

———. 1983. Magicians of Manumanua. Berkeley.

Anuak Politics, Ecology, and the Origins of Shilluk Kingship

L. Lewis Wall

Most of the articles in this collection focus primarily upon political phenomena and analyze the impact of social and cultural contexts upon them. But we must not ignore the fact that human behavior has to operate in both a human-built environment and a natural environment, and Wall's essay stresses these natural or ecological factors. He raises the possibility of two historically similar political systems that diverged and became more complex or hierarchical due to favorable environmental factors. One society, the Shilluk, inhabited an environment that, with technology relatively similar to the Anuak, were able to increase in population and accumulate more resources. The Shilluk, in turn, developed a different political system.

Although Wall's view of political ecology may be too narrow and ahistorical, he does raise issues of comparative significance. One of the primary issues imbedded in his presentation is why ranking hierarchy emerges with the control of ritual prestige among the Shilluk and not among the Anuak.

THE CULTURAL AFFINITIES between the Anuak and Shilluk peoples of the Upper Nile have been known for some time. The close relationship between their languages has been established beyond doubt (Westermann 1912: 30–32; Tucker and Bryan 1948: 12–13, 23) and the historical traditions of both peoples tell of their common descent from two brothers who quarrelled and separated (Hofmayr 1925: 62; Evans-Pritchard 1940a: 9; Crazzolara 1950: 42–4). There are many other social and cultural similarities as well. Evans-Pritchard, in his 1948 Frazer Lecture, and Lienhardt, in a subsequent article (1955: 32), have suggested a

130

common historical and structural relationship between the political systems of these peoples. The purpose of this article[1] is to investigate further the relationship between the Anuak and Shilluk and to give one possible explanation of how Shilluk kingship could have developed out of a political system similar to that presently found among the Anuak, with particular reference to the ecological factors involved.

The Anuak

The Anuak have been described by Evans-Pritchard (1940a; 1947) and Lienhardt (1957, 1958).[2] They number between 30,000 and 50,000 people straddling the Sudan-Ethiopian border and living along the Pibor, Sobat, Gila, Akobo, Agwei, Oboth, and Baro rivers, with the majority of the population settled in Ethiopia. They live in small isolated village communities rarely exceeding 500 persons. Economic life centers around the cultivation of millet, maize, and other crops. Although their vocabulary gives evidence of a pastoral past, they are a sedentary people today with little interest in cattle or livestock—a fact which contrasts remarkably with their Nuer, Dinka, and Murle neighbors, all of whom are pastoralists. Sheep, goats, and fowls are raised by the Anuak, but are not of great economic importance. Each village raises enough crops for its own needs and little else. As Evans-Pritchard wrote (1940a: 22): "A predominantly agricultural economy means that each village community is a self-subsistent group, so that there is no necessity for them to have economic inter-relations."

Ecology combines with agricultural self-sufficiency to promote the isolation and independence of each village group. Northwestern Anuakland is lower and flatter than the regions to the southeast and consequently is subject to flooding during the rainy season, when the area is crosscut by deep watercourses and wide swamps. As a result, the western regions are sparsely populated and some village communities are forced to move either due to flooding or to drought. Communication between villages is usually difficult and is almost impossible during the rains. As one moves east, however, the open savannah gradually gives bay to higher forested land with better water supplies and no flooding. More favorable conditions have led to a greater density of settlement. Villages are located closer together and there is more cooperation and interaction among them.

Considering these conditions it is not surprising that the most important political unit among the Anuak is the village. "The absence of large organized political groups is consistent with the type of country in which Anuak live and their modes of livelihood" (Evans-Pritchard 1940a: 15).

The view of the village as the limit of their social world is manifested in the fact that it is the fundamental unit of defense and that no mechanisms exist for obtaining compensation for deaths occurring in fighting between villages. Although the Anuak are grouped into a number of non-exogamous clans, clanship holds little significance in Anuak life. Villages are usually associated with one lineage of a clan and there is little contact among lineages of the same clan in other villages. In each village there is a lineage which is said to be the "owner" of the land (*kwai ngam*), the original inhabitants and the founders of the village. In smaller villages there may be only one resident lineage; but larger villages may have more than one, the others being regarded as "guests" of the *kwai ngam*. Ideally (but not necessarily) this lineage should be the dominant political lineage (*tuong duong*) from which the village headman is chosen. Only male members of this traditional headman's lineage whose biological fathers have served as headmen are eligible for the position.

Since the village represents the limit of everyday Anuak experience, it is not surprising that the village headman should be the symbol of the village. He is the focal point for village loyalty and expresses the uniqueness, unity, and exclusiveness of each village vis-à-vis its neighbors. He controls the village drums and the beads of office. Great formal respect is paid to him. He is never allowed to sit directly upon the ground. Special vocabulary exists for many of his possessions and the buildings of his homestead, which are decorated with carved ornamental poles and grass screens. Those who approach him must do so on their knees and address him respectfully. The headman also has a number of deputies and "court officials" attached to him, and the youths of the village often group themselves around him as temporary followers and retainer (*luak*).

The impression should not be given, however, that village headmen are hereditary autocratic rulers. They remain in office only so long as their rule is beneficial to the community. A headman has many obligations to his village, the most important being the generous distribution of food and gifts to his people. A headman retains power only so long as he commands the following of the majority of the village population. He guides his village largely by consensus and force of personality rather than inherent power. He must therefore develop an efficient system of patronage within his village; and this, ultimately, leads to his downfall by exhausting his personal resources. When he has become poor or "stingy" the Anuak see this moment as the opportunity to replace him through an *agem* or "village revolution," and he is deposed in favor of another member of the ruling lineage whose father was a headman. The ousted headman must then flee the village, taking with him only what he can carry, usually seeking refuge in a nearby village where he has maternal kin and there hoping for a triumphant return from exile when the people grow tired of his successor. The fact that any son of a former headman is eligible for office, coupled with the steady and persistent drain on personal resources imposed by the office, leads to a frequent turnover in village headmen and a constant Anuak preoccupation with the machinations of local politics.

Among the southeastern Anuak, however, a different political system is found. Although all villages have a headman, in this part of the country headmen must compete for power with a noble clan, the *nyiye*. The nobles are members of a single patrilineal clan spread throughout Anuakland who have displaced traditional headmen in many villages. According to Anuak myth (Evans-Pritchard 1940a: 76–79; Lienhardt 1955: 36–37) this noble clan was founded by a mysterious man named Ukiro who appeared in the river one day and was captured by the Anuak, who took him to their village and made him their ruler at the expense of an unpopular headman. Ukiro brought with him five bead necklaces, four spears, two stools, a spear-rest, a drum, and a few other objects, now lost, which have taken on important ritual functions. The most important of these objects is the *ucuok* necklace. To become eligible to take over the headmanship of a village a noble must first be invested with these ritual emblems. Investiture is open only to the sons of those nobles who have themselves been invested. Once invested, a member of the *nyiye* may be invited to replace a headman in the aftermath of a village revolution.

These revolutions occur fairly frequently and mirror tensions among the various rivals for the headmanship of a village. Since many Anuak villages are inhabited by several lineages, only one of which may supply the headman, village politics reflects lineage rivalries. Therefore a lineage residing in a village but not itself supplying the headman may invite a noble to come and reside as its "guest" and candidate for headmanship. All male members of the noble clan who have been invested with the emblems are eligible to become ruling nobles and consequently are rivals with each other. Agnatic links between nobles therefore are generally not very useful in the political process; but since patrilineal descent is the prerequisite for membership in the noble clan, maternal relatives play an extremely important cross-cutting role in the removal of a headman and his replacement by a noble. Non-ruling lineages in a village having maternal ties to members of the noble clan will often invite them to their village as candidates for headmanship and pay for the cost of their investiture with the noble emblems. The noble then takes up residence in the village, marshalls his support, and waits for the moment when a revolution will occur and he will be asked to replace the older line of traditional headmen. Of course he may or may not be successful in this and the

resulting interplay of individuals and situations results in a series of relationships, ranging from villages in which the noble clan is the "owner" of
the land and its traditional rulers (as well as being nobles) to situations in
which nobles are merely residents with no political importance at all
(Evans-Pritchard 1947: 81–83).

All nobles are treated with respect by the Anuak, but if a noble suc-
ceeds in establishing himself as the new head of a village this respect is
intensified. He assumes all the trappings of the traditional headman but
these are elaborated to include a larger ceremonial etiquette and a larger
entourage of court officials and retainers (*luak*), composed mainly of
armed youths dedicated to the noble who relish the excitement and
prestige of court life. Retaining the favor of these youths (and that of the
village as a whole) is no easy task. The noble, like the headman, must
curry favor through gifts, generosity, and a shrewd appreciation of where
the political realities of the moment lie. To do anything at all he must
move the people with him; he cannot act on his own caprice. Although a
noble, he is bound by the same strictures of political process as the
headman. This is often expensive. For example, Evans-Pritchard reported
(1947: 78) one noble who was forced to sacrifice no less than eight oxen
from his tiny herd within the first few months of his tenure in office in a
bid to keep public support. When the villagers tire of a noble they cannot
simply depose him by force. The only way to remove him is to persuade
him to leave of his own accord or to invite another noble to come and
rule in his place. This noble then has the sanction to attack his rival and
drive him out, or kill him.

The Anuak noble clan, then, may be looked upon as a single "lineage"
of potential ruling headmen scattered throughout the country instead of
localized in just one village. They are bound together by their common
ancestry and are bound to the villages in which they establish themselves
by links of maternal kinship. Investiture with the noble emblems gives
clan members their full status as nobles and allows them to enter the
political process; therefore the man who controls the emblems controls
investiture. This is extremely important because it determines the flow of
eligible candidates into the political system.

According to the historical information collected by Evans-Pritchard
(1940a: 76–107) there have been five main phases in the history of the
Anuak noble clan. In the earliest period the noble possessing the emblems seems to have retained them until he died, at which time they
passed on peacefully to his son. This process was eventually disrupted by
dynastic wars in which the owner of the emblems was slain by his
successor. As Evans-Pritchard pointed out, this led to the spread of the
noble clan, since the noble in possession of the emblems would not

allow his kinsmen to reside in the same village with him. They were forced out into the countryside, generally residing with their maternal uncles. In the last century this process stabilized somewhat and the emblems tended to remain in one lineage of the noble clan to the exclusion of other lineages. Occasionally they would pass to a different lineage through peaceful means, such as when cognatic links between the parties were involved. Generally, however, there were wars between rival lineages. The introduction of firearms around 1900 altered this situation and led to the increasing centralization of power in the hands of three powerful nobles and the formation of loose village coalitions. This situation persisted until 1921 when the British began to administer the region and interfered with the political process. Initially this strengthened the position of the man who controlled the emblems, but soon they were removed from the control of any one man and the traditional system, which had been developing towards greater and greater centralization, was ended.

The Shilluk

The Shilluk number some 110,000 people living on the west bank of the White Nile from a point roughly twelve degrees north latitude south to Lake No, a distance of about two hundred miles. To date no satisfactory anthropological monograph has appeared on the Shilluk although various authors have written excellent articles on their life and institutions, particularly Pumphrey (1941) and Howell (1941, 1952).[3] The land inhabited by the Shilluk is open savannah high enough to be free from flooding throughout the year and fertile enough to support a large, nearly continuous, string of settlements running along the river. While possessing considerable numbers of cattle, the Shilluk are in the main agriculturalists who grow millet, maize, and various kinds of beans and pumpkins in sufficient quantities to feed a large population. The combination of fertile land and a lack of flooding makes possible a high density of population which contrasts strongly with the desolate surrounding lands. For example, the explorer Georg Schweinfurth, who was not prone to exaggeration, wrote of his 1869 visit to Shillukland (1873: 85):

> No known part of Africa, scarcely even the narrow valley of the Nile in Egypt, has a density of population so great; but a similar condition of circumstances, so favorable to the support of a teeming population, is perhaps without parallel in the world. Everything which contributes to the exuberance of life here finds a concentrated field—agriculture, pasturage, fishing, and the chase. Agriculture is rendered easy by the natural fertility of the soil, by the recurrence of the rainy seasons, by irrigation, effected by an

atmosphere ordinarily so overclouded as to moderate the radiance of the sun, and so retain throughout the year perpetual moisture.

The Shilluk are divided into approximately one hundred exogamous patrilineal clans. These clans are not territorially defined but are scattered about the country. Only the lineages comprising the clans have any real relationship to residential patterns. The family homesteads (*gol*) or individual lineage members are grouped together to form hamlets of agnatically related kinsmen. Such a hamlet may be comprised of as many as fifty homesteads. Ultimately these scattered hamlets form larger "settlements" (*podh*) with a clearly defined territory and common pastures and fishing areas. In each of these settlements an original or "owner" lineage, called the *diel,* is recognized. Other lineages are said to be the "guests" (*wedh*) of these people.

The main political officials on the lower level are the various lineage heads and the head of the settlement. The settlement chief is chosen, ideally, from the *diel* lineage, although he may be replaced by another more powerful person belonging to a different lineage. This position is hereditary, subject to confirmation by the Shilluk *reth* (king). Above the settlement level Shillukland is divided into eleven districts and two further provinces, Luak in the south and Ger in the north, corresponding roughly to the ceremonial divisions of Gol Nyikang and Gol Dhiang which function at the time of choosing and installing a new *reth*. But the settlement is, as Howell has written (1952: 101), "the largest political unit which has a permanent and stable function in Shilluk society today."

The religious and political head of the Shilluk nation is the king, or *reth*. Each *reth* is thought to be the reincarnation of Nyikang, the Shilluk culture-hero who led them to their present land, and the institution of the rethship is often cited in anthropological literature as an example of "divine kingship" (cf. Frazer 1911: 17–28; Seligman 1911). The supreme being, called Juok is approached through Nyikang—in fact, the personages of Juok and Nyikang are often not clearly separated. Nyikang in his turn is seen as embodied on earth in the person of the king. "The kingship is the common symbol of the Shilluk people and, Nyikang being immortal, an abiding institution which binds past and present and future generations" (Evans-Pritchard 1948: 17). The *reth* is, therefore, the visible expression of the Shilluk nation, the focal point for Shilluk cosmology, and the center of Shilluk politics. While there is no formal cult either of Nyikang or of Juok, the *reth* must perform certain rituals pertaining to the rains, the harvests, and so on. In addition, the *reth* has important legal functions as a mediator of disputes, wielding the moral authority of his office to maintain peace among his people (Oyler 1920; Howell 1952).

The presence of a royal clan leads to certain social distinctions. The majority of the people are *collo,* commoners, as opposed to the *kwar reth,* the royal clan. In addition, there are two other groups, the *bang reth,* descendants of former slaves and retainers of the Shilluk kings linked together by a fictive clanship, and the *ororo,* a small branch of the royal clan disinherited by an early king for treachery to him. The distinctions are not of great importance in everyday living but are significant in terms of the political process. Accession to the rethship is dependent upon two things: royal descent and election by a council of chiefs. Of these two descent is by far the more important. Only the son of a *reth* (*nyireth*) is eligible to succeed to the office. He need not be the son of the currently ruling *reth* so long as his father was at one time king. This means that at any given time there are a number of *nyireth* theoretically eligible to succeed to the office. In fact, it has often been the case that any *nyireth* who could raise a rebellion, kill the ruling king, and install himself in the royal capital at Fashoda could become *reth.* This led to strong structural tensions in the Shilluk political system. For this reason no *nyireth* is allowed to stay the night in Fashoda, and all royal wives are sent to outlying villages upon their pregnancy, there to raise their sons. This procedure has resulted in the royal clan spreading itself across Shillukland, establishing new lineages throughout the countryside which often supplant the ruling lineages in the settlements or hamlets where they become established. As the royal clan is by far the largest clan in Shillukland, comprising about seven per cent of the population, this makes them very important in the political process. Every settlement is likely to have its own "favorite son" *nyireth* whom they are likely to back as a candidate for the rethship. Maintaining oneself as *reth* in the face of this potential opposition requires considerable diplomatic skill in manipulating local rivalries and balancing opposed segments of the royal clan.

Upon the death of a *reth* these tensions are manifest in the process of selecting his successor. The new *reth* is chosen from among the *nyireth* by a council of division chiefs, ritually grouped into the ceremonial moieties of Gol Dhiang and Gol Nyikang. Westermann (1912: 122–124) and Hofmayr (1925: 145–146) both suggest that this was done randomly; recently more democratic measures have been introduced (Howell and Thomson 1946: 27–37). However, there is no doubt that in previous times the joint assent of the northern and southern sections of Shillukland had to be obtained. When this did not happen, civil war was likely to break out between the opposing factions, as happened in the last century when *reth* Kwatker was deposed by the Turkish *mudir* of Fashoda and Ajang Nyidhok was installed as a puppet ruler, never accepted as legitimate king by the southern Shilluk (Howell 1952: 102–3).

Once the successor has been tentatively agreed upon there is a lapse
of about one year prior to his installation to allow the necessary preparations for the installation ceremony to be completed.[4] The death of the
reth means that the spirit of Nyikang has been released and is now abroad
in the country. Of this the Shilluk say *piny bugon,* ("there is no land"), or
as Evans-Pritchard has explained it (1948: 10) "the center of the Shilluks'
world has fallen out." The process of installing a *reth* is, therefore, largely
a process of persuading the spirit of Nyikang to enter the new king and by
so doing to reanimate the land and give his consent to the recreation of
the order of Shilluk society. This concept of renewing or recreating
Shillukland is the heart of the ceremony. The country is divided into two
opposed halves, Gol Dhiang in the south—the half associated with the
reth-elect—and Gol Nyikang in the north, associated with Nyikang himself, being the place where he ascended to the heavens in the midst of a
great thunderstorm at the end of his stay on earth. Each half forms a mock
army and they both march toward a common meeting place at the center
of Shillukland, just outside the royal capital of Fashoda. The army of Gol
Dhiang is preceded by the *reth*-elect; the army of Gol Nyikang is preceded by effigies of Nyikang and his sons, Dak and Cal. The spirits of
Nyikang, Cal, and Dak are thought to animate these effigies at this time.
The journey symbolically recreates the myth of the Shilluk migration and
the founding of Shillukland by Nyikang and his sons (cf. Oyler 1918). On
the outskirts of Fashoda the *reth*-elect and his party cross the watercourse
of Arepujur and are there beset by the army of Nyikang in a mock battle.
Nyikang is victorious and the candidate is taken captive into the capital.
Here the ceremony of installation takes place. The new *reth* is given
possession of the ritual objects of kingship: the sacred spear of Nyikang,
beads from the Nuba mountains said to have been part of his daughter
Adwai's bridewealth, a silver ring taken in battle, and especially the sacred stool. The effigy of Nyikang dances up to the stool and is seated
upon it, with the *reth*-elect bowed down in front of it holding the legs.
The effigy is then lifted off the stool and goes with the effigies of Dak and
Cal into a special shrine. The *reth* is seated upon the stool and invested
with the sacred emblems. Howell and Thomson write (1946: 62), with
reference to the installation of *reth* Anei Kur: "The act of substitution
upon the stool symbolizes to the Shilluk the possession of the *reth* by the
spirit of Nyikang, and we saw that the *reth* was seized with a trembling fit
at the critical moment, and certainly appeared to be in a dazed condition
immediately afterwards, when he walked across to the temporary camp
opposite the shrine." Following this installation the *reth* is kept in seclu-
sion under the joint supervision of the chiefs of the north and south, and
is bathed alternately with hot and cold water so that his rule will be

moderate and not subject to extremes. He is also given a girl, called the *nyakwer,* to symbolize the union of Nyikang and the land. All the fires in Fashoda, which have been extinguished, are rekindled, representing the departure and return of stability, light, and new life. The Shilluk world is recreated.

The Origins of Shilluk Kingship

An examination of the respective political systems of the Anuak and Shilluk leads one to the conclusion that there is a common structural, if not an actual historical, relationship between them. Anuak politics, with its competing systems of headmanship and nobility, can be looked upon as an embryonic form of the Shilluk rethship, and it seems not unlikely that the political system of the Shilluk was at one time very much like that found in Anuak villages which, for ecological and historical reasons, went through an accelerated process of development.

A comparison of certain features common to both systems tends to confirm this. For example, in both cases eligibility for the position in question, be it noble or *reth,* depends upon direct patrilineal descent from a previously invested predecessor. Actual accession to a position of power depends upon "election," in the case of the Anuak by being asked to come replace a village headman or, in the case of the Shilluk by being asked to succeed to the kingship by a council of chiefs. Among the Anuak the maternal kin of the noble play an exceedingly important role in his investiture and form the power base from which he may spring to replace the headman. The fact that the Shilluk *nyireth* are brought up in the villages of their maternal kin and the fact that the *reths* seem to have ruled from their maternal villages prior to the establishment of the capital at Fashoda (Lienhardt 1954: 141; Seligman 1932: 47) seems to indicate an analogous situation at an early period in Shilluk history. In more recent times we may note that a dissatisfied *nyireth,* in raising a rebellion against the king, was supported in large part by his local (generally maternal) community. This seems to indicate stresses in the Shilluk polity similar to those found among the Anuak (Lienhardt 1955).

There are parallels as well in the ritual and ceremonial aspects of Anuak nobility and the Shilluk rethship. Both the noble clan of the Anuak and the royal clan of the Shilluk trace their ancestry to semi-divine person-ages having intimate ties with the river. Ukiro, the founder of the Anuak nobility, simply appeared one day out of the water and was later captured and made ruler of an Anuak village (Evans-Pritchard 1940a: 76–79; Lienhardt 1955: 36–37). Nyikang, founder of the Shilluk nation and the first *reth,* was the daughter of Nyikaya, a water spirit, half woman, half crocodile, still venerated among the Shilluk and thought to have the capacity to judge right and wrong in legal cases through trial by ordeal (Banholzer and Giffen 1905: 197). Among both peoples certain ritual objects legitimate the office holders: spears, beads and drums among the Anuak; spears, beads, bracelets, and the sacred stool of Nyikang among the Shilluk. Special vocabulary exists for use in the court of the Anuak nobles (Evans-Pritchard 1940a: 66); likewise there exist certain "royal language conventions" for the court of the *reth* (Pumphrey 1937). Anuak nobles are buried in a different fashion from ordinary Anuak and the graves, as well as trees near them, are respected (Evans-Pritchard 1940a: 70–75). Among the Shilluk this practice has been elaborated to the point where the graves of dead *reths* are maintained as special shrines associated with the spirit of the *reth* and with Nyikang, attended by hereditary caretakers (Seligman 1911).

These similarities can be fitted together into a larger whole when the broad outlines of Nilotic history are considered. According to the common tradition of the Anuak and Shilluk peoples they arrived in their present lands as the result of a great migration. The leader of this movement was Nyikang, the Shilluk culture-hero. One of the chiefs with Nyikang was his brother Gilo, with whom he had a great quarrel. Gilo and his followers separated from the others and moved away to found the Anuak people (Seligman 1932: 109; Evans-Pritchard 1940a: 9–10; Hofmayr 1925: 62). This story forms part of a much broader tradition of the early history of the Nilotes in which they migrated from a homeland in the south. Father J. P. Crazzolara has collected the traditions of most of the Lwo-speaking peoples of East Africa, to which group the Anuak and Shilluk belong, and has pieced together a general outline of their early history through a comparative analysis of these materials (Crazzolara 1950). From this information, and that presented by Hofmayr (1925) it appears that the Shilluk and the Anuak migrated from their southern homeland to their present location some time in the sixteenth or seventeenth centuries.

The social and political organization of these early migrants was undoubtedly loose, even as it is among most Nilotic peoples today.[5] Probably they were pastoralists moving northward with their herds of cattle, similar in many respects to the present Nuer and Dinka tribes who seem to have been the first Nilotes to reach the area (Crazzolara 1950: 15; Ogot 1964: 287–288). As the Shilluk-Anuak group spread out they settled in sedentary communities, gradually abandoning their cattle in favor of an agricultural economy. Although their languages contains many cattle-related words indicative of a nomadic past, today the Anuak possess virtually no cattle and have only the slightest interest in them. Indeed, there is a myth in which it is said that while God granted cattle to all the people, the Anuak killed theirs and so today are cattleless (Evans-Pritchard 1940a: 20). In similar fashion the Shilluk, while maintaining herds, do not leave their permanent settlements to follow them and possess many fewer cattle than do their Nuer and Dinka neighbors (Howell 1950: 100). Their economy is far more agricultural than pastoral. The adoption of such a sedentary way of life necessitated certain changes, the most important of which was the adoption of the village (as opposed to the cattle-camp) as the fundamental unit of social life and the creation of the village headman—a type of office unknown among the nearby Nuer and Dinka. The village became the main unit of defense. A dominant lineage supplied the headman. All in all, the system was probably like that now found among the scattered village communities of the western Anuak.

Ecological conditions vary throughout this area and affect settlement patterns. The territory occupied by the present-day Anuak is not conducive to a high population density, particularly in the western regions. Here villages remain fairly isolated, self-contained units, frequently fortified by moats and stockades (Evans-Pritchard 1940a: 16–17). In southeastern Anuakland the villages are located more closely together and a higher density of population obtains as a result. Among the Anuak ecological conditions deem to set certain limits on the size of villages with resultant effects in local politics. As Lienhardt has written (1958: 26):

> Since economic difficulties within a village tend to be reflected in changes of headmen, it is probable that this way of reducing the size of a village by division has a necessary economic function which the Anuak themselves do not recognize. The evidence suggests that it has been the largest villages which have been sundered by disagreements over the headmanship, and that such villages have been hosts to many "guests," and have thus probably begun to increase in size beyond the possible local resources of land and food.

In striking contrast to these conditions the Shilluk occupy a highly favorable ecological niche capable of supporting a large densely settled population. As the Shilluk moved across the Nile they left the low swampy areas behind them and were able to form a nearly unbroken line of settlements stretching some two hundred miles along the west bank of the river, from Muomo to Tonga. Among these Nilotes, then, the areas of sparsest population are the least centralized politically. Scattered villages, each forming an individual polity, are the rule in western Anuakland while the more densely populated lands of the southeast harbor the competing systems of headmanship and nobility, with the villages linked together through a common sentiment about the noble emblems and a common respect for a noble clan. Among the Shilluk, who have the greatest density of settlement, a single royal clan is spread throughout the countryside and the people pay honor to a king who is the visible symbol of their nationhood.

In the earliest times it seems likely that the Shilluk lived in villages presided over by a headman coming from a dominant lineage; but the density of population, ease of communication and travel up and down the river, closeness of villages to each other, and a common cultural heritage undoubtedly led to a greater feeling of unity among the Shilluk than was found in the much more sparsely settled regions to the south. Neighboring villages must have maintained frequent intercourse with each other, and such contact would have taken on increased importance if particular clans or lineages competed with each other for power in these regions. The size of the royal clan at the present time indicates that it must have begun spreading early and voraciously, and it is easy to see how the villages of Shillukland could have been drawn together into a system of ritualized politics similar to that found among the southeastern Anuak. Replacing a headman with a member of the royal clan would give local political activity an impetus which would carry on outside the particular village in question. The royal clan would have served as the focal point for uniting the people and led to the development of a centralized political system, the creation of the rethship. A need to unite against a common enemy would have spurred the process on, and as the Shilluk began to interact with one another in this manner the elaboration of myth and ceremony centering on Nyikang and the *reth* would have given them a common ritual ground expressive of their growing unity as a people.

Such a view accords with Shilluk traditions. The first *reths* held court in the villages of the maternal kin by whom they were raised. At his time no one man had been able to muster sufficient power to create a central seat for the rethship. Opposition from collateral lineages of the royal clan probably made the position of the reigning *reth* somewhat precarious. In an unstable political situation the benefits of ruling from the village of one's maternal kin would have been obvious. However, *reth* Tugo, the ninth or tenth Shilluk king (his position varies in the king-lists), is credited with establishing the royal capital at Fashoda and with instigating the full ceremonies of investiture at a time when the Shilluk were at war with the neighboring Dinka (Hofmayr 1925: 72–74; Crazzolara 1950: 134; Lienhardt 1955: 41; Ogot 1964: 299). Tugo had a reputation as a great warrior (as did his predecessor Tokot) and it seems likely that the break with the traditional practice of ruling from the home of his maternal kin was brought about by military necessity. Tugo's military prowess, coupled with the threat of Dinka incursions into Shilluk lands, gave him a strong enough base to push the incipient tendency towards ritualized political leadership to its ultimate conclusion. The "divine kingship" was born. Gradually the *reth* assumed more and more ritual functions, becoming in essence the "high priest" of the Shilluk people with responsibilities at the time of harvest and obligations as a rainmaker (Seligman 1932: 80–82), in addition to his position as a military leader and functionary of justice. These religious duties have no parallel among the Anuak. The development of a single focus for the social order in this manner was mirrored and undergirded by the mythology of Nyikang, who symbolized the *reth* and his relation to the Shilluk order (cf. Oyler 1918b; Lienhardt 1954). The *reth* became the symbol of the Shilluk people as a whole, and with this newfound unity they were able to organize a powerful military machine, at least nominally controlled from Fashoda, which enabled them to establish their suzerainty for hundreds of miles up and down the river. Population density, favorable ecology, and a higher level of political organization than that found among any of their neighbors allowed the Shilluk to dominate the upper reaches of the White Nile until the coming of the Turks in the early nineteenth century (cf. Mercer 1971).

To the south their Anuak cousins lagged behind. Sparsely settled in isolated village communities they only gradually developed common political ties. Fragmented, the Anuak were helpless in the face of widespread Nuer raiding—something with which the Shilluk were never bothered (Evans-Pritchard 1940b: 132). Only with the introduction of firearms toward the end of the last century did the nobility-influenced system of Anuak politics begin to move towards centralization, a process which was interrupted and then stopped by the intervention of British administration. Among the western Anuak no such system developed. It is likely that, given time, the noble clan might have extended itself through that area and gradually united the Anuak people into a single body politic; but it is highly doubtful that the Anuak could ever attain the level of organization found among the Shilluk.

In sum, it appears that in comparing the Anuak and Shilluk peoples of the Nile basin, we see a common political structure developing at differential rates, affected mainly by ecological variations in the lands they occupy, with the historical end result that one group, the Shilluk, have emerged into full nationhood while the Anuak have remained less aware of the common ties that bind them together as a people. Hocart (1936) suggested that government originated out of a ritual organization designed to secure life for the community. It seems that in the case of Shilluk kingship we have an example of central "government" emerging from just such a system of ritualized politics.

NOTES

1. I am indebted to Dr. Godfrey Lienhardt of the Institute of Social Anthropology at Oxford University for supervising the research that led to this paper, and for many helpful remarks pertaining to it.

2. The account of the Anuak which follows is based upon these sources.

3. The account of the Shilluk which follows is based upon these sources.

4. These two accounts have been abstracted to provide the following account of the installation ceremony.

5. General surveys of the Nilotes may be found in Seligman (1932) and Butt (1952). Early history and political traditions for the Nilotes as a whole are treated in summary fashion by Ogot (1964).

BIBLIOGRAPHY

Banholzer, W., and J. K. Giffen. 1905. Appendix: History and Religion of the Shilkluks. The Anglo-Egyptian Sudan, Volume 1, ed. C. Gleichen, pp. 197–199. London.

Butt, A. 1952. The Nilotes of the Anglo-Egyptian Sudan and Uganda. London.

Crazzolara, J. P. 1950. The Lwoo, Part 1: Lwoo Migrations. Verona.

Evans-Pritchard, E. E. 1940a. The Political System of the Anuak of the Anglo-Egyptian Sudan. London School of Economics Monographs in Social Anthropology, No. 4.

———. 1940b. The Nuer: A Description of the Modes of Livelihood and Political Institutions of a Nilotic People. London.

———. 1947. Further Observations on the Political System of the Anuak. Sudan Notes and Records 28: 62–97.

———. 1948. The Divine Kingship of the Shilluk of the Nilotic Sudan. Cambridge.

Frazer, J. G. 1911. The Dying God. The Golden Bough, Vol. III, (3rd. ed.). London.

Hocart, A. M. 1936. Kings and Councillors: An Essay in the Comparative Anatomy of Human Society. Cairo.

Hofmayr, W. 1925. Die Schilluk: Geschichte, Religion and Leben eiones Nioten Stammes. Wein.

Howell, P. P. 1941. The Shilluk Settlement. Sudan Notes and Records 24: 47–67.

———. 1952. Observations on the Shilluk of the Upper Nile: The Laws of Homicide and the Legal Functions of the Reth. Africa 22: 97–119.

———. 1953. Observations on the Shilluk of the Upper Nile: Customary Law—Marriage and the Violation of Rights in Women. Africa 23: 94–109.

Howell, P. P., and W.P.G. Thomson. 1946. The Death of a Reth of the Shilluk and the Installation of His Successor. Sudan Notes and Records 27: 5–85.

Lienhardt, R. G. 1954. The Shilluk of the Upper Nile. African Worlds: Studies in the Cosmological Ideas and Social Values of African Peoples, ed. C. D. Forde, pp. 138–163. London.

————. 1955. Nilotic Kings and Their Mothers' Kin. Africa 25: 29–42.

————. 1957. Anuak Village Headman I: Headmen and Village Culture, Africa 27: 341–355.

————. 1958. Anuak Village Headmen II: Village Structure and Rebellion, Africa 28: 23–36.

Mercer, P. 1971. Shilluk Trade and Politics from the Mid-Seventeenth Century to 1851. Journal of African History 12: 407–426.

Munroe, P. 1918. Installation of the Ret of the Chol (King of the Shilluks). Sudan Notes and Records 1: 145–152.

Ogot, B. A. 1964. Kingship and Statelessness Among the Nilotes. The Historian in Tropical Africa, ed. J. Vansina, R. Mauny, and L. V. Thomas, pp. 284–304. London.

Oyler, D. S. 1918a. Nikawng and the Shilluk Migration. Sudan Notes and Records 1: 107–115.

————. 1918b. Nikawng's Place in the Shilluk Religion. Sudan Notes and Records 1: 283–292.

————. 1920. The Shilluk Peace Ceremony. Sudan Notes and Records 3: 296–299.

Pumphrey, M.E.C. 1937. Shilluk 'Royal' Language Conventions. Sudan Notes and Records 20: 319–321.

————. 1941. The Shilluk Tribe. Sudan Notes and Records 24: 1–45.

Schweinfurth, G. 1873. The Heart of Africa, Volume 1. London.

Seligman, C. G. 1911. The Cult of Nyakang and the Divine Kings of the Shilluk. The Fourth Report of the Wellcome Tropical Research Laboratories at the Gordon Memorial College, Khartoum, Volume B, pp. 216–238. Khartoum.

Seligman, C. G., and B. Z. Seligman. 1932. The Pagan Tribes of the Nilotic Sudan. London.

Tucker, A. N., and M. A. Bryan. 1948. Distribution of the Nilotic and Nilo-Hamitic Languages of Africa. London.

Westermann, D. 1912. The Shilluk People: Their Language and Folklore. Philadelphia.

Strategies of Legitimation and the Aztec State[1]

Donald V. Kurtz

A state is a historical political phenomena and, therefore, is histori-cally limited. The overwhelming number of societies that anthropolo-gists study do not have political characteristics of a state. Therefore, there are fundamental political differences between societies that have states and those that do not. Kurtz lists the political elites' strategies for making their political control over inhabitants not only effective but, even more critically, legitimate. The political elite control economic resources and allocate them in a manner that satis-fies the populace and also increases their ideological control. These strategies involve maintaining cultural distinctions and manipulat-ing symbolic events.

In the course of time, a state must convince its subjects of legiti-macy. In order for a state political sphere to function and reproduce the relations of production, it must create ideologies and institutions that maintain social distance and authority through both a central-ization of power and a political socialization of the populace.

THIS PAPER ANALYZES the process by which early states attempt to become legitimate employing the Aztecs of Mexico as a specific case in point. The aim here is to describe how early states survive after they emerge, particularly with the purpose of understanding the array of sym-bolic and materialistic activities in which leaders of early states engage, such as promoting economic production and establishing a state priest-hood. The survival of a state and such activities by its leaders seem to be related. The epistemology, in fact, is fundamentally political; a quest for resources upon which the power and authority of state leaders rests and by which they endure. Yet, while some of the actions of leaders are obviously political, such as the elaboration of government and the codification of laws, others are less so and raise some questions regarding their political import.

For example, in early states sumptuary laws favoring the rulers and elites are codified (Kurtz 1978, 1981). The sexual activities of citizens become a concern of state authorities (Y. A. Cohen 1969). Institutions, such as schools, that are not indigenous to stateless societies emerge (Y. A. Cohen 1970). State leaders try to influence the organization of local level kinship, religious, political and other institutions (Adams 1966). To provide a more synthetic explanation of these and related phenomena, this paper argues that these actions are directed toward a primary state goal—legitimacy—and comprise the process of legitimation.

Legitimation refers to the means by which the leaders of a state acquire the support of the population over which they rule. The process entails the implementation of a variety of strategies by which state leaders attempt to shift the allegiance and support of the people from local level organizations to the state and mobilize these populations in the service of the state. A state that has not been able to acquire the support of its polity may survive and govern but its survival will be precarious. Following suggestions by Swartz, Turner, and Tuden (1966) that legitimacy is the outcome of a process, I argue that legitimation is the result of several strategies that can be demonstrated empirically and explained by existing anthropological theory.

Legitimacy and Legitimation

Anthropologists have expressed interest in the concept of legitimacy and legitimation only recently (Kurtz 1978, 1981; Orenstein 1980; Swartz, Turner, and Tuden 1966). Most nonanthropological discussions regarding legitimacy are abstract and philosophical and tend to focus on the role of ideology in promoting authorities' right to rule and functional concerns with sociopolitical stability and cohesion (Easton 1965; Parsons 1969; Weber 1954). But notions of a validating ideology and sociopolitical stability are static conceptualizations that ignore the complex dialectic underlying legitimacy. In any case, analyses of legitimation are almost nonexistent.

Legitimacy is an achieved condition, the consequence of legitimation. Swartz et al. (1966) make clear that legitimacy refers to a type of support and is the result of an intricate process and suggest that legitimacy derives from the implementation of strategies that political leaders use to attempt to attain goals. A fundamental goal of state politics is acquisition of support; i.e., either the active or passive compliance of citizens with state policies and goals. It is my contention that support is the underpinning of legitimacy and provides the most fruitful concept for understanding legitimation. This paper attempts to demonstrate the dialectic involved in the development and acquisition of such support.

Support comes in many guises. It may be given directly by an individual or group to the existing authority structure or indirectly, in which case it is mediated through some intervening process or object of support, such as ideology (Swartz et al. 1966). However, all support is fragile and subject to change as the social and political environment changes (Easton 1965; Swartz et al. 1966). It responds to events and the actions of leaders and rests in part on the threat of coercion. But undue coercion may be counterproductive, for individuals and groups who provide support at one moment may be moved to support an alternative political structure. To mitigate this leaders develop strategies to marshal support. These involve calculated risks, for actions in one arena may detract from support in another.

Nettl (1967) has suggested that legitimation represents a mobilization by the state of its nation's citizens and institutions. Indeed, state agents do play a critical role in co-ordinating activities of citizens in tasks that shift their support from local level organizations to the state itself. Yet, few states have attained complete legitimacy. In protohistoric states, crises of legitimacy are not well documented, but inferences may be drawn from ethnohistorical data which suggest that even in early states legitimation is orchestrated by political leaders in a protracted dialectic.

Concepts and Hypothesis

State and nation, although inseparable functionally, are distinct analytic entities. A state is an organization of bureaucracies over which most commonly a single office presides. The occupant of that office is the head of state and the major actor in state political affairs and rituals. Below the head of state exists a political bureaucracy dedicated to governing a subordinate population (Y. A. Cohen 1969).

Nation refers to a socially and culturally differentiated population that resides in a variety of communities within a more or less firmly demarcated territory. Part of that population comprises a social class that is politically and economically dominant; its members staff the state bureaucracy. The subordinate population, or lower classes, comprise another social category toward whom the state directs strategies designed to win support. A major source of potential threat to state support resides in the conditions of state and national inchoateness; i.e., the condition in which autonomous organizations that the state either has not been able to sub-vert or assimilate persist and threaten it (Y. A. Cohen 1969). Therefore, the extent to which legitimacy is attainable is always a matter of degree due to inchoateness.

In order to become legitimate, early states have to overcome inchoate-ness at two levels: the nation and the state (Kurtz 1981). National incho-ateness is marked by heterogeneity based upon regional differences, like language diversity, ethnic plurality, religious affiliation, and resident kin or nonkin organizations. Within the latter, leaders, symbols, and ideolo-gies exist that may detract from the support citizens should provide the state (Claessen and Skalnik 1978; Y. A. Cohen 1969). State inchoateness is manifest in the incomplete formulation of government institutions de-signed to execute public policy and manage public affairs (Rounds 1979; Webster 1976). A state tries to overcome inchoateness by acquiring suffi-cient resources to supplant local centers of autonomy and mobilize citi-zens in its support. Inability of a state to overcome inchoateness and acquire the support of its population is a major threat to its legitimacy and, therefore, survival.

As a working hypothesis, I argue that legitimation of political author-ity is in large measure a consequence of the ability of authorities to generate, control, and allocate economic and symbolic resources in pur-suit of public and private goals (A. Cohen 1969, 1974; Nettl 1967). Then, following Firth's (1973) suggestion that the anthropological study of symbols should link symbols to specific social structures and events, let us view legitimating strategies as articulating the material and symbolic domains of political activity. For example, the state attempts to develop an economy that will satisfy the material needs of its citizens and provide it with resources to carry out public policy. A major goal of state eco-nomic policy is to mobilize the labor of its citizens to produce goods and commodities above the per capita requirements of the population. These gross surpluses then may be coordinated by the state and deployed strate-gically in ways that increase its power and influence (Adams 1966; Kurtz 1974, 1978, 1981). The positive feedback between the resources on which state power rests and the planning and mobilization it undertakes, all conditions being equal, tend to augment legitimacy. Since conditions are rarely equal, symbols come to play a strategic role.

The articulation of local and state institutions concerned with activi-ties, such as market exchange, enforcement of conformity, and education, provide points of critical disjunction in the relationship of the state and local level (Befu 1965). Symbols are likely to occur in situations of disjunction because they overcome contradictions (A. Cohen 1974; Firth 1973). The state pours its symbolic resources into the disjunction between state and local institutions in order to redirect the support of its citizens. A panoply of uncommon state symbols emerge to communicate to citizens state values and expectations: patriotism, hard work, self sacrifice. The head of state and subordinate functionaries, such as priests, create and manipulate symbols just as they themselves become symbols in rituals that reaffirm state authority in order to constantly renew citizen allegiance. Actions by the state are aimed teleologically at reducing inchoateness by either welding rival social structures, such as lineages and local religious cults, into the structure of the state or replacing them with those of state derivation.

The process is not linear. That is, the state does not fulfill one strategy before embarking upon another. It moves when and where it can, ideally triggering a positive feedback that continually generates support. Success depends upon the inchoateness a state confronts. In general the process is slow and few states are ever completely legitimate. The Aztec state was no exception to this pattern, as I will demonstrate.

Legitimation Strategies

The process of legitimation contains five overlapping strategies: a planned mobilization of the nation's economy; establishment of social distance between rulers and ruled; validation of state authority, consolidation of state authority and power; and political socialization of citizens. These strategies were carried out by the Aztec state over nearly 150 years (1376–1520).

Economic Development

Even in early states economic planning is the keystone to state development. Planning derives from a conscious awareness of desirable goals and involves strategies to achieve them expeditiously. It employs a variety of symbols—redistribution, markets, prices, goods—aimed at reducing local autonomy and welding the population into a unified nation. Finally, it usually is directed at urban populations, for it is among them that such symbols communicate most effectively.

The economic foundation of the Aztec state was laid by successive emperors in the first century of its existence, approximately 1375–1475. The last fifty or so years, 1475–1520, was a period of political and economic consolidation. Economic and social transformations over this 150 years suggests considerable planning. Tenochtitlan was a planned city that gradually emerged as a dominant symbol of developing Aztec hegemony (Calnek 1972:111; Duran 1964:32) and as a center for institutional innovations by the state. During Acamapichtli's reign (1376–1396), the market system of Tenochtitlan-Tlatelolco was organized and began to come under state control. Trade was encouraged by the state and some *pochteca,* a specialized category of traders, conducted business on its behalf in international ports of trade on the frontiers of the empire (Berdan 1982:31–35; Bray 1977:383; Chapman 1957; Kurtz 1974; Sahagun 1950–1969, BK. 9). Specialization in production was encouraged and resulted in increasing bifurcation between peasants and urban craft specialists (Calnek 1972:114; Hicks 1982; Kurtz 1974). Nobles, the primary entrepreneurs of Aztec society, engaged in buying and selling land, invested in craft manufacturing, and other business ventures (Carrasco 1961:491; Caso 1963:871; Kurtz 1974). Slaves provided an important source of energy. They were concentrated in the service of well-to-do citizens, such as the *pochteca.* Military expansion aimed at acquiring additional revenues was continuous.

The first century of the Aztec State (1376–1476) was a period of remarkable technological development, especially hydraulic innovations engineered by the state. Chimalpopoca (1415–1428), the third emperor, acquired a supply of fresh water for Tenochtitlan, a resource critical to the growth of the city (Duran 1964:45). Construction of *chinampas* continued and probably expanded along the lakes' shores (Calnek 1972). Irrigation was extensive, and under Moctezuma I a dike was constructed across Lake Texcoco to alleviate flooding of Tenochtitlan and separate saline from fresh waters (Berdan 1982:23; Gomara 1954:144; Soustelle 1961:32).

Of incalculable economic significance was the acquisition by nobility of private lands and the assumption by the state of the right of eminent domain (Caso 1963:868; Kurtz 1974), which could be invoked as state needs required. Following independence from the Tepanecs, the Aztec nobility claimed most of the Tepanec land for themselves, thus acquiring private holdings that were disproportionate to their numbers in Aztec Society (Bray 1977:382; Caso 1963:867; Tezozomoc 1944:35–37). The nobles subsequently augmented these holdings with lands acquired through conquest (Zorita 1963:111–125). By and large, lands of the nobility were worked by tenants.

Almost every Aztec citizen paid some tax to the state, either in work or kind. Corvée labor was required on roads, public buildings, royal palaces, state projects, and the emperor's lands (Zorita 1963:111ff). Artisans paid in kind with goods they produced. Tributes in the form of raw materials, subsistence goods, luxury items, and manufactured products were appropriated from conquered peoples to supplement the state treasury (Chapman 1957; Duran 1964:102; Kurtz 1974). Proceeds from these taxes flowed into the state's coffers and subsidized other state policies.

Some of these revenues were redistributed to the people, although probably less than one half filtered down to Aztec citizens (Kurtz 1974). During famines and droughts the state provided citizens with food from its warehouses (Duran 1964:148). The state gave gifts, awarded titles, and granted rights to land to individuals who served it well (Duran 1964:70), subventions which tended to co-opt their local allegiances. The state obviously was aware of the political credit which it earned through redistribution and subventions.

Markets were the major mechanism by which goods were provided to the people. The market system continued to expand and modernize, subject increasingly to state manipulation and the forces of supply and demand (Kurtz 1974; Sahagun 1950–1969, BK. 8:67–69). People were required by law to attend the markets and sell their produce and goods in them in order to ensure that provisions would be available (Duran 1971:274–276). Markets also were centers for a variety of state activities which complemented their economic functions: public announcements, religious rituals, dispensations of justice. They symbolized the concern of the state with its citizens, as well as its increasing control over their affairs (Duran 1971:273ff; Kurtz 1974). An important step in mobilizing the market system in the service of the state was effected in 1473 when the great market at Tlatelolco was absorbed into the Aztec political economy. Among other benefits, this provided the state with the means to continue expansionist policies aimed at acquiring additional revenues (Duran 1964:78–80, 91ff).

Aztec political economy suggests that a viable economy is imperative in permitting a state to rule and that economic development in early states is conscious, directed, and planned by individuals in power. Only by building an economy that is sound and sensitive to the needs of its people can an inchoate state hope to attain legitimacy. The economy subsidizes the power of the state and the strategies by which it pursues legitimacy.

Social Distance

Following the emergence of the state its leaders attempt to effect a real and cognitive distance between themselves and the polity (Y. A. Cohen 1969; Kurtz 1978, 1981). The distinction between rulers and ruled may be formalized through laws and reflected in differences in life style, moral exclusiveness, ritualized patterns of behavior, myths concerned with descent and exclusiveness, and access to *desiderata*. The establishment of social distance between rulers and ruled serves different functions and seems to be essential to the well-being of the state.

The formalization of behavior distinctive to different categories of

Aztec society probably began during the period of incipient statehood. Descent and myths justifying distinctiveness are important indicators of social distance. Succession to the head of state through a distinctive royal line was established under Huitzilhuitl, the second emperor (Duran 1964:72; Rounds 1979; Zorita 1963:92). After independence from the Tepanecs, myth and legend were used to establish the exclusiveness of the rulers (Duran 1971:299). From the reign of Moctezuma I (1440–1469) emperors were vested with divine status (Caso 1963:865; Duran 1964:168; Sahagun 1950–1969, BK: 6:52).

The law code that Moctezuma I bequeathed the nation established the moral exclusiveness of the rulers (Berdan 1982:37; Caso 1963:867; Duran 1964:118). The first clause of Moctezuma's code asserts that the emperor should not appear in public except on special occasions (Duran 1964:131). Nobles were tried in special courts and for the same offense a noble was punished more severely than a commoner; with greater privilege went greater responsibility (Berdan 1982:49; George 1961; Sahagun 1950–1969, BK. 8:41). Commoners, however, were bound by restrictive sumptuary laws. Nobility were distinguished from commoners by clothing, jewelry, emoluments of prestige, and a sybaritic life style in general (Berdan 1982:49–50; Cortez 1928:66, 77; Duran 1964:129, 131–132; 1971:435; Sahagun 1950–1969, BK. 8:23ff). Ritualized patterns of deference and demeanor between rulers and ruled had become extremely formalized by the reign of Moctezuma II (1502–1520). Commoners were required to relate to nobility in special ways; they had to prostrate themselves before the emperor and were neither permitted to speak nor look at him. Even the nobility approached him bowed, with eyes lowered (Cortez 1928:27; Duran 1964:224; Motolinia 1950:212).

Preferential access to economic *desiderata* by the ruling class, such as land, slaves, tenant farmers, and corvée symbolized the distinction between rulers and ruled and compounded economic differences. Commoners, for example, were not permitted to own more land than they could work in person; nobles could buy and sell land and employ commoners as laborers (Bray 1977:383; Caso 1963). Commoners also were subject to different education than nobles (Berdan 1982:88–90; Zorita 1963:135–136), and were thus allocated to inferior social roles.

Social distance affirms the class structure and symbolically demarcates and distinguishes rulers from commoners. It creates an aura of state authority, enhances the respect and obedience which the state demands, and symbolizes the right of a few to rule many (Y. A. Cohen 1969; Kurtz 1978, 1981). Although social distance reduces potential conflict between rulers and ruled which familiarity is likely to breed, it also entails risk. Physical and cognitive distance between the state and its citizens may impair the identification of citizens with the state and create a credibility crisis. However, proximity of rulers to ruled may reduce the ability of the state to govern, since, as noted, it is unlikely to be able to meet the expectations of its citizens. These risks are ameliorated by other legitimating strategies.

Validation of Authority

The elaboration of a state religion is one of the more dramatic changes that the early state effects. It is a major step in developing the state's values and ideology, and supernatural sanction for legitimate state authority. The linchpins of this institution are state priests. The Aztec state priesthood recruited novitiates from both sexes and apparently all classes of society (Berdan 1982:130) as a means of co-opting local level allegiances. In the forefront of the state's legitimating strategies, priests provided the Aztec state with direct support and served as objects of indirect support for the population at large. They were dedicated to formulating a theology that provided direction to the state, imbued it with a numinous quality, and extolled the virtues of state and nation.

By the time of the Spanish intrusion, Aztec priests were attempting to define the state pantheon more precisely; providing many gods with more specific personalities, and merging attributes of the gods into a more unified concept, perhaps that of a single God (Caso 1937:20; 1958:23). They were attempting to elevate *Huitzilopochtli* to a preeminent place in the pantheon, probably to serve as a unifying symbol for state, nation, and empire (Caso 1937:9). As well as connoting social distance, a correlative symbol of state unity was the deification of the Aztec emperors.

The Aztec state also exploited the strong popular sentiment in central Mexico that the Toltec dynasty was the sacred source of legitimate power and authority. From the time of Acamapichtli, a Toltec prince, Aztec rulers stressed that they were the legitimate heirs of the Toltec Dynasty. State priests, among others, tied Aztec to Toltec myths and legends in order to extend the historical depth of the state (Caso 1958:84; Duran 1964:13ff, 141–143; 1971:299; Sahagun 1959–1960, BK. 2). Some myths, such as those that bound the commoners in service to the rulers following the war of independence, validated the rights of the ruling class and provided a charter for Aztec class structure as it emerged after independence (Duran 1964:57–58).

With the establishment of the state the customary symbols of the rulers' majesty, morality, and responsibility to the gods were elaborated and redefined. At the investiture of the head of state, high priests admonished him of his obligations and duties (Zorita 1963:93–94). Priests could invoke the wrath of the gods upon rulers who were evil or otherwise unfit to rule (Sahagun 1950–1969, BK. 6:25; Zorita 1963:93–94).

A covert but powerful symbol of priestly support for the state was the vow of celibacy. Celibacy symbolizes the total commitment to God and state by a few persons who willingly disenfranchise themselves from mundane society and who place their service to God and state above any concerns for themselves. Whether secular and/or religious, celibacy appears to be sponsored by early states (Y. A. Cohen 1969). During training Aztec novitiates remained celibate; for certain members of the priesthood celibacy may have been a permanent condition (Berdan 1982:131–132).

Consolidation of Authority and Power

The early state consolidates its authority and power by developing legal, political, and religious institutions that convey state values to its citizens, and state agents infiltrate local organizations to ensure their entrenchment. In general, the state attempts to reduce the influence of local organizations on the people and to mobilize its citizens behind its policies. There are three major features to this strategy: the codification of laws and elaboration of legal institutions, extension of state political influence over local affairs, and intervention of the state religion into the religion and affairs at the local level.

LAW. The relationship between the codification of law by early states and the embellishment of formal legal institutions suggests an indispensable legitimating strategy (Kurtz 1981). Early states codify laws for several reasons: (1) to prescribe the behavior of citizens and the relationship between state and citizen; (2) to define citizenship and the rights that derive therefrom; (3) to validate the class structure by providing differential legal treatment for persons of different status; and (4) to legalize the right of the state to act against sources of inchoateness, such as kinship associations and secret societies. An increasing number of crimes are considered to be against the state, a legal interpretation which supercedes traditional law (Kurtz 1981).

Moctezuma I is considered to be the law giver of Aztec society. His code encompasses an array of legal prescriptions and norms, defining among other attributes the mutual obligations between state and citizen (Duran 1964:131; George 1961). Personal vengeance was forbidden; only state agents could exact punishments. Persons who aided a wrongdoer or contributed to a crime were equally responsible with the guilty party. The law code designated crimes against the state and social order, such as treason and unauthorized use of dress or insignia of nobility. Crimes against the moral order included drunkenness, prostitution, and homosexuality. Crimes against persons included homicide, theft, and property damage (Duran 1964:131–132; 1971:282ff; George 1961; Sahagun 1950–1969, BK. 2:100; BK. 8:41–42, BK. 10).

Aztec law was enforced through a hierarchy of courts. Local courts commonly were convened in market places. Above them were an appellate court, a supreme court, and two special courts, one of which heard cases restricted to problems in Tenochtitlan while the other reviewed local court decisions. Military courts disposed of cases against commoners and nobility who committed crimes in time of war (Duran 1964:122; George 1961; Zorita 1963:124ff). Judges appointed by the emperor presided over the courts (Sahagun 1950–1969, BK. 8:54). The emperor was the ultimate judicial authority. He rendered decisions when the special courts reached an impasse and approved all death sentences.

POLITICS.   With sufficient resources and a legally sanctioned right to act the state can extend its political influence and neutralize that of local organizations. Overt opposition by local organizations to state authority is not a prerequisite for preemptive actions by the state. State behavior toward the *calpullis, pochteca,* and nobility suggest that the state perceived them as potential threats. *Calpullis* probably were endogamous clan organizations (Bray 1972:175; Carrasco 1971:363–371) and as such probably claimed the strong allegiance of their members. As state power developed the influence of *calpulli* officials in state government declined, and *calpulli* kinship associations were increasingly subjected to state control (Bray 1972:176; Carrasco 1971:365; Hicks 1982). Able-bodied Aztec males were liable for military service (Berdan 1982:79; Sahagun 1950–1969, BK. 2:212–214). Headmen of noble descent and state priests were appointed by the state to *calpulli* political and religious organizations. Heads of wards were charged with supplying corvée labor and royal edicts were sent to them to be transmitted to the people (Duran 1971:201). Although individuals' rights to land were determined by their status within a *calpulli,* one's status within a *calpulli* increasingly was determined by the state (Hicks 1982).

Upon marriage an individual was inscribed in the *calpulli* register for tax purposes (Carrasco 1971:357; Zorita 1963:367–369). The state may have been restricting polygynous unions (Carrasco 1971:367–368; Duran 1971:435), to reduce the potential to expand kinship structures. Courts were reluctant to grant divorces. These actions reaffirmed the strength of the monogamous household, the social structure that threatens the state least.

The *pochteca* were intimately involved with state economic, military, and political affairs. Some served as judges in courts convened in marketplaces. They also were more powerful and richer than most other Aztec *calpullis* (Sahagun 1950–1969, BKS. 4–5:87). Leadership was hereditary. They had their own courts, judges, gods, rituals, and festivals (Berdan 1982:31–34; Chapman 1957; Sahagun 1950–1969, BK. 9). Because they represented a very firmly bounded social group in possession of considerable power and influence, it is not difficult to see how the state might consider them a potential threat, and why they were subject to state regulations.

The state restricted the interaction of the *pochteca* with other Aztec citizens, functionally segregating them in their own wards. Certain categories of *pochteca* were not allowed to trade in public markets. Others were required to trade only in certain commodities, such as slaves. In general, the economic activities of the *pochteca* took place on behalf of the state in international ports of trade (Chapman 1957; Sahagun 1950–1969, BK. 9:17–18).

The head of state established alliances with neighboring states through marriage (Duran 1971:435; Motolinia 1950:25). This may have been especially important in the early stages of state development. Acamapichtli is reputed to have married twenty daughters of the chiefs of the clans that comprised Aztec society. From these unions presumably descended the original nobility of Aztec society, and some ultimately may have become heads of wards and *calpullis*. Itzcoatl granted titles, privileges, and high offices to his noble relatives, thereafter restricting participation of commoners in state bureaucracies (Caso 1963:866–867; Tezozomoc 1944:35–37). By the reign of Moctezuma II the nobility had grown in size considerably, due largely to the appointment of persons of low status to "knighthood" as reward for service to the state. In a move suggesting that this burgeoning petty nobility may have posed some threat, Moctezuma II removed such entitled nobility from state posts, denied privileges to others, and executed many of questionable birth. The bureaucracy was restructured and access to state offices was denied to all but pedigree nobles (Berdan 1982:46; Carrasco 1971:361; Duran 1964:222–226).

RELIGION. Early states are comprised of state and local level religions that are related dialectically. The state religion sanctifies the legitimacy of state government and is a source of real and symbolic power that the ruling class manipulates to impose its values on all citizens. Local religions validate structures and organizations with which they are associated. Both may be polytheistic but local level polytheism may harbor theologies that provide justification for local organizations that may threaten state authority. Polytheism is a manifestation of inchoateness against which the state reacts.

Aztec religion comprised state and local polytheism (Bray 1977:393).

This condition persisted despite attempts by the state to overcome it. State priests attempted to reduce state and local polytheism and replace or integrate local *calpulli* and kin based religions with the state religion. Yet some of these activities promoted polytheism, for the state had a policy of incorporating the major deities of conquered peoples into its pantheon (Caso 1937:8). While this welded subject peoples into the Aztec state and empire, it also created an increasingly chaotic state pantheon.

The state priesthood was hierarchic. At its apex high priests were dedicated to major gods (Caso 1958:82). The head of state and other high officials also presided as priests in important state ceremonies (Caso 1937:54, 1958:82). State priests were involved in local level affairs and may have exercised a loose suzerainty over the priesthoods of tributary communities, even occasionally imposing Aztec cults upon them (Nicholson 1971:436). Although *calpulli* kin groups worshipped their own gods, state priests infiltrated their cults (Carrasco 1971:363; Caso 1958:90; Duran 1964:32).

Priests forced obedience to state norms, using the threat of divine retribution against nonconformers (Duran 1971:274). Priests attended court to ensure that religious observations concerned with the law were carried out and that justice was dispensed with the approval of the gods (George 1961:39). In some instances oaths to the gods were accepted as truth of the testimony being given (George 1961:39). Priests also serve as judges and military commanders (Caso 1937:54, 59; 1958:85). Complementing the preceding strategies were others aimed at socializing citizens regarding state expectations.

Political Socialization

If efforts by the state to inculcate its citizens with values which will ensure their support were accomplished easily, other legitimating strategies would be unnecessary. The fact that socialization is not accomplished easily is suggested by the investment the state makes in political socialization in material and symbolic resources. Political socialization as explored here differs from what has been assumed previously (see Easton 1965; Greenstein 1965; Weber 1954). As conceptualized here, socialization in early states presumes the complementary and contradictory practices of benevolence, information control, and terror. The state attempts to ensure support by dramatizing what it can do for the loyal citizen (benevolence), what the citizen should do for the state (information), and the consequences for citizens who do not conform to state expectations (terror).

BENEVOLENCE. Wittfogel (1957) suggests that any activities by early states that outwardly appear to benefit the people are designed explicitly to maintain the ruler's power and prosperity and cannot be considered benevolent. Still, considerable evidence suggests that early states do act benevolently toward their citizens, if only to bind citizens to the state (Claessen and Skalnik 1978). But it also is clear that the motivation for benevolence is not always altruism.

Sahagun (1950–1969, BK. 8:59; BK. 10:13) claimed that Aztec rulers and nobles generally were benevolent. Certainly the Aztec state directed several subventions at its citizens, such as distributing food in times of shortage and at certain state ceremonies (Bray 1977:390; Duran 1964:144–147; Sahagun 1950–1969, BK. 8:44). Rewards in titles and land for state service obligated individuals to the state (Duran 1971:174). Public works, such as irrigation, flood control, roads, and temples not only provided goods and services to the citizens (Duran 1971:201), they were symbols of the state's concern with its people. They also had practical consequences. Irrigation and flood control enhanced agricultural production, a major source of state revenue. Roads expedited the movement of goods to market, *pochteca* to trade zones, and troops to conquest (Sahagun 1950–1969, BK. 11:267–268; Zorita 1963:73). Construction and maintenance of temples and other public buildings appeased the gods, organized people's labor according to state directives, and supported priests and other state functionaries. Perhaps more than any other aspect of legitimation, state benevolence fulfills a functional paradigm that depicts reciprocal obligations between state and citizen as a major source of legitimacy (Easton 1965; Parsons 1969).

INFORMATION. Early states controlled the dissemination of selected information among their citizens, aimed in large measure at inculcating them with state values (Y. A. Cohen 1970; Kurtz 1981). The Aztec state maintained a firm control over information (Duran 1964:141–143) and disseminated it in a variety of ways. Aztec markets served as centers of communication because many people could be contacted there at any one time. State edicts and announcements were promulgated in them. Local and high courts convened there and criminals were tried publicly (Kurtz 1974; Sahagun 1950–1969, BK. 2:100).

The state also used schools to convey information to young children. The law code of Moctezuma I declared that all city wards would have schools and prescribed the curriculum (Duran 1964:132). It stressed training in religious and military matters, manners, morals, hard work, and discipline. Priests controlled education in both the *calmecacs* (the schools for noble children) and the *telpochallis* (the schools for commoners) (Caso 1937:60; 1958:89). Religious and military training were stressed in both schools. However, the *calmecacs'* curriculum was more extensive than that of the *telpochallis'* and was concerned with training

judges, priests, administrators, and military leaders. Both males and females received formal education. School attendance for boys, at least, was
compulsory (Berdan 1982:88–90); Carrasco 1971:356–257; Sahagun
1950–1969, BK. 6:209). Females were trained in *calmecacs* to become
priestesses. The instruction in *telpochallis* was an extension of training
received in the home (Sahagun 1950–1969, BK. 6:171ff), and its students
provided a major source of corvée labor for the state (Berdan 1982:90;
Carrasco 1961:485; Sahagun 1950–1969, BK. 8:54). Education above all
was aimed at creating a good citizen. Intellectual curiosity was not stimulated, the inculcation of state values and conformity were the goals (Caso
1937:60; 1958:85–87; George 1961; Sahagun 1950–1969; BK. 6:209;
Torquemada 1964:113–117).

The state also appears to have promoted Nahuatl as a national language from early in the 15th century (Offner 1979). By the 16th century
it apparently was attempting to establish it as a *lingua franca* for the
central highlands (Heath 1972). The imposition of a national language
would be an important unifying force for the nation. To what extent
Aztec schools were promoting this is not clear.

Information also may be conveyed through other channels. Public
trials and punishments, for example, symbolize the consequences for
nonconformity. These and other activities are best considered in the final
mode of socialization—state terror.

TERROR. The value of terror as a means of socialization is summed
up in the saying attributed to an anonymous Chinese of the Confucian
era: "Kill one, frighten ten thousand." State activities that evoke terror
among citizens convey a message regarding consequences for nonconformity. Terror may be an aspect of the politics of any state; it occurs most
commonly when the legitimacy of an established state is threatened or
when a state is extremely inchoate. Under these conditions the state tries
to regulate areas of its citizens' behavior that in more secure states by and
large are overlooked.

State terror in Aztec society increased after the Tepanec war. While it
is difficult to measure this terror, or ascertain variations in its application,
by the reign of Moctezuma II state terror had increased noticeably. During his reign spying on Mexican citizens as well as potential enemies was
common state practice (Duran 1964:210ff, 227–229; Sahagun 1950–
1959, BK. 8:57).

One characteristic of terror in early states is a severity of punishment
exceeding what might seem to be just and reasonable. Theoretically
punishment demonstrates the power of the state. The Aztec state prescribed death for crimes such as theft, drunkenness, fornication, adultery,
and others (Berdan 1982:96–98; Duran 1964:131–132, 223, 1971:124,

282ff; George 1961; Motolinia 1950:75; Sahagun 1950–1969, BK. 2:100; BK. 8:43, 69). Most executions were public and carried out in market places. Although execution for theft might be understandable, the concern the state had with its citizens' drinking habits and sexual activity is more difficult to explain. Perhaps if a state thinks it can control fundamental areas of its citizens' affective behavior, it has taken a giant stride toward control of other, less affective areas of their lives, such as their productive labors.

The state held extended kin jointly liable for certain transgressions by their members, especially if they were sufficiently heinous to nullify the individual's right to citizenship. For lesser offenses an individual's family might suffer to the extent that their house was destroyed (Sahagun 1950–1969, BK. 8:44). For more serious offenses, such as treason or aiding a traitor, the offender might be executed, all family property confiscated, and kin subjected to punishment (Berdan 1982:38; George 1961; Sahagun 1950–1969, BK. 8:44, 57; Zorita 1963:132).

The nobility was not exempt from subtle forms of persuasion. From the reign of Moctezuma I, each emperor required that a certain number of lords and children of lords attend the court for part of each year (Cortez 1928:94; Zorita 1963:104, 111, 160). While the purpose for this service is not clear, enforced attendance at court does encourage obedience and allegiance of the nobility (Befu 1965). Aztec courtiers who did not comport themselves appropriately might be killed (Duran 1964:223). In effect, courtiers became state hostages.

Although the most common explanations for human sacrifice among the Aztecs center around religious activity and, more recently, ecological considerations (Harner 1977), political explanations have been rare. Bourdillon (1980:23) and Berdan (1982:111–118) recognize a connection between human sacrifice and political power in states. Although Aztec human sacrifice clearly had religious import, for them and other early states generally it was also an exercise in the demonstration and use of political power and a subtle feature of the repertoire of terror the state employed in the socialization of its citizens. This is suggested by several factors.

Aztec human sacrifice was public, justified, enforced legally, religiously sanctioned, and conducted on behalf of the state. It increased steadily after the Tepanac war and seemed to correspond to Aztec territorial expansion (Berdan 1982:118; Kinman 1952). Sacrifice also was carried out at all Aztec state and religious functions and at the death of heads of state and other important functionaries (Kinman 1952: Sahagun 1950–1969, BK. 2). State priests, the head of state, and other important officials actively participated in it (Duran 1964:178; Kinman 1952). Berdan

162 DONALD V. KURTZ

(1982: 112) comments that "Everyone was a potential candidate for sacrifice." But individuals whose status as citizens was clear and unambiguous almost never were sacrificed. Common sacrificial victims were prisoners of war, criminals, slaves, children and adults of both sexes (Berdan 1982:114; Kinman 1952; Motolinia 1950:63–66; Sahagun 1950– 1969, BK. 2). War prisoners clearly were not citizens. Sacrifice of prisoners demonstrated Aztec political power and hegemony. On occasion, enemy heads of state were invited to Aztec ceremonies where they watched the sacrifice of their own captured warriors (Duran 1964:194– 195). While their sacrifice may have had religious connotations, their deaths also demonstrated the fate of those who defied Aztec military might (Hicks 1982). Thus human sacrifice was an important symbolic aspect of Aztec state politics.

As social undesirables criminals held dubious citizenship, as they do in most states. Slaves often had been criminals, as well as debtors and indigents. Neither slaves nor criminals fulfilled normative expectations of the ideal Aztec citizen (Sahagun 1950–1969, BK. 10, BK. 6). Sacrifice of these individuals also tended to demonstrate state power and convey a message regarding the possible fate of anyone who did not live up to Aztec ideals of citizenship.

More ambiguous is the sacrifice of children and adults. Religious considerations well may have been pre-eminently important in these contexts. Still, in state societies generally, children rarely are considered to be full, responsible citizens. Further, Aztec adults prior to their sacrifice were symbolically divested of their human social status (*ergo* citizenship) and allocated that of a surrogate deity. The fact that mature, responsible individuals holding a clear and unambiguous status of citizen rarely were sacrificed suggests a subtle symbolic relationship between state and citizen. A good citizen was made a god prior to sacrifice; a less desirable person was expendable.

Many aspects of terror are more symbolic than real. While the right to employ terror is legally sanctioned, to what extent coercive laws are enforced is not always clear, or even important. There is little evidence that joint liability or the death penalty for adultery were used commonly but it is important that such laws were codified. They can be applied as the state deems necessary.

Conclusions

This paper has explored the process by which the Aztec state attempted to attain legitimacy. The focus has been upon legitimation, not on legitimacy. The paper suggests that support is a key concept for understanding legitimation. Legitimation is accomplished through a series of strategies by which the state attempts to acquire the support and allegiance of its citizens.

The legitimation of a state is based on its ability to control sufficient resources and mobilize its citizen's labors and its nation's institutions and to permit it to create and manipulate an array of uncommon symbols. State economic policies are aimed at increasing production above per capita requirements of the population. Surplus goods and commodities are mobilized by the state and provide it with the means to pursue legitimating strategies, a major goal of which is the reduction of the influence of local level organization upon the citizens. Symbols intervene and imbue every phase of the process. Their interdigitation with the material aspects of legitimation appears to be necessary for the state to attain legitimacy.

Legitimating strategies do not follow one upon the other. Perhaps the only necessary first step is increased state control over the nation's economy. This provides the state with resources that permit it to pursue other strategies which, ideally, interact systemically in a positive feedback. If legitimation is successful inchoateness is reduced and legitimacy is increased. Some states are more successful than others but few states become indelibly legitimate. Legitimation is an ongoing process. It is never a permanent condition. Some states are more successful than others.

NOTE

1. I thank Hans Claessen, Jean-Claude Mueller, Sudarshan Seneviratne, Bill Washabaugh, and Pat Gray for critical comments on this paper.

BIBLIOGRAPHY

Adams, R. Mc. 1966. Evolution of Urban Society. Chicago.

Befu, H. 1965. Village Autonomy and Articulation with the State. Journal of Asian Studies 25:19–32.

Berdan, F. 1982. The Aztecs of Central Mexico: An Imperial Society. New York.

Bourdillon, M. F. C. 1980. Introduction. Sacrifice, eds. M.F.C. Bourdillon and M. Forces, pp. 1–28. London.

Bray, W. 1972. The City State in Central Mexico at the Time of the Spanish Conquest. Journal of Latin American Studies 4:161–185.

———. 1977. Civilizing the Aztecs. The Evolution of Social Systems, ed. J. Friedman and M. H. Rowlands, pp. 373–398. London.

Calnek, E. 1972. Settlement Patterns and Chinampa Agriculture at Tenochtitlan. American Antiquity 37:104–115.

Carrasco, P. 1961. The Civil-Religious Hierarchy in Mesoamerican Communities: Pre-Spanish Background and Colonial Development. American Anthropologist 68:483–497.

———. 1971. Social Organization of Ancient Mexico. Handbook of Middle American Indians: Archaeology of Northern Mesoamerica, Part I, pp. 349–375.

Caso, A. 1937. The Religion of the Aztecs. Mexico City.

———. 1958. The Aztecs: People of the Sun. Translated by Lowell Dunham. Norman.

———. 1963. Land Tenure Among the Ancient Mexicans. American Anthropologist 65:863–878.

Chapman, A. 1957. Port of Trade Enclaves in Aztec and Maya Civilizations. Trade and Market in the Early Empires, ed. K. Polanyi, C. Arensberg, and H. Pearson, pp. 114–153. Glencoe.

Claessen, H.J.M., and P. Skalnik. 1978. The Early State. The Hague.

Cohen, Abner. 1969. Political Anthropology: The Analysis of the Symbolism of Power. Man 4:217–235.

———. 1974. Two Dimensional Man. Berkeley.

Cohen, Y. A. 1969. Ends and Means in Political Control: State Organization and the Punishment for Adultery, Incest, and Violation of Celibacy. American Anthropologist 71:658–687.

———. 1970. Schools and Civilizational States. The Social Sciences and the Comparative Study of Educational Systems, ed. J. Fischer, pp. 55–147. Scranton.

Cortez, H. 1928. Five Letters: 1519–1526. Translated by J. Bayard Morris, ed. Sir E. Dennison Ross and Eileen Power. London.

Duran, Fray D. 1964. The Aztecs: The History of the Indians of New Spain. Translated with notes by Doris Heyden and Fernando Horcasitas. London.

———. 1971. Book of the Gods and Rites and the Ancient Calendar. Translated and edited by Fernando Horcasitas and Doris Heyden. Norman.

Easton, D. 1965. A Systems Analysis of Political Life. New York. Firth, R. 1973. Symbols: Public and Private. Ithaca.

George, R. H. 1961. Crime and Punishment in Aztec Society: An Examination of the Criminal Law-Ways of the Aztecs as a Reflection of Their Dominant Value Orientation. Unpublished masters thesis. Mexico City College (Currently University of Americas).

Gomara de, F. 1954. Historia General de las Indias. Segunda Parte obras Maestras. Barcelona.

Greenstein, F. I. 1965. Children and Politics. New Haven.

Harner, M. 1977. The Ecological Basis for Aztec Sacrifice. American Ethnologist 4:117–135.

Heath, S. B. 1972. Telling Tongues: Language Policy in Mexico, Colony to Nation. New York.

Hicks, F. 1979. 'Flowery War' in Aztec History. American Ethnologist 6:87–92.

————. 1982. Tetzcoco in the 16th Century: The State, The City, and the *Calpoli*. American Ethnologist 9:230–249.

Kinman, K. M. 1952. Historiography of Human Sacrifice among the Aztecs and Mayas. A Special Topic Paper Presented to the Graduate Council of the Centro de Estudios Universitarios of the Mexico City College in Partial Fulfillment of the Requirements for the Degree of Master of Arts.

Kurtz, D. V. 1974. Peripheral and Transitional Markets: The Aztec Case. American Ethnologist 1:685–706.

————. 1978. The Legitimation of the Aztec State. The Early State, eds. H.J.M. Claessen and P. Skalnik, pp. 169–190. The Hague.

————. 1981. The Legitimation of Inchoate States. The Study of the State, eds. H.J.M. Claessen and P. Skalnik, pp. 177–200. The Hague.

Motolinia, T. 1950. History of the Indians of New Spain. Translated and edited by Elizabeth Andros Foster. Westport.

Nettl, J. P. 1967. Political Mobilization: A Sociological Analysis of Methods and Concepts. London.

Nicholson, H. B. 1971. Religion in Pre-Hispanic Central Mexico. Handbook of Middle American Indians: Archaeology of Northern Mexico, Part I. 10: 395–446.

Offner, J. A. 1979. A Reassessment of the Extent and Structuring of the Empire of Techotlalatzin, Fourteenth Century Ruler of Texcoco. Ethnohistory: 231–241.

Orenstein, H. 1980. Asymmetrical Reciprocity: A Contribution to the Theory of Political Legitimacy. Current Anthropology 21:69–91.

Parsons, T. 1969. Politics and Social Structure. New York.

Rounds, J. 1979. Lineage, Class, and Power in the Aztec State. American Ethnologist 6:73–86.

Sahagun de, B. 1950–1969. Florentine Codex: General History of the Things of New Spain (12 books). Translated by A.J.O. Anderson and C. E. Dibble. Santa Fe, N.M. and Salt Lake City, Utah (originally written in 1569).

Soustelle, J. 1961. Daily Life of the Aztecs on the Eve of the Spanish Conquest. Stanford.

Swartz, M., V. Turner, and A. Tuden. 1966. Political Anthropology. Chicago.

Tezozomoc de, H. A. 1944. Cronica Mexicana. Notas de Manuel Orozco y Berra. Mexico.

Torquemada de, Fray J. 1964. Monarquia Indiana. Mexico.

Weber, M. 1954. Max Weber on Law in Economy and Society. Translated by S. Shils and M. Rheinstein. Edited by M. Rheinstein. Twentieth Century Legal Series, Vol. 6, Cambridge.

Webster, D. L. 1976. On Theocracies. American Anthropologist 78:812–828.

Wittfogel, K. 1957. Oriental Despotism: A Comparative Study of Total Power. New Haven.

Zorita de, A. 1963. Life and Labor in Ancient Mexico: The Brief and Summary Relation of the Lords of New Spain. Translated and with an Introduction by Benjamin Keen. New Brunswick.

The Structure of Violence
Among the Swat Pukhtun[1]

Charles Lindholm

*Violence is never the sole means of control within a society, but it is
a frequent method of resolving conflict or exerting power. In state
societies, violence is the prerogative of the power structure and not
allocated to smaller groupings within a society. In nonstate societies,
violence is not controlled on a societal level, and feud and blood
revenge is carried out by discrete units, usually kin groupings,
within the society. Obviously, many factors affect the degree and frequency of violence in societies, and the frequency rate of violence
varies from ethnographic area to ethnographic area. The literature
demonstrates that the Middle East is an area where violence is employed for many reasons. From Lindholm's article, one can deduce
that the relations between groups and individuals rely heavily upon
overt conflict for regulations and status. One may hypothesize that
the instability between social groupings is one factor that influences
the frequency and that the disparity of power relationships between
individuals induces violence.*

*The violence described by Lindholm centers on cleavages of
factions that express struggles centered on land and followers. The
violence may be symptomatic of an incomplete and uneven state
presence in Swat Valley and the contentions that are expressed in a
fragmented and localized power struggle.*

VIOLENCE, STRUCTURED THROUGH institutions of feud and warfare,
is perhaps the most important formative element in Middle Eastern segmentary lineage societies. As organizations of "disequilibrium in equilibrium" (Hart 1970:74), these societies become coherent in relations of

lineage opposition. In other words, "The tribe is not organized except for offence and defence; except in war and in matters ultimately connected with war, the licence of individual freewill is absolutely uncontrolled" (Robertson-Smith 1903:68).

The ideal form of the patrilineal segmentary lineage system unites groups and individuals through descent from a common male ancestor. Those who share an ancestor are obliged by the tie of blood to defend one another against outsiders or more distant relatives. In theory, coalitions in opposition can unite thousands, or even millions, of putative lineal relatives in warfare, as the British, French and, more recently, Soviet colonialists have discovered. The same mechanism operates as well at the very lowest level of the genealogy, grouping brothers against patrilateral parallel cousins. In its ideal form the system has a boundless capacity for fusion and fission, "since even the nuclear family is a miniature of the larger social system" (Murphy and Kasdan 1959:27).

But the ideal pattern in which every segment at every level is structurally equivalent is mitigated in reality by differentiation in the vital matters of revenge and warfare. Among the Bedouin of Cyrenaica, for example, the nuclear family is not responsible for blood vengeance. That duty falls upon the coresident lineage segment which is related to the victim up to the fourth or fifth ascending generation. Likewise, the members of this group share blood money and are held culpable for any homicide committed by a member (Peters 1960:31). More inclusive segments function only as landholding units and rarely, if ever, unite in blood disputes, while lineage groups within the coresident segment appear to fission rather than fight. A similar distinction is seen in Iraq (Fernea 1970). In fact, violence against close agnatic relatives is generally disallowed in Middle Eastern societies, though the rule is sometimes very laxly observed, as among the Berbers of the Rif where "vengeance killings within agnatic lineage groups... occurred too often simply to be dismissed as exceptions to the rule" (Hart 1970:70).

Among the Pukhtun people of Swat in Northern Pakistan violence is more highly structured than in the cases reported elsewhere in the Middle East. The Pukhtun of Swat are the descendents of nomads who conquered the region some 400 years ago, reducing the local inhabitants to helots. The Pukhtun themselves became sedentary agriculturalists, relying on their own labor and that of their dependents to produce subsistence crops of rice, wheat, and, later, maize. Land now is scarce, but this problem appears to be fairly recent. Traditionally, the region was one of "ordered anarchy" with numerous and ephemeral small-scale leaders in every village, each deriving his position from personal ability and strength. Early in the twentieth century a central government was superimposed over this structure of shifting alliances (Barth 1959a; Ahmed 1976; Wadud 1963), but in the last decade this government has weakened considerably, allowing the old segmentary system to reassert itself (Lindholm 1979).

Within this setting relations between groups and between individuals are structured in large measure by degrees of violence. Inside the nuclear family, men and women confront one another in a continuous struggle for dominance. Women, as incoming wives, seek to retain their lineage honor and to control their new home. For men, the task is to subdue the wife or, failing that, to humiliate her. The husband has the trump card in this battle, since he can take a second wife, thereby shaming the first and all her lineage. The woman's response may be violent, as she is not allowed divorce. Overt fighting, as well as covert use of magical spells against her rival, are the woman's weapons. Should she fail to drive out her cowife, she may vindicate herself by poisoning her husband, and men with two wives who die of "cholera" are often rumored to have been murdered, although public accusations are rarely made.

On their side, men are permitted and encouraged to beat their wives regularly. Only if bones are broken is a woman allowed to flee to her family, and even then she must return to her husband after a year or so. Outright murder of wives, however, is very uncommon, since her lineage would avenge her death. The few cases of wife murder involved women without close male relatives. But there is a caveat to the rule of lineage vengeance for the death of a lineage woman; if the woman has been sexually promiscuous or acted in a manner which is scandalous, her own patriline will reject and even shoot her. (For more complete data on Pukhtun marriage see Lindholm & Lindholm 1979.)

Violence in the nuclear family is not limited to husband and wife. Fathers, sons, and brothers have relations of hostility, despite the formal respect and service the younger must always offer the elder. In a relationship typical of patrilineal society (Denich 1974), brothers are rivals for the father's land and squabble among themselves and with the father for a share. These conflicts, though causing ill-feeling, do not often end in real fighting because a man's brothers and father are his most certain allies in any outside clash and it would be self-defeating to kill them. As an example, there is one case within recent memory of my informants where a man did kill his brother. The motive was greed for the brother's wealth and lust for the brother's wife, who was the killer's accomplice. The killer inherited both and was safe from revenge since he himself was the closest relative of the murdered man. But without allies he was unable to protect his gains, and a local strong man deprived him of his property and his new wife, and drove him from the village.

Killings of fathers and sons are more frequent than killings of brothers. Two fathers were reportedly killed by their sons in recent memory, and there was an attempt by a son to kill his father during the time of field-work. The attempt failed, and the son is presently in jail on his father's complaint. In another case during the fieldwork, a large landlord shot and killed his son because the son had refused to give a share of his rice harvest to the father's mother, the victim's own grandmother. The wife of the dead man asked that the killer be prosecuted, but her brothers-in-law pressed her to drop the case, which she was obliged to do. These cases were all over land, but sexual jealousy and seduction of wives within the extended family also can cause murder, as Ahmed (1980) notes.

Violence within the family is thus of two types: that directed towards affines and that directed towards agnates. The former is part of a larger pattern of lineage enmity which is acted out in the hostile relationship of husband and wife and may lead to a feud if the wife is killed without sufficient cause. The latter derives from internal rivalry over property and women and may also escalate to murder, but does not involve revenge, since the killing has been committed by the closest possible agnate.

The next level of violence is between close patrilateral parallel cousins. This is the most deadly relationship in Swat. Of the seventeen killings of men by men which I recorded during fieldwork, seven were killings either of close patrilateral parallel cousins or of the servants of these cousins. In addition, there were numerous fights between cousins which ended short of killing. The tension between cousins is such that the kinship term of reference, *tarbur,* is synonymous with "enemy."[2] The enmity between cousins derives from their claims to the land of their common grandfather. Their holdings are adjacent, and each will try to push the holdings of the other back by trickery or force. As an example, two cousins had neighboring plots. The cousin whose field was more distant from the village walked to his field on an ancient pathway which verged on the plot of his *tarbur.* There was a simmering dispute over the right to this narrow path which ended in gunfight and the death of one of the men's sons.

Disputes express or question dominance and power. It is an axiom among the Pukhtun that *tarbur* do not fear one another. A man whose cousin has become wealthy and powerful will feel pressure to pick a fight with him to display his own strength. The most devastating feud ongoing during fieldwork was one which began with a boy's refusal to let his second cousin play soccer with him. This insult led to a fight which spread to the boys' fathers. At the close of the fieldwork three men were dead and the fields of both families had either been sold for weapons or else left fallow as the remaining men sought to eliminate their rivals.

Among elite Pukhtun who have a claim to local leadership, a feud must be carried through to its bitter conclusion, which usually entails the ruin of all the participants.[3] Outsiders, who are jealous of a dominant family, will sometimes try to precipitate such a feud. In one village, unauthorized use of a room in the men's house by some young men for a rendezvous with a prostitute led to a beating by the owner of the room, who was the uncle (FFBS) of the young men. This was followed by a series of escalating retaliatory actions, culminating in the jailing of one of the young men. Soon thereafter, the uncle's valuable stand of apple tree saplings was cut down in the middle of the night. The village waited to see what the uncle, a notoriously bad-tempered man, would do, but, after consultation with his brothers, he decided to do nothing. "Thank Allah, I have many enemies," he told me, "they would like to see me ruined in a fight with my *tarbur*. Perhaps these enemies cut down my trees." This case exemplifies a repeated motif in Swati politics; that is, the role of the manipulatory third party.

Although the elite must maintain a feud to the last man, less powerful lineages may allow themselves to be pressured to reach a settlement. In the case of the cousins feuding over the pathway, the village *jirga* (council of elders from elite families) prevailed on the father of the dead boy to accept a blood payment and forswear revenge against his *tarbur*. The opponents in this case were clients of local Pukhtun patrons who feared that they might be drawn into an escalating conflict. They therefore pressed their clients to accept a truce. A similar case concerned two landless cousins employed by rival Pukhtun as tenant farmers on adjoining strips of land. A fight between the client families ended in the death of two men, but the patrons forced a reconciliation.

It is important for the *jirga* to reach a compromise in cases involving poor clients since the honor of the patron is at stake. Even in fights which have nothing to do with his interests, a patron is obliged to enter the fight on his client's behalf in order to keep his credibility as a leader. Fights between servants, like fights between children, can lead to destructive battles between Pukhtun families. Every effort, therefore, is made to arbitrate fights among clients.

Barth (1959a) and Ahmed (1976) provide extensive discussions of the role of so-called saints in mediating disputes in Swat. My data suggest that such figures, who are generally non-Pukhtun claiming a religious heritage, do not intervene in disputes within a village between cousins. If the disputants are poor or weak, then the village *jirga* will try to mediate; if the participants are Pukhtun, particularly if they are elite Pukhtun with pretensions to leadership, no mediation is attempted. It is considered inevitable that the fight will end in the death or exile of one family and the financial ruin of the other. Saints, it seems, mediate in disputes which go beyond the village limits.

Unlike the Berbers cited by Hart (1970), the Pukhtun do not consider violence between near patrilineal relatives to be abnormal. Furthermore, in contradistinction to the cases considered by Fernea (1970) and Peters (1960), Swat Pukhtun take revenge directly on the man who committed the murder and perhaps, after he has been killed, on his sons and father as well. The notion of group responsibility is not developed, and retaliation, even in cases which do not involve *tarbur*, is directed to specific individuals. Pukhtun will wait many years to take revenge on a particular person. For example, a man was killed in a fight in the early 1950s. His killer offered the victim's family blood money, which was accepted. But for a Pukhtun, blood money, or even the donation of a woman, is never adequate compensation for death. Blood demands blood. Thus, after nearly thirty years, the son of the murdered man killed his father's killer while the old man was lying, helpless and immobile, in a hospital bed.[4] This act, which led to the permanent exile of the killer, was much praised by the Pukhtun men.

It is evident from the above history that vengeance need not involve daring. Rather, it is accomplished by stealth or betrayal. Courage is not in the act of killing so much as it is in the willingness to take the ruinous consequences for the sake of cleansing one's honor.

Rivalry between cousins and the focusing of revenge on individuals and nuclear families instead of on larger groups limits the escalation of blood feuds in Swat. Other forms of violence, however, involve more inclusive groups both inside and outside the village.

All Swati villages are divided into neighborhoods (*palao*). A very small village may have only one *palao*, but most have three. Two of the *palao* are generally larger and more powerful than the third. Each neighborhood in turn is subdivided into *tul*, or wards, also usually three in number. These *tul* are dominated by and named after a particular leader who, with his close relatives and clients, heads a faction which must be represented in village *jirgas*. The *tuls* in a neighborhood, though in opposition, can join together in action against another *palao*. Of course, all is not peaceful within the *tul* either, as *tarbur* compete with one another for leadership and prestige. Thus the political organization of the village is perhaps best conceived as small circles of patrilineal kin, residing near one another, and acting together in opposition to other circles of the same scale.

Complementing and complicating the formal segmentary system is a dualistic party structure (*dullah*) which cross-cuts the *tuls* and *palao*. It strongly resembles the *liff* alliances of the Berbers (Montagne 1973).

Gellner (1969:67) doubts the existence of the *liff* at the village level, and claims the system functions, if it functions at all, between villages. Hart (1970:42–45) also sees the *liff* working primarily to balance the uneven distribution of power within tribal units by means of external alliances. He (Hart 1980:45) notes that " 'temporary' *liff*... operating within a clan, a subclan, or a local community, could and did shift and change." The Pukhtun, like the Berbers, speak of the dual parties as if they were concrete entities; indeed, each individual sees the tribal world divided into those who are for and those who are against his party. In Swat, the parties are named after their local leader's clan, so that the parties have different names throughout the valley. Each village *dullah* connects with a web of alliances throughout the region so that a powerful leader will be able to name members of his party in 50 villages or more.

These parties are not formally structured. They are simply a statement, couched in universal and abstract terms, of the fluid oppositions and alliances of individuals. A man sees his party as a tool in his own personal struggle against his enemies, particularly his *tarbur*. Barth (1959a:2) states that enmity between cousins takes precedence over segmentary merging in Swat; "the opposition between small, closely related segments persists in the wider context, and these segments unite with similar small segments in a pattern of two party opposition, not in a merging series of descent segments." In this Barth has reified individual strategy into a structural principle and has incorrectly given impermanent alliances priority over the principle of the unity of patrilineal segments. In actual fact, party alliances are set aside in cases of blood revenge. No man would support the murderer of his *tarbur* under any circumstances, even if the killer were a longtime party ally. The limited range of revenge rights obscures, but does not obliterate, the unity of blood groups in Swat. While a man may not actively seek vengeance for a wrong done to a cousin, he certainly would not stand in the way of revenge being taken[5] because the *tarbur* is not only one's enemy but also, in the proper circumstances, a reliable support. A man without *tarbur* stands naked to the assaults of genealogically more distant enemies, and while strong *tarbur* provoke jealousy they also evoke pride and confidence.

Barth's (1959b) overvaluation of the opposition between cousins results in a static picture of Pukhtun social structure; oppositions balance out in a no-win game as the manipulations and defections of players tend toward stalemate. This long-term leveling process is institutionalized in the dyadic *dullah* system. But in pursuing his analysis, Barth ignores the triadic patterning of *palao* and *tul* and the dialectical development of differential power relations institutionalized within these forms. In the long run, Barth's picture of stalemate is accurate, but in the short run good players gain positions of dominance and prestige. Obviously, some families become strong simply by out-reproducing others; some men are particularly brave, intelligent, or Machiavellian; and some clans are lucky or skilled at manipulation. Uneven development belies the picture of balance offered by Barth's concentration on the party system.

The mechanisms of party formation provide a processual view of Swati political process. Certainly a man opposes his *tarbur*, but he often has several *tarbur*. He has a choice of enemies and allies and joins or wars with his cousins according to his own advantage. The shifting dyad covers a triadic form consisting of ego, his momentary allies and his momentary enemies. This same pattern is found at every level of Swati society. For example, although each village is divided into two parties, the party lines do not simply bisect the village. Rather, one *palao* will mostly follow the party of its most able *tul* leader, a second *palao* will mostly support the rival party, while a third *palao,* weaker in numbers, will oscillate between the two sides, playing off the opponents and hoping they will exhaust themselves in the combat. The same pattern is repeated with the *palaos* themselves as the three *tuls* vie for dominance. At a regional level, the motif again recurs. Regions are usually made up of three "brother" clans; two strong and one weak, which are cross-cut by *dullah* alliances. At all these levels the potential power of the weak but manipulative third party is evident,[6] and the role of the troublemaker, discussed earlier, is a structural concomitant of the Swati social order.

Within the village politically violent action is always possible but rarely occurs. A murder, whatever the cause, leads to revenge. As mentioned above, political alliances then drop away and the affair becomes one of feud between two nuclear families. Much more likely in village politics was exile. Should one family become overwhelmingly powerful, their disgruntled *tarbur* would flee the village to find temporary refuge with a nearby ally. The refugees would encourage their host to plan warfare on their home village in hopes of humbling their proud relatives.

Exile, while sometimes lengthy, was almost always impermanent. The exiled party was never totally accepted by its hosts on the grounds that "a man who would betray his own kin would certainly betray us as well." Furthermore, the exiles had no rights in land in their host's territory, while their claim to land within their own village continued in force. Eventually, the exiles would tire of living on charity and return home to claim their patrimony. Sometimes they had to return as supplicants, but more often they were invited back by their *tarbur* in order to strengthen the manpower of the village. Occasionally, the exiles returned as members of an invading army and used the strength of their new position as conquerors to settle old grievances.

Violence between villages varies according to the genealogical distance between them. Villages which are closely related have a ritualized form of warfare which formerly occurred at the close of Ramadan, the Muslim month of fasting. The villages were paired according to genealogical and spatial proximity—the two attributes are considered isomorphic in Swat—and the young men would meet in a field to fight with slingshots. There were always a number of injuries and sometimes a death. No revenge was taken for these fatalities, which were seen as accidental. In these fights the youth of the whole village participated together regardless of party affiliation.

Fighting between more distantly related villages was considerably more violent and was known by the people themselves as *jang* (warfare). Whereas ritual war was within the group of "brother" villages, real warfare was between "brothers." It was to these more distant villages, who could wage real warfare, that exiles fled. Fatalities in these wars could be quite high, as the fighting parties rallied their allies and bodyguards for attacks on opposition strongholds. Deaths in such wars, however, did not involve revenge or even lasting enmity. Conversely, killings committed by turncoat *tarbur* who had joined the enemy were avenged. For example, in the last great intervillage war (around 1900) one ambitious man joined the village's enemies. With his help, the enemy group invaded the exile's home village, and during the occupation, the traitor killed two of his cousin's bodyguards and destroyed a great deal of property. Later, with the aid of allies and defections from the enemy, the defeated party regained strength and recaptured its home base, once again balancing the regional distribution of power. The exile was banished by his allies, who did not want the responsibility of protecting him from vengeance. He was obliged to return home and allow two of his sons to be killed in compensation for his crimes. He accepted this punishment as just, rejoined the village jirga, and retained a position of prestige in the village. His grandsons are presently among the most powerful men in their neighborhood. It is significant that the exile's erstwhile allies were not held responsible for deaths which occurred in this war. Also noteworthy is the Swat attitude toward betrayal. The exile, having failed to win power by manipulation within the village, took the risk of moving the conflict onto the intervillage arena. His treachery was seen locally merely as a political ploy which failed and not as anything particularly reprehensible. This matter-of-fact attitude toward betrayal, so difficult for the Westerner to understand, is simply a realistic acceptance of the structurally motivated individualism of Swati politics.

The causes of large-scale wars seem generally to have focused on exiles. Men who had killed a *tarbur* or women who had shamed their husbands would flee to the protection of a powerful family, which was obliged to offer protection. If this refuge was violated by enemies of the refugee, then the host might become involved in a feud with people who were remotely related to him. Such an event could bring together very large lineage/village groups (Barth, 1959a:122). Also, exiles could instigate a war by throwing themselves on the mercy of their host and demanding that he avenge any wrong which had been done them.

Of course, as Sillitoe (1978) notes, political leaders can manipulate situations to further their own political ambitions. Ambitious and courageous men with aptitudes for strategy favored warfare since it increased their local authority and prestige. The role of the protector, however, is ambiguous and malleable. He can choose to stress his place as mediator between the refugee and his or her pursuers. As a supposedly disinterested outsider, he could try to work out some sort of settlement to end the situation amicably. Or, conversely, he could use the exile's complaints to justify beginning a war. Then again, the ability of the host to use the situation for his own advantage is limited by external circumstance as well. A host who is reluctant to fight will be forced to it should the refugee be attacked, for instance.

The rewards of war at this level were primarily for renown. Certainly there were material benefits of success, and Swati elders recall pillaging the fields of defeated villages. But homes were never ransacked, and men forced into exile left their valuables in the care of local religious men with the full expectation of returning to reclaim them. Rather than wealth, the winner's prize was the carved columns to the loser's men's house, which were carried away as emblems of victory. Successful warriors did not expect to hold on to their conquered territory, since their very success meant that former allies would defect, join the defeated group, and rebalance the system. The end result of the several intervillage wars recorded was a "great name" for the war leaders and their families, but no apparent aggrandizement of their property.

It is in situations of intervillage war that the saintly class of religious mediators became arbitrators. While the village *jirga* mediated disputes between nonelite within the village, and feuds between proud *tarbur* were left to run their tragic, but quite restricted, course, war between villages could not cease without the intervention of an external noncombatant saint, whose mediation allowed both sides to back off without undue loss of face. The fact that these mediators were rewarded with land grants which lay between the potentially warring villages indicates both the primary role of the saints and the relative lack of land pressure during the era of warfare. It is noteworthy that this land was reclaimed by strong Pukhtun clans several generations later when land pressure began to be felt. This reclamation did not infringe on the property rights of anyone except the dispossessed saints and so did not lead to increased warfare. Thus, by removing land from the tribal property and deeding it to weak saintly lineages, the Pukhtun, consciously or otherwise, provided themselves with a land reserve from which powerful lineages could draw in the future without violating the rights of any group that could offer serious resistance.

This is not to suggest that land pressure does not lead to warfare. In fact, fighting occurring in Swat between Pukhtun landlords and their tenants is directly related to land pressure. The Pukhtun, increasing in population, often wish to remove their tenants or to increase tenant rents. The tenants, encouraged by a stress on tenant's rights under the mildly socialist regime of the Pakistan People's Party (which fell in 1977) now claim the land as their own. The weakness of the military government in Swat has allowed tenant revolts in the region to persist, but this type of warfare between classes is new to Swat. Previous battles were between proud Pukhtun leaders who fought for lineage pride and prestige. In this earlier form of war neither land nor property was permanently confiscated, and looting of produce was sporadic and not of great importance in terms of subsistence, as evidence by the absence of reports of hunger during intervillage wars.

In the past, there was another type of warfare which was much more destructive. This was war between regions, and it grew from the same causes which led to intervillage war; that is, the exile of a group which then sought the intervention of an external third party to redress the balance of power. In this case, the third party entering the fray was not simply another village, but another district. In Swat, as I have argued elsewhere (Lindholm 1977), the external third party was the State of Dir. Dir ruled by hereditary kings, gladly provided sanctuary for Swati exiles. Under favorable circumstances, the army of Dir would join with the exiles, invade Upper Swat, and establish rule there. But Dir was not content simply to redress the balance. The King of Dir wished to annex Swat, and began exploiting his victory by levying taxes and confiscating wealth. The Pukhtun remember these invasions as times of severe scarcity and hunger. Eventually, Dir's exactions led to an activation of the segmentary principle of unity against invasion. The Swati parties united (usually under the leadership of a non-Pukhtun religious charismatic) in a war of resistance and Dir was driven out. Three such wars are recorded in the past 150 years.

A final type of war, also destructive, involved expansion rather than defense. For structural reasons, the segmentary lineage system is one which tends to expand at the expense of its less well organized neighbors

(Sahlins 1961). The Pukhtun of Swat conquered their weaker neighbors to the north, the fierce Kohistani peoples. This expansion ceased in the mid-1800s as the harshness of the terrain, the lack of booty, and the ferocity of the Kohistani resistance all combined to defeat the Pukhtun armies. Pukhtun wars of aggression apparently were led by strong men anxious to raise their personal prestige and accumulate a following through leadership in battle and redistribution of spoils. At this late date, it is difficult to discern exactly who followed such men, but it seems that great war leaders were temporarily able to unite fighting men of many different lineages in loose alliances brought together for the sake of conquest. The secular leadership of expansionist warfare appears to be in marked contrast to leadership in wars of defense, which often arises from saintly lineages and relies upon religious exhortation to encourage resistance.

Conclusion

Violence in Swat is highly structured along several lines; the stress on revenge, the utilization of types of mediating bodies and leaders, and the scale of genealogical distance and corresponding physical propinquity of the rival elements. Far from every genealogical level being a replica of every other, each more inclusive patrilineal segment has its own specific rules of violence for hostilities with segments of equal scale. Moreover, relations involving revenge take precedence over other forms of violence and opposition, so that a death in a village party dispute dissolves the parties and leads to a personal vendetta between two nuclear families. In intervillage wars, as well, murders by *tarbur* are avenged, while those by more distant enemies are not. The formal patterning of revenge thus acts to restrict the range of feud and violence.

Behind the structuring of violence lies the Swati social order which focuses on the nuclear family as a relatively autonomous unit within the egalitarian structure of the segmentary lineage system. The shifting dual parties superimposed over the triads of *tul, palao,* and clan reflect the reality of uneven development and the manipulation of alliances on the ground. This system allows great flexibility on the part of individual players. Structural cohesion is maintained by the ties of blood and the obligation to revenge. Though highly restricted, this obligation is the kernel of the social order, and provides the minimal stability necessary for system continuance.

Barth (1959a:84) notes that the range of blood responsibility was formerly wider, but has narrowed "in line with the general political trend whereby descent groups are losing their corporate political functions, and also with the legal principles exemplified in the courts of the neighboring administered territories." Twenty five years after Barth's field-work, revenge continues to be taken by the Pukhtun. The problem is not the change of the system, but its persistence, despite the existence of law courts. In fact, early in the reign of the local central government, death sentences were carried out by the nearest relative of the victim, thus satisfying both law and custom. Revenge as a central cultural value can not be understood through historical analysis or through efforts to find first causes. Rather, a descriptive portrait of the Swati social order puts the revenge motif into its proper context and demonstrates its centrality within the total society.

Following Geertz (1973), I contend that the systematic description of social order has analytic value in that a pattern is postulated which has predictive power. For example, during the 1977 national elections which were marred by serious bloodshed throughout Pakistan, it was possible to accurately predict that Swat would remain relatively peaceful due to the precedence of revenge over party. It was also possible to predict that the Pukhtun vote in Swat would split in the traditional balanced opposi-tion of the *dullah.* The model of individual manipulation within the system accounts for the shifting loyalties which characterize Swati poli-tics, as well as for the long-term balance of the system, since alliances alter to level any overly powerful element. The role of third parties as mediators, manipulators, and unreliable allies is also apparent in the model.

NOTES

1. Research for this paper was undertaken in 1970 and 1977 with support from a Fulbright-Hayes Predoctoral Dissertation grant, the National Science Foun-dation, and a Henry Evans Travelling Fellowship from Columbia University. The fieldwork areas are Shamizai and Sebujni Districts in Northern Swat.

2. The seventeen killings include a killing of a friend, three killings of affines, two killings within the nuclear family, four killings in the ongoing war between tenants and landlords, and seven killings of *tarbur* or *tarbur*'s servants. Of these killings, six occurred during my fieldwork, while the remainder occurred be-tween 1970 and 1977. These are the killings of which I have good histories, and by no means exhaust the list.

3. Contra Barth's (1959a:82–85, 125) cases of village leaders embroiled in blood feuds, the leaders I interviewed all claimed not to engage in any revenge fights. In fact, it is a mark of an elite lineage that it avoids feuds whenever possible since it is recognized that such fights are ruinous. Genealogies of village leaders do show deaths by violence but not in the violence of feud. Rather, leading men

were killed in intervillage wars or in battles with Dir. Despite the impression generally created by ethnographies of the Pukhtun (including my own), violence is quite rare and everyday life is certainly more courteous and safer (Bourdieu 1974) than ordinary life in many supposedly less violent societies.

4. The killer in this case was said to have waited so long to take revenge because he was prudently saving money to support his family after his inevitable exile from Swat.

5. Black-Michaud (1975), following Barth (1953), argues for a dichotomy between vengeance killing, which does not involve corporate responsibility, and feuding, which does. For the Swat, this dichotomy is too radical. Rather, there is a continuum of support, from the obligation to blood revenge incumbent on the nuclear family of the victim to the withdrawal of the victim's more distant relatives from positions of alliance with the killer. A similar argument is made by Salzman (1978) against Peters's (1967) claim that segmentary lineage theory falls to allow for the actual importance of affinal ties. "There is a difference in the weight of affinal ties between situations in which a man will not support his agnates against his affines and in which a man will actively support his affines against his agnates" (Salzman 1978:62). Degree of support is the vital factor, and men in Swat do not support their affines or their party members in cases of blood revenge.

6. When Swat was ruled by a King, his method of retaining power was to grant a stipend and military backing to the weak third parties at the village and district levels. Khan Badhur, whom Barth (1959a) discusses at length, was a leader of this type.

BIBLIOGRAPHY

Ahmed, A. 1976. Millenium and Charisma Among Pathans. London.

———. 1980. Pukhtun Economy and Society: Traditional Structure and Economic Development in a Tribal Society. London.

Barth, F. 1953. Principles of Social Organization in Southern Kurdistan. Oslo.

———. 1959a. Political Leadership Among Swat Pathans. London.

———. 1959b. Segmentary Opposition and the Theory of Games: A Study of Pathan Organization. Journal of the Royal Anthropological Institute 89:5–21.

Black-Michaud, J. 1975. Cohesive Force. New York.

Bourdieu, P. 1974. The Sentiment of Honour in Kabyle Society. Honour and Shame, ed. J. Peristiany, pp. 193–241. Chicago.

Denich, B. 1974. Sex and Power in the Balkans. Women, Culture and Society, ed. M. Rosaldo and L. Lamphere, pp. 243–263. Stanford.

Fernea, R. 1970. Shaykh and Effendi. Boston.

Geertz, C. 1973. Thick Description: Toward an Interpretive Theory of Culture. The Interpretation of Cultures, ed. C. Geertz, pp. 3–30. New York.

Hart, D. 1970. Clan, Lineage, Local Community and the Feud in a Riffian Tribe.

Peoples and Cultures of the Middle East: Vol. II, ed. L. Sweet, pp. 3–75. Garden City.

Lindholm, C. 1977. The Segmentary Lineage System: Its Applicability to Pakistan's Political Structure. Pakistan's Western Borderlands, ed. A. Embree, pp. 41–66. Durham.

———. 1979. Contemporary Politics in a Tribal Society: An Example from Swat District, NWFP, Pakistan. Asian Survey 19:485–505.

Lindholm, C., and C. Lindholm. 1979. Marriage as Warfare. Natural History 88 (8):11–20.

Montagne, R. 1973. The Berbers. London.

Murphy, R., and L. Kasdan. 1959. The Structure of Parallel Cousin Marriage. American Anthropologist 61:17–29.

Peters, E. 1960. The Proliferation of Segments in the Lineage of the Bedouin of Cyrenaica (Libya). Journal of the Royal Anthropological Institute 90:29–53.

———. 1967. Some Structural Aspects of the Feud Among the Camel Herding Bedouin of Cyrenaica. Africa 37:261–282.

Robertson-Smith, W. 1903. Kinship and Marriage in Early Arabia. Boston.

Sahlins, M. 1961. The Segmentary Lineage—An Organization of Predatory Expansion. American Anthropologist 63:322–343.

Salzman, P. 1978. Does Complementary Opposition Exist? American Anthropologist 80:53–70.

Sillitoe, P. 1978. Big Men and War in New Guinea. Man 13:252–271.

Wadud, M. 1963. The Story of Swat. Peshawar.

Class, Politics, and Family Organization in San Cosme Xalostoc, Mexico[1]

Richard W. Miller

Political anthropology focused increasingly in the postwar period upon peasant societies. Peasants are small agrarian producers who, with familial labor and simple equipment, provide for their own consumption and for the demands of an agrarian class and state elite.

Miller's article documents a situation in which community, family, and household structure in San Cosme reflect the ability of wealthy peasant families to monopolize access to state controlled resources, leading in turn to increased social differentiation in the village. The article shows the vulnerability of rural populations before the external agents of power. Although San Cosme is a product of the land reform associated with the Mexican revolution, impoverishment and its pervasiveness reflect that reform must be a permanent process or, as in this case, the peasants will again lose politically and economically.

Eᴛʜɴᴏɢʀᴀᴘʜɪᴄ ᴇᴠɪᴅᴇɴᴄᴇ ᴄʟᴇᴀʀʟʏ indicates the presence of some form of extended family in nearly every Mesoamerican community. Nutini (1967:387–391) estimates the incidence of extended family forms to vary between 20 and 30 per cent of the total number of households found within the region, yet as Nutini (1976:10) also notes, the analysis of the structure and function of the extended family in Mesoamerica has not received much attention and our knowledge of the forms, variations, and dynamics of these groups is not well developed.

Anthropologists have developed several explanations to account for variations in the structure and function of the family. These variations are most often explained in terms of demographic variables, including the developmental cycle of the family (Fortes 1949; Goody 1958), economic variables (Collier 1975; Goldschmidt and Kunkel 1971; Goody 1976; Netting 1965; Nimkoff and Middleton 1960; Pasternak, Ember, and Ember 1976; Sahlins 1957; Wolf 1966), or in terms of the urbanization-secularization process (Goode 1963; Kahl 1968; Redfield 1941).

Among Mesoamericanists two basic models have been used to explain variation in the incidence of extended families. One was developed by Redfield (1941), who used a rural-urban continuum model to explain the higher incidence of extended families in rural areas compared to the greater prevalence of nuclear families in urban areas. Redfield reasoned that the disintegration of communal forms of labor, civic enterprises, and religious rites along with the introduction of a market economy and more emphasis on individual achievement would reduce the importance of extended families. Nutini and White (1977:366–373) have adopted this model to explain the variations in community family structure in the Tlaxcalan area of Mexico where Indian communities tend to have a higher incidence of extended families compared to the more acculturated communities.

A second model, one based on economics, is used by Collier (1975:76) to explain the decline of extended families among the Maya of Chiapas. Focusing his attention on the agricultural economy of the region, Collier postulates that patrilocal extended families and patrilineal organization will be found in areas where land is still a valuable resource and available in sufficient quantities that it can be used to bind families together through inheritance.

Arizpe (1973) also uses an economic model to explain the low incidence of extended families (25 per cent) and the high incidence of nuclear families (68 per cent) in the Indian community of Zacatipan in the Sierra de Puebla. While recognizing that large extended families are correlated with large landholdings, Arizpe proposes that the size of the domestic unit will be a direct relation to the optimal size of the productive unit, especially the optimal size of the labor group needed, given the conditions of the regional economy. In the area of Zacatipan, coffee production has become increasingly important, and the smaller work groups it requires has led to a reduction in the size of the domestic units found in the area.

This essay reports on the family organization of a stratified, basically mestizo community located in the northern part of the Mexican state of Tlaxcala. Here a group of wealthy peasants is the most secularized group in the community. They own large amounts of land and practice mechanized, commercial agriculture. However, they tend to live in large extended families. On the other hand, the poorer peasants of the community, who have retained many traditional Indian beliefs and practice subsistence agriculture on small plots of land, have a high incidence of nuclear families.

The data presented here suggest that the high incidence of extended families among the wealthy peasants is only partially explained by economic factors and the secularization process. Instead, it is the class system of the community and the local political process, especially the way classes and the political system articulate with state and federal institutions as important sources of resources needed at the local level, that is of primary importance in the structure and function of the extended families among the wealthy peasants.

With few exceptions (Hawkins 1975; Goldschmidt and Kunkel 1971), anthropologists have not examined external factors and the integration of local communities and higher level institutions as important factors in the social organization of rural communities. And as Yanagisako (1979: 175–176) notes in her review of family studies, seldom has stratification been recognized and taken into consideration in the analysis of family structure. The findings of this study indicate that variations in family structure and function in the community studied are due less to the secularization process or to economic variables such as the size of landholdings or productive units and due more to class relations at the local level and the way these relations are politically maintained by ties to higher level state and federal institutions.

The Community of San Cosme Xalostoc

San Cosme Xalostoc is a *municipio* (township) located in the northern part of the state of Tlaxcala. It has a population slightly in excess of 7,000. Although recent population growth has reduced family holdings and forced many to seek work in nearby factories, Xalostoc is still an agrarian community with an average of three and one-half hectares of land per family.

Corn and barley are the principal crops, and farming requires land plus several other expensive instruments of production. A form of traction is needed—either draft animals or a tractor—plus two types of plows, a cultivator, fertilizer, and some means of transporting the crop from the fields to the household. These are minimal instruments and are used in the production of all crops grown in Xalostoc. Additional items such as threshers and mulchers are often used. In short, agriculture in Xalostoc is more mechanized and intense than in other areas of Tlaxcala or the Central Highlands. Yields are correspondingly high with corn production averaging two and one-half metric tons per hectare in a good year and barley yields averaging around three metric tons per hectare.

Xalostoc is a class stratified community, and the class system is based on agricultural production and access to land and the various instruments of production. Census data (*Censo Agricola, Ganadero, y Ejidal* 1970) show that privately held land amounts to 30 per cent of the land in the *municipio*. These lands are divided into 675 units. Only 34 of these units exceed five hectares, but they account for 44 per cent of all private land in the community. The remaining lands are divided into small plots, most of which are less than a single hectare.

The other 70 per cent of the municipal land is in *ejido* and amounts to 3,093 hectares. These lands have been added to the community since the 1910 Revolution as part of the national land reform program. Ultimate title of these lands rests with the federal government, and the local peasants are granted usufruct rights which are heritable. However, these lands may not be bought, sold, rented, or generally worked by someone other than the grantee. *Ejido* lands are divided into equal shares among 1,103 recipients.

While the class structure of Xalostoc is indicated in the unequal distribution of private lands, it also has developed around and is supported by production in the *ejidos*. Class relations have formed in the *ejidos,* not over the control of land, which is impossible given federal law, but over the control of the instruments needed to work the land. Most *ejidatarios* (grantees of *ejido* land) have only small units of land, even when their private holdings are taken into consideration, and such small units of land produce only a meager income that is barely enough to feed a family for one year. Supplemental income must be sought to meet clothing, medical, and other expenses. Under these circumstances, the purchase of draft animals, plows, cultivators, fertilizers, and so forth is not possible. The cash needed to make these purchases is unavailable; credit is impossible to obtain; and small parcels of land make the purchase of these implements uneconomical. As a result, the peasant with little land is left without the means to initiate and complete the agricultural production cycle.

Lacking the means to purchase capital, the poor peasant must rent it by entering into an agreement with a wealthier peasant who owns an excess of capital. With large landholdings, the wealthy peasants derive profits which allow them to purchase agricultural capital. Furthermore, they often can obtain credit to make these purchases by using their lands as collateral. In fact, as they have increased their profits, they have purchased additional capital, far more than they need to work their own lands, with the intention of renting it to poor peasants.

Several types of contracts are established between the owners of capital and the poor peasants. First there is outright rental for a cash payment; however, most are too poor to afford even this. A second agreement involves the use of capital in exchange for a portion of the crop at harvest. The portion of the crop given in payment will vary with the amount of capital provided; usually one-third or one-half of the crop is given as payment. A third agreement involves the rental of land by a poor peasant to a peasant with the capital needed to work the land. Although illegal, all of these arrangements also are made with *ejido* land. These agreements increase the returns to capital, which is owned by the wealthy peasants, while reducing the returns to the land of the poor peasants. It does indeed make agriculture possible for the poor peasant, but it does so on terms that are highly lucrative for the wealthy who own the instruments of production.

The wealthy of Xalostoc have not only increased their land holdings to the maximum size possible given the land tenure conditions of the *municipio,* they have also invested in all types of agricultural machinery and have come to control primary access to the basic instruments of production necessary to complete the agricultural cycle. As a result, they have become the dominant force in the agricultural economy of the community. The profits from agriculture have been so great that they have been able to invest in several nonagricultural businesses. They have established stores that sell both general and specialized items. Furniture stores, hardware stores, an auto parts store, the local pharmacies, and the major general merchandise stores are all owned and operated by the wealthy peasants of the community, allowing them to control the sales of necessary goods produced outside of the community. In other words, most commercial activity in the community is dominated by the same group that controls agricultural production.

Family Organization Among the Wealthy Peasants

The wealthy peasant is defined as one who owns enough land plus the necessary tools to be able to initiate and complete the agricultural cycle without the need to borrow or rent any instrument of production. The sample used here includes only those families with at least ten hectares of land plus the assorted implements needed to work the land. Only thirteen families fall into this category. These same families also have held important political offices within the community and at least one member of each family has served as municipal president and/or *ejido* commissioner.

Household Organization

The wealthy peasants live in two types of households. The first is the single household compound which consists of a single structure with one roof. All those living in this unit share a common entrance and many of the rooms within it. Usually such a compound houses a single nuclear family, but sometimes it may include extended family arrangements.

The second type of household is a multiple compound which contains two or more structures which may or may not share a common roof. These different structures serve as the residences of two or more nuclear families living in some form of extended family arrangement. All share a common entrance, and a single wall will usually surround the entire compound. There may be some sharing of facilities, but most of the units are separate and rooms such as kitchens, bedrooms, and the bath will not be shared.

The numbers of families found in these household arrangements are listed in Table 1. The seven extended families living in the multiple compounds are all patrilocal extended families, and the extended families found in the single compounds are bilocal extended families. These figures indicate that the wealthy peasants of Xalostoc live predominately in extended family arrangements. Average household size is accordingly large.

The high incidence of extended families is not consistent with secularization models or the findings of Nutini and White (1977) for other areas of Tlaxcala. The wealthy peasants of Xalostoc do not hold many traditional beliefs, indeed, their ideologies are very secular. They do not participate in the local cargo system or in other traditional rites. And their integration into the national market economy is nearly complete. Therefore, the explanation for their family structure cannot be found in the secularization process. Economic factors, most often cited to explain family structure, can partially account for this pattern of family organization.

TABLE 1
Distribution of Household Types

Type of Compound	Number	Number of Families	Average Household Size
Single	6	13	—
Nuclear Family	4	4	5.3
Extended Family	2	9	25.0
Multiple Compound			
Extended Family	7	21	11.8
TOTAL	13	34	12.8

Economics, the Productive Unit, and Household Organization

Economics has played an important role in the household organization of the wealthy peasants of Xalostoc. This group of peasants came from a group of prerevolutionary independent middle peasants who were active participants in the Revolution and who took advantage of the postrevolutionary decline of the hacienda to expand their own land holdings and commercial activities. In the years following the Revolution, they purchased many hacienda lands, and led the movement to establish *ejidos* under the national land reform program. During these years they also invested in agricultural equipment, mechanized their own operations, experimented with new breeds of livestock, began to use chemical fertilizers, and were successful in obtaining significant amounts of federal agricultural credit. Profits from agriculture eventually led to investments in nonagricultural businesses, and this group has become the leading merchants and financiers of the community. The development of these numerous business and commercial activities has had an effect on the household organization of the wealthy and in several ways is responsible for the extended families in which they live.

The expansion of business activities since the Revolution has enabled the heads of the wealthy households to provide business and work opportunities for members of their families. In a country such as Mexico, where the rates of unemployment and underemployment are so high, few have access to employment much less the ability to provide work for others. The wealthy of Xalostoc have been expanding their businesses for several decades and have been able to provide new opportunities for family members as they were added to the household. Since patrilocal residence is the preferred form of postmarital residence, sons live with their father and usually engage in management activities involving one or another of the father's businesses. Since the business activities of the wealthy are so extensive and varied, many people are needed to work and manage them. This puts the households of the wealthy in constant need of workers; sons fulfill this need. They begin to work in family businesses at an early age and continue to do so following marriage. They help manage the businesses, do much of the daily work in them, and are consulted about important decisions involving the household's business affairs.

In cases where sons do not become directly involved in family businesses, they pursue professional careers. Their educations are financed by their fathers, and in nearly all cases, they return to the community to live and practice their professions. This has been the case with the local physicians and most of the lawyers. In these cases, a man not only pays for his son's education, he also helps him develop important political and professional contacts at the state and federal levels. Financial aid needed to purchase offices and pay for other costs of starting a profession in the community are provided by wealthy household heads.

The wealth and resources of the wealthy peasants have been important in creating large extended families among this group, and the case of Xalostoc would seem to fit similar cases described by Netting (1965), Nimkoff and Middleton (1960), and Sahlins (1957) and conform with findings in other areas of Mesoamerica (Arizpe 1973; Collier 1975). In Xalostoc, however, sons do eventually leave their natal homes and establish independent nuclear families. The ability of wealth and resources to bind these families together is limited, as an examination of the developmental cycle of these families will show.

The Developmental Cycle of the Family and the Unit of Production

As previously noted, when sons marry, they usually are already living with their fathers and working in their father's businesses. As a result, they have no direct control over resources. Upon marriage, most sons set up an independent household budget and, if they have not done so before, arrange to receive an income for the work they do for their fathers. Eventually they will use this income to set up businesses of their own.

In the early years of the marriage, patrilocal residence is convenient for both a man and his son. The household head benefits from the trusted and loyal help his son provides. A son benefits from a stable source of employment and the use of his father's often comfortable household facilities. At this point in the developmental cycle, the two families work closely as a single productive unit. However, a son's primary goal is to save enough money to begin his own business and to establish his own household.

When a second son marries and resides patrilocally, the first son begins to become independent from his father. The first step usually involves the purchase of a separate stove and the establishment of separate rooms and facilities within the compound. It is at this point that tensions between father and son are the greatest. The father wishes to keep his son as a worker and manager in his own businesses; the son, on the other hand, wishes to develop his own businesses, work for himself, and increase his wealth.

What finally decides the issue is the system of inheritance in Xalostoc. Without exception, all of the wealthy peasants will not, nor do they intend to, allow their offspring to inherit from them until they die. They do this to preserve the family businesses, their power over their family and in the community, and to guarantee their security and comfort in their old age. Knowing this, a son will fight to establish his own independent businesses, ones he can control and from which he can derive a source of income, power, and community status.

A compromise is reached in these situations, and a wealthy man will lend capital and other assistance to his sons in order to enable them to set up their own businesses. In this way the sons will be able to acquire their own businesses, and a father can still retain some measure of control over his sons while protecting his property from being fragmented by early inheritance. The father's assistance may permit sons to establish an entirely separate business, or to take over and further develop one of the family's current businesses. In either case, a father will lend his son money, help him acquire credit, give him advice, finance his educational career, use political contacts to help him find jobs in the government, and see that they receive a share of the community's *ejido* lands as well as have access to sources of agricultural credit.

The youngest son is the only exception to this pattern. Being the youngest, he is expected to live with his parents, share a household budget with them, care and manage the family businesses, and eventually inherit the household compound and most of the land or major family businesses. The only exceptions to this involve the two wealthiest families in the community. In the case of these two families, all sons have established neolocal residences and have entered into separate businesses at the time of their marriages. The vast wealth and important political contacts of the heads of these two households have enabled these men to establish their sons in separate businesses and households without going through a period of patrilocal capital accumulation.

Currently, the patrilocal extended families among the wealthy include a youngest son, who has little independence and maintains close economic and social ties with his father, often sharing many household facilities, a common kitchen, and a common household budget. Also included in current patrilocal extended families is another son, who has begun a course of independence. He has started to develop his own family businesses, has a separate budget, a separate kitchen, and will eventually, usually with the marriage of still another brother, form a separate household. The wealth of these families has made possible the formation of extended families with three constituent families and a long developmental cycle.

Although the wealthy live in large extended families, these families are only partially related to the optimal size of the productive units found within the regional economy. When a father and one son live in a common household, they work together and cooperate in the family businesses, but with the exception of the youngest son, all sons have the goal of establishing separate businesses and begin to do so while they are still living patrilocally. In fact, in all of the cases of patrilocal residence, one son has already established an independent business and is no longer a functioning member of the household economy. In other words, extended families contain two different productive units. A father and his youngest son work one unit; a second son works the other. Since the business interests of these families are so extensive, hired labor is frequently used. In many ways there is little point in speaking of the family in Xalostoc as a productive unit. The family may form the managerial nucleus of various productive enterprises, but even within the household units one can find separate businesses with separate managements.

This does not mean, however, that these separate families are without important and continuing ties. In fact, many strong and important ties continue to bind these families into cooperative social units. Following Nutini (1967:241–243), these families can be called non-residential extended families when sons live in separate residences, for even following residential separation, these families continue to function together in many important ways.

Politics, Class, and the Non-residential Extended Family

The four nuclear families living in single household compounds could be considered as parts of non-residential extended families. Furthermore, nearly all of the extended families among the wealthy are parts of larger non-residential extended families. While there is no longer residential unity, and distinct economic interests define each of the component nuclear families, there still is considerable unity and frequent, almost daily, visiting among these families. The economic functions of the non-residential extended family may not be great, as sons and daughters have become established in separate productive units, but a man and his sons still consult each other in important business decisions.

Lacking strong economic ties or mutual business interests, the real force that binds these families together is a political one. Although they all may be active in distinct businesses, all need political power and political contacts for their businesses to grow and prosper and to maintain their class position within the community. The government of Mexico is directly or indirectly involved in nearly every facet of the economy from directly entering into production as with steel or indirectly influencing the course of investment through subsidies, taxation, special credits and concessions, the setting of prices, the support of infrastructural development, and sundry other activities (see, for example, Hansen 1971; Vernon 1965; Wilkie 1970). Since the 1910 Revolution, the government especially has intervened in the area of agricultural production. It has developed a system of land redistribution, agricultural banks, regulated the prices of agricultural produce, financed and constructed important agricultural infrastructure, and made the use of advanced machinery possible in many rural areas. Governmental intervention in the economy has affected the local economic activities of Xalostoc in profound ways. Competition for governmental concessions, loans, credits, and favors touches every business and nearly every economic activity. Therefore, local political power and ties to state and federal agencies is critical to the successful functioning of any business, and the wealthy families in Xalostoc are tied together by their common need for the political strength that will help them maintain and increase their wealth and preserve their class position within the community.

Since most of the land in Xalostoc exists as *ejido,* politics plays a significant role in agricultural production. *Ejido* lands are acquired through the government, and the local *ejido* commission grants these lands to individual peasants. Since the wealthy rent their agricultural machinery in often illegal ways for use in the *ejidos,* control over the governance of the *ejidos* is vital to their interests. The federal government through its local representatives also grants agricultural credit, issues crop insurance, provides low-cost machinery, subsidizes irrigation, promotes the development of new animal and crop hybrids, and provides fertilizers to increase productivity. In non-agricultural areas, government loans are provided for small businesses, and the government grants business concessions, issues permits, and engages in many other activities in support of community businesses. Furthermore, control over the local government provides community leaders with access to state and federal funds, which are own used illegally for personal benefit. Finally, the community has produced many professionals over the past several decades, and many of these people work in some capacity for the state or federal government. Acquiring these positions requires political contacts, and families without such contacts are at a disadvantage in their professional and business careers. So while the various family members among the wealthy may have formed distinct businesses, divergent business interests, and varied professional activities all maintain an active interest in developing governmental contacts and acquiring political power to maintain their class position. It is in the pursuit of these political goals that much of the cohesion among families is found.

At the municipal level, political influence is important, for many state and federal agencies have local representatives. The *ejido* commission, the municipal government, and the national political party along with its several divisions are all represented in the community. Therefore, control of local politics is important, and one of the main units of political organization and activity is the family. Wealthy families act in unison in political matters. Together with their numerous contacts and supporters among the ranks of the poor peasants, they compete for political advantage in the community. Their primary goal is the control of local political resources and access to higher level authorities.

To achieve these goals, families must unite with other families to gain enough political strength to control local political processes. It is in these political struggles that family cohesion becomes great and brothers, sons, and fathers work together toward common goals. The wealthy have controlled community politics since the Revolution, and among these families one or two have held the most power, have had the most wealth, and have had the greatest number of political contacts outside of the community. Other families, while having less wealth and power, do play an important role in community politics. Since the Revolution they have formed a coalition among themselves that has dominated community politics. However, while they have been able to dominate community politics, the dozen or so families that form this coalition have fought among themselves for prominent position within the political structure of the community, and it is in these struggles that family unity becomes important. Families with the greatest political influence locally are in the best position to reap the spoils of the political system and to develop important high-level contacts in the state and national government. The political history of the community is replete with examples of particular families trying to place their family members in key political positions within the community.

Since local political offices are the channel through which state and federal funds reach the community, the struggles to control these offices are great, and families must form alliances to control them. No one family, not even the most wealthy and powerful, has enough power to control the outcome of political events and must form alliances with other families to influence the outcome of political decisions. Alliances are formed by promises of secondary positions within the government, special concessions, or placement on important local political committees. Whatever the outcome, the political spoils of the community will be distributed according to the sets of alliances that form during the political process. The success of a family in this struggle will depend upon its unity and its subsequent ability to reward followers. More than any particular business interest, the need for political unity and the need to perform as a political group is what binds wealthy families together into extended and nonresidential extended families.

Family Organization Among the Poor Peasants

Poor peasants in Xalostoc differ from the wealthy peasants in many signifi-cant ways. First, they all lack enough land and capital to support their families through agriculture. For purposes of this study, only families with land totaling no more than three hectares will be considered. Over 95 per cent of the peasants of Xalostoc have less than five hectares, and 60 per cent have less than a single hectare. These peasants not only lack land, but they also lack the tools needed to work the land. They either rent the necessary tools of production or they give up part of their crop in exchange for the use of these tools. Some have left agriculture to become permanent factory workers and rent their land. Those who have become permanent factory workers will not be considered here.

Even during the best of times, harvests usually will not support the families of poor peasants and they must seek additional sources of in-come. They may work as field hands in the fields of large landowners; they may work in one of the numerous nonagricultural businesses in the community; or they may seek work in one of the nearby urban centers. Usually they work in all of these areas, finding only sporadic work in any one of them. In the end, they find themselves in constant search for work and just barely able to maintain their families.

Household Organization

The poor peasants live in two types of household compounds. The first is a single compound which may contain a single nuclear family or two or more nuclear families living in an extended family arrangement. The second type of household is the multiple compound which is occu-pied by an extended family, usually patrilocal. Here there is a marked lack in sharing of facilities, and a separate household budget is usually kept for each family. Two-thirds of the families among the poor live in nuclear families. Of the one-third that are extended families, about half live in multiple compounds and half live in single compounds. This contrasts with the high incidence of extended families found among the wealthy peasants of the community, and it is what one would expect from a secularized community such as Xalostoc.

Economics and the Developmental Cycle of the Family

Most extended families among the poor result from a brief period of postmarital residence; usually this is patrilocal. Only the youngest son is expected to live in permanent patrilocal residence, and these form most of the cases of extended families living in single compounds. The lack of strong economic, political, or religious functions played by families has resulted in few extended families forming. In most cases a son resides with his father following marriage, but with few economic resources, a man is unable to provide for his sons. The family land usually consists of only a few hectares and cannot support a larger productive unit or a social unit larger than a single nuclear family. As a result, sons usually establish a separate economic career before marriage. They most likely enter into a course of sporadic work, seeking and sometimes finding work in diverse places, usually for brief periods of time. By the time they marry, they have already become independent of their fathers. In fact, since their fathers are unable to support them, sons must obtain some source of independent employment before they marry. The brief period of patrilocal residence is seen as a time for the accumulation of enough assets to construct a separate household. As a result, household budgets are kept separate. There is very little economic cooperation, political unity, or religious effort to bind extended families of the poor. The exception to this is the case of the youngest son, who is expected to live in permanent patrilocal residence, care for his parents in their old age, and take over the compound when they die. In these cases an extended family forms a single compound and the various facilities plus a common household budget will be shared. However, like the multiple compounds that form with sons other than the youngest, economic, political, and religious ties among the families of the single compound are also weak. Often the youngest son will have different sources of employment from his father.

Unlike the extended families of the wealthy, those of the poor contain only two families per household. Facilities are not adequate to support additional families. The period of postmarital residence is also brief. A married son will set up an independent household when the marriage of a brother becomes imminent.

The strong social ties found among the families of the wealthy are absent among the poor. The relationship among brothers is tenuous at best. Often there is fighting over family property and inheritance. Without significant economic, political, or religious functions, the social interaction of brothers is limited to life crises events. Only the sentiment of kinship serves to unite them, but even this is strained by fighting over family resources. The same lack of social interaction applies to father and son. With little resources, a father cannot provide employment or educational opportunities for his children. Therefore, when sons reach adulthood, they must find an independent source of income. Often this means migration in search of work, creating a geographical as well as an economic distance between families. Finally, the poor have little political power within the community and usually align with one of the wealthier families for political favors. It is not uncommon to find brothers and even father and sons aligned with different factions within the community.

In comparison, it must be noted that the families of the poor engage in diverse economic pursuits, and in this they do not differ from the wealthy. The productive unit does not bind the wealthy into extended families any more than it does the poor. In neither group does the productive unit play an important role in the functioning of the extended family, except in the case of the youngest sons who reside in permanent patrilocal residence. What makes the families of the wealthy cohesive is that their diverse business interests are controlled, owned, and operated by them in their own interests. They need sources of capital to establish and run them, and these resources are often obtained through the political process. It is, therefore, in common political interests, and only secondarily in common economic interests, that these families are more cohesive. The poor, while also engaged in diverse businesses, enter as workers and employees. They do not own their own businesses, nor do they make decisions about them. Even their agricultural businesses are not self-sufficient because they lack the fundamental means of production. As a result, economic activities among the poor tend to divide families and separate them geographically, producing the pattern of nuclear families found in the community.

This pattern of nuclear family formation contrasts somewhat with that found by Nutini and Murphy (1970) in other areas of the Tlaxcala-Pueblan Valley where extended families tend to form as a result of labor migration. In many cases, migrant workers in Xalostoc leave their wives to live in nuclear family households. However, these households are often spatially and socially close to other households, forming non-residential extended families. However, social interaction in these larger families primarily involves women who help each other meet daily expenses and labor needs in managing domestic chores.

Conclusions

Extended families exist in nearly every community in Mesoamerica from the rural villages to the urban-industrial centers, yet we know little about the social conditions that regulate the structure and function of these extended families. The rural-urban continuum model of Redfield and the secularization model of Nutini are only partially useful. These models work reasonably well for the area of Tlaxcala proper (Nutini and White 1977:369), and they also seem to apply to other Indian communities such as Chignautla in the Sierra de Puebla (Slade 1976:171). However, there are areas where the model fails. The Indian communities of

Hiutzilan (Taggart 1971:135) and Zactipan (Arizpe 1973:159–160) both have a low incidence of extended families.

The most common alternate models have been based on economics (Arizpe 1973; Collier 1975). However, the data from Xalostoc indicate that economics can only partially explain the family organization of the community, and it appears that the conclusion reached by Gross and Kendall (1983), that multiple factors are involved in determining family structure, would also apply to Xalostoc.

Among the poor peasants the secularization process has weakened many forms of community activity that once required family co-operation. But economic factors have also been important. The declining land base of the peasant family has weakened the importance of the family as a productive unit, and meager resources have created conflict and disputes among brothers over inheritance of family property. Furthermore, the need to seek wage labor outside of the community has dispersed family members while placing them in diverse occupations.

While the wealthy peasants have been influenced by the secularization process, the secularization model cannot explain the high incidence of extended families among this group. Here economic factors can explain some features of family organization. The extended families that form in the early phases of the developmental cycle are the result of sons working in and managing family resources. However, given the nature of the inheritance system in Xalostoc, sons quickly seek to establish separate, independent businesses, and they begin to do this in the later stages of the developmental cycle. As a result, the strong cohesion found among families, both those sharing a common residence and those not, cannot be explained in terms of the size and functioning of productive units.

The evidence presented here indicates that both stratification and institutions external to the local community are important factors in the family organization of the wealthy peasants. Specifically, it is in the area of political activity that these families unite in order to obtain important resources controlled by state and federal political institutions. These resources are necessary in all of the diverse economic activities of these families and access to them through the political system is necessary to maintain their class position within the community.

NOTE

1. Fieldwork was conducted between February 1975 and October 1976, and this time period represents the ethnographic present in this study.

BIBLIOGRAPHY

Arizpe, L. 1973. Parentesco y economia en una sociedad Nahua. Mexico.

Censo Agricola, Ganadero, y Ejidal. 1970. Secretaria de Industria y Comercio: Direccion General de Estadisticas. Mexico.

Collier, G. A. 1975. Fields of the Tzotzil: The Ecological Bases of Tradition in Highland Chiapas. Austin.

Fortes, M. 1949. Time and Social Structure: An Ashanti Case Study. Social Structure: Studies Presented to A. R. Radcliffe-Brown, ed. M. Fortes, pp. 58–84. Oxford.

Goldschmidt, W., and E. J. Kunkel. 1971. The Structure of the Peasant Family. American Anthropologist 73:1058–1076.

Goode, W. J. 1963. World Revolution and Family Patterns. New York.

Goody, J. R. (ed.). 1958. The Developmental Cycle in Domestic Groups. Cambridge.

———. 1976. Production and Reproduction: A Comparative Study of the Domestic Domain. Cambridge.

Gross, J. J., and C. Kendall. 1983. The Analysis of Domestic Organization in Mesoamerica: The Case of Postmarital Residence in Santiago Atitlan, Guatemala. Heritage of Conquest 30 Years Later, ed. C. Kendall, J. Hawkins, and L. Bossen, pp. 201–228. Albuquerque.

Hansen, R. D. 1971. The Politics of Mexican Development. Baltimore.

Hawkins, J. P. 1975. Ethnicity, Economy, and Residence Rules: Class Differences in Domestic Systems in Western Highland Guatemala. Family and Kinship in Middle America and the Caribbean, ed. A. Marks and R. Romer, pp. 251–334. Leiden.

Kahl, J. A. 1968. The Measurement of Modernism: A Study of Values in Brazil and Mexico. Austin.

Netting, R. McC. 1965. Household Organization and Intensive Agriculture: The Kofyar Case. Africa 35:422–429.

Nimkoff, M. F., and R. Middleton. 1960. Types of Family and Types of Economy. American Journal of Sociology 68:215–225.

Nutini, H. G. 1967. A Synoptic Comparison of Mesoamerican Marriage and Family Structure. Southwestern Journal of Anthropology 23:383–404.

———. 1968. San Bernardino Contla: Marriage and Family Structure in a Tlaxcalan municipio. Pittsburgh.

———. 1976. The Nature and Treatment of Kinship in Mesoamerica. Essays in Mexican Kinship, ed. H. G. Nutini, P. Carrasco, and J. M. Taggart, pp. 3–27. Pittsburgh.

Nutini, H. G., and B. L. Isaac. 1974. Los pueblos de habla nahuatl de la region de Tlaxcala y Puebla. Mexico.

Nutini, H. G., and T. D. Murphy. 1970. Labor-Migration and Family Structure in the Tlaxcala-Pueblan Area, Mexico. The Social Anthropology of Latin America: Essays in Honor of Ralph Leon Beals, ed. W. Goldschmidt and H. Hoijer, pp. 80–103. Los Angeles.

Nutini, H. G., and D. R. White. 1977. Community Variations and Network Structure in the Social Functions of Compadrazgo in Rural Tlaxcala, Mexico. Ethnology 16:353–384.

Pasternak, B., C. Ember, and M. Ember. 1976. On the Conditions Favoring Extended Family Households. Journal of Anthropological Research 32:109–123.

Redfield, R. 1941. The Folk Culture of Yucatan. Chicago.

Sahlins, M. D. 1957. Land Use and the Extended Family in Moala, Fiji. American Anthropologist 59:449–462.

Slade, D. L. 1976. Kinship in the Social Organization of a Nahuat-Speaking Community in the Central Highlands. Essays on Mexican Kinship, ed. H. G. Nutini, P. Carrasco, and J. Taggart, pp. 155–186. Pittsburgh.

Taggart, J. M. 1972. The Fissiparous Process in Domestic Groups of a Nahuat-speaking Community. Ethnology 11:132–149.

Vernon, R. 1965. The Dilema of Mexico's Development. Cambridge.

Wilkie, J. W. 1970. The Mexican Revolution: Federal Expenditure and Social Change since 1910. Berkeley.

Wolf, E. R. 1966. Peasants. Englewood Cliffs.

Yanagisako, S. J. 1979. Family and Household: The Analysis of Domestic Groups. Annual Review of Anthropology 8:161–205.

The Oaxacan Village President as Political Middleman[1]

Philip A. Dennis

Societies consist of varieties of social categories or groups, each with differing membership and resources. In many societies, these are differing societal levels containing discrete governmental institutions. Dennis describes how individuals play particular roles in bridging these social groupings. His article portrays the village president as a political middleman. In this structural position, he theoretically acts as an impartial honest broker and transmits information and resources between segments of the society. One can see that this position easily lends itself to self-aggrandizement.

The village president in this case, according to Dennis, links his village to national institutions of party and bureaucracy. However, one must consider the effects of several variables such as population growth, capitalist agriculture, technical and bureaucratic change which could convert this political position into directly exploitative patron-client relationships.

SINCE THE EARLY colonial period, national governments in Mexico have organized relationships with Indian villages through a class of intermediaries—*caciques*, village *alcaldes*, *municipio* presidents, and other "political middlemen." Such a policy of "indirect rule" served the purposes of the colonial government very well: local authorities would continue to administer the lives of the Indian population, thus sparing the Spanish government the trouble; and at the same time the Indian communities would serve as readymade units from which labor and tribute could be exacted (Wolf 1957) The effect of the policy was to emphasize the unity and solidarity of the village community, and to make of critical importance the roles linking the villages and higher levels of government.

The national government in recent times remains no less dependent on political middlemen. Friedrich (1968) has shown, for instance, that the contemporary *caciques* of Tarascan Michoacan derive a large part of their authority from their ability to interpret for the *ejidatarios* crucial sections of the Agrarian Code; at the same time they mobilize the villagers on behalf of the government on crucial political occasions. In other peasant societies political middlemen apparently play similarly crucial roles. In Java, for example, Geertz's (1960) Muslim *kijaji* legitimizes the secular government's programs in the eyes of the pious villagers, while transmitting to the government the villagers' conservative and religiously defined political objectives. Wolf (1956: 1075) has stated that, in general, such political middlemen "stand guard over the crucial junctures or synapses of relationships which connect the local system to the larger whole."

Some recent work on political middlemen has stressed the power and influence which may sometimes accrue to such positions. Loffler (1971) describes an Iranian peasant leader remarkable for his forcefulness and initiative in defending the rights of his constituents, and in introducing modern innovations to his village. This man is successful partly because of his personal abilities, and partly because he fills the vacant niche of true mediator, relating the peasant village directly to the highest authorities, and by-passing the traditional but unresponsive power hierarchy. Bieler (1973) describes two more mundane types of middlemen: the Portuguese priest and travel agent in Toronto. These men become power figures in the ethnic community by filling out tax and immigration forms, giving legal advice, and generally acting as translators and advisors for their Portuguese countrymen. In the process, of course, they assure themselves of a clientele.

In these examples we see the middleman capitalizing on his position as sole intermediary between different but related social systems. His ability to operate effectively in both systems is the key to his success. He must be able to speak different languages, behave appropriately in both village and government office, and manipulate the symbols of two different cultures. These kinds of abilities define the middleman's role (Swartz 1968). Since there are relatively few individuals with such abilities, we might expect to find that many middlemen are uniquely capable of filling their intercalary niches, and that they gain power through control of crucial relationships.

However, the opposite possibility is that in his position the middleman becomes trapped between different and contradictory sets of expectations. While operating successfully in two different social systems may sometimes imply power, it may also require considerable dexterity. The middleman may have to face in two different directions at once, in Wolf's (1956: 1076) phrase. In this case we see not individuals manipulating roles for their own benefit, but struggling to deal with the difficulties of their roles. This situation would seem to occur where the middleman does not have unique control over crucial synapses of relations, and is in fact highly expendable. Middlemen who are elected or appointed to their positions and who hold them at the pleasure of their constituents, are especially likely to be vulnerable. This paper examines the role of one such middleman: the Oaxacan village president, who must answer both to his fellow villagers, and in the case of intervillage land disputes, to district and state authorities. After presenting the president's dilemma, I will discuss the possible solutions, including the "radical" solution of temporarily abandoning one's post.

Intervillage Land Feuds

Villages in the Valley of Oaxaca, Mexico, are strong, corporate social units of the type described by Wolf (1955). Although they participate in a common marketing system, they are highly endogamous, and they exhibit a striking kind of cultural autonomy. Informants always point out differences in the "customs" of neighboring communities: different saints' days and ways of celebrating *fiestas,* different costumes and dialects of Zapotec, and different economic specializations. Surrounding villages are also known by their "character:" the residents of a village are known, in general terms, as progressive or staunchly traditional, hospitable or hostile, trustworthy or insincere. These character stereotypes are both a result of and a folk explanation for the bitter disputes between communities.

Village political systems are organized around the concept of service and the ideal of equality. Every adult male is a "citizen" of the community, with an equal voice and vote in decision making. Periodic assemblies of the citizens are held to discuss important issues, with the elected village officials presiding. Most villages of any size are classified as independent political units, whether or not they have the 2,000 inhabitants legally required (Pérez Jiménez 1968: 9), and as a result they have an elaborate system of local political offices. The village president is chief officer of the *Ayuntamiento* or village council. Together with the *Comisariado,* the official in charge of communal resources, he bears the greatest share of responsibility for village governance. The president and *Comisariado* and members of their committees are elected for a period of three years, after which they must be allowed a period of "rest" before being asked to serve again. Men earn prestige from serving in the elected posts, but there is no pay, and after service they return to their everyday occupations as ordinary citizens. Respect in the community, experience in lesser posts, and the financial resources to take time away from farming are the main prerequisites for election. The president's position is the most important, but there are also many lesser positions and committees. The vigilance committee, for example, conducts periodic patrols of the community boundaries to insure that no trespassing has taken place.

Villages hold their lands in communal tenure, and they are ever-ready to dispute an invasion by neighboring communities. References in the literature (Lewis 1951: 238, 244; Beals 1945: 17–18) suggest that intervillage conflict is prevalent in other parts of Mesoamerica, but the Zapotec villages of Oaxaca are perhaps most notorious for their land disputes (see Wolf 1967: 306). These disputes sometimes continue for decades, even centuries, over the same tracts of land, and may involve considerable bloodshed. One feud between the villages of Amilpas and Soyaltepec has lasted about 300 years (Dennis 1973).[2]

The most violent episodes in such land disputes are the *tumultos,* or brawls, which erupt periodically along the disputed borders. They are usually spontaneous affairs which occur when crowds of men are massed along the border (during a land survey, for instance); insults begin to be exchanged, rocks are thrown, and soon a small battle rages. Taylor (1972: 84–85) mentions that the colonial land surveys (the *vistas de ojo*) "almost invariably" provoked resistance and interference by Indians who believed they were being dispossessed. Colonial authorities attempted to deal with the problem by permitting only village officials to be present, but surveys and boundary marking ceremonies remained, then as today, very tense affairs. Less commonly, *tumultos* begin as armed invasions by the men of one village, who seek to recover land they believe to be unjustly occupied by men of the opposing village. When the opponents come out to defend their lands, a full-scale armed clash may develop. Such *tumultos* may result in many casualties, especially in recent times when villagers fight with modern firearms.

In the history of Amilpas and Soyaltepec, recorded *tumultos* have occurred in 1694, 1792, 1830, 1909, and 1910. Various *tumultos* with other neighboring villages have also occurred, as well as a great deal of violence on a smaller scale. Four men from Soyaltepec were executed by Amilpeños in 1928 after being apprehended cutting timber on Amilpas' mountain land. In 1965 an Amilpas man was murdered near the village boundary by Soyalpeños who resented his attempt to divert water flowing downstream onto Soyaltepec land. Massed crowds of men from the two villages came close to fighting at several points during the government imposed land settlements of the 1940s. Battles and less spectacular forms of conflict over land are thus a regular, highly patterned feature of the Oaxacan cultural landscape.[3]

The President as Middleman

In these Oaxacan communities, the village president acts as a political middleman.[4] The district, state, and federal governments consider him the official representative of the community, and they normally deal through him in any matter concerning the village: public projects such as schools, questions of larger political allegiances, disputes over village boundaries and land ownership. The villagers also regard the president as a crucial intermediary with the government, particularly in the case of land disputes. He is expected to defend the lands by preparing and delivering official documents, bribing government officials, and gaining the favor of powerful *patrones* outside the village. A good president should not be afraid to go into the highest offices, and he should be able to argue eloquently and convincingly in his community's behalf. As we shall see, he is able to put these same abilities to good use in protecting himself.

In acting as the community's representative, however, the president's fellow citizens concede him no real political authority. Within his own village, a president must act in terms of consensus and co-operation. He cannot command the other citizens to do anything which they have not already agreed to in public assembly. He can call them together, argue for his own position, and determine their will; but he cannot enforce his own opinions over those of the other citizens. Should he overstep his authority, he is likely to be accused of corruption; presidents are always suspected of accepting bribes from opponents in other villages, stealing money from the public treasury, misspending funds collected in assembly for bribes or legal fees, or otherwise making use of their position for personal gain. Insistence on one course of action against community wishes is likely to be interpreted as stemming from a vested personal interest. Many past Amilpas and Soyaltepec presidents are believed to have sold out their communities, duping their fellow citizens while allowing valuable land to be stolen. At the least, an overbearing president will be accused of arrogance and conceit. The community is then free to depose him, by force if necessary, and replace him with someone more likely to represent accurately the community's wishes. In extreme cases, an arrogant or dishonest president may be banished from the village or even killed by angry villagers. An Amilpas case from the 1950s involved a former president and prominent citizen. It became known that this man had gone to Oaxaca, over the heads of the current Amilpas officials, to secure an order preventing a public pipeline from passing across his property. This action was seen as an outrageous attempt to circumvent the community authorities, acting in the public interest, for purely personal and "egotistic" motives (i.e., to avoid a small loss of land). It was also interpreted as confirmation of widespread suspicion that the man had acted dishonorably in the past. He was forced to leave the village, and, although his wife and family remain, informants say he would risk being killed if he returned. Well aware of the sanctions his community can bring to bear, the average president is content to act only as spokesman for the general consensus.

The district and state governments have quite different expectations of the village president. In general, they hold him responsible for the actions of people in his community. In the case of land disputes, he is expected to prevent conflict while higher authorities settle the dispute, and to notify them of any situation which gets out of his control. If a *tumulto* occurs between villages, the presidents of the communities involved may be jailed as punishment for failure to control their constituents. Following a large-scale *tumulto* in 1910, the presidents of both Amilpas and Soyaltepec spent three months in jail, until the villagers could raise enough money to have them released. Following the 1928 murders the Amilpas president and two other village officials were sent to jail for a year. In part, the president and other village officials may be seized because they are the only individuals who can be identified after incidents in the feud: it would be impractical to jail all the men of a village for participating in a *tumulto*. In addition, however, the district government holds the president responsible because he is expected to be able to control his citizens; an intermediary who has no control over his constituents is of little use to the larger government. The assumption seems to be that the president can act like an authoritarian *ladino* leader, imposing his will on the villagers and enforcing even unpopular decisions. In Zapotec Oaxaca, at least, village presidents cannot behave in this way.

Here we have an interesting dilemma. The president must act in terms of consensus and co-operation in dealing with his fellow citizens. He cannot order them to do anything, or prevent them from doing anything, but nevertheless he is held personally responsible for their actions by higher authorities. Thus it comes about that in inter-village feuding, the citizens often "compromise" their president.

> (Does the president order the people to defend their land?) Even though the
> president doesn't say anything, it is the citizens who go out. A group of fifteen
> or twenty gets together, and even though the president gets angry and tells

them not to go, why should they obey him? They compromise the poor fellow. And he is the one who is responsible, for what if they kill someone? [Soyaltepec informant] The president is in his office, he doesn't know what things his sons may be doing. Of course if they do something violent, something wrong, the blame will be thrown on him. [Amilpas informant]

The president's dilemma is similar to that of the contemporary African chief as described by Fallers (1955). In occupying his political status the president or chief must answer to two different and contradictory sets of expectations. This is a difficult task, and one which takes its toll of presidents as it does of chiefs. Unlike the African chief, however, the Oaxacan village president does not internalize both contradictory sets of role expectations. He does not expect to be able to behave like an authoritarian leader, even though he knows the government expects it of him. Consequently, he does not suffer the psychological problems of the chief, who must rationalize to himself two different and incompatible standards for his own behavior. The predicament of the Oaxacan village president is in the realm of action; his foremost task is to protect himself in a difficult situation.

Solutions to the President's Dilemma

The first and most obvious solution to the dilemma is to avoid being president at all. In fact, men go to great lengths to avoid serving in any of the more important village offices. They take trips away from the community during the time for elections and instatement. They involve themselves in lesser positions, such as the religious *cofradias,* since there is a rule that no one should have to serve in two positions at the same time. And when elected, they protest vociferously that they are not qualified, or that other men are more experienced, or that they don't have the full support of the village. At an election for *Comisariado* in Soyaltepec in 1970, all the candidates for the committee were conspicuously absent from the assembly, and a search was begun to literally drag them out of hiding. They were finally brought before the assembly and notified of their election, which they unsuccessfully protested to the government official supervising the proceedings. Other villagers responded to their discomfort with chuckles of commiseration. The reluctance to serve in local political offices has usually been interpreted as due to the time and expense involved. These are certainly important factors, since there is no pay for service and a great deal of time is lost from farming. However, I believe reluctance to serve is based partially on recognition of the difficulties inherent in the role itself. As president, an individual is much more likely to be caught between conflicting standards than to gain power and influence. The best he can hope for is to preserve himself unscathed, hoping his village will not "compromise" him and that his reputation as upstanding community member will emerge relatively untarnished.

Once in office village officials must adopt another strategy for dealing with the dilemma: to argue as forcefully as possible for actions likely to be acceptable to the government. For instance, when trespassers from opposing villages are apprehended on the land, the president might argue that they be captured and turned over to higher authorities, instead of being executed. The Soyalpeños in the 1928 incident were executed by the vigilance patrol from Amilpas, apparently with the president's approval. A more shrewd president would have argued against execution, realizing he himself would be held responsible, and perhaps have avoided a year in prison. In a similar incident of 1792, Amilpas trespassers were captured by Soyaltepec and imprisoned by district authorities who supported the Soyaltepec action.

An eloquent president may be quite effective in bringing the assembled citizens around to his point of view. His eloquence is, in fact, his chief means of implementing his opinions. Since he has no real power, he must rely on his ability to argue, persuade, and hopefully to prevail upon, the assembled audience of his fellow citizens. In Amilpas assemblies which I attended, the president continually emphasized his role as defender of the village interests, while urging citizens to follow the course he proposed, which he claimed was in their best interests. Because of the ideal of community service, the president must phrase his arguments in terms of community welfare, and not in terms of mere self-protection; but a persuasive president should be able to show that avoiding conflict for which he will be held responsible is also the wisest course of action. He can argue that pressing forward with petitions, bribes, and litigation— a task in which he is already engaged—is really the most effective way to achieve community objectives. The eloquence which makes the president an effective intermediary also enables him to deal with his own community.

A third general strategy is to avoid, as much as possible, potentially dangerous conflict situations. Men who have been important in village political history have not been conspicuous as conflict leaders while actually in office. It was while acting as private individuals (*particulares*) that they played a prominent role in actual confrontations with the opposing village. The leader of the Amilpas vigilance patrol in 1928, who was chiefly responsible for the execution, had previously served as village president but occupied no important position at the time. As village officials, men are seemingly reluctant to "compromise" themselves, whereas by "moving a conflict" as private individuals they are compromising someone else, namely, the current officials.

When the president finds himself in a completely untenable situation because of conflicting role expectations, the ultimate solution is to abandon his post temporarily. This is simply a variant of the third general type of strategy, i.e., avoiding conflict situations, but it is a spectacular and interesting variation on the theme. Abandoning his post is appropriate behavior when a *tumulto* breaks out which the president cannot control, but for which he will be held responsible. In such a case, abandoning one's post is an expected, almost institutionalized pattern of behavior, and it is viewed as a shrewd and entirely commendable strategy on the part of the president. Valentín Mendoza, a famous president of Amilpas during the 1909–10 period, is supposed to have been especially good at this.

> One time about 11:00 they began to fight in *Arroyo de Popote*. When Valentín heard that the villages were fighting, he got on his horse and went to Etla. When he got there, neither the *Jefe Político* nor the *Agente del Ministerio Público* were there. They were at a banquet in San Juan del Estado. Valentín went on up there. Then, when the battle was over here, and Soyaltepec went to accuse the Amilpas president, the *Jefe Político* said, "Why, Valentín was with me in San Juan del Estado!" Said Valentín, "I didn't see that, I can't give any account of it." "How could he have been fighting," said the *Jefe Político,* "if he was at the banquet with me?" Valentín had a good head on his shoulders [Amilpas informant]

In this case Valentín, the president, "uncompromised" himself by establishing an incontrovertible alibi.

Abandoning his post seems to be viewed as clever strategy because it preserves the president's integrity for the more important business of carrying on litigation through the government. It would be foolish for the president to be out fighting with the rest of the citizens when, by establishing an alibi, he could remain an effective intermediary with the government, able, perhaps, to defend the very citizens involved in the *tumulto*. To involve himself personally in violence would be counterproductive in terms of the welfare of the other citizens. I had assumed at first that a president would act as a conflict leader, taking all active part in the violent aspects of the dispute. Informants assured me that this was not the case.

> (Should the president be in the front of the conflict?) The president? No! The president is in reserve, looking for the way to defend his people. [Amilpas informant]

It is the government's expectation that the president will act as a conflict leader, but such all expectation is unrealistic given the president's awareness of the constraints under which he operates. No competent president would be caught in such an affair, for, apart from bearing the brunt of the responsibility himself, he would also eliminate the possibility of continuing to act as an effective intermediary. In effect, the president temporarily abandons his post in order to retain it longer.

A president is not supposed to be "fierce" or "violent" (*bravo*) like the men who participate in *tumultos*, but shrewd and intelligent, something of a "country lawyer." Another anecdote about Valentín illustrates these qualities very well. At one point in the feud Valentín rode to Etla to bring the soldiers, when violence seemed imminent. As the soldiers prepared to come, he sent word back to the Amilpeños to hide their firearms. When the soldiers arrived, they found the armed Soyaltepec men along the border, and promptly confiscated their firearms, leaving the still armed Amilpeños at a great advantage. A president thus fights most effectively, not with a gun or *machete,* but with his head, assisted, where possible, by documents, bribes, and village *patrones.*

Conclusion

The Oaxacan village president's position as political middleman is recognized as a difficult one, particularly in the case of intervillage disputes. Unlike more familiar middlemen, he gains little power, and on the contrary must exhibit considerable dexterity in dealing with the contradictory expectations of fellow villagers and higher authorities. Men are reluctant to attempt the role; those who are successful at it must be able to preserve themselves as effective intermediaries, by arguing persuasively for actions acceptable to their superiors, by avoiding personal participation in violent incidents, and at times by temporarily abandoning their post to escape responsibility.

NOTES

1. A preliminary version of this paper was presented at the symposium on "Ethnic Communities, Dominant Systems, and National Integration" at the 32nd annual meeting of the Society for Applied Anthropology, Tucson, Arizona, April, 1973. I am grateful to Drs. Edwin Eames, Vera Green, Janet Moone, and other participants in the symposium, for their comments and criticism.

2. I spent fifteen months in Amilpas and Soyaltepec in 1970–71 doing field work. My research was supported by a National Institute of Health Traineeship (Grant No. 1256) through the Department of Anthropology, Cornell University. The names of villages and individuals have been changed in this paper.

3. Several large scale *tumultos* were reported in the Oaxaca newspapers during the course of my research. In a *tumulto* between San Sabastían Abasolo and Santa María Guelaxé three men were killed (*Oaxaca Gráfico,* Nov. 16, 1970), and several others killed in follow-up incidents. I gathered what information I could about such active feuds from a distance, while studying in detail the relatively dormant dispute between Amilpas and Soyaltepec.

4. Other village officials, especially the *Comisariado,* play a similar but less important kind of role. I have focused on the village president as the official with the most responsibility, and therefore most likely to be trapped in the position of political middleman.

BIBLIOGRAPHY

Beals, R. L. 1945. Ethnology of the Western Mixe. University of California Publications in American Archaeology and Ethnology 42: 1–176.

Bieler, C. 1973. The Institutions of Portuguese-Canadian Integration in Toronto; or, Where is Multiculturalism? Paper presented at the 32nd annual meeting of the Society for Applied Anthropology, Tucson, Arizona.

Dennis, P. A. 1973. An Inter-Village Land Feud in the Valley of Oaxaca, Mexico. Unpublished Ph.D. dissertation, Cornell University.

Fallers, L. 1955. The Predicament of the Modern African Chief: An Instance from Uganda. American Anthropologist 57: 290–305.

Friedrich, P. 1968. The Legitimacy of a Cacique. Local-Level Politics, ed. Marc J. Swartz, pp. 243–269. Chicago.

Geertz, C. 1960 The Javanese Kijaji: The Changing Role of a Culture Broker. Comparative Studies in Society and History 2: 228–249.

Lewis, O. 1951. Life in a Mexican Village: Tepoztlan Restudied. Urbana.

Loffler, R. 1971. The Representative Mediator and the New Peasant. American Anthropologist 73: 1077–1091.

Pérez Jiménez, G. 1968. La institución del municipio libre en Oaxaca: prontuario de legislación orgánica municipal. Mexico.

Swartz, M. J. 1968. The Political Middleman. Local-Level Politics, ed. Marc J. Swartz, pp. 199–204. Chicago.

Taylor, W. B. 1972. Landlord and Peasant in Colonial Oaxaca. Stanford.

Wolf, E. R. 1955. Types of Latin American Peasantry: A Preliminary Discussion. American Anthropologist 57: 452–471.

———. 1956. Aspects of Group Relations in a Complex Society: Mexico. American Anthropologist 58: 1065–1078.

———. 1957. Closed Corporate Peasant Communities in Mesoamerica and Central Java. Southwestern Journal of Anthropology 13: 1–18.

———. 1967. Levels of Communal Relations. Handbook of Middle American Indians 6: 299–316. Austin.

Patronage and Community-Nation Relationships in Central Italy[1]

Sydel F. Silverman

As a political framework becomes more complex, the problem of control of the entire entity looms large. The multiplicity of levels and their different groupings pose an integration problem. Silverman puts this dilemma into ethnographic perspective, suggesting that in Italy a system of patronage which developed was a potential path to emerging nationhood or the creation of a functioning state.

Electoral politics, together with an expanding state, may either destroy or co-opt patron-client politics. The patterns by which the vertical structure of loyalty and power break down and become redirected are central issues for anthropology as it grapples with the way communities are integrated into national and transnational power configurations.

ONE OF THE most strategic yet formidable problems in the anthropological study of complex societies is the relationship of the parts to the whole of such societies. Most attempts to tackle this problem have been concerned primarily with those parts which are localized social systems, or communities,[2] interdependent with though analytically separable from the whole, a national social system. The community and national levels of sociocultural integration of Steward (1955: 43–63), the discussion of tensions between pueblo and state by Pitt-Rivers (1954: 202–210), the community-oriented groups and nation-oriented groups of Wolf (1956), and the local roles and national roles of Pitkin (1959) are only a few examples of this recurring contrast, the social analogue of the great-tradition/little-tradition approach to complex cultures. Such a model immediately sets the task of formulating the interaction between the two systems.

210

One of the more promising efforts to describe this interaction has been the concept of the "mediator," an individual or group that acts as a link between local and national social systems. Wolf introduced the idea of the cultural "broker" in a discussion of data from Mexico, defining as "brokers" the "groups of people who mediate between community-oriented groups in communities and nation-oriented groups which operate through national institutions" (Wolf 1956: 1075). The mediating functions which Wolf emphasizes are economic and political, and he traces a succession of three phases in the post-Columbian history of Mexico during which these functions were carried out by different groups in the society. In his review of peasant-society research published the same year, Redfield (1956) observed that a recurrent phenomenon in many societies is the existence of a "hinge" group, administrative and cultural intermediaries who form a link between the local life of a peasant community and the state of which it is a part. The concept of the mediator is relevant to many studies of "part-societies" which exist within a larger encompassing whole. It describes the pivotal chiefs within colonial nations, whose positions derive from earlier periods of tribal autonomy, as well as the elites looked up to by peasants, deriving from a historical balance between two stable classes; the formal agents of national institutions, who penetrate into communities from distant capitals, as well as the upwardly mobile villagers who move into positions in national institutions.

In the analysis of material collected during field work in a Central Italian community, the concept of the mediator proved to be most pertinent for understanding the relationship of the community to the larger society during a particular period. However, it was found that if this relationship is followed over time, not only are there changes with regard to the groups which perform mediation functions, as Wolf (1956) showed for Mexico, and the roles through which mediation is effected, as Geertz (1960) showed for Java, but there are fundamental changes in the structuring of links between community and nation. These changes suggest that the concept of the mediator is most useful if defined narrowly and thus restricted to a particular form of part-whole relationship.

The concept refers to a status which functions as a link between a local system and a national system. In interactional terms, the mediator may be seen as one to whom action is originated from the national system and who in turn originates action to the local system; to some extent, the direction is reversible, the mediator still being the middle element. However, if the mediator were to be defined merely as anyone who acts as a means of contact between the systems, it would include such a wide range of phenomena as to become virtually meaningless. Moreover, such a definition would obscure the important differences between various kinds of contacts which may exist.

Wolf (1956: 1075) referred to the "brokers" as persons who "stand guard over the critical junctures or synapses of relationships which connect the local system to the larger whole." By taking Wolf's terms in their full implications, it is possible to arrive at a more precise definition. First of all, the functions which those who are defined as mediators are concerned with must be "critical," of direct importance to the basic structures of either or both systems. For example, a person who brings awareness of a new fashion in clothing from the national into the local system would not by virtue of this function alone be considered a mediator, even though he does act as a communicational intermediary. Second, the mediators "guard" these functions, i.e., they have near-exclusivity in performing them; exclusivity means that if the link is to be made at all between the two systems with respect to the particular function, it must be made through the mediators. As a result, the number of mediator statuses is always limited. To the extent that alternative links become available, so that the mediators lose their exclusive control of the junctures, they cease to be mediators. These two criteria, critical functions and exclusivity, limit the extension of the concept. Persons who provide contact between the two systems but who do not necessarily fulfill both criteria will be referred to here as "intermediaries." While the terminology is clumsy, it is felt that there is an important distinction which needs to be made between the broader category, "intermediary," and the special kind of intermediary, the "mediator."

It seems to be general that there is a rank difference between the mediator and the other persons in the local system who are involved in the mediated interaction. The mediators may take on their function because of previous possession of a higher rank, or they may achieve a higher rank as a result of assuming the mediator role. In either case, the relationship between the local and the national system assumes a "vertical" form.

The concept of the mediator was developed out of the study of particular kinds of societies, those to which anthropologists first turned when they began to move beyond the primitives, namely complex societies which still retain a strong "folk" element. That it is within such societies that the concept finds its widest applicability suggests the possibility that it may represent a form of part-whole relationship peculiar to the preindustrial state society. It is obvious that in a society at a pre-state level of integration there would be little necessity for mediators. On the other hand, the existence of mediators implies that the local units are separate from each other and from the larger society to the extent that a limited group can have exclusive control over the connections between part and whole—a situation associated with preindustrial societies. However, if the mediator is characteristic of this sociocultural level, it may be expected to be replaced by other kinds of community-nation interaction with further integration of the national society.

The present discussion explores this possibility. It examines the traditional mediators in the community of Colleverde, a patron group, and traces the impact of contemporary national development upon them. It attempts to show that "mediators" can best be understood as elements of a particular form of part-whole relationship, one which exists at a particular level of development of complex societies but which is superseded with further development.

The Community

Colleverde (a pseudonym) is an Umbrian *comune* near the geographical center of Italy, about 50 kilometers from the provincial capital, Perugia, and approximately 550 kilometers north of Rome. The medieval castle-village which is the functional center of the community is situated on a hilltop overlooking the valley of the Tiber. The countryside of the *comune* covers a wide range of environmental variation, from a strip of level plain along the banks of the Tiber (about 550 meters above sea level), through a region of low and medium hills, to the woods, meadows, and wasteland of a high-hill zone (up to 650 meters). In 1960, Colleverde parish (one of two parishes in the *comune,* each of which may be considered a separate community) had a population of 1,885 in 465 households. About one-fifth of the inhabitants live in the village, the remainder on dispersed farms in the surrounding countryside.

About 80 per cent of the active population are agriculturalists. The majority work self-contained farmsteads, most of which comprise between two and fifteen hectares. Except for minor variations due to altitude, each farm produces the entire range of local crops and animals: wheat, olives, wine grapes, maize, a variety of minor crops grown for human and animal subsistence and for renewal of the land, meat calves (which since the advent of tractors after World War II have been rapidly eliminating the work oxen which were formerly raised), pigs, a few sheep, and barnyard fowl. In addition, industrial crops (tobacco, sugar beet, and tomato) have been introduced on a small scale in the irrigated tracts of the plain. Of these products, only the wheat, calves, and industrial crops are raised primarily or exclusively for sale. At least two-thirds of the land is cultivated under the *mezzadria* system of share-farming, while the remainder is worked by peasant proprietors, tenant farmers, and a few wage-laborers.

The *mezzadria* system is based on a contractual association between a landowner, who furnishes the farm (including cleared land, farmhouse, outbuildings, and livestock) and advances all working capital as needed, and a peasant family who provide labor and the minor equipment. All other expenses and the income of the enterprise are divided between them, theoretically half and half; in 1948 the peasant's share of the income was raised by law to 53 per cent. As compared with other sharecropping systems, the *mezzadria* is distinguished by three elements: the integrated farm, the family labor unit, and the active participation in investments and operation of the enterprise on the part of both owner and cultivators.

The integrity of the farm and the major dependence upon a family for its labor requirements imply a recurrent imbalance between the number of working hands and the size of the farm. Adjustment is made primarily by a movement of families among farms as major changes in family size occur. Partly because large households traditionally were advantageous to the *mezzadri* (enabling them to work a larger farm),[3] the ideal household consisted of a patrilocal extended family, in which all sons brought their brides to live in their father's household and in which authority and economic control were vested in the family head. Although during the past few decades the largest households have been breaking up, more than half the *mezzadria* families still have at least one married son residing in the parental household. In the community as a whole, however, only a third of the households consist of extended families, and the predominant form is the nuclear family.

The community is economically and socially heterogeneous. The fundamental principle of settlement pattern, the segregation of village center and countryside, demarcates the most pervasive social division, the people of "inside" and those of "outside." This cleavage is occupational: those who do not work the land (landowners and administrators of agricultural properties, professionals, clerks, merchants, artisans, and laborers) as against those who do. It is the major correlate of social-class differentiation: the *signori* (the local upper class) and a middle group consisting of the working people of families resident in the village for generations, as against the great lower class. It describes, in general, political party alignments within the community: the Right and Center as against the Left. To some extent it parallels a difference in the spirit of religious participation: the "cynical" (in the view of the Colleverdesi) as against the devout. It is also a cultural division, for the village is regarded as the seat of civilization surrounded by rusticity, bringing *civiltà* (that which is "civilized," in the sense of "citified") to the countryside and bestowing the aura of *civiltà* on the whole community.

Patronage

Until the recent postwar period, the mediation of relations between Colleverde and the larger society was the function of a patronage system. Before discussing this function, it will be helpful to describe the general features of traditional patronage in the community. Patronage patterns are familiar to all the older contemporary Colleverdesi, whose recollections (supplemented by local historical documents) were the basis for the following reconstruction. However, only vestiges of them remain today.

Patronage as a cross-cultural pattern may be defined as an informal contractual relationship between persons of unequal status and power, which imposes reciprocal obligations of a different kind on each of the parties. As a minimum, what is owed is, protection and favor on the one side and loyalty on the other. The relationship is on a personal, face-to-face basis, and it is a continuing one.

As is the case in other cultures where a patron-client relationship receives explicit recognition, patronage in Central Italy is not coterminous with all the meanings of the term for "patron" (cf. Kenny 1960: 14–15; Foster 1963: 1282). In Colleverde, the term *padrone* is applied to: (1) the legal owner of something, for example a house or a dog; (2) one who controls something, such as the mistress of a household, or one who has self-control; (3) an employer, when reference is made to him by or to an employee; (4) the grantor of a *mezzadria* farm, whether or not he is actually the landowner and whether or not there is anything more than minimal contact with the cultivators; (5) a guardian deity; and (6) a patron in a patron-client relationship.[4] However, all of these usages which refer to one person as the padrone of another describe potential bases for the formation of a patron-client relationship.

The most important patron-client relationship in Colleverde was that between the parties to the *mezzadria* arrangement. The relationship developed informally, by extension of the formal terms of the contract. A peasant might approach the landlord to ask a favor, perhaps a loan of money or help in some trouble with the law, or the landlord might offer his aid knowing of a problem. If the favor were granted or accepted, further favors were likely to be asked or offered at some later time. The peasant would reciprocate—at a time and in a context different from that of the acceptance of the favor, in order to de-emphasize the material self-interest of the reciprocative action—by bringing the landlord especially choice offerings from the farm produce, by sending some member of the peasant family to perform services in the landlord's home, by refraining from cheating the landlord, or merely by speaking well of him in public and professing devotion to him.[5] Or the peasant might be the first to offer his "favors," in anticipation of those he would later have to ask of the landlord. Whether or not a true patronage relationship developed from the *mezzadria* association depended upon the landlord's inclination, his need of support, and his place of residence (or the length of an absentee owner's yearly sojourn in Colleverde).

The *mezzadria* association was particularly conducive to the development of a patronage relationship, for the institution had the effect of bringing landlord and peasant into long and personal contact with each other. The minimum duration of the contract is one year, but typically it persists for several years, and traditionally it was common for a farm to be occupied by the same family for many decades and even for generations. The landowner's role as director of the enterprise requires his continuing interest and his physical presence much of the time. Some proprietors employ managers (*fattori*), who range from unskilled foremen and commercial agents to highly trained agricultural technicians, but traditionally even when this was the case the landlords maintained close contact with their farms. In contrast to the typical situation in southern Italy, the landowning class throughout the *mezzadria* area has a strong tradition of active interest in agriculture; for example, many receive higher education in fields which equip them for the management of their property. There is, in fact, a marked tendency to glorify their attachment to their land and "their" peasants.

Until recent years, the owners of Colleverde's land were the nucleus of the village population, constituting a local upper class. In other communities of the area, those proprietors who did not reside in the rural centers lived in the nearby towns and small cities and often retained part-time residences near their band. Thus the landlords were accessible. Moreover, close and continuing contact between landlord and peasant was encouraged not only by the necessary interaction related to the operations of the farm but also by the cultural definition of the *mezzadria* relationship. The association was ideally a personal and affectionate tie ranging far beyond the formal contract covering the enterprise, a tie between two families, one the protector and benefactor and the other the loyal dependent. To the peasant, the landlord was the most immediately available person to turn to for economic aid or for knowledge about the world outside. To the landlord, a patronage relationship was at the least a great convenience. It provided a check against being taken advantage of, a check that was cheaper, more reliable, and in any case a useful supplement to supervision by *fattori*. It facilitated contacts with the peasant and contributed to the day-to-day efficiency of the enterprise. Finally, it was a means of controlling potentially disruptive influences from the outside. It is significant that the paternalism of the *mezzadria* landlords has often been pointed to as a factor in delaying the spread of labor agitation to the Central Italian hill region for several decades after its onset in many agricultural areas of the nation about 1870 (Bandini 1957: 77–78).

A peasant whose own landlord was unavailable or who was unable or unwilling to dispense favors occasionally turned to other landowners. More common was the formation of a patron-client relationship between lower-class persons who were not *mezzadri* and a local landlord or other local person of high status and power. The potential client would approach one of the *signori* with a request, or he might attempt to establish the relationship first by presenting him with some small gift or by making himself available to run errands or help out in various ways. Such relationships, although they did not center about common participation in an agricultural enterprise, resembled and may be said to have been patterned after the landlord-peasant relationship.

The patron-client relationships in Colleverde differed from those which Foster observed in Mexico in one important respect. An essential aspect of such relationships in Tzintzuntzan is that they are dyadic; they can exist only between two individuals: "Ego conceptualizes his obligations and expectations as a two-way street, he at one end and a single partner at the other end" (Foster 1963: 1281). In Colleverde, however, the dyad was not the only or even the most frequent form. When the relationship was formed between *mezzadria* landlord and peasant, the landlord became patron not to an individual but to an entire household. His obligations automatically extended to all members of the peasant family, unless some member specifically rejected his own obligations as client. On the other hand, the wife of the landlord became *la padrona*, and she was expected to adopt the role of patroness, especially toward the women of the peasant family. To a lesser extent, other members of the landlord's family were also treated as patrons and sometimes accepted the obligations of patronage. These extensions of the patron and client roles to whole households were not the result of independently established contracts; they were more or less automatic, although the other persons were not strictly bound to accept the role.

Furthermore, there was in Colleverde the concept of an individual (or a married couple or family) becoming patron to a group made up of unrelated persons. Traditionally, there were several community associations and organized projects (an important example was the 40-member band) which were initiated and/or maintained by local *signori,* who were considered their patrons. Such persons gave economic support and political protection to these groups (not to their members as individuals).

Similarly, certain *signori* regarded themselves and were generally regarded by others as patrons of the community, with the responsibility to
provide benefits for the community as a whole. One way in which this
was done was by leaving a will providing that part of their patrimony be
used in specific ways by the community. Such endowments were a major
source of public funds and community charities.

The Patron as Mediator

The descriptions of patronage systems in various cultural settings suggest
that one of the most important aspects of the patron's role is to relate the
client to the world outside the local community. Pitt-Rivers (1954: 141)
emphasized this point in his analysis of an Andalusian village: "It is, above
all, [the patron's] relationship to the powers outside the pueblo which
gives him value." In Andalusia, a structure of patronage links the authority
of the state to the network of neighborly relations and balances "the
tension between the state and the community" (Pitt-Rivers 1954: 154–
55). Kenny (1960: 17–18), writing about Castile, observed that the patrons are validly described as "gatekeepers," for "they largely dominate
the paths linking the local infrastructure of the village to the superstructure of the outside urban world." In general, the patrons described from
recent times in Spain and Latin America, and those of traditional Central
Italy, are mediators in the full sense of the definition adopted here. Their
functions are critical ones, for they have an essential part in the basic
economic and political structures of the society. Moreover, persons become patrons precisely because their capacity to perform these functions
is virtually exclusive.

It would appear, in fact, that patrons are particularly well adapted to
performing the function of mediation between the local and the national
system. The patron usually has a distinctly defined status in both systems
and operates effectively in both. Furthermore, the relationship between
patron and client is stable and durable. As Foster has pointed out, continuance of the relationship is assured by never permitting a balance to be
achieved between the obligations of the parties; the account is never
settled, but rather each constantly wins new credits which will be re-
deemed at a future time or incurs new debts which must later be paid.
Stability of the patron-client tie is reinforced by its patterning after a kin
relationship, the patron becoming "like a father" in obligations to and
respect due from the client (as the close connection between "patronage" and "paternalism" suggests). Personalized terms of address are used,
there generally are affective overtones to the relationship, and frequently
there is a denial of utilitarian motives and an insistence instead upon the

non-priced demands of "loyalty," "friendship," or being "almost like one of the family." (One Colleverdese woman explained her economically advantageous relationship with her patroness with the statement, "We are old friends, so we always ask each other for favors.") In societies where social mobility is limited and where kinship therefore cannot function as a link between the local and the national system (cf. Friedl 1959), patronage provides a close, highly sanctioned, and self-perpetuating relationship between different social strata as a link between the systems.

Nevertheless, the data from Colleverde suggest that this aspect of patronage is a fairly recent acquisition. Until the unification of Italy in 1860, mediation of the client's dealings with the outside was only a minor aspect of the patron's role. The patronage system had its basis in the peasants' dependence upon the landlords, who historically were the peasants' sole recourse to physical protection and economic aid. However, under the domain of the States of the Church, the community had only tangential relations with the larger political unit, and for most Colleverdesi the sphere of social interaction extended no farther than the nearby market towns and a radius of neighboring communities within which there were cycles of fairs and religious festivals. Certainly for the lower classes extra-local contact was minimal, and there was little necessity for mediation.

After 1860, however, the new nation began the task of knitting together the separate regions and communities. The degree of contact between the national and the local system increased steadily, and more and more the nation encroached into the lives of Colleverdesi of all classes. The governmental bureaucracy entered the community, bringing to the peasants the bewildering demands of official papers and legal codes and occasionally offering equally bewildering economic benefits. New roads and railroads brought outsiders into the community and took Colleverdesi out. Obligatory military service and temporary labor opportunities in other areas took men to distant parts of the nation. To some the developing national institutions meant potential jobs, both within the community and outside it. In order to deal with their expanding world, the lower-class Colleverdesi needed help. The peasants turned to those who had always aided them. Persons who had no landlord, or whose landlord was unwilling or unable to help, sought other sources.

Of the functions performed by the patrons during the period from 1860 to 1945, some represent a continuity with the earlier role of the landlord: lending money or guaranteeing loans, giving employment, helping to provide dowries for the daughters of the client families, providing medicines and helping to obtain medical services. However, to these were added many new functions involving the mediation of contacts with the world outside the community. The patron filled out the papers which were required at every significant step in the individual's life, and he spoke to bureaucrats on his client's behalf. As government benefits were introduced, the patron was needed to obtain them. For example, Sra. M., whose husband was killed during World War I, tried in vain for months to collect a government pension for war widows, and only after her patron spoke of her case to the appropriate officials did she succeed in getting it. The patron interpreted the law to his client and offered advice. If there were trouble with the authorities, the patron would intervene. Many cases could be cited of persons who were arrested by the *carabinieri* and released after intervention of the patron, and of others who were sentenced to prison and for whom the patron obtained pardons.

If a client had to go out of the community for any purpose, the patron would recommend him to some acquaintance at the destination. In fact, all dealings with institutions or persons outside the local system required personal recommendations from a mediator.[6] When M.'s grandfather tried to get the local tobacco concession, when R. applied to a military specialists' school, when F. took his deaf sister to a physician in Rome, when P. as a young man went periodically to the coastal plain to seek work, when T. took his bride to Perugia to choose a coral necklace—all would have considered it foolhardy to do so without a recommendation from a respected contact, and to get a recommendation a patron was needed. As jobs in the national institutions expanded, access to them was also a matter of recommendations, and this remained no less true even after adoption of the *concorso* system, an open competition for available jobs based on examinations.

In the patronage patterns of traditional Colleverde which were vividly recalled by older informants, the mediation functions were, in fact, the major importance of the patron. For example, the most valuable patron was neither the wealthiest nor the most generous, but the one with the best connections. Yet this aspect of the patron's role was elaborated only in the late nineteenth and early twentieth centuries. It was only after the community became incorporated into a complex nation, a nation which made demands upon and offered opportunities to individuals and which required extensive contact between the local and the national system, that the dominant features of "traditional" Colleverdesi patronage emerged.

In general, the patrons of Colleverdesi in the 1860–1945 years can be characterized as a small group of local *signori,* no more than a dozen heads of households at any given time. Most were *mezzadria* landlords, owning as little as two or three small farms or as much as several hundred hectares of land. Some of the landlords also occupied professional or administrative positions of authority in the community, as schoolteachers, pharmacists, physicians, tax collectors, priests, and elected administrators. In addition, some of these positions were held by non-landed members of local landowning families, who also formed part of the patron group. The non-land-owning patrons also included a few bureaucrats and professionals (the *comune* secretaries, two of the pharmacists, a physician, and some of the priests), who came to Colleverde from other towns in Umbria.

The patrons were not an aristocratic group, although a few landowning families traced remote kinship ties to Umbrian nobility. New members were recruited from the commercial class of the towns and cities of the region, for it was this class that throughout Umbria was taking over the holdings of the traditional landowners and educating its sons for the burgeoning bureaucracy and the professions. There was little mobility into the patron group from the lower classes of Colleverde, for the sons of the prosperous peasants and artisans who were able to purchase land, even those who acquired substantial holdings, were not accepted as true *signori,* nor were they likely to possess the connections with *signori* in other communities which were an important foundation of patronage power. Despite their ties and sometimes their origins outside the community, the patrons were fully a local group. They lived in Colleverde, and their identification with it was strong.

Each patron performed a wide range of mediation functions, the same individual often being for his clients at once the economic, political, social, and ideological link to the larger society. As a group, the patrons controlled virtually all the critical junctures between the local and the national systems. Colleverde's economic relationships with the rest of the nation were for the most part the concern only of the major landlords. This follows from the duality of the traditional *mezzadria* economy: only the landowners sold produce on the market, while the peasants' share was consumed for their own subsistence. Direct participation in the political life of the nation was limited to the patrons. The mayor and the administrative council of the community were selected from this group; they were elected, but until well into the twentieth century few persons other than the *signori* were eligible to vote. Moreover, it was primarily members of this group, who acted as local representatives of the state, for local jobs in the bureaucracy were passed from one member of the elite to another. Even the religious ties of the community to the Universal Church were to a large extent in the hands of the patrons. Not only were the priests of Colleverde themselves often part of the patron group (as major landlords holding the several Church-owned *mezzadria* farms and usually as members of landowning families), but the patrons constituted the lay leadership of the local Church, and many had kin connections with Church officials throughout Umbria and in the Vatican.

The patrons had numerous social relationships based on kinship and friendship extending beyond the community, and they practiced frequent inter-community visiting. The peasants, in contrast, maintained only rare ties of closest kinship outside the immediate area. Finally, because the patrons were long the only literate persons in Colleverde, they were the carriers of the national culture, and values and ideas filtered down through them to the rest of the community. In sum, this group were mediators precisely because they had, almost exclusively, direct access to the nation and because they occupied those formal positions which were the links between the local and national systems. In turn, this control of the mediation functions was the primary source of their power to exert patronage.

Looking outward from the community, the mediators' relationships with the national system were of two kinds. First, the local patrons had extensive ties with near and distant kinsmen, friends, and business associates—social and power equals to themselves—in other village centers, in towns, and in cities of the region. These were continuing relationships based on reciprocal, equivalent obligations. Second, the Colleverdesi patrons, as well as their equal numbers in other communities, were themselves clients to more powerful, higher-status patrons. These higher patrons did not function at the village level but belonged to the spheres of town and city. Thus, through a hierarchy of patronage (cf. Kenny 1960: 22–23; Gillin 1962: 37), Colleverde was linked to the higher units of organization within the nation.

The structure of the traditional relationship between Colleverde and the larger society may now be summarized. A small group of local upper-class families, the nucleus of which were the major landowners of the community, functioned as mediators. Although they considered themselves as Colleverdesi and were active in community life, they were also participants in the national society. Within the local context they acted out the national culture, creating—of a village of only 300 inhabitants—an urban-like, "civilized" center in the rustic countryside. Interaction between the mediators and those in the community for whom they mediated was based on a continuing and intimate patron-client relationship, which was an extension of the landlord-peasant relationship defined by the land-tenure system. Because of the nature of this relationship and the constant presence of the patrons, the clients were strongly aware of a wider social sphere without direct participation in it. Thus, the countryside was linked to the village (and the village lower class to its upper class) by the vertical bond of patronage, while the village was in turn linked to the outside through the patrons' participation in two kinds of networks: horizontal ties with equivalent members of other communities and vertical ties through hierarchies of patrons operating at progressively higher levels of national integration.

This description is an example of only one form that a part-whole relationship through mediators can take. Such a relationship varies significantly in at least five different ways. First, there is the tie between the mediators and those in the local system for whom they mediate, which need not be one of patronage. Not only are there other mechanisms by which the connection with a mediator may be established (such as kinship, ritual kinship, employment, or political appointment) and other cultural rationales for maintaining the connection, but the mutual rights and obligations and the kind of interaction involved may be different. The relationship may be limited to specific areas rather than as wide-ranging as the patron-client tie; the interaction may be sporadic rather than fairly continuous; and the quality of the relationship may be more or less emotionally intense than that between patron and client in Colleverde.

Second, the nature of the mediators themselves may vary greatly— their history, their traditions, and the manner in which they are recruited and replaced. For example, a mediating group recruited from economically successful peasants would be quite different from the patrons of Colleverde, a landowning class with quasi-aristocratic traditions.

Third, there is variation in the particular functions which the mediators perform and in the way in which these functions are combined. A political functionary whose main business is the collection of taxes is a mediator of a very different kind from the Colleverdesi patrons, whose functions touched every aspect of life. In the case of Colleverde, all mediating functions were combined and performed by the same group, but at the opposite extreme there might be a separate mediator for each function.

Fourth, the size of the mediating group may vary, determining a smaller or larger number of channels into the local system. In Colleverde there were multiple channels, intermediate between the extreme possibilities of a single individual as mediator and a situation in which each household has its own links to the national system.

A fifth dimension of variation is the kind of relationship of the mediators to the local system and the degree of their integration into it. The patrons of Colleverde were fully a part of the local system and locally resident. However, mediators may also be part of the local system yet not reside in the community, they may reside locally but remain detached from the local system, or they may be outsiders with only tangential relationships to the local system.

The Elimination of Mediators

In the period since World War II there have been fundamental changes in the relationship between the Central Italian rural community and the larger society. The patrons of Colleverde, the traditional mediators between the local and the national system, have been pushed out of the strategic link positions. However, they have not simply been replaced by other emerging groups. Rather, it may be said that there has been change in the nature of the links between community and nation.

In contemporary Colleverde there is no longer a patron group. In part this is the result of the economic decline of the families which formed the nucleus of this group. A century ago, all but a minor part of the landed property in the community was concentrated in their hands. With time, however, there has been a continuing increase both in the total number of landowners and in the proportion of land owned by persons of non-local or lower-class origin. These changes began with the inheritance provisions of the Civil Code of 1865, which required that a large portion of the patrimony be divided equally among all children. A high birth rate and a declining mortality rate among the landowning families during the late nineteenth century contributed to the subdivision of inheritances. By the turn of the century some of the landlords had fallen into debt, and mortgaged land gradually passed to members of the urban commercial class and to estate agents who were able to exploit their employers' indebtedness. At the same time, and particularly in the years during and after World War I, a number of local peasants and other landless individuals were able to acquire small amounts of land, through profits from agriculture or through wage labor or commercial ventures. After World War II this trend was intensified; it was accelerated by laws encouraging peasant proprietorship, but mainly it was the result of the rising values of livestock, the expansion of cash crops, and wage-labor opportunities in a nearby tobacco factory and in the industries of northern Italy, Germany, and France.

The present distribution of land ownership indicates an absence of any substantial holdings in the hands of either local descendants of the traditional patron families or other local residents who might have taken over the role of the patrons. The contemporary holdings fall into three general categories, according to size. The major landlords, four individuals with holdings of about 500 hectares each, are all outsiders—absentee owners, none of whom was raised or lived for any length of time in Colleverde, and whose relations to their peasants and the community in general are impersonal. Four landlords have what may be considered medium-sized holdings (about 35 to 50 hectares). All are Colleverdesi by birth and residence, but none is of a traditional landowning family, and none thinks of his role as properly one of patronage or is regarded in this way by others in the community (they are scornfully referred to as "*signori* merely through money," as opposed to the "true *Signori*, through birth and mentality"). Among the owners of small holdings are many of the descendants of the old patron group, some of whom still live in Colleverde, frugally, and some of whom have moved into bureaucratic and professional positions in larger centers, returning to the community for summer holidays and for retirement in their old age.

Thus the economic decline of the traditional patrons has not been accompanied by the emergence of any new group to assume an analogous role, for there is no longer any local concentration of wealth sufficient to provide the foundation of a patron group. Moreover, of the most prosperous persons in the community today, none either belongs to the tradition of patronage or has the social status to which the patron role is appropriate.

In the absence of a patron group, what has become of the traditional functions of the patrons? Many of the functions of economic assistance have been taken over by the state. Instead of the favors of a patron, there are governmental credit institutions, a national health plan, an official charitable organization supported by land set aside for this purpose by the government, assistance for infants and nursing mothers, sickness and disability benefits, old-age pensions, and special allotments during agricultural crises and other times of special need. Other institutions which will be mentioned below (political parties, syndicalist organizations, and the Church) also offer assistance on a limited scale.

The primary concern here, however, is with the mediation functions formerly performed by the patrons. Some of these have been eliminated entirely in the postwar period, as persons of all classes and categories have been brought into direct participation in the national system. The partial incorporation of the *mezzadri* into the market economy (the last occupational category to be so affected), the movement of political activity into the piazzas and bars of the community consequent upon universal suffrage, the emphasis upon individual membership in a Universal Church at the expense of community-wide, locally oriented religious activity— these are all manifestations of the general process of the integration of separate communities into a national unit, which implies an increasing degree of non-mediated participation in national life. The most important specific developments in Colleverde which have facilitated this increase in non-mediated participation have been inexpensive means of transportation (particularly local bus service and the motorcycle), the expansion of literacy and elementary education which provide the basic skills of participation, and radio and television which bring knowledge of the larger society even to the immobile and illiterate.

Nevertheless, the individual Colleverdesi continues to be related to the national system through a number of indirect links as well. These indirect links, corresponding to the formal positions and informal roles through which the patrons acted as mediators, have been taken over by other groups, both from within and outside Colleverde.

The elective administrative positions of the community have been held since the first free elections after World War II primarily by *mezzadria* peasants, as a result of the consistent victories of the Communist-Socialist coalition ticket. The only group which has any possibility of succeeding to local political control, the members of the organized political opposition, consists mainly of the upwardly mobile sons of peasant proprietors, artisans, and merchants.

The local bureaucratic positions are filled today through the *concorso* system, the effect of which is to recruit more and more personnel from the lower classes and to distribute them over an ever expanding geographic range. Thus many of the jobs in Colleverde which are subject to the *concorso* are occupied by nonlocal persons. The *comune* secretary (an administrative position second in importance only to the elected mayor), the civil police officer, the head of the post office, the tax collector, several of the schoolteachers, the doctor, the veterinarian, the midwife, and (as everywhere in Italy) the *carabinieri* are outsiders. All these positions, with the exception of the *carabinieri,* were traditionally held by members of the local landowning families. Other bureaucratic functionaries in Colleverde—clerks in the town hall, the postal clerk, and the excise-tax official—are local persons, the educated sons of lower-class families. Only the pharmacist, who is a woman, and some of the teachers are descendants of the traditional patron group.

In addition to occupying these formal positions which are links between the local and the national systems, the patrons also acted as informal intermediaries for individual clients. Today there are several national organizations which perform this function in Colleverde, assisting individuals to deal with the world outside the community, providing advice and, to a lesser extent, recommendations and intervention. Since the establishment of free elections, various political party groups have attempted to outdo each other in offering conspicuous services, and intervention with the higher powers is the most potent of these. Labor unions and other syndicalist organizations, which act to protect the interests of their members, have also re-emerged since the war.

Although most of the twenty or more national and regional organizations which have some formal representation in Colleverde exist there by name only, three or four are regularly resorted to for help by Colleverdesi. Among these groups, one sponsored by the Church is of particular importance. The local Church has been a vigorous partisan in the postwar political conflict in the community, and in its bid for popular support it has been an innovator of various services and projects. In order to counteract the drawing power of the favors offered by the Leftist organizations, the priest organized a local chapter of A.C.L.I., the national Catholic labor organization. Today an official of the provincial A.C.L.I. comes to Colleverde once a week to offer advice of any kind to any member, such as aid in claiming a pension or guidance to men seeking temporary work abroad.

There are still in Colleverde some vestiges of personal, informal patronage by local individuals rather than by institutions. Occasionally a landlord in relation to a peasant, or an employer to an employee, will take on special obligations as intermediary or protector. However, even in the rare cases where such a relationship persists over a period of several years, the patronage functions actually performed are restricted to particular areas and limited by the usually slight power of the patron. Much more characteristic of landowner-*mezzadro* relationships today is the merely superficial observance of command and deference behaviors; in fact, the use of the term *padrone* often becomes almost sarcastic, reflecting the landlord's failure to fulfill the functional obligations of a patron.

In general, two kinds of personal patrons may be distinguished in the community today. In the first place, there are a few individuals who consider themselves patrons and who have deliberately tried to take on patronage roles in the traditional form. One, the wife of a prosperous merchant (who like his wife is of lower-class parentage) has several clients to whom she gives gifts of food and loans of money and for whom she helps to obtain employment; however, she is dependent for these gifts and loans upon whatever she can set aside while managing her husband's store, over which she has no formal control. Another, a retired public official descended from an old landowning family, is for several people a source of advice on matters relating to law and government. Similarly, the pharmacist is sought for advice by a number of lower-class persons, but like the retired official her role is restricted to specific areas. Each of these individuals is limited by his actual power. Having little to offer the clients and little more than personal satisfaction to receive, none has succeeded in more than simulating the role of the traditional patron.

In addition, there are some persons who have the power to perform important patronage functions. Personal intermediaries are still required in dealing with the national government and other powers outside the community. It is through recommendations that most jobs are obtained, official matters settled, and so on. For example, since the rapid increase in the number of persons qualified for white-collar and professional work has greatly intensified competition in the *concorso* system, the selection is determined largely by recommendations, performance on the examinations being only a minimal qualification. The most valuable local sources of recommendations are the political party secretaries and the priest. As in the traditional patron-client relationship, these new intermediaries exchange favors for loyalty, namely political support. However, unlike the traditional patronage forms, these relationships are functionally specific and of brief duration. Alignments shift frequently as favors are bestowed where most profitable in return for temporary support (ultimately, votes).

It has been seen that new groups have moved into positions which enable them to act as intermediaries. Can the change, therefore, be best understood as a shift from one kind of mediator to other kinds? If "mediators" are defined as persons who have exclusive control over the functionally important junctures between the local and the national systems, the answer to this question must be negative. Instead of a small patron group who alone have direct access to the national system and thus control all connections with it, there are today separate ties for each functionally distinct aspect of the interaction between local and national systems, and with regard to each aspect there are many different ties which are alternative links. The clerk whom one sees about collecting government insurance benefits is not the same person as the official agent to whom one sells surplus wheat. Moreover, if the clerk's response is unsatisfactory one can go to an official of the union of *mezzadri* or to the A.C.L.I. center in the Church; similarly, if one prefers, the wheat may be sold to an independent merchant or to the landlord instead of to the official agent. The number and diversity of indirect links to the larger society, and particularly the existence of alternative possibilities, preclude the presence of mediators.

In addition to the increase in indirect links, there has also been a qualitative change. Today, a large proportion of the indirect links are structurally horizontal, relating persons of equivalent rank and social category. Ties between persons of particular occupational groups in various communities throughout the region and nation have been strengthened and institutionalized in the syndicalist organizations. Politically, the major identification of individual Colleverdesi is as members of social and economic interest groups which cut across communities. The political intermediaries—the elected administrative officials, the bureaucrats, and the grantors of favors—are drawn from all social strata and to an increasing degree from the lower rungs. Outwardly extended social relationships based on kinship and friendship are no longer restricted to one class in Colleverde but are maintained at least to some extent by all segments of the population. This trend has been intensified by the postwar outmigration of many Colleverdesi families (most of whom moved to towns and cities in Central Italy), which has meant to their relatives and close friends still in Colleverde numerous new ties with other centers— ties which it was possible and pleasurable to maintain through visiting back and forth on holidays. Thus, from the point of view of the Colleverdesi peasant of today, the national society is known and partici- pated in not primarily through an upper-class landlord, but through the mayor who is also a peasant, the labor union confined to *mezzadri,* other formal organizations composed of lower-class persons, and relatives and friends who live in other towns.

In sum, the traditional mediators have not simply been succeeded by new groups in the society taking control of the "critical junctures," nor has such control simply passed to persons occupying different roles from that of the traditional mediators. New groups have become intermedi- aries and new roles have appeared through which persons may act as intermediaries, but there has also been occurring a fundamental shift in the form of relationship between the local and the national systems. The junctures can no longer be "guarded" by any group. Direct participation by individuals in the national system, alternative links between the sys- tems, and structurally horizontal links are basic elements in the emerging form.

Conclusion

Twice in the recent history of Colleverde there has been an intensifica- tion of contacts between the community and the larger society. The first time, in the years following the unification of Italy, the interclass bond of patronage became the basis of the linkage between the local and the national systems. Mediators guarded the junctures between part and whole, at once facilitating contacts between community and nation and limiting the access of local persons to the larger society. The second time, in the period after the Second World War, a new part-whole relationship developed. Horizontal, outward ties were strengthened at the expense of vertical, local ties. Diverse, competing intermediaries, as well as an in- creasing degree of non-mediated participation in the national society, replaced the mediators. The kind of change which can be observed in Central Italy is undoubtedly occurring in many industrializing nations. It may be that the mediator represents a general form of community-nation relationship characteristic of an early phase of development of nation-states, a form which regularly gives way as the process of integration of the total society advances.

NOTES

1. The field work on which this paper is based was carried out in a rural community of Central Italy from August, 1960, to September, 1961. The project was supported by a predoctoral fellowship (MF-11, 068) and grant (M-3720) from the National Institute of Mental Health, United States Public Health Service. A more detailed description of the community is given in my doctoral dissertation (Silverman 1963).

The term "Central Italy," following the agricultural-economic definition adopted by the National Institute of Agrarian Economics (Italy), designates the large area extending over the sub-Appenine hills of Emilia-Romagna and the hills and plains (but not the mountains) of Tuscany, Umbria, the Marches, Latium, and Abruzzi-Molise north of the province of Campobasso (Istituto Nazionale di Economia Agraria 1956: facing 108).

2. The boundaries of the local system are not precisely coextensive with the community, since a local system may include regular relationships between members of different communities and since any community in a complex society has within it some representation of the national system. However, this paper will follow the common practice of using the term "community" interchangeably with "local system."

3. The upper limit of household size was about twenty members. The average size, based on estimates from a population register covering the period 1881–1907, was seven or eight. Today, the average *mezzadria* household consists of about six members.

4. In the third, fourth, and sixth instances, the term may also be used for address. Alternatively, the *padrone* may be addressed in the respectful form of using the given name preceded by *Sor* or *Signora* (rarely, *Sora*). In Colleverde, as in Foster's community, there is no specific term for "client."

5. Until the reforms of recent years, the *mezzadria* contract required a number of "extra" obligations of the peasant to the landlord, including gifts of fowl and eggs in specific quantities at different times of the year and various forms of unreimbursed labor in the landlord's household. Thus it is not always apparent whether a peasant's offering was the fulfillment of the formal *mezzadria* contract or part of a voluntary patron-client relationship. However, the essence of the latter was that the quantity or value of the goods and services given exceeded the formal requirements.

6. The recommendation, the importance of which has diminished only slightly though the channels have changed, is a request for a personal favor to the recommender, and it is not at all concerned with the qualifications of the person on whose behalf it is made. The value of a recommendation depends first upon

the status of the recommender, second upon the closeness of his connection to the addressee, and third upon the closeness of the connection between the recommender and the recommended.

BIBLIOGRAPHY

Bandini, M. 1957. Cento anni di storia agraria Italiana. Roma.

Foster, G. M. 1963. The Dyadic Contract in Tzintzuntzan, II: Patron-Client Relationship. American Anthropologist 65: 1280–1294.

Friedl, E. 1959. The Role of Kinship in the Transmission of National Culture to Rural Villages in Mainland Greece. American Anthropologist 61: 30–38.

Geertz, C. 1960. The Changing Role of Cultural Broker: The Javanese *Kijaji.* Comparative Studies in Society and History 2: 228–249.

Gillin, J. P. 1962. Some Signposts for Policy. Social Change in Latin America Today, pp. 14–62. New York.

Istituto Nazionale di Economia Agraria. 1956. La distribuzione della proprieta fondiaria in Italia, v. 1: Relazione generale, a cura di Giuseppe Medici. Roma.

Kenny, M. 1960. Patterns of Patronage in Spain. Anthropological Quarterly 33: 14–23.

Pitkin, D. S. 1959. The Intermediate Society: A Study in Articulation. Intermediate Societies, Social Mobility, and Communication, ed V. F. Ray, pp. 14–19. Proceedings of the 1959 Spring Meeting of the American Ethnological Society. Seattle.

Pitt-Rivers, J. A. 1954. The People of the Sierra. London. Redfield, R. 1956. Peasant Society and Culture. Chicago.

Silverman, S. F. 1963. Landlord and Peasant in an Umbrian Community. Unpublished Ph.D. dissertation, Columbia University.

Steward, J. H. 1955. Theory of Culture Change. Urbana.

Wolf, E. R. 1956. Aspects of Group Relations in a Complex Society: Mexico. American Anthropologist 58: 1065–1078.

Egalitarianism in an
Autocratic Village in Israel[1]

Harvey E. Goldberg

Rarely is there a uniformity of belief or complete consistency in all areas of a society. In an Israeli village individuals hold contradictory views about how authority is allocated. At times, and in particular social contexts, an egalitarian attitude prevails. Other times, autocratic control dominates. Both of these political stances add to the functioning of the community.

The issues of ethnicity and class are constant qualifiers of citizenship in the contemporary nation-state. Goldberg indicates how differing ethnic, immigrant, and class cultures may provide differing models and issues for national politics, particularly political mobilization.

THE TERM "EGALITARIAN" frequently occurs in discussions of the ethos of social relations in Middle Eastern communities (Adams 1957; Antoun 1968; Bourdieu 1966; Hamady 1960: 103–151; Peters 1965: 125; Stirling 1966: 222). Egalitarian relationships are viewed as opposed to "authoritarian" relationships, but a number of writers have suggested that equality and autocracy frequently coincide and, indeed, may complement each other. Bateson (1935: 181–183) states that symmetrical schizmogenesis (based on equality) and complementary schizmogenesis (e.g., dominance), when coexisting within one society, may countervail each other and jointly serve to maintain the stability of the society. More recently, Pitt-Rivers (1963) has explored the concept "egalitarian" and cited a number of cases in which individuals or groups are equal in one sphere (e.g., "before God" or in a sports match) while they are quite unequal in others (e.g., in political power or wealth). With particular reference to Middle Eastern society, Berger (1964: 274–276) has pointed to the egalitarian and authoritarian aspects of Arab political institutions, suggesting that autocratic political control may be necessary to counteract fierce egalitarian tendencies. The present paper continues this line of inquiry by describing and analyzing autocratic and egalitarian aspects of the social structure of a village in Israel and pointing out relationships between them.[2]

In pursuing this argument, I will first present (after giving some background) a model of the community as political autocracy. Next, I will consider an alternative model, namely that of a community divided into competing and theoretically equal patronymic groups. This latter model will be rejected, but not without leaving some uninterpreted data. I will then describe some of the features of egalitarian interaction in the community followed by an interpretation of the patronymic group model in terms of an egalitarian ethos. Finally, some of the links between the autocratic structure and the egalitarian ethos will be analyzed.

Background

The community discussed is an immigrant village with the fictitious name of Even Yosef. The families of Even Yosef constitute a "transplanted community" that originated in two neighboring villages in the Gharian district of Tripolitania, Libya (Goldberg 1967c; Slouschz 1927: 115–153) and settled in Israel in 1951. These villagers are presently living in a *moshav* or small-holders' co-operative. Various aspects of the Israeli community have been described and discussed elsewhere (Goldberg 1967a, 1967b, 1967c, 1969a, 1969b).

A *moshav*[3] is a cooperative community established to promote farming as the primary occupation of its members. The nuclear family is the basic social and economic unit, but the various households are bound together by mutual aid as well as by common agricultural credit, supply, and marketing services. In each *moshav* an equitable division of the means of production (land, water, and capital) is maintained.

A *moshav* is also a unit of local government. Authority over various aspects of village affairs is vested in the general assembly of adult members, which decides upon matters of principle and policy. The implementation of policy is entrusted to a committee of the *moshav,* assisted by other committees and an administrative staff. The *moshav* committee is chosen by the general assembly in free, universal, and secret elections.

This brief description pertains to the formal aspects of *moshav* organization as it developed in the pre-state period of Palestine (Weingrod 1962a: 118–119). This organizational framework provided the basis for the founding of 274 new villages in Israel from 1948 to 1958. Most of the settlers of these new villages were immigrants, coming from many countries of Europe and the Middle East. The concrete social forms that evolved in each instance were a product of the interaction of the cultural predisposition of the immigrants and the formal *moshav* organization. Many aspects of *moshav* organization were interpreted in terms of traditional forms of social interaction "imported" by the immigrants (Weingrod 1962a: 126–227). In Even Yosef, the reshaping of *moshav* organization according to traditional patterns is salient in several spheres, two of which are particularly relevant to the autocratic nature of the community and will be discussed here. The first concerns the relationship of the community to the environing society and governmental bureaus, and the second concerns the status and role of the community leader.

Community Political Structure: The Autocracy Model

The Community and the Environing Society

The Gharian Jewish community of Tripolitania was a minority group that constituted less than 1 per cent of the population of the Gharian district. The majority of the (approximately) 45,000 residents of the Gharian were Arab Moslem peasants whose principal crops were olives, figs, and barley. In the 1930s the Italian government established agricultural colonies in the region (Epton 1963: 96; Italian Library of Information 1940: 62–77).

The relationship of the Jewish community to these other groups conforms neatly to the "mosaic pattern" described by Coon (1958: 206). In this system the cultural and social autonomy of "ethnic" groups is coupled with economic interdependence. The Jews were blacksmiths, shopkeepers, itinerant hawkers, and tinkers who serviced the needs of the agricultural population. Although the Jews owned some land and flocks, they were primarily dependent for food on the produce of the Arab food growers. Coexisting with this economic interdependence was the social and cultural autonomy of the Jewish community (cf. Briggs and Guede 1964: 14–20). The degree of this autonomy is perhaps reflected in the preservation of a distinct Jewish dialect of Arabic within the relatively small speech community of 400 people (cf. Blanc 1964: 12–16).

The migration of the Gharian Jewish community from Tripolitania to Israel involved, from one point of view, a transition from minority-group to majority-group status and the shift from membership in a confessional minority to citizenship in a national state. From other points of view, however, the community remained isolated and autonomous from the Israeli socio-cultural environment.

From the very beginning of their migration, the Gharian Jews attempted to remain together insofar as was possible. In Israel, close to 90 per cent of the original community managed to regroup and settle in Even Yosef. The *moshav* situation, in itself, minimizes the contact of the immigrant villagers with the wider society, as compared with immigrants to urban areas (see Matras 1965: 51). Moreover, the villagers themselves have forged few links with outside individuals and groups. Since settling in Even Yosef, only two individual families have left the community.[4] Community endogamy has been over 90 per cent (Goldberg 1967b: 178). Although many of the men were forced to work outside the village in the early years of settlement, most of them today spend their entire working day within the village boundaries.

Associated with these demographic facts is a set of attitudes reflecting the villagers' continuing indifference to and ignorance of the environing society. The *moshav* is tied to, and dependent on, many different bureaus which supply resources vital to the functioning and growth of the community (Weingrod 1962b: 75–76).[5] Most of the people of Even Yosef, who benefit from the resources provided by these agencies, have little information about their nature or their rights and obligations vis-á-vis the villagers. For example, few of the villagers realize that they own shares in the marketing co-operatives. When representatives of these bureaus appear in the village, the villagers reveal little conception of their function. The bureaus are labeled an indiscriminating "they" or are called "the *sochnut*" (the Jewish Agency), the bureau that deals most directly with the agricultural activities and the development of the village. In general, the villagers are at a loss to explain many aspects of the political life of the *moshav* in which they do not directly participate.

Culturally, too, there is a minimum of interchange between the adult members[6] of the community and the wider society. About one-third of the village families receive a daily newspaper. Few people travel into town to see movies or engage in other leisure activities. The radio is used primarily to listen to Arabic broadcasts (from Israel and from the Arab countries). Arabic is the language spoken among the villagers and is the first language learned by the children. In short, Even Yosef is a community with few ties to its socio-cultural environment.

Autocratic Leadership in Even Yosef

Though the villagers of Even Yosef are socially and culturally insulated, the village as a whole nevertheless maintains complex administrative and economic ties with the "outside world." The maintenance of these ties is made possible by the activities of one individual who occupies the status of external secretary (*mazkir*) of the community. According to the *moshav* constitution, the *mazkir* should be nothing more than the main administrator of village affairs. In Even Yosef, however, the role of *mazkir* has been transformed into that of a chief executive who has extensive decision-making powers in the village (Goldberg 1967a: 43–50). One individual has held the post of *mazkir* from the founding of the *moshav* to the present,[7] and he is the political and cultural "broker" (Wolf 1956: 1075) par excellence. From his control of the channels of information and resources he emerges as the only significant political figure in the community.

All observers of village life, including the villagers, the extension workers, and the ethnographer, concur in this assessment of the autocratic nature of the community. The extension workers refer to the secretary as "king," while some of the villagers affectionately call him "our dictator" or "prime minister." A few examples of the *mazkir*'s dominance of village affairs indicate the power associated with his position. His control of communication channels to the outside is illustrated by an incident involving the village telephone. The only telephone in Even Yosef is located in the *moshav* office. There are usually a number of villagers gathered around the office who can easily listen to any telephone conversation. Any important information communicated by telephone is eventually passed on to the *mazkir*. Recently a member of the *moshav*, driving a newly purchased tractor, collided with the horse of another villager, and the owner of the horse immediately went to the *moshav* office to telephone the police. The *mazkir*, who happened to be in the office at the time, dissuaded the fellow from notifying the police, promising that everything would be settled satisfactorily within the *moshav*. The tractor driver would most probably lose his license, he argued, and thereby be cut off from an important source of income. The owner of the horse complied with the *mazkir*'s request. Had the tractor driver lost his license, he would not have been able to repay the *moshav* the money he had borrowed to purchase the tractor. By virtue of his access to the telephone, the *mazkir* not only aided the driver but protected the *moshav*'s interest in him and his tractor.

Most of the financial affairs of Even Yosef are left in the hands of the *mazkir*. He also has considerable control over the financial affairs of the individual families. Every year the *moshav* members receive a dividend from the income of the co-operative citrus grove. The amount given to the members and the installments in which it is paid are decided by the *mazkir*. Last year the portion promised to the villagers was paid four months behind schedule, and no one could offer any explanation except that the *mazkir* decided that the payment had to be delayed.

The *mazkir* limits control over his financial decisions by circulating misinformation or by allowing misinformation to be circulated by others. During the field investigation the villagers of Even Yosef expanded their holdings by occupying neighboring uncultivated land. Before this land could be of any use it had to be leveled by bulldozers, divided into plots by a surveyor, and supplied with irrigation lines. The *mazkir* arranged for these preparations, and no one else in the village knew exactly what expenses were involved. The *mazkir* asked that 1£150 per season be paid to the *moshav* for renting the land. The villagers provided the ethnographer with varying explanations of the high rent. Although most of them were erroneous, the *mazkir* make no attempt to clear up the misconceptions.

The decision-making power of the *mazkir* is further augmented by his domination of the *moshav* committee. According to *moshav* law the *mazkir* is bound by the decisions of the committee, but in Even Yosef the committee is frequently only a "rubber stamp" for the decisions of the *mazkir*. The law requires that a quorum of at least half of the committee members be present at a meeting (in Even Yosef this means five out of nine men); minutes must be kept at each meeting, and the committee members in attendance must affix their signatures to the minutes. In Even Yosef the committee meetings are run by the *mazkir*. While the positions of "secretary" and "committee head" are legally quite distinct, these two roles are not differentiated in the eyes of most of the villagers, and are both associated with the status of *mazkir*. Moreover, the *mazkir* also serves as the "recording secretary" at the committee meetings, compiling the minutes as the meeting progresses. At the end of each meeting the minutes are signed and validated by the other members of the committee in a perfunctory manner without attempting to examine their contents. And if a quorum is lacking at any meeting, the necessary signatures are added by the absent members at some convenient future time.

An Alternative Model: Patronymic Groups in Even Yosef
Village Patronymic Groups

More examples of the autocratic workings of the community can be adduced. At this point, however, I wish to raise the following question: Would an analysis of the status and role of the *mazkir* exhaustively describe the political organization of the community? I will begin discussing this question by briefly considering the patronymic groups[8] of Even Yosef.

Table 1 lists the main patronymic groups of Even Yosef. As may be seen, 35 per cent of the villagers belong to one patronymic group, Hajaaj; 28 per cent belong to Hasaan; and 15 per cent belong to Guweta. One common model of Middle Eastern social organization, in the minds of Middle Easterners and of anthropologists, is that of political structures based on the balanced (or unbalanced) opposition of two, or more, patrilineal descent groups (Patai 1962; but see Peters 1967). Also, research in Middle Eastern *moshavim* in Israel has sometimes found communities segmented into factions based on descent principles or quasi-descent principles such as country or town of origin (Weingrod 1962a: 123–124; Weintraub and Lissak 1964b: 135–136). The data of Table 1, then, immediately suggest that Even Yosef may be divided into three *hamula* or political patri-groups.[9] This type of political organization, in which power is distributed among a number of groups, differs widely from the autocratic model outlined above in which political power is concentrated into one status that is occupied by a single individual for a long period of time.

The data collected on the social life of Even Yosef, however, do not confirm the *hamula* hypothesis of political organization. No land or water rights are vested in the patronymic groups. Economic co-operation follows affinal ties more often than it follows patrilineal links (Goldberg 1967a). There is no patronymic group endogamy (Goldberg 1967b: 180–181). Patrilateral political loyalty usually does not extend beyond the "expanded family" (Goldberg 1969b), and members of the various patronymic groups elect one another to the *moshav* committee. Between the level of the expanded family and the community there are no significant political groups. The relationship of the *mazkir* to the whole community is the dominant political configuration in the village. No other status or group challenges the position of the *mazkir*. This configuration seems to be the "direct descendant" of the traditional political structure in Tripolitania (Goldberg 1967c: 211–215).

TABLE 1
The Main Patronymic Groups of Even Yosef

Patronymic Group	Number of Families	Percentage
Hajaaj	35	35
Hasaan	27	28
Guweta	15	15
Others	22	22
TOTAL	99	100

The Puzzle of the Kin Group of the Ten Brothers

This brief portrait of the autocratic political structure of Even Yosef would be accepted as accurate by most of the villagers. A few individuals, however, in response to my questions about kin factions, stated that there was one kin-group in the village that acted as a political unit. This group, with the patronym *Hajaaj,* consisted of ten brothers. The three oldest were the sons of one mother, and the seven youngest were sons of another. Nine of these brothers were married, and they ranged in age from 57 to 23 years. Their father was reputed to be 100 years old.

The few individuals who talked about the political activities of the ten brothers complained that "they control everything." One man stated that "they run the *moshav* and the *mazkir* is in their hands." These people pointed to the fact that one of the brothers had been given the job of operating the *moshav* tractor during the citrus harvest and that several other brothers had received sizable loans from *moshav* funds. These sources of income and credit, of course, enhanced the economic position of the brothers.

Most of the villagers, however, denied that the *mazkir* granted favors on the basis of kinship and did not admit the existence of kin-based cliques. Faced with conflicting interpretations of *moshav* political organization, I attempted to collect data on cases in which the ten brothers acted as a political unit.

During the one and one-half years of my research in the *moshav,* I observed (as opposed to heard about) only one instance of concerted action on the part of patrilineally related relatives. This took place at a meeting of about half of the *moshav* members. The village had acquired temporary rights to a new tract of land (see above). This land was to be divided, by lottery, among those families that wanted additional land. Before the meeting, the villagers had informally decided that new plots would be given only to those families who would personally farm the land. Land would not be allotted to anyone who intended to rent his plot. One individual, Hlafu[10] the butcher, had registered his intention of securing a new plot, but there was a certain amount of suspicion that he did not plan to engage in the manual labor necessary to cultivate the land. Among those suspicious of Hlafu's intentions were several of the ten brothers.

About 40 individuals had gathered in the *moshav* office to participate in the lottery and determine which plots would be assigned to which families. When it was Hlafu's turn to receive a plot, one of the ten brothers shouted that he should get no land because he had no intention of farming it himself. Hlafu retorted saying: "Who do you think you are? You and your brothers grabbing all the jobs! You are not worth a fraction of me." A second brother joined in and said that Hlafu should be fined several thousand pounds for speaking in that manner and making a scene in the village office. Hlafu again retorted, and a third brother chimed in. This brother, who was a member of the committee, said, however, that everyone should calm down and that Hlafu would get what was coming to him as a member of the *moshav*.

Later, when Hlafu discussed this incident with me, he said that "they all supported one another because they are brothers." This case, I repeat, was the only overt manifestation of the political solidarity of brothers that I observed. In order to interpret the activity of the brothers it is necessary to understand their resentment of Hlafu. This leads us to a consideration of the egalitarian aspects of life in Even Yosef.

Egalitarianism in Even Yosef

Egalitarianism and Economic Innovation

During the initial years of the *moshav*'s existence the villagers purchased meat, to the extent they could afford it, in the neighboring town. During this period Hlafu took the initiative of establishing contacts at the local slaughterhouse. After several years he purchased a second-hand meat refrigerator from a butcher he had met. He installed this refrigerator in his home, converting one room into a butcher shop. This meant that his family of 10 souls (himself, his wife, his father, and several children) had to confine themselves to three rooms of living space. He became the primary supplier of meat to the village.

On his weekly trips to the slaughterhouse Hlafu met many cattle merchants. He brought these dealers into contact with villagers who had cattle for sale, and for each deal he received a commission from both the villager and the merchant. These activities were one of the sources of resentment which many villagers bore him. Hlafu had a monopoly of the meat business. While the villagers had the option of buying their meat in town, in spite of him, this would have increased the cost to them because Hlafu undersold the town butcher and the trip to town involved some expense and a good deal of time.

Hlafu had begun his economic venture at his family's expense. He was one of the last in the village to add new items of comfort to his home such as modern furniture, indoor toilet facilities, and a washing machine. At a time when other people were adding extra rooms to their homes to accommodate expanding families, Hlafu forced his family into cramped quarters to make room for the butcher shop. He profited on the cattle deals by "just talking" while everyone else was "breaking their back" in the fields.

More important, however, Hlafu did not hesitate to inform any villager of his opinion of him and antagonized people who "had to work with their hands while he worked with his brains." Some people said that half the village were not on speaking terms with him. A number of men would never enter his shop but, instead, sent their children or wives on meat-purchasing errands.

One individual who was not on speaking terms with Hlafu was a man named Disi, who was 30 years old and the father of one son. The average number of children for men in his age category was four to five. Disi, while not an unpopular man, also experienced the criticism of his peers when attempting to "get ahead." Even Yosef has many large families (Goldberg 1967b: 178) with the consequence that the women spend many hours washing clothes. Disi was the first individual in the village to purchase a washing machine (this was in 1963). Neighbors and relatives quickly came to inspect this new item of technology, and their first reaction was critical. The women said to Disi's wife that it did not clean clothes as thoroughly as manual washing. The men said to Disi: "Why does your wife need a machine? You only have one child."[11]

These expressions of disapproval were not without ambivalence. By the end of 1964, close to 60 per cent of the village families owned washing machines, and I conjecture that the figure today is in the vicinity of 90 per cent. The cases of Hlafu and Disi exemplify how economic innovators, in production and consumption, respectively, are subjected to the leveling criticism of their peers. The initial criticism, however, is often followed by attempts to imitate the innovator.

Equality, Shame, and Interpersonal Relations

Gossiping, backbiting, and ridicule are common mechanisms of egalitarian social control in small communities (Gluckman 1963: 312; Foster 1965: 305). In Even Yosef, face-to-face confrontations (as between Hlafu and the brothers at the meeting) are relatively rare. Although there is much criticism of others, particularly anyone who attempts to raise his position in the economic or prestige pecking order, this criticism is usually not forthright but indirect.

The villagers of Even Yosef openly recognize this feature of their interpersonal relationships. They say that shame and embarrassment (*haashim*) govern much daily interaction. A person will not directly criticize his neighbor even though he feels the latter has wronged him. Rather he will discuss the matter with other members of the community and avoid face-to-face "embarrassment." Another common shame-saving technique is to send children on errands which potentially involve a "loss of face," as Disi and other villagers do when they send children to buy meat from Hlafu (cf. Hotchkiss 1967: 716). Sometimes villagers sent their children to me asking a special favor, such as to take them on a long trip. I might easily refuse the children and later both the father and I could pretend that "nothing happened between us."

The avoidance of face-to-face confrontation also occurs with regard to economic conflicts. As noted above, the village obtained temporary rights to a new tract of land. This was divided among approximately 40 families and a temporary irrigation network was set up to bring water to the new fields. The new plots, however, strained the water supply available to the village. If everyone tried to irrigate their plots at the same time very little pressure was available for any one plot. The water reached the new plots through a main pipe line which then branched into two lesser mains, one servicing the upper plots and the other bringing water to the lower plots. When one of the main branches was turned off, there was adequate pressure for the other set of plots. No schedule, however, was established for alternating the water supply between the upper and lower plots.

Initially the villagers handled this dilemma in the following manner. One group would come to the juncture point and shut off one of the main branches, thereby directing water to their own set of plots. Sometime later, after the first group had left, a group from the opposite set of plots would come and reroute the water to their fields. Later still, the first group would return to direct the water in their own favor, and so forth. Oddly enough, despite this hydraulic tug of war, the two groups never appeared at the juncture at the same time and no group switched the water in the presence of the opposing group.

When I asked the villagers to explain the situation, several people were quite explicit about "the rules of the game." Each group was well aware that the other group was turning off the water, but, so long as they did not meet at the juncture point, they could all claim that "someone was fooling around with the water." The villagers rerouted the water "behind one another's backs" in order to avoid a conflict-producing situation and not because they believed they had successfully concealed the facts about who was tampering with the irrigation system. After about a week of maneuvering, the villagers asked the *mazkir* to establish a definite irrigation schedule for the new fields.

The villagers are quite cognizant of the nature of their interpersonal relationships. They claim that everyone in the village is "ashamed" of everyone else. "Shame" is one of the major reasons they offer to explain the political inactivity of the majority of the community. Everybody is "embarrassed" to speak up to the *mazkir*. A man who has performed an economic service for a relative is "embarrassed" to ask for payment. If a family wishes to refuse a marriage offer made for their daughter, they say "she is too young to get married" in order to avoid giving an embarrassing rebuff. The term "embarrassment" or "ashamed" constantly is used to interpret social interaction in the community.

Some villagers see the pervasiveness of embarrassment in community interaction as a function of the kinship network. "Everyone here is related to everyone else," they say, referring to both consanguineal and affinal links. Several people utilized the image of a net in depicting the interrelationships of the village families. Relatives, of course, try not to engage one another in embarrassing situations.

Egalitarianism and Prestige

That the villagers attempt to avoid situations which will publicly embarrass people, or show one person to be the inferior of another, does not mean that the community of Even Yosef is not concerned with social ranking. On the contrary, the egalitarian emphasis is the obverse of a persistent concern with rank and prestige.

One of the primary factors in determining social rank is, of course, wealth (Goldberg 1969b). Village norms do not tolerate an ostentatious display of wealth, but individuals may hint at their growing affluence in subtle ways which do not invite leveling attacks. For example, Halifah Zubit, one of the first people in the village to own a truck, sometimes drives to the village store in the evening to purchase a pack of cigarettes. He may not need the cigarettes at the particular time, but he does not miss the opportunity to let others know that he owns a truck.

Ownership of a tractor is also a significant indicator of wealth. More than a dozen families own tractors, either singly or in partnership. In some instances, when tractors are utilized during most of the work week, they represent economically sensible investments (Goldberg 1969a). The average *moshav* farmer, however, does not need a tractor regularly. It is wiser for him to hire a tractor from time to time when needed. Nevertheless, a number of villagers, hesitant to invest in productive enterprises outside the village, have purchased tractors for their farms. These tractors, which sit idle most of the time, are an economic liability but still serve to bring prestige to their owners.

Washing machines have also become significant status symbols in the village. Most families own locally produced machines, while the *mazkir* and one other villager named Bachu, own Italian-made automatic machines, which cost nearly twice as much as the Israeli models and thus clearly indicate the wealth of the owner. In short, the egalitarian ethos of Even Yosef does not grow out of an absence of concern with prestige but refers to the lively and continual participation in the village ranking system.

Egalitarianism and Politics

The villagers of Even Yosef, though they seek wealth and prestige, are quite cautious with respect to political power. They do not want power because it means responsibility and vulnerability. Those who are elected to the *moshav* committee are glad to accept the prestige which accrues to that position but do not, by virtue of their election, become important participants in the decision-making processes of the community. Aside from the prestige involved, the villagers are glad to be elected to the committee for two further reasons. First of all, membership in the committee sometimes provides an avenue to economic gain and, second, membership in the committee may be instrumental in institutionalizing rules that actualize the egalitarian ethos of the community.

Elections for the *moshav* committee were held once during my stay in Even Yosef. Two individuals were elected who had not served on the previous committee. They were Halifah Zubit (the truck owner above) and Eli Hasaan. Halifah, at an earlier date, had purchased a movie projector. At one of the first meetings of the new committee he proposed that the *moshav* provide entertainment for the youth and show films once a week. This program was adopted and Halifah got the contract to show the films. At the same meeting, the committee had to select an individual to work on the *moshav* tractor during the coming citrus harvest. This job had been held the previous year by one of the ten brothers (above). The new committee did not, however, select the Hajaaj brother again but chose, instead, another person who was the economic partner of Eli Hasaan.

Later, when I asked the Hajaaj brother in question what he thought of the new committee, he replied that "they were no good and they were only out for themselves." He asserted that Halifah Zubit and Eli Hasaan colluded, each voting for the other's economic advantage. I did not attend this committee meeting, but my guess is that there was no conscious "deal" between Halifah and Eli. Rather, Eli was probably "embarrassed" to vote against Halifah's movie proposal, and Halifah to vote for a tractor driver other than Eli's partner. In any event, it is clear that the *moshav* committee is perceived as instrumental in furthering one's personal economic position. The villagers do not campaign actively to be elected to the committee, but they do not hesitate to exploit this position if they are elected.

The committee is also used to establish rules aimed at egalitarian leveling. One such rule was mentioned above, namely, that new land be allotted only to families who would farm the land themselves. Another instance has to do with Bachu, the wealthy villager with the Italian washing machine. During the 1963–64 citrus harvest a new method of shipping oranges from the groves was initiated. This involved the use of large crates which could not be lifted manually. In order to move them there was developed a hand-operated hydraulic fork-lift which could be harnessed to a horse. These lifts cost several thousand pounds apiece, and the *moshav* purchased four of them. Bachu got the idea that if he personally purchased a lift he could rent it to the *moshav* as well as use it on his own land. Other villagers were resentful and suggested to the committee a rule that the *moshav* should use only its own lifts and should not rent any from private individuals. As Bachu was the only person who owned such a lift, it is clear that he was the target of this rule.

Egalitarianism and the Patronymic Group Model

The Ten Brothers Interpreted

The preceding section, I believe, provides some of the clues to understanding the case of the ten brothers. Villagers often participate in the political process with nonpublic goals in mind. Similarly, the political activities of others are frequently interpreted primarily as instrumental to their private economic advancement. The egalitarian ethos of the community provides no justification of direct criticism of another's economic success. Rather, leveling attacks against economic advancement are transformed into other types of criticism, notably complaints about political machinations. The statement that the ten brothers "run the village" should be restated as "some of the ten brothers are rising rapidly on the scales of economic and social success."

The father of the ten brothers, who is the oldest man in the village, began his career as a humble blacksmith in the Gharian. Over a period of about 50 years he significantly improved his economic position. He became one of the large-scale merchants (as opposed to itinerant peddlers) in the community and built an olive press on the main street of the village. After the beginning of the Italian colonization in the 1930s (Italian Library of Information 1940: 62–77), he was one of three villagers to import diesel engines to power his olive press. Initially, his older sons were partners in his business enterprises.

Along with its accruing wealth, his family also grew in prestige. His eldest son was appointed "assistant shaikh"[12] under the British Military Occupation. However, the family was still considered *nouveau riche*, partly owing to the recency of their wealth but also because they had not consolidated and legitimized their social position by assuming roles of religious leadership and learning specialized religious skills (Goldberg 1969b).[13]

The migration to Israel, in 1949–1951, brought about a general economic leveling of the community (Goldberg 1969a; Weingrod 1962a:

125–126). For many of the families, their new economic position was as poor as it always had been, but some of the older elite families who experienced this sudden economic decline nevertheless retained some of the prestige of their former social standing.[14] In the case of the family of the ten brothers, the economic leveling attendant upon migration seemed most appropriate to the egalitarian ethos of the community. The ten brothers, in the eyes of many of the villagers, returned to the economic position "in which they belonged."

Despite the setback, a number of the brothers, in Israel, recapitulated the successful career of their father. They learned the techniques of modern agriculture and devoted themselves to the labor necessary for successful farming. They were receptive, also, to the economic and managerial skills called for by *moshav* organization (Weintraub and Lissak 1964a: 115–120). Some of them also exploited nonagricultural sources of income such as truck driving, operating a tractor, guarding the citrus grove, and assisting with administrative details in the *moshav* office. The brothers, along with other enterprising villagers, pressed the *mazkir* for loans, and the latter tended to give extensive credit to those who demonstrated economic initiative and success. In short, many of the ten brothers "made food" in relatively few years and consequently earned the envy of the other villagers.

A Survey of Models of Community Political Structure

My interpretation, then, of statements such as "the ten brothers run the village," is that they do not portray accurately the village political structure but rather reflect the resentment of certain villagers toward the economically "aggressive" brothers. To test this interpretation, I decided to survey which villagers held which political opinions and extracted from my field notes all the statements that had been made to me about village politics. I found that I had sampled the opinions of 33 *moshav* members, two resident nonmembers, and two ex-residents of the village. These individuals do not constitute a systematic sample; they were selected in an ethnographic fashion, namely, by seeking individuals who, it seemed, would further my understanding of *moshav* political organization. The sample is undoubtedly biased in that it contains a relatively large number of individuals who are active in village politics, and it is probably biased in containing a relatively high proportion of people who have come into conflict with one or more of the ten brothers. It is therefore interesting to compare some attributes of this sample to the attributes of the universe of (male) *moshav* members. Table 2 presents the distribution of patronymic groups in my "political opinion sample" and does not differ widely from the distribution of these groups within

Patronymic Groups in the Political Opinion Survey

Patronymic Group	Number of Families	Percentage
Hajaaj	15	41
Hasaan	9	24
Guweta	6	16
Others	7	19
TOTAL	37	100

the village as shown in Table 1. The average age of villagers in the sample is 38 years, whereas the average age of all village members is 44 years. Within the total village, 28 per cent of the members have served on the committee at one time or another, whereas 38 per cent of the sample have served as committee members. The social significance of these two differences is that the sample overrepresents politically active villagers and probably also people who are "trying to get ahead."

In order to add an extra measure of objectivity to the evaluation of the political opinion data, I asked a graduate assistant[15] to rate the opinions as to whether or not the subject thought that the ten brothers controlled the village. After completing his initial judgments, I suggested that he reevaluate the ratings and take into consideration data not included in the extracted field notes. The second set of judgments resulted in the following ratings:

Rating	Number
Ten brothers do not control village	17
Ten brothers do control village	7
Insufficient information	9
Opinions expressed by ten brothers themselves (not rated)	4
Total	37

In four out of the "insufficient information" cases I confidently assigned the rating of "do not control." The set of combined ratings yields 21 out of 28 people, for whom ratings were made, who do not think the ten brothers run the village. Table 3 lists the seven individuals rated as believing the ten brothers do control the village and some data concerning each of them.

A perusal of Table 3 suggest that many of the individuals listed either aspire to social rank that they have not yet achieved (D Guweta, I Hajaaj),

TABLE 3
Villagers Rated as Believing Ten Brothers Control the *Moshav*

AB	Elected to the *moshav* committee twice, in 1952–53, but not re-elected since. Works primarily as a small-scale construction contractor outside village. A non-Gharianite.
C Hajaaj	His wife is the sister of the last *shaikh* of the Gharian Jewish community (1942–1949). Relatively prosperous in the Gharian as a merchant, and relatively poor in Israel.
D Guweta	A non-Gharianite but raised by his sister in Even Yosef. No longer lives in Even Yosef. He is one of the most achievement oriented villagers whom I met.
E Guweta	Former farm-work coordinator of the village (about 1954–1955). Often elected to the *moshav* committee but rarely attends meetings.
Bachu Hasaan	The wealthiest farmer in the village, his income coming solely from agriculture.
GH	A non-Gharianite. His family suffered many medical misfortunes, and he is dissatisfied with the welfare and insurance payments. He is subject to the severe criticism of the other villagers because of his unwillingness to work in agriculture (he was an itinerant peddler in Tripolitania). He eventually left the *moshav*.
I Hajaaj	Son of the *mazkir*. Lives in a neighboring "Yemenite" *moshav*. He is not highly regarded by the villagers, particularly in comparison to his father.

or aspire to regain a rank which they once occupied (AB, C Hajaaj, E Guweta, GH?). From a social psychological perspective they may be characterized as experiencing "status inconsistency." Thus Bachu Hasaan is highly respected for his agricultural skills but does not have the overall prestige that his wealth would suggest. Similarly, AB and E Guweta are held in regard for their knowledge of the "outside world" (Goldberg 1969b), as indicated by their election to the *moshav* committee, but neither of them feels that his economic position is commensurate with his prestige rank. Research has suggested that "status inconsistency" is related to a preference for change in the distribution of power (Goffman 1957), or is associated with holding certain views of the structure of society (Landecker 1963: 221). In the case of Even Yosef, it seems, status inconsistency is related to the political opinion that the village is controlled by the ten brothers.

Discussion: Egalitarianism and Autocracy

Thus far I have discussed village egalitarianism in its relationship to economic, political, and prestige ranking and have shown how the egalitarian ethos is linked to the minority view of village politics being controlled by the ten brothers. The present section will explore more fully the relationship between egalitarianism and political autocracy after briefly considering certain aspects of egalitarianism and economics.

Egalitarianism and Economic Rank

Foster (1965), in his formulation of the Image of Limited Good, has shown that egalitarian leveling is common to peasant communities in many areas of the world. It is difficult for me to judge to what extent the leveling behavior in Even Yosef is governed by a Limited Good cognitive orientation, though it is interesting to note the presence of symptomatic traits such as rumors (I would not call them "tales") about finding hidden treasures (Foster 1965: 306). The Gharian Jews, however, have long been familiar with buying and selling as a source of profit, and their own economic development in Israel would, it seems, call into question the validity of a zero-sum world view that they might have had. Moreover, in certain ways, the egalitarian ethos seems to work for positive economic development and not only toward leveling.

It was noted above that innovations are often imitated quickly by the villagers. The agricultural extension worker successfully exploits this "keeping-up-with-the-Joneses" motivation in diffusing new agricultural techniques within the community. Sometimes slavish imitation leads to waste, as in some cases of tractor buying cited above. Another instance occurred when two wealthy farmers attempted to compete with Hlafu's butcher business and built a shop to contain a new refrigerator and meat counter that they purchased. Their partnership dissolved after a week, and the new butcher shop remained unused. In other cases, however, egalitarian motivated imitation has led to the acceptance of improved techniques of farming and marketing.

Similarly, egalitarianism serves to raise the consumption standards of the villagers. Villagers are "shamed" into providing their families with the same new comforts that neighbors and relatives have acquired. In one case the advance in living standards was channeled through the political structure. A number of people wished to replace the original concrete floors of their homes with stone tiles, the standard flooring material in Israeli homes. After some discussion, it was decided that every home in Even Yosef ought to have tiled floors. The village's reputation would be stigmatized if a few families, who could not afford a new floor, retained the cement floor indicative of the status of new and poor immigrants. The task of tiling the village homes was delegated to the *mazkir* so that the issue would not depend upon individual initiative. The *mazkir* implemented this program, and today every building in Even Yosef boasts a tile floor.

This case illustrates the villagers' belief that the poor should also share in the development of the village. Similarly, a number of people insist that loans be extended to the poorer villagers ("who really need them"), as well as to the better-off villagers who seek to realize even greater profits (cf. Weingrod 1962a: 127). While the *mazkir* grants large-scale loans to the latter type of individual, he allows the members of the committee to vote modest loans to the poorer villagers for whom the money represents welfare more than funds for investment.

In summary, egalitarian leveling may curb the economic advance of some villagers, but just as often it promotes the economic development of others. In the political sphere, too, egalitarian oriented activity may serve both to support the autocratic community structure and to provide checks on excessive inequality.

Egalitarianism and Political Leadership

In the "political opinion survey" described above, ten individuals spontaneously explained the political inactivity of the majority of the villagers in terms of "shame and embarrassment." People do not question the decisions of the *mazkir* because they "are embarrassed in front of him." Issues are not discussed openly at public meetings because opposition to a point of view is interpreted as a brazen attack on some other person's interests. The younger farmers, who feel their interests are not adequately represented on the *moshav* committee, bemoan the fact that they lack leadership because "everyone is ashamed to speak up."

Anyone who does attempt to assume leadership risks the embarrassment of being shouted down or ridiculed. On the other hand, a person who will not assume leadership, after much complaining about decisions and policies, is also criticized for his lack of "blood." A certain villager, who was elected to a committee a number of different years, was frequently criticized for not voicing his opinions in public. This individual, and others, do not "speak up" at public gatherings because they lack confidence in the strength of their support. A person who is wealthy, or who has many relatives, may be somewhat more willing to challenge public opinion or the *mazkir*. Those who lack such supports fear that, were they to voice their opinions publicly, their supporters would silently "back down" and leave them exposed in embarrassing solitude. Moreover, by openly challenging the opinion or decisions of the *mazkir*, a person presumes to be of equal status to him (cf. Bourdieu 1966: 197–200). Few villagers are willing to risk the exposure to shame implied in that sort of challenge.

The egalitarian ethos, then, serves to encourage prestige competition among the members of the community while inhibiting challenges to the position of *mazkir*. Leveling competition among many individuals and families also emphasizes the importance of a status which stands above personal and particularistic loyalties. In short, egalitarian activity serves to maintain the position and facilitate the effectiveness of the community leader.

On the other hand, because the *mazkir* is assured of his position, he is expected to refrain from wantonly shaming those below him (cf. Bourdieu 1966: 207). This may be illustrated by briefly considering the status of the internal secretary in Even Yosef. This position involves a great deal of responsibility and relatively little authority, in comparison to that of the *mazkir*. The latter makes the major decisions regarding the allocation of resources within the community, whereas it is the task of the internal secretary to assure that these resources are in the right place at the right time, e.g., that the irrigation system is working, that there are crates available for the harvests, that poultry is delivered to the market. The internal secretary is in daily contact with the villagers, while the *mazkir* spends much of his work week in towns where the central bureaus are located. The former, therefore, bears the brunt of much of the daily bickering and leveling challenges of *moshav* life.

The position of internal secretary has been held, for about nine years, by an individual named Nissim, who is five years younger than the *mazkir* and is the age-mate of some of the active farmers. Though he is generally respected, he is considered fair game for egalitarian challenges, and people do not hesitate to insult, curse at, and argue with him over minor inconveniences. Nissim belies that the villagers are not angry with him personally, but that "they just act that way when they are annoyed." He explains that it is necessary to "treat them as your children," that is, gradually coax them out of their "temper tantrums." He claims that both he and the *mazkir* are able to keep aloof from this sort of bickering but states that few other villagers have that ability.

Many villagers agree that Nissim's willingness not to reciprocate in egalitarian exchanges is an essential ingredient to his maintaining the position of internal secretary. Two individuals held similar jobs before him, but neither of them lasted more than a few years. These individuals took the egalitarian challenges and insults "to heart" and were not able to withstand the pressures. One informant explained that Nissim, whose family was one of the wealthiest in the Gharian, was confident of his social rank in the community and was thus able to shrug off these challenges. The preceding petty administrators, less sure of their social positions, could not confidently remove themselves from the area of competition. Rather, he explained, they removed themselves from their positions of minor leadership.

Another implication of the egalitarian ethos is that the *mazkir,* whom everybody acknowledges to be "superior," ought not to ostentatiously display reminders of his status. Rather he should be "quiet" and modestly conduct himself with dignity. Were he to communicate "loudly" the fact of his high position, e.g., by excessively beautifying the outside of his home or by purchasing an automobile for leisure and display, this would immediately bring forth leveling criticisms. Similarly, the villagers allow the *mazkir* to enjoy modest, but illegal, "kick-backs" on supplies he brings into the village, so long as he is discreet and does not publicly flaunt the fact of his tight political control.

"Consent," writes Lévi-Strauss (1964: 303), "lies at the origins of power." The villagers of Even Yosef, though inheriting culturally an auto-cratic political structure, are quite aware of how this structure operates. As among the Nambikwara (Lévi-Strauss 1964: 305), "it is as if, having handed over to him certain advantages, they expect him to take entire charge of their interests and their security" (see also Goldberg 1967c: 214–221). If the villagers feel that the *mazkir* has assumed too much power, there are various ways in which they can communicate to him that he, too, is not completely free of egalitarian demands.

Formal *moshav* organization has provided the *mazkir* with authority far greater than that of the *shaikh* of the Gharian Jewish community. On the other hand, the *moshav* also provides the means of disposing of a *mazkir* who does not meet expectations. Everyone is well aware that the *mazkir* can be voted out, though few have seriously contemplated replac-ing him. He is by far the best qualified individual for the position in terms of his knowledge and of the respect and loyalty he commands. Con-versely, the *mazkir* has threatened to quit in order to quiet complaints about the way the *moshav* is run. These complaints, of course, are not voiced directly, but the *mazkir* is quickly apprised of murmurings of discontent. One such incident concerned the holding of *moshav* funds. While the majority of village funds exist "on the books" or in banks, a certain amount of cash is kept on hand to meet necessary cash payments to individuals. A number of years ago the *mazkir* kept these funds in his home. Many villagers began to complain and insisted that, while the *mazkir* made the major decisions with regard to the disposition of funds, the funds should be held by someone else. This, in fact, was the tradi-tional system in Tripolitania, where the *shaikh* made the major decisions about the use of synagogue funds but the funds themselves were kept in the home of the community treasurer (*gabai*). The *mazkir* acceded to these demands, and the funds were transferred to the home of Nissim (the internal secretary). In other instances as well, such as insisting upon greater publication of the proceedings of committee meetings, the villagers succeeded in getting the *mazkir* to agree to greater democratization of *moshav* organization. These organizational changes are quite minor, however, and the village continues to be, unquestionably, an autocracy. Nevertheless, the periodic raising of such demands may be viewed as a ritual which communicates the message that, in a very real sense, the *mazkir* rules by consent.

Summary

Several heretofore implied points of view should be stated in summarizing the argument of this paper. The village of Even Yosef, simple and undifferentiated as it may appear, cannot be comprehended by any one model. The model of autocracy and the model of egalitarianism both are accurate and relevant. Moreover, the village has also been analyzed as a "stratified" community (Goldberg 1969b), giving yet a third perspective to its social structure. In formulating these models I have observed behavior and have noted explicit statements by the villagers about the way their community "works." These native models, while providing basic insights, do not necessarily represent social reality and are not, in themselves, the end point of analysis (Peters 1967). It should be emphasized, however, there exists not one model of the political structure of the community in the minds of the villagers, but several (though some "deeper" analysis might reveal an underlying unity). In dealing with this variation in explicit political models, I have tried to place the political views held by individuals in their relevant social contexts. Thus the view of the community as organized into kin factions is interpreted as congenial to those individuals who suffer from status inconsistency. In Lévi-Straussian parlance, this model of community organization is a "myth" which solves the contradiction of the ideal that everyone is equal and the reality that some people enjoy greater economic, social, and political rank than others.

In summary, the political structure of Even Yosef is notably autocratic. The power associated with the status of *mazkir* is based on his control of resources and communication channels which link the community to the central bureaus. Coexisting with this autocratic structure, however, is a lively system of egalitarian interaction, particularly in the economic and prestige spheres. Economic egalitarianism aims at leveling those who are getting ahead, but I do not believe it is a major factor in retarding economic development (Goldberg 1969a). Conversely, egalitarianism implies the sharing of wealth with those who might otherwise slip back into dire poverty. Egalitarian interchanges, however, are quite relevant to maintaining the political structure of the community. The prestige compe-

254 HARVEY E. GOLDBERG

tition among individuals and groups reinforces the political position of the *mazkir* while it simultaneously dramatizes the egalitarian values which should guide him in the conduct of his office.

NOTES

1. An earlier version of this paper was presented at the annual meeting of the Middle East Studies Association, December, 1967, in Chicago. The data presented are derived from field work conducted from October, 1963, to April, 1965. This research was supported by a U.S. Public Health Fellowship (grant »MH-07876) from the National Institute of Mental Health.

2. The term "autocratic" is used in preference to "authoritarian." The latter has been used widely in reference to a personality constellation (Adorno et al. 1950), whereas in the present context I focus on regularities of social interaction, not personality functioning. The most appropriate, but not completely accurate, anthropological designation of my area of concern is with an egalitarian ethos. Egalitarianism, in this context, is a useful label that suggests "the emotional quality of socially patterned behavior" (Honigmann 1954: 42–43) to be described in greater detail. Associated with the emotional tone of egalitarian activities are cognitive and conative components, so that at times the term "egalitarian ethic" would be equally appropriate.

3. The following two paragraphs are a paraphrase of Weintraub's (1964: 4) brief description of the formal organization of the *moshav*. More material on immigrant *moshavim* (plural) may be found in Ben-David (1964), Deshen (1965), Minkovitz (1967), and Weingrod (1962a, 1962b, 1966).

4. Nineteen families, however, left Even Yosef as a group. This was due to the growth in population from 416 at the end of 1951 to 809 at the end of 1963. By this time there was considerable pressure on the land, particularly from young families who were living with their parents. For several years the need was felt to find additional farms on which the young families could support themselves. These families insisted on settling another *moshav* as a group, rather than agreeing to settle individually in a number of different *moshavim*. A suitable village was finally found, and in the winter of 1963 the nineteen young families left Even Yosef to take up residence in the new *moshav* located in a neighboring region.

5. Some of these bureaus are the Jewish Agency Settlement Department, the Ministry of Agriculture, the Jewish National Fund, the marketing co-operatives, the National Religious Party, the Auditors Union, the Association of *moshavim,* National Insurance, and the Water Company.

6. This description refers primarily to the adult members of the community. The village youth are discussed in Goldberg (1967a).

7. This statement requires some qualification. From the founding of Even Yosef in 1951 through 1956 the present *mazkir* served as the internal secretary of the village, and the external secretary (*mazkir*) was an individual named Hai

Haddad. Haddad had been a prominent member of the Jewish community of Misurata (a coastal Tripolitanian town) and was responsible for bringing five of the nine non-Gharianite families to Even Yosef. Haddad and the present *mazkir* controlled the village until 1956, when the former died, since which time the present *mazkir* has ruled unchallenged. Most of the villagers neglect to mention Hai Haddad unless quizzed intensively about village history.

8. A patronymic group is a set of families sharing a patronym. They may or may not claim to be related to one another. Likewise, they may or may not function as social units.

9. Here I follow the suggestion of Cohen (1965: 118) that the term *hamula* refer primarily to the political aspects of a patrilineage or patronymic group.

10. The names of all living individuals are fictitious.

11. Given the Middle Eastern emphasis on progeny, this is a fine example of how "a person can . . . cut another member to the quick by a seemingly innocent statement" (Gluckman 1963: 314).

12. This was an honorific status which did not share the power of the main *shaikh*.

13. The family did, however, take steps in this direction. One of the sons began to serve as a sexton in Tripolitania. Another son was initiated into the village burial society in Israel.

14. See Willner (1962: 227–228), Deshen (1965: 76–81), and Minkovitz (1967) for examples of intra-community prestige relationships surviving the migration to Israel.

15. I wish to acknowledge the assistance of Michael Malina in this phase of the research and his criticism of an earlier draft of this paper.

BIBLIOGRAPHY

Adams, J. B. 1957. Culture and Conflict in an Egyptian Village. American Anthropologist 59:225–235.

Adorno, T. W., et al. 1950. The Authoritarian Personality. New York.

Antoun, R. T. 1968. On the Significance of Names in an Arab Village. Ethnology 7: 158–170.

Bateson, G. 1935. Culture Contact and Schismogenesis. Man 35: 178–183.

Ben-David, J. 1964. Agricultural Planning and Village Community in Israel. UNESCO, Arid Zone Research 23. Paris.

Berger, M. 1964. The Arab World Today. New York.

Blanc, H. 1964. Communal Dialects of Baghdad. Harvard Middle Eastern Monographs 10. Cambridge.

Bourdieu, P. 1966. The Sentiment of Honour in Kabyle Society. Honour and Shame: The Values of Mediterranean Society, ed. J. Peristiany, pp. 191–242. Chicago.

Briggs, L. C., and N. L. Guéde. 1964. No More For Ever: A Saharan Jewish Town.

Papers of the Peabody Museum of Archaeology and Ethnology, Harvard University, 54.

Cohen, A. 1965. Arab Border-Villages in Israel: A Study of Continuity and Change in Social Organization. Manchester.

Coon, C. 1958. Caravan: The Story of the Middle East. New York.

Deshen, S. 1965. A Case of Breakdown of Modernization in an Israeli Immigrant Community. Jewish Journal of Sociology 7: 63–91.

Epton, N. 1953. Oasis Kingdom: The Libyan Story. New York.

Foster, G. 1965. Peasant Society and the Image of Limited Good. American Anthropologist 67: 293–315.

Goffman, I. 1957. Status Consistency and Preference for Change in Power Distribution. American Sociological Review 22: 275–281.

Gluckman, M. 1963. Gossip and Scandal. Current Anthropology 4: 307–316.

Goldberg, H. 1967a. Acculturation, Continuity and Youth in an Israeli Immigrant Village. Unpublished Ph.D. dissertation, Harvard University.

———. 1967b. FBD Marriage and Demography Among Tripolitanian Jews in Israel. Southwestern Journal of Anthropology 23: 176–191.

———. 1967c. Patronymic Groups in a Tripolitanian Jewish Village: Reconstruction and Interpretation. Jewish Journal of Sociology 9:209–225.

———. 1969a. Domestic Organization and Wealth in an Israeli Immigrant Village. Human Organization (in press).

———. 1969b. Elite Groups in Peasant Communities: A Comparison of Three Middle Eastern Villages. American Anthropologist (forthcoming).

Hamady, S. 1960. Temperament and Character of the Arabs. New York.

Honigmann, J. 1954. Culture and Personality. New York.

Hotchkiss, J. 1967. Children and Conduct in a Ladino Community of Chiapas, Mexico. American Anthropologist 69: 711–718.

Italian Library of Information. 1940. The Italian Empire: Libya. New York.

Landecker, W. 1963. Class Crystallization and Class Consciousness. American Sociological Review 28: 219–229.

Lévi-Strauss, C. 1964. Tristes tropiques. New York.

Matras, J. 1965. Social Change in Israel. Chicago.

Minkovitz, J. 1967. Old Conflicts in a New Environment: A Study of a Moroccan Atlas Mountain Community Transplanted to Israel. Jewish Journal of Sociology 9: 191–208.

Patai, R. 1962. Dual Organization. Golden River to Golden Road: Society, Culture and Change in the Middle East, pp. 177–250. Philadelphia.

Peters, E. 1965. Aspects of the Family Among the Bedouin of Cyrenaica. Comparative Family Systems, ed. M. Nimkoff, pp. 121–146. Boston.

———. 1967. Some Structural Aspects of the Feud Among the Camel-Herding Bedouin of Cyrenaica. Africa 37: 261–282.

Pitt-Rivers, J. 1963. The Egalitarian Society. Proceedings of the Sixth International Congress of Anthropological and Ethnological Sciences 2: 229–233. Paris.

Slouschz, N. 1927. Travels in North Africa. Philadelphia. Stirling, P. 1966. Turkish Village. New York.

Weingrod, A. 1962a. Reciprocal Change: A Case Study of a Moroccan Immigrant Village in Israel. American Anthropologist 64: 115–131.

———. 1962b. Administered Communities: Some Characteristics of New Immigrant Villages in Israel. Economic Development and Cultural Change 11: 69–84.

———. 1966. Reluctant Pioneers: Village Development in Israel. Ithaca.

Weintraub, D. 1964. A Study of New Farmers in Israel. Sociologia Ruralis 4: 3–51.

Weintraub, D., and M. Lissak. 1964a. Physical and Material Conditions in the New *moshav*. Agricultural Planning and Village Community in Israel, ed., J. Ben-David. UNESCO, Arid Zone Research 23: 102–128. Paris.

———. 1964b. Social Integration and Change. Agricultural Planning and Village Community in Israel, ed., Ben-David. UNESCO, Arid Zone Research 23: 129–159. Paris.

Willner, D., and M. Khols. 1962. Jews in the High Atlas Mountains of Morocco: A Partial Reconstruction. Jewish Journal of Sociology 4: 207–241.

Wolf, E. 1956. Aspects of Group Relations in a Complex Society. American Anthropologist 58: 1065–1078.

Conflicting Political Models
in a Swiss Commune[1]

Daniela Weinberg

In a complex political field, various social groups and their political representatives may have different political goals. In a state, lower political elements may perhaps disagree with projects or aims of the higher levels. These inevitable disagreements lead to a constant reshuffling and restructuring of leadership positions and the composition of the groups. These competing political aims are a dynamic of change in all systems, and it is difficult to envision a political institution where harmony between these two levels prevails.

Political parties at the local level have to consider the interest or pressure groups of the locale which may not always coincide with national platforms or party images. Where, however, the national party is strong or local conditions are in flux, the national or managerial party, or bureaucracy, may be able to separate local leaders and followers and enforce new roles and models.

THE POLITICAL SYSTEM of a complex society is subtle and elusive. Beneath the structure and order of governmental institutions and political parties there is a fuzzy region of indirectness, ill-definition, and informality. We may think of this shadowy area beneath the surface as the *milieu intern* (Bernard 1957)—the "internal environment" of the system which acts as the last bastion of regulation before the system yields to adaptation and change, or death.

It is here, in this little studied region of a political system, that we may find what Dimen-Schein (1978:377) calls "emergent intermediate structures like ethnic groups and neighborhoods" which help to reduce the monolithic power of the state over the individual. These informal "struc-

258

tures of everyday life" coexist with the formal structures of government and politics. Although they may be only recently "emergent" in those Western societies dominated by a centralist model of government, they have always existed—indeed, they predate formal structures—in Alpine societies, traditionally localist in their political ideology.

This paper is about the clash between centralist and localist models of political organization in a Swiss mountain commune. It documents the breakdown of a self-regulating cultural system as it teeters on the threshold of change, between the informal processes of localism and the formal structures of centralism.

Bagnes is a large, multivillage commune which replicates the cultural diversity of the Swiss nation-state. The outsider sees the commune as a single political, geographic, religious, and linguistic unit. The commune is perceived by its own citizens, however, as a pluralist society in miniature—*"notre republique bagnarde"* (our Bagnard republic). In the native cognitive mapping, the commune is divided into five regions, differentiated ecologically and culturally. Its twelve villages are further discriminated linguistically by phonemic contrasts barely audible to an outsider. Villagers have a strong sense of *campanilismo,* the identification with one's own "bell tower" that has been described for Italian villages (Silverman 1975:16).

In many ways, then, these villages of Bagnes are like Dimen-Schein's (1978) "ethnic groups and neighborhoods." They have a distinct cognitive reality within the commune but no formal recognition on the outside. And, as we shall see, they constitute the "internal environment" of the commune insofar as they ensure the continuing identity of the political system.

The informal power of the villages is balanced against the formal authority of the official political apparatus of government and party in a small-scale replica of the Swiss federalist system. Like the 25 cantons of the Swiss state, the villages of Bagnes have voluntarily surrendered some of their autonomy to the commune in order to benefit from the advantages of scale. Integration of these semiautonomous communities is effected at the commune level through several important and ancient institutions. Certain lands, for example, are held in common by all commune citizens—the forests and high pastures on the upper slopes of the valley walls. Government and administration exist only at the commune level, in the form of two bodies of elected representatives. Political integration appears in two official political parties which have existed in essentially their present form and strength for over 100 years. But these integrative mechanisms are incomplete in their control functions. The high pastures, for example, although commune property, are held in perpetual usufruct by individual villages. The representatives elected to governmental bodies have been steadfastly loyal to their local (village) constituents. And the apparent political integration at the commune level has been under constant threat from extrapolitical allegiances at the village level.

This interplay between unity and diversity acts as a check against, on the one hand, a dominant central authority, and, on the other, a centrifugal anarchy. Similarly, at the village level, checks operate to prevent concentrations of power. Political factions and interest groups in the village are always in flux because their members participate simultaneously in various economic and social institutions with crosscutting memberships (Wiegandt 1977).

As long as the environment remained relatively constant, this self-regulating system functioned well. In the last few decades, however, the commune of Bagnes has been subjected to pressure from a rapidly changing environment. As agriculture has declined and commerce and tourism have increased in importance, the financial and administrative complexities of commune government have grown. In 1964, the majority Conservative Party recruited a young Bagnard—an engineer living and working in another canton—to run for commune government. Four years later, this man was elected commune president and fulfilled the apparent goal of his recruiters by reorganizing commune administration following a centralist model.

Although the president's stated intention was to increase administrative efficiency, the effect of his reforms was political. Citizens lost their advocates on the commune council and found themselves removed from direct access to the decision-making process. The centralist model began to eclipse the localist model. Formal structures replaced informal processes. The "intermediate structures . . . of everyday life" (Dimen-Schein 1978) were vitiated. The self-regulating system was rendered impotent.

I begin this essay with a description of the traditional Bagnes village before 1930 and the subsequent economic changes that eroded village autonomy. Next I discuss the operation of traditional informal political processes, revealing the chronic conflict between the political party and the villages. The next two sections describe the 1968 reorganization of the formal structure and the political effects of these changes. In the final section, I discuss the resulting loss of regulatory capacity of the cultural system.

Village Autonomy Before 1930

The Commune of Bagnes is located in the Pennine Alps of southern Switzerland, in the French-speaking half of the bilingual (French and

German) Canton of Valais. The population of 4,800 is distributed among twelve villages and several hamlets. The traditional (pre-1930) economy of Bagnes was based on dairying and grain cultivation, supplemented by kitchen gardening and small-scale viticulture. Pressure on the restricted carrying capacity of the harsh Alpine environment was reduced through late marriage, celibacy, and seasonal migration. Until early in the twentieth century, the commune was geographically isolated and inaccessible, economically self-sustaining, and endogamous. Seasonal contact with neighboring communes was maintained through the contiguity of high summer pastures and, with more distant communes, through ownership of vineyards in the Ahone valley. Occasionally, itinerant artisans and pilgrims passed through the valley, and native seasonal migrants and mercenaries brought news from the outside.

Even within the valley, among its dozen villages, isolation prevailed during the long months of winter. With summer came movement and contact, especially among villages clustered in a local area. Economic and affinal ties were established, and these villages formed social as well as geographic regions within the valley. Each village, nevertheless, maintained its distinctiveness as an economic, social structural, and even dialectal unit.

The village was virtually the minimal social, economic, and political unit in that it was relatively self-sufficient and autonomous. Money was appropriated from the commune, but villagers decided on its allocation and implemented their decisions through a locally elected manager (*chef de travail*). The manager was in charge of public works in the village such as snow clearance, road repair, and fire-fighting. Other village officials were responsible for maintenance of the chapel. The elected representative to the commune council was regarded as the advocate of his village, serving its unique interests and needs. During his four-year term on the commune council, he acted as spokesman, both for the village as a whole and for any of its individual members. As a "village president" (in the native metaphor) he heard and tried to resolve grievances between village and commune. Interpersonal conflicts were resolved within the village segments in which they arose—neighborhoods, co-operative dairies, communal bread-baking groups, and co-operative summer-pasture and irrigation associations.

Articulation with the Outside World

Today—in the village of Bruson, for example—the only viable segments remaining are the economic co-operatives concerned with summer pastures, dairying, and the cash crops (strawberries and raspberries) intro-

duced in the 1930s. Most of the traditional mutual-aid functions of neighborhoods have been eliminated with the introduction of governmental
social welfare programs and modern plumbing, and through a reduced
emphasis on agriculture as a primary source of income. The irrigation co-
operatives atrophied and disappeared with the decline of agriculture.
Bread-baking became a commercial enterprise, and, since the death of
the village baker in 1968, bread has been brought in from outside and
sold in the two village shops. Although villagers still elect a manager to
oversee public works, much of his domain has been preempted by commune and canton: road work, for example, is now the specific charge of a
villager employed by the canton.

With post-World War II economic prosperity, tourism and related
industries have relentlessly removed men from agriculture, leaving wives
and children to maintain the traditional ideal of self-sufficiency through
self-provisioning (Weinberg 1975). Even the agricultural co-operatives,
once the mainstay of community independence, are now linked to and
regulated by canton-wide co-operative associations. In a similar way, the
commune councillor, far from performing his traditional function as village president and advocate, is now merely a political party cadre and a
specialized executive of commune government.

This transformation of the role of councillor is related to the economic development of the commune and the concomitant decline in
village autonomy. But the immediate precipitating factor in this change
was the deliberate manipulation of normative and pragmatic ideals (Bailey 1969) by powerful political figures in the commune. In 1968, the
majority Conservative Party succeeded in reducing the number of commune councillors from fifteen to eleven through a communewide election. The Conservative commune President then streamlined the work
assignments of the council accordingly and consolidated the twelve village electoral units into five multi-village "regions." In a final move toward concentration of political power, the Conservative Party reorganized itself by replacing the traditional twelve "sections" of the party with
five multi-village "circles." Before examining these structural reforms in
detail and considering their effects on the commune, I will discuss informal political process in Bagnes.

Informal Political Process

The Conservative Party of Bagnes has held a comfortable and unchallenged
majority of 65–75 per cent in the commune council for the past 120 years.
Its only significant rival, the Radical Party,[2] has been content to play the role
of established loyal opposition. This balance of power has been maintained

for several reasons. In the native view, the differences between the parties are slight and mainly historical; the Radicals had their origins in the anticlerical liberalism of the early nineteenth century. Today, however, with official separation of church and state accomplished, this difference is not significant. In addition, both parties have always stood for similar values and programs because the commune population itself was not divided into socioeconomic strata with competing interests.

Each party recruits new members on the basis of kinship. Political affiliation is an ascribed characteristic of the individual, passed from father to child. As part of one's patrimony, it is, ideally at least, not subject to choice or change.

The persistence of the two parties is further guaranteed by their informal identification with voluntary associations and commercial establishments in the commune. There are two communewide "political" brass bands, and any village large enough to support more than a single café has two with contrasting "political color." In the past, other local associations with "political" identity included privately owned banks, mutualist insurance societies, and village shops (Weinberg 1976).

The weight of history, kinship, and partisan voluntary associations and institutions has virtually eliminated political rivalry between the two parties. But the history of each party is characterized by internal dissidence and factionalism. This comes about, in spite of the rich multiplicity of parapolitical party supports, because of a countervailing set of allegiances which crosscut and undercut loyalty to party. At the cantonal level, these extraparty allegiances form opposing interest groups based on language (French vs. German), ecology and economy (mountain vs. lowland), regionalism, and interpersonal conflict. In the Commune of Bagnes, these extraparty interest groups are defined by economy, region, village, and rivalries between kinship groups. Some of the groups thus defined are: leftbank vs. rightbank, head of the valley vs. mouth of the valley, commercial-touristic vs. agricultural, the five cognitive-geographic village clusters, one's own village, and, in a few villages, the "family clan" with which one is traditionally allied (Weinberg 1976).

Conflict Between Party and Village

During commune elections, a voter will take his or her ascribed party ballot into the voting booth and may then choose to "modify" it by crossing out one or more names, or by writing in names of candidates that appear on other parties' ballots. The voter will use this modification procedure to favor a covillager or to express some other personal preference for or against a candidate. The candidate's party membership holds a very low priority in the voter's mind. A voter will always vote for the native son, or daughter, even if that candidate has been presented by the other party. Under the proportional representation voting system used in Bagnes, this modification procedure allows the voter to maintain party loyalty and, at the same time, to have a direct impact on which of the party's candidates will be seated.[3] In spite of the vigorous objections of party officials, almost half the ballots in any commune election are modified. Although party discipline and strength may be subverted, important normative ideals of Swiss democracy are upheld: voter independence, polling booth confidentiality, voting for the best person regardless of party affiliation, guarding against monopolies of power, and promoting youth and women (since 1970) in the political arena.

These normative values, taken together with extraparty loyalties and legal requirements, make the pre-election period a time of great stress for each party. The crucial decisions to be made are the number of candidates to present and the choice of candidates.

As to number, each party tries to present at least as many candidates as now occupy seats on the council, in the expectation that they will win at least that many seats once again. The law limits the maximum number of candidates to eleven—the total number of council seats available. Within this numerical range, both normative values and pragmatic considerations must be taken into account. The "democratic" and legal norms dictate that the maximum number of candidates be presented in order to offer the widest possible choice to voters, to enable the widest representation of villages, and to provide for potential replacements in cases defined by the law (incompatibility, conflict of interests, resignation, or death). But the more candidates the party presents, the more losers it will have. It seems reasonable to present one or two candidates beyond the minimum number on the off chance of winning an additional seat but too many additional candidates puts a strain on party loyalties and creates interpersonal conflict within the village party organization which names the candidates.

The choice of candidates is not so difficult. The party has clear criteria such as: gender (there should be a few women on the ballot), age (a preference for youth), village origin (to assure wide representation), commune citizenship ("authentic Bagnards"), occupation (a preference for self-employed people whose time is more flexible, and for agriculturalists who represent commune tradition), personal popularity, and a clean party record. Desirable personal qualities include: interest in politics, experience, capability, education, eloquence (*beau parleur*), cleverness *(habileté)* and responsibility *(sérieux)*.

But the single most important quality of a prospective candidate is the willingness to run. A candidate is willing if he or she sees a good chance of winning. The fear of defeat is dramatically articulated in the figurative use of the verb *luger* (which may be specific to the Alpine region)—literally, to sled rapidly downhill, and, by evocation, to make a fool of oneself by being roundly defeated. Too many names on the ballot will discourage potential candidates. In addition, incumbents are hesitant to run for a second term because of the observed effects in such candidacies: the councillor becomes associated in the voter's mind with all the unpopular decisions of the council (*"on se salit"*—literally, "one dirties oneself") and, in the next election, drops to a lower place on the list of winners or even becomes a loser. In addition, a potential candidate for the minority Radical Party may be reluctant to run for fear of reprisals on the job.

The candidate who agrees to run, and then wins, finds that being a councillor is time-consuming and costly in money and personal reputation. Bagnards recognize that public office-holding necessarily transforms the office-holder. While some councillors are viewed as selfless and dedicated, others are believed to have adroitly exploited their position for personal gain. For the potential candidate, only the slight aura of honor and the satisfaction of serving the community can offset the risks involved—first in running for office, and then in occupying that office.

With the problems of the ballot solved, the party enters the election at the mercy of the voters and their extraparty allegiances. In past elections, intravillage dissension in the form of competing family clans or economic rivals has sometimes resulted in nonrepresentation of a village on the council and ensuing bitterness against the party. In other cases, village solidarity behind a native candidate was sufficiently strong to weaken and even defeat other candidates on the party ballot. Village political solidarity is memorialized in a local, probably apocryphal, tale of a commune councillor who, throughout his four-year term of office, energetically courted the support of a certain village other than his own. All these villagers promised to vote for him in the next election. The election results, however, showed that he had received only one vote from that village. When he confronted villagers with this fact, each one insisted that *he* had voted for him (Courthion 1903:161–2).

Whether conflict-ridden or solidary, the village is of critical importance to the party. The events of 1968 presented the Conservative Party with an ideal solution to the problem: the elimination of the village from commune politics.

Formal Structural Change

Change began in 1964 with a major reorganization of commune administration. In 1968, the Conservative commune president completed and stabilized the reorganization by regrouping the twelve villages into five electoral-administrative regions, corresponding to the cognitive-geographic regions of the valley. Then, by commune-wide vote, the number of councillors was reduced from fifteen to eleven. The Conservative Party supported the reduction, which was carried by a two-thirds majority in all the villages except Bruson where it was opposed in the same proportions.

Supporters argued that reduction in council size would have the effect of increasing the responsibility and reliability of each councillor. And, indeed, after the vote for reduction the commune president reduced the number of council committees from 25 to eleven by consolidating those with similar functions. The three previous committees concerned with schools of various types (elementary, secondary, home economics) were fused into a single committee called "School and Parish." Earlier committees devoted to youth activities, sports, and recreation were fused into a single new committee called "Physical Education." These two new committees were further grouped under the larger heading of "Cultural Policy." Another new committee fell under the heading of "Social Policy;" six others under "Development Policy;" and the last, the Finance Committee, stood alone as the base of all the others.

The President's rationale behind this arrangement of council committees was twofold: first, to create a more logical division of labor, more responsive to the needs of the commune; and second, to assure an equal distribution of responsibility among the councillors. Each councillor is now president of one committee and a member of three or four others. Each committee consists of either three or five members, including, respectively, two or three councillors of the majority Conservative Party.

The President regarded this reorganization as a positive step toward centralization, necessary in view of the economic development and ever-increasing complexity of commune affairs and finances. He conceded, however, that the new organization made administrative specialists of the councillors, who had once been village spokesmen. Villagers are now more likely to take their problems directly to the councillor in charge of the appropriate committee rather than to their own village councillor. Villages no longer have their own budgets and are now wholly dependent on the central commune government. The new system, while elevating the councillors to the more important position of technical-administrative specialists, has removed them from their voting constituents. So the councillors, too, are now more dependent on their sponsoring parties.

Political Effects of the 1968 Reorganization

Opposition to the reduction of council size was based on the political implications of what was presented as merely a streamlining of administrative structure. These fears were justified by the results of the 1968 commune elections, immediately following council reduction. The century-old party proportions were maintained in the new council: instead of ten Conservatives and five Radicals, there were now seven Conservatives and four Radicals. Although the absolute number of Radicals on the council was now only four, the Radical Party suffered a smaller relative loss than did the Conservative Party—losing only 20 per cent of their councillors, compared with the Conservatives' 33 per cent. On the other hand, only four of the five newly organized regions were represented by the minority party. The Conservatives, however, with their seven council seats, more than adequately represented the five regions and could even afford to give heavier representation to some than to others.

The traditional electoral and political units, however, were not regions but villages. These were officially wiped out in the final step in this series of changes. The Conservative Party, imitating its reorganization of commune administration, now reorganized itself by consolidating its twelve village "sections" into five multi-village "circles." As a result of these administrative and political reforms, Conservative villagers gave up council representation and political control of their own councillors to the Conservative Party. In the past, ten of the twelve village sections were represented by Conservative councillors. Now only seven are represented in the commune council. Thus, only 58 per cent (instead of 83 per cent) of the villages send Conservative councillors to the commune council.

More serious, however, is the effect of the new system on the villages' control over nominations of council candidates. When there were fifteen seats on the council, the Conservatives usually won ten of them. Thus, the party presented twelve candidates to the voters—essentially, one from each village. Now, with only seven of the eleven seats expected, the party presents nine candidates, and the villages are no longer the nominating units. The five Conservative circles choose the candidates, according to a specific formula of apportionment: the four largest circles are permitted to name two candidates each, while the smallest (Bruson) names only one candidate.[4]

Of these nine candidates, only seven (or at best eight) can expect to be elected. The most likely to lose is the candidate from Bruson. He or she must work especially hard to maintain the support of village constituents in the face of the councillor's new, highly specialized function on the commune council. The candidate does have certain advantages, however, over fellow candidates from other circles. First, Bruson has more continuity than the other four circles because its composition has not been changed from the pre-1968 section. Second, the very smallness of the circle makes for greater unity in backing the candidate, who is known to all constituents either through kinship or other associations. Last, a kind of underdog effect enhances this natural solidarity: Brusonins would support almost any candidate of theirs rather than lose all representation in the commune council.

At the 1968 pre-election meeting of the Bruson circle, members seriously debated the advisability of presenting any candidate at all, since the risk of loss was so great. Some members suggested offering their single candidacy to a neighboring circle to fill, in the hope that the other circle would reciprocate in the next election. Finally, in a spirit of optimism and courage, the circle decided to present a candidate of its own. The rest of the meeting was devoted to persuading someone to be that candidate—a difficult task in light of the new payoff matrix. In the election, the Bruson candidate not only won a seat but placed third out of the nine Conservative candidates. This was a result of his commune-wide popularity, but, more importantly, of the villagers ignoring party lines and backing their native son candidate.

The other four Conservative circles did not fare so well. Each of them consists of three or four villages and hamlets. Potential candidates from these circles must court voters of villages other than their own and compete with native sons and daughters of those villages. Incumbents who seek a new candidacy must, in addition, overcome the distance between themselves and their constituents created through the reorganization of the council and its committees. Prospective candidates, whether new or incumbent, must rely more heavily on party backing and present themselves as party, rather than village, representatives.

The new system thus strengthens the Conservative Party while weakening the position of individual candidates. It is of little consequence to the party which candidates are nominated and eventually elected. The party can, therefore, exert pressure on and control the behavior of its councillors. Because of the nature of party recruitment, by inheritance and ascription, the party is assured the stability of its voting support. Through the newly strengthened internal discipline, the party can better maintain control of the commune council and propagate its own policies. The reorganization of the commune was itself such a party policy, put into effect by a particularly strong Conservative president. The new system centralizes not only commune administration but also political control within the Conservative Party. Through this double process of streamlining (political and administrative) the majority party sought to assure its continuing majority status within the commune.

The Conservative Party has not, however, succeeded in obliterating the village level and thus neutralizing the effects of extraparty allegiances. Although the party officially disengaged the relationship between village and council by introducing the new level of region, there is evidence that the traditional cognitive system of politics is still in effect. Thus, in the 1972 elections, more than half the ballots of both parties continued to be modified. The two losing candidates on the Conservative ballot were victims of intravillage conflict: in one case between family clans, and in the other between economic rivals. And one of the largest and most Conservative villages in the valley, because of internal clan dissent, failed entirely to elect a councillor.

On the morning after the 1972 elections, one of my staunchly Conservative informants in Bruson effectively demonstrated the persistence of divisive forces in the party. She gleefully summarized the election results by saying that "three from the left" had won. For a moment, I was confused, since there is nothing remotely leftist in the ideology of either of the two parties. Then I realized that she was referring to the left bank of the river, her own side of the valley. These three victorious candidates were a Conservative from a nearby village, the incumbent Conservative from Bruson, and a Radical from the nearby hamlet of Le Sappey. Thus, the intended replacement of the village level with the region has been nothing more than an intermediation: in effect, a superposition of conflicting political models, modern centralist upon traditional localist.

Discussion

This paper has been concerned with three components of a political system: the commune government, the majority political party, and the village. An important link among these three is the commune councillor. I have shown how the party attempted to strengthen itself and increase its control over commune government at the expense of village control over representatives in government. I have described the transition from councillor as village president to councillor as party pawn. In the past, the councillor enjoyed a double power base—moral in the village and transactional in the party (Bailey 1969). With the elimination of the village level in party organization, the councillor is left without a moral base of support and is entirely dependent on the transactional. In addition, the transformation of job description from village representative to commune specialist further decays the councillor's traditional base of support in the village.

Models of decision-making have also been radically transformed. In the past, the commune council, although ideally a collegial unit, was in fact an arena council (Bailey 1965) consisting of spokesmen for opposing interest groups. The councillor derived his support from the small, face-to-face, solidary, consensus-based village community. In many cases, the councillor was essentially the head of a kinship group, the "family clan." The political and administrative reorganization of 1968 imposed a new image on commune politics. The commune, rather than the village, is now the minimal political unit serving the people directly.

The village remains a moral, consensus-based unit, but a new stage for conflict has been introduced at the level of the multivillage region. In effect, the reorganization created a second arena council in addition to that of the commune council. The five villages not represented by Conservative councillors correctly view themselves as being in competition with the other villages, competition for the now-scarce resource of political representation. Because those five villages might be any of the twelve in any given election, all twelve villages are engaged in competition to achieve or to maintain political representation.

The Conservative Party intended the region to replace the village not only as the new structural unit, but also as the new cognitive unit. Party discipline and unity, always difficult to maintain in the face of extraparty allegiances, were now to be in force in an inevitable arena-type council. The opposition among local groups, once expressed and contained in the commune council, was now recreated at the local level of the region. The party further amplified conflict by neutralizing the political effectiveness of the village councillor. Villages thus lost political representation in two ways: having no councillor at all, or having one who was a party pawn.

The localist model of the Swiss political system depends not only on autonomy at the lowest level of organization but also on direct communication with the highest level. At each level of the system, we find both formal structures and informal processes—the former providing stability and the latter variety. The combination of stability and variety, of structure and process, promotes adaptability in the system as a whole and enables it to respond smoothly to environmental change.

In Bagnes, extrapolitical allegiances at the village level had always prevented the formation of permanent foci of power in the commune. The informal expression and management of conflict at the local level ensured the maintenance of formal institutions at the commune level. As Dimen-Schein (1978:377) suggests, "people's command over their cultures is most effectively realized through control over these structures of everyday life."

The reorganization of the commune in 1968 introduced the region without destroying the village. The result was a three-level hierarchy in which formal control flowed from top to bottom while informal processes continued to exist at the lowest level. With these processes officially detached from the system, however, they no longer serve a homeostatic function but appear instead as gratuitous conflict, dissent, and self-interest.

NOTES

1. This paper is based on research conducted between 1967 and 1975, a period of important political and economic change in the Commune of Bagnes. Although I am confident of the broad outlines of my analysis of the political system, I have little specific information about events since that time.

2. I employ local usage when I speak of the "Conservative" and "Radical" parties. The Conservative Party recently affiliated with the European Christian Democratic Party and officially adopted its name. The older term, "Conservative," however, is still used widely in Bagnes. The Radical Party was officially called "Radical-Socialist" until 1972 when the Socialist members joined the cantonal Socialist Party and presented their own ballot in commune elections. Even before the split, however, the cover term "Radical" was commonly used. In any case, neither "conservative" nor "radical" should be read as a descriptor of political ideology but only as a local label.

3. In the Swiss proportional representational system, the ballots are counted first to determine relative party strength (and the corresponding number of won seats) and second, to determine the relative strength of individual candidates (and establishing a rank ordering for actual occupancy of party seats).

4. As a result of a 1972 cantonal law revising election regulations, the villages lost control over the actual voting process as well. The new law requires that votes be counted at the commune, rather than the village, level. In the past, village election officials were able to make very good guesses about the local outcome of an election. As voters cast their ballots, the officials checked off their names on a master list of eligible voters. Since party affiliation is fixed, it was only necessary to look at this list in order to determine the outcome. In addition, the art of undetectable election frauds is highly developed in the Valais. One of these, the barely visible marking of the ballot, depends on the fact that official ballots may be acquired outside the polling place and in advance of the election date. Parties may distribute ballots to their constituents, along with pre-election promotion materials. If these ballots are (illegally) marked, and if votes are counted at the village level, then it is relatively easy for the local party cadres to control how their people vote. Obviously, it was this potential for violation of normative beliefs that prompted the new legislation in 1972.

BIBLIOGRAPHY

Bailey, F. G. 1965. Decisions by Consensus in Councils and Committees. Political
    Systems and the Distribution of Power, ed. M. Banton, pp. 1–20. London.
———. 1969. Strategems and Spoils: A Social Anthropology of Politics. New York.
Bernard, C. 1957. An Introduction to the Study of Experimental Medicine. New
    York. (original publication 1865).
Courthion, L. 1972. Le Peuple du Valais. Lausanne. (original publication 1903).
Dimen-Schein, M. 1978. Ethnography, Teaching and Creativity. Reviews in Anthro-
    pology 5:365–379.
Silverman, S. 1975. Three Bells of Civilization: The Life of an Italian Hill Town.
    New York.
Weinberg, D. 1975. Peasant Wisdom: Cultural Adaptation in a Swiss Village.
    Berkeley.
———. 1976. Bands and Clans: Political Functions of Voluntary Associations in
    the Swiss Alps. American Ethnologist 3:175–189.
Wiegandt, E. 1977. Communalism and Conflict in the Swiss Alps. Unpublished
    Ph.D. dissertation, University of Michigan, Ann Arbor.

Popular Devotions, Power, and Religious Regimes in Catholic Dutch Brabant[1]

Mart Bax

*Mart Bax details the waxing and waning of a particular Dutch Ro-
man Catholic shrine over five hundred years. In the changing role of
the bureaucratic corporate Catholic Church, many adaptations and
resistances to feudal, Protestant, and finally secular and multi-
religious national regimes have occured. Ownership and jurisdiction
of the shrine reflected interactions between the interests of the local
Catholics, the Dutch state, Brabant, and the institutional needs of the
Catholic Church. This evolution, as described by Bax, could be further examined by observing the nature and intensity of religious beliefs and practices and the social groups and strata that carried and
expressed them.*

SINCE THE EARLY 1970s, pilgrimages and processions in honor of traditional patron saints have gained increasing popularity among the people
of rural North Brabant, Netherlands. Every year, thousands of visitors are
drawn to more than 70 shrines and "powerful" images in this almost
exclusively Catholic southern Dutch province; the chapels of convents
and monasteries have become overcrowded, whereas church attendance
has steadily declined.[2] In short, the official belief of the established
church, with its lore and standardized liturgical practice, has been
steadily losing ground to popular belief.

At first sight this revival appears to be a curious anomaly. After all, the
dominant perspective—in contemporary times still adhered to by Christian (1972) for Spain and by Weber (1979) for France—implies an almost unilinear development; popular representations and practices disap-
pear in the face of increasing integration and modernization. But a grow-

ing number of publications about similar forms of popular religion demonstrates that North Brabant is not unique. Similar processes have been observed in France, Germany, Belgium, Spain, and Italy (Ahrens 1977; Blijlevens 1982; Bonnet 1973; Donders 1979; Haarsma 1977; Isambert 1975; Metz 1979; Pannet 1974; Rousseau 1977). These authors observe a tendency toward repopularization among Catholics whenever the Church becomes well-established and its doctrines and liturgical practice become standardized. Curiously enough, although they explain these developments in terms of modernization, they also acknowledge that more systematic and detailed empirical research is necessary if there is to be deeper understanding. Evidently, then, the modernization theory is not very useful for the exploration of this problem.

It is remarkable that this field has hardly been approached from a political point of view in terms of power relations.[3] A recent exception is Asad (1983), who argues that the evolution of representations, experiences, and practices is intimately connected with power processes in the religious field and its wider social environment and, consequently, anthropologists should begin by investigating these power processes, their specific historical conditions, and their immanent forces. The present article takes this perspective and makes an effort to clarify the changing status of a canonized saint and his devotional cult vis-à-vis the liturgical cult and the sacramental rituals of the established church in a Brabantian rural community. Specifically, it seeks to explain how and why this formerly widely accepted complex of practices and representations came to fall into disfavor and to be branded as superstition, why it has never disappeared altogether, and how and why it has made such a spectacular comeback in recent years.

The argument is guided by the following theoretical propositions: (1) the status of religious practices and representations is determined by the power balance between the groups that constitute a religious configuration; (2) the study of the changes in the power balance in and between the constituent groups can provide greater insight into the changes of the status of these practices and representations; (3) a religious configuration is not an isolated entity, but is related to other, more comprehensive configurations; and (4) changes of the latter influence the leeway and social strength of each of the parties or groups that make up the religious configuration. The article first describes the evolution of the cult in terms of a competitive process between two types of religious specialists (the diocesan and the monastic clergy) in the present municipality of Berghem/Roersel between 1490–1982.[4] The second part explores the conditions and forces that account for the emergence and further development of this competitive process. In the context of the Dutch state formation process, diocesan regime-building seems to be a major determinant.

The Evolution of a Saint and His Devotees
Emergence, Expansion, and Peak (1490–1876)

The mere mention of St. Gerlach's name in the small, rural town of Roersel touches a tender nerve. Many people praise him for his protection and the prosperity he has brought to the community; others shrug their shoulders, observing that "the phenomenon" has only caused undue commotion, discord, and foolishness. Although many people want nothing to do with St. Gerlach, he remains the patron saint of the town. His evolution is closely connected with that of the Fathers of W., a local branch of an old order, who came from Munsterland (Germany) to Roersel around the middle of the fifteenth century. The Fathers obtained land from the local lord and enjoyed his protection.

Monastic sources tell how, around 1470, a serious epidemic in the district took many lives. With their herbal knowledge, the Fathers did whatever they could but the disease continued to take a heavy toll. One night, an older monk had a vision: a man in a shining robe ordered him to go to Munsterland and bring back what was needed. The monk went to the monastery there and obtained a piece of bone that reportedly belonged to the Blessed Gerlach, the patron saint of the order. Back in town, the inhabitants prayed to St. Gerlach for his intercession with God and shortly afterwards the mysterious disease disappeared from Roersel. In gratitude the townspeople built a chapel dedicated to the saint and looked after by the Fathers of W. The local lord offered a silver shrine for the relic and it was placed on the altar. Gerlach became the local patron saint and his chapel acquired the status of parish church, where liturgical cult and devotional practice went hand in hand. Every year, his *dies natalis* was celebrated with an impressive procession but on ordinary days many people also came from far and near to call for aid, to ask for protection from disease and other perils, or to render homage for blessings received. Until the last quarter of the nineteenth century, the church and monastery flourished, trade and commerce thrived and brought great prosperity to the rapidly growing town. Since then, however, Gerlach "has gone through many trials," as present-day protagonists put it.

Waning Influence (1876–1965)

The first attack on St. Gerlach came from Berghem, a small town some three kilometers from Roersel. In 1876, the provincial authorities combined Roersel and Berghem into one municipality, with the latter as the administrative center. (Rumor has it that prominent citizens of Berghem were behind this.) The town hall was to be built there, which was why, it was argued, the parish church should in Berghem as well. But since it was too small for a separate parish, Roersel would have to be incorporated. In accordance with the new diocesan policy aimed at a parochial organization strictly separated from "secondary" devotional practices, the new parish of Berghem/Roersel was created and its church was consecrated by the bishop himself. The Fathers of W. obtained a letter from the diocese with the unequivocal message that they were discharged from their duties regarding the spiritual care of the faithful. Thus, at one stroke, the segregation of liturgical cult and devotional practice had become a formal religious fact. But this must have been unacceptable to many of the faithful, for individually and in groups they continued to visit their beloved saint.

Shortly afterwards, St. Gerlach was dealt another blow; public meetings and processions could only be held with the permission of the local secular authorities and, despite repeated requests, the Fathers were never granted permission.[5] Consequently, the public processions in honor of St. Gerlach came to an end, though for many years the veneration was continued behind the monastic walls and still drew large numbers of people.

In 1897, the monastic community lost another important resource; its monopoly over local education. The provincial board of education ordered the school to be closed and instructed the municipal authorities to set up a new one in Berghem with staff to be appointed and supervised by the parish priest and the church board.[6]

The control of St. Gerlach and his priestly servants over the faithful declined in still other respects. In 1883—on diocesan initiative, as is noted in the parish memorandum book—a confraternity of the Blessed Sacrament was set up to promote the adoration of Christ and His sacramental gifts. The association held weekly night masses which were primarily intended for men, though women were not prevented from celebrating the "Holy Secrets." Membership was not compulsory but the faithful were strongly encouraged to join. (Elderly informants still remember that in their parents' days, the parish priests used to announce from the pulpit who had joined the confraternity and who had not.) Every year, in the third week of July, a procession was held in which almost the entire population took part. Up to World War II, it expanded in size as ever more groups and voluntary associations, organized and supervised by the church, put themselves under the protection of the Blessed Sacrament. The citizen soldiery, the brass band, the Farmers' Union with its rapidly expanding economic branches, and the sporting club, all joined in and thus generated a close-knit network, firmly linked to the parish church and its priest. Together with a circle of local notables—people still note the oligarchical clique of families that emerged in those days—the priests ruled the community with an iron fist. Deviant attitudes and practices were not tolerated, as the following case illustrates.

The Gevers family owned a small grocery shop in Berghem and a few acres of grazing land. William, the eldest son, was doing well at school and since he took an interest in spiritual life, he was noticed by the parish priest. As an altar boy, he was charged with the most honorary tasks, and at confirmation class he was called an example to his peers. Visiting his parents, the priest observed that the boy should go to the preparatory seminary. His parents were hesitant because of the expenses, but the priest told them not to worry for he would find a way. William himself, however, was more interested in the Fathers of W. Once with his mother, and more often with an elderly aunt from Roersel, he had visited St. Gerlach's chapel. "The miraculous and very special atmosphere, full of grace," as he puts it, impressed him deeply. Indeed, he was so fascinated that he decided to become a monk. His parents were frightened when he told them. His father in particular tried to make him change his mind " 'for the sake of the family." William thought his father informed the priest. For once, after mass, the cleric asked him whether it was true what he had heard. William assented, whereupon the priest replied that this was "nonsense;" he was "too bright a boy to be cooped up in that gloomy building." But William persisted. One day, he informed the priest that after much pondering and praying, he had obtained a sign from heaven that he could not resist. The priest objected that it was all "superstition" and "boyish romanticism," that it was against his father's wishes and that he must have been "talked to by those refractory monks." But it did not help. In 1923, twelve-year-old William donned the garb of the Fathers of W. and took the name of Cornelius. "At that time, I could not suspect what my decision would lead to but later it became clear to me how hard people can be," says the now elderly monk. The mortgage on his father's land was terminated and the local bank refused a new loan. At school his siblings were ostracized and his father lost the patronage of several good customers. The Gevers family was evermore stigmatized and finally had to move to another area.

The loss of the care for the public liturgical cult and the increasing intertwining of secular spheres of life with the parochial organization rang in an era of a "hidden apostolate" for the personnel of the monastery. What did this comprise, how was it organized, and why did it attract faithful parishioners? "In anybody's life," Father Hubertus observes, "particular occasions turn up when he longs for personal contact with God and his visual appearance. Nobody can do without this." In times of personal crisis, he meant, people would come to the monastery. Usually these visits were related to diseases or other problems in family or business life. Special protection was sought for young children and pregnant women, and until recently, small peasants would call for a Father to "lead" their cattle.[7]

The ritual at the monastery consisted of the following elements. First, the troubled person told his problems in the confessional. Then he received Holy Communion, whereafter St. Gerlach's shrine was visited, worshipped, and kissed. Next, one was blessed by one of the Fathers, who gave some holy water, a picture of the saint, and a special prayer to be recited for nine days. Then the visitor was reminded of the offertory box and requested to inform the community of the time when his prayers had been answered. In addition to these forms of communication between patron, intermediaries, and client, masses for the dead constituted another important raison d'etre for St. Gerlach's servants.[8] Again, though less frequently and usually at night, a Father was sent for to give spiritual assistance at the house of a sick or dying person.

In these hidden forms of communication between the monastery and the faithful, *zelatricen* (female propagandists) must have played an important role. These women (middle-aged or older and as a rule unmarried or widowed) had a particular bond with the monastery and their life style to some extent lent them a reputation of sanctity among certain circles of the population. After personal crises and miraculous help, these women had taken the vow to dedicate their lives to the service of St. Gerlach. After their weekly eucharist at the monastery, they were instructed on how to help their fellow mortals. This included trying to find out which people had personal problems, looking them up, and telling them about the miraculous help they themselves had obtained through the intercession of St. Gerlach. The "Blessed Ones," as the monastical diary refers to the clientele, could obtain a small replica of St. Gerlach, a small oil lamp, and a bottle with blessed water. The lamp and bottle could be refilled on the saint's birthday.[9] Local written sources do not disclose the reactions of the parish priests but the life story of Marie Therésè might give an impression.

> Prior to her joining the Community of St. Gerlach, her name was Sophie van Genderen. As a seventeen-year-old girl, she married Hermanus van Genderen, a farm-hand at a big farm near Berghem. As a young girl, she had visited the chapel with her mother. She still remembers that, time and again, the parish priest had remonstrated her mother on her behavior. Her husband was furiously against her going to the Fathers; it would certainly get them into trouble. For three years, Sophie had in vain been waiting for a child. Then she made up her mind and with the help of an aunt (a *zelatrice*) found her way to the chapel, where she supplicated St. Gerlach

for his intercession so that she might have a baby. At home she prayed every day to a small replica her aunt had lent her—much against her husband's wishes. Some six months later, Hermanus died in an accident at the farm, leaving a lonesome wife behind. She went to confession and the priest forbade her any contact with the monastery. But the twenty-year-old woman needed help and comfort, and since she could not obtain it from the church, as she observes, she was drawn back again to the chapel. When this news reached the priest, he summoned her to stop those "superstitious practices," for otherwise he would have to take other steps. Sophie, however, was restless and continued visiting the monastery and its chapel. After some time, the parish priest's words came true; Sophie lost her parish assistance and was evicted from her (church-owned) little cottage. With monastical help, she was accommodated in Roersel, and up to her seventieth year she worked as a maid in the monastic buildings. As Marie Thérèse, she joined the Community of St. Gerlach, which consisted of some twenty women at the time. Ever since, she has been zealous for "her" saint and his prompt and prodigious powers.

Up to the early 1960s, the local religious field was thus characterized by two religious regimes, unequal in strength and composition. On the one hand, there was the local branch of the diocesan regime, headed by secular clerics and focused on the liturgical cult and the sacramental rituals. It was not only the official but also the dominant and strongest regime. Numerous spheres of life were tightly connected with the ecclesiastical organization. Together, they constituted a strong and close-knit network from which it was difficult to escape. On the other hand, there was a secondary or subordinate regime of loosely organized devotees, supervised by the monastic clergy and their patron saint. Not until the middle of the 1960s did the first signs of a changing power balance begin to manifest themselves, as will be illustrated in the next section.

Increasing Polarization and a Shifting Balance (1965–1975)

THE SISTERS OF B. AND THE AGED PEOPLE'S WELFARE WORK. In the early 1950s, the monastic community was confronted with serious problems. The monastery saw its number of novices decline to a critical joint. Consequently, it had to close its small training college, resulting in a loss of labor and income. The Fathers looked for alternatives and "Providence was with them," as they put it. With a grant from a "grateful devotee"—a large entrepreneur-cum-politician from a southern city, whose life had been saved through prayers and help from St. Gerlach— the Fathers decided to turn part of the buildings into a rest home for the aged. Negotiations with a small convent of the Sisters of B., confronted with similar personnel problems, resulted in a partnership. The Sisters would look after the aged and a separate convent building for the Sisters would be created. The community would be semi-autonomous, though in spiritual matters it would fall under the jurisdiction of the Fathers. Meanwhile, canvassing for aged clientele started in the parish and region and many people enrolled. Some twelve months before the opening of Gerlachshave, as the new complex came to be called, the home was almost subscribed, with many local aged among the clientele. Suppliers and lay personnel spontaneously offered their services. The new complex was opened and consecrated by a German bishop and the General Superior of the order.

Gerlachshave was a thorn in the flesh of the young parish priest, Oerlemans. The cleric had reportedly tried to prevent the plan from materializing, protesting to the diocese that double cloisters were against the ecclesiastical rules, but he did not succeed. The monastery and convent were separated by a wall, whereas the grounds of the convent were the property of the Sisters of B. Oerlemans tried again when it appeared that ever more parishioners combined their Sunday mass observance with a visit to their parents or grandparents in the rest home. In a letter to the monks from the church board, it was pointed out that administering the sacraments to the parishioners was not in the Fathers' jurisdiction. The board was to bring the case to the bishop's notice.

THE SPLIT IN THE FARMERS' UNION.   In 1969 the parochial branch of the North Brabant Christian Farmer's Union (NCB) held its annual meeting, with the election of a new executive as one of the main issues. For some years, tensions had been growing among its members because agrarian modernization had forced many small farmers to fold and look for other jobs, in construction work and industry. Only a patch of potatoes or vegetables and a few pigs had kept these exfarmers in the Union, though for a long time they had felt that its policy did not coincide with their interests. Consequently, many considered withdrawing from it. Matters came to a peak as a result of a case that had nothing to do with the agrarian sector, though it clearly reflected the increasingly contrasting interests.

A proposal was introduced that the NCB, being the major local organization, should promote recreational facilities for the aged, as there was no community center or any other local facility for them. The people who made the proposal, some exfarmers, suggested contacting Gerlachshave to jointly set up a recreation center, and this was loudly seconded by some others. According to an exmember who attended the meeting, parish priest Oerlemans, honorary President of the Union, spoke at length that this was altogether out of the question; that the NCB was an association for the farmers and their interests, and that the unity of the parish had seriously been damaged by the "refractory behavior of the Fathers." A tumultuous debate followed in which religiousness was mixed with farmers' interests. The "fat farmers" were accused of jobbery, rubbing shoulders with the priest, and being blind to the problems of their old colleagues who, for economic reasons, had been forced to sell their land. Pent up hatred and envy must have burst forth and the meeting ended with a blazing row. Some 50 exfarmers resigned from the Union. They set up a small purchase co-operative and, together with their families, began to attend mass at the chapel. A new religious community began to take shape around St. Gerlach.

THE ESTABLISHMENT ON THE OFFENSIVE. Afraid of a further loss of influence and convinced that they were right, the parochial establishment (Oerlemans, some local notables, the church board, and the leaders of the Farmers' Union) decided to respond and expose the dissidents as unorthodox. The first blow took the form of an article in a regional weekly, disputing the authenticity of St. Gerlach's relic. A "correspondent" wrote that he had been informed that the relic might be false. A thorough investigation in the archives of the Munsterland mother-house had failed to prove that the Roersel relic originated from that house. Indeed, the very authenticity of the relic of the mother-house was challenged; no deeds of sale or donation were produced. The article concluded that "a formerly widespread and highly valued practice could now be only attributed with folkloristic value." (The local grapevine has it that the article was written by the old school headmaster, a loyal adherent of the parish church and a close friend of Oerlemans.)

In 1973 the same weekly published an article questioning the saintly status of Gerlach. The new *Calendarium,* set up in Rome, did not mention Gerlach. Thus, it was argued, the Holy Church did not recognize this saint; therefore, the veneration should be stopped. The following week, the periodical contained a long letter to the editor in defense of St. Gerlach. The Congregation for the Rites, to be sure, had provided general directives for the Universal Church, but the article stipulated that it was up to the local churches and monastic orders to adapt them to local circumstances. It was also explained that St. Gerlach's name was still registered in the *Martyrologium,* implying that the Holy Church recognized his saintly status.

Early in May, 1974, this more or less theological skirmish took an abrupt, violent turn. The story circulated that the parish priest, Oerlemans, when visiting an old woman, saw a small statue of St. Gerlach. Infuriated and uttering curses, he was alleged to have lifted it and smashed it on the floor. The news, spreading like wildfire throughout the community, must have caused great commotion. Many messages about weeping statuettes of St. Gerlach are said to have been registered at the monastery. Also, parts of the church doors were tarred (allegedly by protagonists of St. Gerlach). Some local people maintain that the old woman found her broken statue miraculously repaired the next morning. Whatever the case may be, the iconoclasm and its aftermath had generated further polarization. For the group of St. Gerlach devotees grew larger and stronger, while uncertainty and partisanship began to split the community of the official parish church.

Back Again Into the Front-Stage (1975-present)

The open ecclesiastical resistance and vilification marked the beginning of an epoch of increasing prosperity and flourishing for St. Gerlach and his devotional cult. According to the Fathers, the prodigious cure of Peter van Iersel, the twelve-year-old son of a large farmer-cum-alderman, had been a primary cause. The boy suffered from a serious blood disease; a hopeless case, the doctors had told his parents. At their wits' end, they took the advice of an old grandaunt and took the boy to the chapel. Together with the entire monastic community, they prayed ardently to St. Gerlach to intercede. Shortly afterwards, much to the doctors' amazement, the boy began to recover. The grateful parents, since then devout members of the chapel community, have devoted a great deal of time and other resources to the public rehabilitation of the saint. On their initiative, a petition for a public procession in honor of St. Gerlach is said to have been sent to the provincial authorities. Permission must have been granted, for ever since 1976, a public procession has been held, with growing attendance.[10] Many local associations changed sides when the procession of the Blessed Sacrament was abolished. Their members blame the parish priest for depriving them of their only opportunity to publicly march through the streets. Oerlemans himself, hardly prepared to discuss the matter, deplores what he calls "the present schism in the parish." He observes that the procession has been postponed on the urgent request of the diocese "to prevent further problems."

Several years ago, the Fathers initiated another public religious ceremony; the blessing of motor cars. Every second Saturday in June, large numbers of motorists from the town and the district have their cars blessed. The ceremony provides special protection against increasingly dangerous traffic but it also encourages careful and responsible driving. Some 200 persons, united in the Confraternity of the Blessed Gerlach, meet several times a year for instruction, devotion, and retreat with special masses. (The rear windows of their cars bear a small protection sticker—an example to others.)

Thus, more and more parishioners have become involved in an increasing number of ways in the devotion of St. Gerlach, and the religious spheres of liturgical cult and of devotional practice are united once again. Whereas in former days one could visit St. Gerlach and his relic only in secrecy, nowadays (1982) three public and ritually rich Sunday masses in the extended chapel are barely enough for the growing numbers of faithful. Only some 30 per cent of the faithful have remained loyal to the parish church.

Clericalization and the Unforeseen Effects of an Emancipation Movement
By Way of Competition Toward a Dominant Clerical Regime

For almost 200 years—until the end of the eighteenth century—Catholic North Brabant was discriminated against in many respects by the Protestant-dominated government (Geyl 1964; Goudsblom 1967; Rogier 1956). Downgraded to a colonial status, it was heavily burdened by taxes. The diocesan organization had been abolished, monks and nuns had been evicted, and their possessions confiscated. There were also laws making provisions for placards prohibiting the public celebration of the Roman Catholic faith. During that period, the diocesan clergy and the order priests were involved in a more-or-less hidden rivalry for clientele. The monastic priests, however, were in a more favorable position. In addition to all the local and regional shrines, they controlled the majority of the parishes (Juten 1935; Krüger 1872–1878; Schutjes 1870–1876). In spite of its regulations, the government was unable to deal adequately with the highly mobile and internationally organized monastic circuit. The main reasons for the dominance of a monastic regime (though in disguised form, for monks dressed like ordinary citizens) were: (1) lack of personnel and proper training facilities for diocesan clerics; (2) fragmented government administration; and (3) a corrupt bureaucracy that accepted large sums of protection money from rich monasteries abroad.

By the end of the eighteenth century, however, the power balance began to change in favor of the diocesan clergy due to two related developments. First, because of Napoleon's operations in present-day Belgium and France. Second, the Dutch government, afraid of these military pressures from the south, strove for more internal unity and therefore provided the diocesan clergy with greater freedom and support. Napoleon's vigorous and highly effective anti-Catholic policy brought the steady influx of monks and other resources (mainly from present-day Belgium) to a halt when the area became part of his empire. Many clerics of Dutch origin fled to North Brabant, including some Louvain seminary professors, Brabantines by birth. Together with the apostolic vicars, and with governmental support, they planned to set up a seminary for diocesan priests and to take over the parochial administration. Within a few years, the new seminary produced increasing numbers of diocesan clerics (Jansen 1976). With these new assets, the fight for hegemony over the parochial administration began in earnest (Bax, n.d.). Systematically, sometimes by force, almost all the "ultramontanian monks" were driven out of the parishes. This offensive, of course, caused the two sections of the Brabantian religious leadership to drift farther apart. Mutual accusations and stigmatization were the order of the day. But a diocesan regime was on its way to becoming well established. By the middle of the nineteenth century, the Dutch diocesan organization was officially reinstated and diocesan priests alone were charged with the parochial administration.

This change in the balance of power brought many monastic clergymen almost below the subsistence level. Turning to a neighboring country was out of the question, for "Rome's henchmen" were very much hunted there. Indeed, quite the opposite movement began to take shape; throughout the nineteenth century, a great influx of monastical male and female personnel took place. They came from Belgium, France, and later from Germany. The hospitable peasant society of North Brabant became packed, so to speak, with them.[11] Initially, the Dutch government adopted the Napoleonic restrictive policy toward monastic personnel. Real monasteries and convents were forbidden, and only female persons who for "spiritual reasons" wanted to look after the poor, the sick, and the aged were allowed some degree of freedom. In principle, the 1848 constitution abolished all the restrictions. So it is not surprising that the growing force of unemployed monks and nuns plunged into this relatively new field, which is now referred to as the "quaternary sector." Schools, poorhouses, hospitals, old-age homes, and infirmaries mushroomed. Middle and eastern North Brabant in particular were fertile fields and even the smallest towns had one or more of these clergy-led institutions.

Evidently, these early manifestations of monastic expansionism were a thorn in the side of the Brabantian prelates and their clerics, who called it "monastical madness." One bishop warned his colleague to put an end to this movement, for "soon there would be many dioceses within his diocese" (Gerlach, n.d.). They were, of course, afraid of an alternative parochial organization that might well be at the expense of their own regime, which, after all, was still in its formative stage. On the other hand, they could not openly obstruct the movement, knowing that the Holy See supported the order clergy. So they were in a fix, so to speak, and at first they did not know what to do about it. After some time, the diocesan authorities decided to fight their opponent with its own weapon. They urged their priests and curates to also set up religious organizations and clergy-run institutions. They defended their policy to Rome by arguing that every possible effort had to be made to "emancipate" the backward peasant population and guide them as well-equipped Catholics into modern Dutch society. (The pope's encyclical letters against liberalism and socialism were very instrumental in this respect.)

After the first half of the nineteenth century, the competition for personnel, lay clientele, and other resources gathered momentum and assumed greater features of a self-sustaining and reinforcing process. Gradually, however, the diocesan camp turned out to be the strongest. Their superior organization, firm discipline, strong internal cohesion, their co-operation with the secular authorities, and their greater numbers of personnel gradually enabled them to encapsulate the smaller and mutually competing monastically run institutions, or to make them dependent in other respects. Only a minority has been able to escape diocesan control (van den Hurk 1977).

Thus, by the early decades of this century, an impressive social configuration had emerged among the Brabantian population, firmly led by the "garbed circuit." It included the sectors of education and welfare, the recreational sphere, most of the political organizations, the Farmers' Union with its multifarious economic branches, the laborers' union, and the employers' association. They were all run by religious personnel or supervised by "spiritual advisors" (diocesan priests), and almost all communication channels converged at one single nodal point—the diocesan headquarters. Locally, the priest ruled with an iron fist. Formerly well-established devotional practices such as pilgrimages and processions in honor of old saints were often discouraged or carefully regulated. The diocesan policy dictated that liturgical cult and devotional practice be strictly separated; masses at shrines and other holy places were rarely permitted, to prevent "possible abuses" it was stated.[12] The monks and nuns locally employed in education and welfare work were eagerly supervised and their ritual activities were safely stowed behind their convent walls. The parish priests watched their contact with the laity with great care and their activities were rashly interpreted as undermining the parochial authority and leadership. Canvassing for monastic novices outside the officially fixed time was looked upon as *schuuperen* (poaching). If monasteries were in need of new personnel for the "foreign missions"—at home they were considered redundant—many parish priests must have stipulated that it was their right and duty to see to the selection. An aged monk observed, "It was always the same old song: the Fathers had to remain in their monasteries . . . they had opted for that vocation; the parishes were most certainly none of their business." "We were caged and muzzled," runs an almost proverbial expression among many older monks.

The Reverse of the Emancipation Movement

A flourishing diocesan regime dominated the Brabantian scene until the early 1950s, when signs of friction, resistance, and decline began to appear. The first symptoms appeared among the clerical elites. Seminary enrollment stagnated and later declined seriously; convents and monasteries were also confronted with a rapid fall in the number of novices (Jansen 1976). Evidently, the priesthood was no longer the highly valued career prospect it had been for so long. Also, anticlericalism emerged among the leading rural laity. This elite, better equipped for many modern, specialized tasks than their "garbed" counterparts, began to resist clerical interference with "worldly affairs," interpreting it as outdated tutelage and not in line with the major tendency in other Catholic areas in the Netherlands. Consequently, the Brabantian diocese urged its clerics to gradually withdraw from those worldly fields. Thus, unforeseen and unintended, the emancipation movement, stimulated by clerical factionalism, had created the conditions for the declining power position of its religious leadership and had contributed to the emergence of a new lay elite.

The movement also entailed changes in religious attitudes and practices. The new elite, quickly adapting themselves to the northern Dutch (non-Catholic) standards of behavior and cultural codes, found it increasingly difficult to participate in public religious performances such as processions and confraternities. They reminded them of bygone times when Brabant was a backward area, suppressed by the Protestant North. Under the pressure of these circumstances, the ecclesiastical authorities adopted a policy aimed at a more restricted spiritual guidance program and a general liturgical sobriety; the teachings of Vatican II were instrumental in this respect.

To the less emancipated Brabantines—the victims of the process of agrarian modernization—the ecclesiastical policy implied a serious loss of identity and orientation (Bax and Nieuwenhuis 1982). They began to feel like strangers in their own parish church, which was run by clerics and a lay establishment with whom they had almost nothing in common. So almost automatically (and no longer constrained by bonds of agrarian dependence) they were drawn to the other section of religious specialists, the monastic clergy and their followers. The latter were only too willing to help. Like their diocesan counterparts, they had also lost many of their functions. Indeed, monasteries and convents had suffered the most from the general declericalization process, for its aging personnel had its educational and welfare functions taken over by better educated lay people and specialized state agencies. Consequently, the raison d'etre of these persons, bound to live in congregations and to conduct an "apostolate in the world," was at stake. In search of new ways to put their religious mission to practice, they found their target groups among the people referred to above.

The consequences of these developments can be traced most clearly in towns like Berghem/Roersel, with the two types of religious specialists operating in one parochial context. The increasing attraction of monastic communities and their devotional practices constitutes an outright threat to the regime of the parish priest, who finds himself between the devil and the deep blue sea, so to speak. Catering to the wishes and feelings of the "simple faithful" more or less implies stating that his opponent, the monastic clergy, is right, which would undermine his own position. Therefore, conforming to the parochial establishment is imperative, but this entails the danger of alienating the ordinary faithful. It is from this perspective that one must understand Oerlemans's emotional reactions and overt insinuations toward the community of the Fathers of W.; they reflect an increasing loss of power. Each new confrontation, however, can widen the gap between the ecclesiastical establishment and the ordinary laity, which in turn improves the chances for monastic communities to expand their regimes.

Conclusions

Popular devotional movements are often explained in terms of spontaneous reactions initiated by the poor and the oppressed. This view might be correct with respect to their initial stages but once the movements have turned into more durable, institutionalized cults authorized by Rome, they must be seen as independent entities whose status and viability are influenced by different agencies and forces. In the preceding pages an attempt has been made to clarify the changing status and social viability of an authorized devotional cult in terms of power by focusing on the long-term competitive process originating from the Catholic religious leadership. This is not to substitute one monocausal explanation (modernization) for another (power), as Asad (1983) convincingly illustrates. Nor does it espouse a simplistic one-way relationship between power and belief. The pursuit of focal points in a power field in order to investigate the status and development of particular devotional cults is a heuristic device that enables us to understand the (changing) inter-relatedness of various causes (economical, political, religious) and to present them in a historically realistic way.

Although each case is historically unique and popular religion is not necessarily monastically promoted religion, and granting that other forces may account for devotional revival, the present case study invites the further examination of similar authorized cults along the lines set out above. The dynamics at work in North Brabant are not unique; indeed, they are at the root of Roman Catholic leadership structure at large. Its dual and in a way ambiguous nature constitutes a potential source of tension, friction, and rivalry. The diocesan or secular priests, supervised by their bishops, are primarily supposed to be in charge of the parochial administration, the liturgical cult, and the sacramental rituals. But the Holy See has never taken any steps to deprive the other section of religious specialists, the monastic clergy, of their sacred mission for the spiritual care of the laity (Kuiters 1958). As both types of priests are entitled to administer the sacraments, in principle they can thus operate in any (religious) field, implying that they are potential competitors. In modern Western European societies, with their relatively stable governments, the field of parochial administration came to be monopolized by the diocesan clergy. The monastic clergy, however, has never disappeared from the religious scene, though they were often seen and treated as mercenary troops at the beck and call of the diocesan authorities. Together, as a result of more or less antagonistic alliances, they have greatly contributed to the integration of backward peasant areas and the emancipation of their population. But unforeseen, this resulted in their losing functions to the laity and the state. To compensate for this loss, the orders have tried to attract clientele in other ways and their own devotional cults were instrumental in this respect. The diocesan clergy, usually more identified with the upper segments of rural society, may view this monastical maneuvering as upsetting the established ecclesiastical order and as poaching in their parochial preserve. They may try to prevent it by emphasizing the orthodoxy and superiority of "their" lore and practice, thus downgrading the orders' "missionary" practices. This, however, implies the risk of estranging the ordinary faithful, the less emancipated groups. These groups may become potential clientele of the opponent, who thus has new reasons for expanding its activities and influence. This is the relatively autonomous religious process that seems to be taking place in many present-day European rural regions. They are reobtaining the status of mission areas and the revival of old devotional cults is only one element in this dialectical process.

Thus, rather than considering the two types of religious specialists to be complementary (which indeed they are from Rome's point of view), or focusing on the needs of the faithful (which means adopting the perspective of the religious specialists), it might be advisable to begin by looking upon these specialists as focal points in specific religious regimes, each of them striving for expansion and consolidation. One might then proceed to hypothesize that it is the power balance between such regimes, in a specific socio-religious field and at a particular time, that influences the status of a certain authorized devotional cult, whether or not it is subordinated and negatively referred to as "popular belief." Abolishing this concept because of its ambiguity, as has been suggested (Christian 1981:178), means excluding the possibility of examining how a particular attitude toward a certain religious form is generated, by whom and for whom.

NOTES

1. Fieldwork for this paper was carried out at intervals between 1978 and 1983. For criticism on an earlier draft, I am indebted to Talal Asad, Jeremy Boissevaln, John Davis, Peter Geschiere, Walter Goddijn, Fons van den Hurk, Jo de Lepper, Mathieu Schoffeleers, Estellie Smith, Peter van der Veer, and Joan Vincent. Errors of interpretation, of course, are mine alone. Shiela Gogal and Kichard Griffiths edited my English writing. The subject matter of this article is sensitive in southern Dutch society. It has been dealt with only in covert and very general terms by clergymen and scholars (e.g., Boelaars 1969; Fortmann 1958; Kuiters 1958; Melief 1958; Van Leeuwen 1969), but the general theme recurs with increasing frequency in *Tijdschrift Nederlandse Religieuzen,* the periodical of the Dutch monastic clergy. For these reasons, and on the urgent request of the monastic community that plays a central role in this article, all the names of persons and places are fictitious.

2. This is evident from a survey conducted in some 30 Brabantian rural communities by the author between 1978 and 1983. (See also Margry 1982.)

3. Christian (1973) pays no systematic attention to the power processes determining why the Catholic Church encourages certain devotional movements and not others. Kertzer (1980) touches on the power struggle between the Church and the Communist Party in Bologna. Sallnow's (1981) article on Andean pilgrimage does view the development of devotional cults as the outcome of power processes, although it gives the impression that the Andean clergy merely are bystanders in that process. Curiously enough, similar power processes are described much more openly for the Late Antiquity and the Middle Ages (Brown 1982; Southern 1972).

4. For the reader who is not familiar with the Roman Catholic Church, it is important to know that its leadership structure includes two types of religious specialists: the diocesan and the monastic clergy. In most countries where the Catholic Church is established, the diocesan clergy, supervised by bishops, are in charge of the parochial administration, including the liturgical cult and the sacramental rites. As a rule, the monastic clergy, members of religious orders who usually live in monasteries, are not involved in the administration of the parishes but in other sorts of religious, educational, and general welfare work. Consequently, they are not under the direct authority of diocesan bishops.

5. The monastical archives indicate that regional secular and diocesan authorities worked hand-in-glove. By various means, they tried to stop the monastical accumulation of wealth, especially in land, which was a widespread phenomenon at the time (Hugenpoth 1861).

6. By government regulations, only qualified teachers (with an official diploma) were allowed to teach at elementary schools. The Fathers did not meet this new requirement so they petitioned the authorities for time to obtain the necessary qualification. The provincial board of education granted them six months' respite, a ridiculously short period. Consequently, the Fathers lost this important privilege.

7. Many Brabantian farmers used to ask a monk to "lead" a cow to the bull to ensure that the cow would give birth to a healthy calf. Usually a small fee (leidgeld) was charged. According to many informants, diocesan priests would have none of this "madness." A small notebook kept by the founder of the Brabantian Farmers' Association (NCB), Father Gerlacus van den Elsen, indicates that this monk earned a regular income from this practice. The diocesan priests I interviewed asserted that they were not acquainted with this local custom.

8. These are contractual arrangements—usually specified in a last will and testament—between a priest and a lay person. The former will say a fixed number of masses a year for the repose of the soul of a client after his death, and the latter (or his relatives) will pay for this religious service. I was informed that, between them, the Fathers of W. said some 300 masses a year. Although both diocesan priests and order clergy say these masses, it is widely held that the Fathers are cheaper.

9. The archives reveal that between 1920 and 1952, over 2,000 statuettes were sold. Some 600 of them found their way to the local population (at the time between 8,000 and 8,500). The statuettes were obtained from a factory in southern Germany.

10. This might indicate that diocesan pressure on the provincial authorities is no longer effective. It is also known, however, that the present bishop takes a sympathetic stand in matters concerning popular devotions. Insiders assert that this has to do with the growing strength of the monastical lobby. Whatever the case, it seems clear that a strong, centrally directed diocesan regime is giving way to a socio-religious configuration with a much more complicated system of power balances.

11. There must have been some 16,000 aliens by the last quarter of the nineteenth century. (Diocesan Archives of Den Bosch, 1290/7/87.)

12. Not all devotional practices were suppressed. Indeed, devotions of the Sacred Heart and the Blessed Sacrament were encouraged, and many parish priests stimulated Marian devotions. But the worship of the Virgin Mary has never been as popular and widespread as in many other European areas. Only three Marian apparitions have been registered in North Brabant since the beginning of this century. They were discouraged by the bishops, and the religious orders were not interested.

BIBLIOGRAPHY

Ahrens, T. 1977. Volkschristentum und Volksreligion. Wiederentdeckung des Mythos für den christlichen Glauben. Frankfurt-on-Main.

Asad, T. 1983. Anthropological Conceptions of Religion: Reflections on Geertz. Man (ns) 18:237–59.

Bax, M. 1985. Religious Infighting and the Formation of a Dominant Catholic Regime in Southern Dutch Society. Social Compass (forthcoming).

Bax, M., and A. Nieuwenhuis 1982. Peasant Emancipation in a Southern Dutch Catholic Area: The Shattering of a Tableau Vivant. The Netherlands' Journal of Sociology 18:25–45.

Blijlevens, A. (ed.) 1982. Volksreligiositeit. Averbode.

Boelaars, H. 1969. De plaats van de religieuzen in de kerk. Nederlandse Katholieke Stemmen 65:318–28.

Bonnet, S. 1973. A hue et à dia. Les avatars du cléricalisme sous la Ve République. Paris.

Brown, P. 1982. Society and the Holy in Late Antiquity. Berkeley.

Christian, W. A. 1972. Person and God in a Spanish Valley. New York.

———. 1973. Holy People in Peasant Europe. Comparative Studies in Society and History 15:106–114.

———. 1981. Local Religion in Sixteenth-Century Spain. Princeton.

Donders, C. J. M. 1979. Some Psychological Remarks on Official and Popular Religion. Official and Popular Religions, eds. P. Vrijhof and J. Waardenburg, pp. 294–322. The Hague.

Fortmann, H. J. H. M. 1958. Gevaren over en weer. Nederlandse Katholieke Stemmen 54:347–352.

Gerlach, P. (n.d.) Geschiedenis der Penitenten-Recollectinen van Dongen. Dongen.

Geyl, P. 1964. History of the Low Countries; Episodes and Problems. London.

Goudsblom, J. 1967. Dutch Society. New York.

Haarsma, F. 1977. Volkskatholicisme en pastoraal beleid in Nederland en Vlaanderen. Tijdschrift voor Theologie 17:391–408.

Hugenpoth tot den Beerenclaauw, J. B. C. C. M. 1861. De kloosters in Nederland. Utrecht.

Isambert, F. 1975. Autour du catholicisme populaire. Reflections sociologiques sur un débat. Social Compass 22:193–210.

Jansen, T. A. J. 1976. De pater op de pastorie. Het aandeel der regulieren in de parochiële zielzorg van Nederland 1853–1966. Nijmegen.

Juten, G. C. A. 1935. De parochiën in het Bisdom Breda (3 vols). Bergen op Zoom.

Kertzer, D. I. 1980. Comrades and Christians. Religion and Political Struggle in Communist Italy. Cambridge.

Krüger, J. B. 1872–78. Kerkelijke Geschiedenis van het Bisdom Breda. (4 vols). Rosendaal.

Kuiters, R. 1958. Pastoors en Paters. Over de verhouding tussen de seculiere en de reguliere geestelijkheid. Nijmegen.

Margry, P. J. 1982. Bedevaartplaatzen in Noord-Brabant. Eindhoven.

Melief, P. 1958. Regulieren en seculieren in ons land sinds 1750. Nederlandse Katholieke Stemmen 54:294–305.

Metz, J. B. 1979. Kirche fur das Volk oder Kirche des Volkes? Eine Frage. Volksreligion—Religion des Volkes, ed. K. Rahner, pp. 76–82. Stuttgart.

Pannet, R. 1974. La catholicisme populaire. 30 ans après "La France, pays de mission?" Paris.

Rogier, L. J. 1956. Katholieke Herleving: Geschiedenis van Katholiek Nederland sinds 1853. The Hague.

Plongeron, B. (ed.) 1976. La Religion populaire. Paris.

Rousseau, A. 1977. La question de la "religion populaire." Recherches de Science Religieuse 65:473–504.

Sallnow, M. J. 1981. Communitas Reconsidered: The Sociology of Andean Pilgrimage. Man (ns) 16:163–82.

Schutjes, L. 1870–76. Geschiedenis van het Bisdom's Hertogenbosch (5 vols). St. Michielsgestel.

Southern, R. W. 1972. Western Society and the Church in the Middle Ages. Harmondsworth. van den Hurk, A. W. 1977. Het verborgen leven van de abdij van Berne in haar parochies. Tilburg.

van Leeuwen, B. 1969. Seculiere en reguliere priesters in de zielzorg. Nederlandse Katholiek Stemmen 65:328–46.

Weber, E. 1979. Peasants into Frenchmen. The Modernization of Rural France 1870–1914 London.

From Cannibal Raid to Copra Kompani: Changing Patterns of Koriki Politics

Robert F. Maher

No society, and therefore no political system, is eternal or unchanging. As the society adjusts to events, these adjustments translate into aspects of the political system—sometimes with surprising results. Maher, in this historical analysis of Koriki society, documents major shifts in political behavior. World War I set into action changes in society that enlarged political boundaries and introduced radical changes in the patterns of leadership. World War II and the introduction of new economic patterns altered the political institutions even further.

Most kinship societies were powerless to resist Western imperialism because they lacked the political and economic organization to make any significant political resistance. Only recently, as the Tommy Kabu movement shows, are new politicians emerging who represent an adaptation of traditional politics to the demands and appropriations of the current regime. In this manner, the specific Koriki experience becomes a part of a more global process. This amalgam and synthesis of two modes of production—one capitalist and colonial and the other tribal and indigenous—is identified as the process of articulation in some Marxist perspectives.

FOR ITS GREATER part the coastal area of New Guinea's Gulf of Papua presents a uniform zone of swamp environment, at least 100 miles long and twenty miles or more in width. It begins in the east with the delta of the great Purari River, which forms about twenty miles of its total span and provides the home for six related tribes which have come collectively to be called the Purari. Separately—and this is the way they have traditionally thought of themselves—they are the Baroi, I'ai, Kaimari, Koriki, Maipua, and Vaimuru. Linguistically, they form a unit of closely related and mutually intelligible dialects. Their cultures likewise reveal a basic similarity throughout, altered only by some local variants on the major contour. Before Australian control, aggressive raiding for heads and cannibal victims dominated relations between most of the Purari tribes. A few professed friendship, e.g., the Kaimari and the Vaimuru, but little of substance in the way of social connections was built upon the relation. In general, except for warfare and the periodic visits of *lakatoi* traders from the Port Moresby area 200 miles to the east, social worlds were tribe enclosed.

After World War II, radical changes developed under the influence of a movement led by an I'ai, Tommy Kabu, who, like many of the younger men, had experienced a wider world during the tumultuous years of the war (Maher 1961a). A particular feature of the Movement was its lack of concern for tribal boundaries. Harmonized with widespread desires among the people of the delta for new conditions of life, the Movement quickly encompassed all of the Purari tribes and extended beyond them to include the small Ipiko tribe and a large part of the more numerous Goaribari. From it a new political and economic unit appeared which was pan-tribal in extent. In its strongest and most inclusive form, it lasted for only a few years, but it left behind a radical alteration in the political institutions of the tribes involved.

Focusing principally upon the important Koriki tribe, this paper concerns itself with the pattern of political leadership as it has developed through Purari life over the last half century or more. It is convenient to distinguish three phases in this development: the circumstances of leadership at the time of contact; its response to the new conditions set by Australian control of the Purari region; and, finally, its reaction to the Tommy Kabu Movement. The first phase will be presented essentially as a reconstruction of the modal aspects of the traditional system. In the two succeeding phases, greater attention will be given to the variation in response under conditions of change.

Traditional Koriki Political Leadership

From earlier reports[1] and from my own materials gathered in 1954–55, it is possible to fill out a description, satisfactory in most respects, of Koriki culture as it was when it first encountered European expansion. Its nature was profoundly influenced by three factors: a Stone Age technology, the swamp environment, and cannibalism. Although limiting in other respects, the swamp provided an abundant food supply in the sago palm.

It also contributed to the efficiency of water transportation. Cannibalism, made a social good by Koriki concepts of reality, created strong social pressures toward solidarity within the tribe as a response to the requirements of defensive and offensive battle. These activities—subsistence, transportation, and war—were carried out by means of stone axes, dugout canoes, and bamboo arrows.

Very little of importance in Koriki culture escaped the influence of these factors. One consequence of relevance here was the settlement pattern. To an unusual extent for Melanesia, the sago subsistence economy and water transportation combined to permit the geographic concentration of the tribal population. The military and ceremonial features of cannibalism made such a concentration highly desirable. At about the time of World War I, Ukiaravi, the principal Koriki settlement, had a population of more than 2,500. The situation was similar among the Kaimari and I'ai, but not among the much smaller Maipua, Baroi, and Vaimuru. The extent to which this is exceptional in Melanesia is clear from the survey of local groupings by Hogbin and Wedgewood (1953, 1954), who found that the largest groups which can be expected to have political unity fell within a population range of 70 to 300, with some exceptional cases of 1,000 or more. To this generalization, the concentrated nature of the lowland Koriki settlement patterns presents a sharp contrast. With the exception of two satellite communities of about 600 persons each, all of the Koriki tribe lived at Ukiaravi in a collection of eight contiguous villages. The entire settlement does not seem to have covered more than thirty acres, a fair part of which was water.

Hogbin and Wedgewood also remarked that there were signs of a population increase in many parts of Melanesia which was leading to a general increase in size of politically significant local groups. Although they were apparently thinking of rather recent events, I have contended elsewhere (Maher 1961b) that the Purari delta was such an area at the time of contact. The dynamic trends observable in the Koriki settlement pattern and social structure of that time seem to indicate a rising population, which I interpret as a consequence of a relatively recent adaptation to the productive swamp ecology.

Villages presented an internal organization of separate polygynous households and a unifying system of exogamous patrisibs (*larava*) grouped in a moiety division. Many sibs were represented in more than one village, and others were known to be descended from other sibs outside their village. Although these circumstances provided some integrative ties between villages, the village kin structure tended to be largely self-contained in its principal functions. An individual identified mainly with his patrisib in his village rather than with its counterparts in other villages. In this respect it was similar to the *iduhu* system of the Western Motu (Groves 1963). Each village was identified by its men's ceremonial house (*ravi*), both physically and in name. In addition, the patrisib structure was represented within the *ravi* by a series of cubicles, one for the members of each sib, and the whole arranged so that those of the two parts of the dual division were placed along opposite sides of the *ravi*. Indeed, the name for the moiety division in Koriki is the same as that for side, *mekai*.

The village was the basic unit in the collective activities of ceremony and war, but since the village itself was internally organized through sib and moiety, the individual found his rights and obligations in any given raid or ritual defined by his position in the kinship structure. War and ceremony, intertwined through cannibalism, were the most important public actions above the level of the family. From this complex of circumstances were derived the statuses and roles of leadership.

Sahlins (1963) has delineated the "big man" as a type expression of Melanesian leadership. Its essential feature is personal power which is achieved, as Oliver (1949) has pointed out, by aggressively exploiting friends and resources. In the process, the "big man" obligates and draws to him a following which supports him in his activities, many of which are community oriented, and thus gives cohesion to Melanesian political life. This contrasts with Polynesia, where the more typical situation is a "chain of command subordinating lesser chiefs and groups to greater, on a basis of inherited societal rank" (Sahlins 1963: 294). While his focus is on political leadership, Sahlins necessarily treats the larger context of the social structure within which politics takes place. In this, the segmental organization of Melanesian society is seen as significantly different in its implications for politics from the marked tendency toward hierarchical structures in Polynesia. These structural differences are related to the contrast in leadership type and, in addition, carry different evolutionary potentials. The segmentalized, personalized, Melanesian form "sets ceilings on the intensification of political authority, on the intensification of household production by political means, and on the diversion of household outputs in support of wider political organization" (Sahlins 1963: 294). On the other hand, the ascribed, hierarchical system so frequent in Polynesia was capable of significant political expansion and did, indeed, expand and intensify its political compass in some places as a response to conditions of European contact.

In discussing social movements in Melanesia, Valentine (1963) constructs a comparable frame of comparison. Within it he draws generalized pictures of political structures in Melanesia and Polynesia resembling those of Sahlins, and goes further in developing their implications for response to the encroachments of European power. In Polynesia, there have been differences in local reactions, "but they are typically recognizable as the predominately secular responses of stratified societies, operating through the instrumentality of pre-existing and sometimes revitalized organs of central authority" (Valentine 1963: 29). But the Melanesian segmentalized structure and "big man" leadership have not been capable of dealing with European authority, and the experience has tended to produce a break with traditional forms of leadership. New forms have developed which have little connection with the past and are capable of encompassing more extensive polities. The most dramatic are the Cargo Cults, but Valentine also sees more recent secular movements as relevant, including, apparently, the Tommy Kabu Movement.

In most respects, Koriki social arrangements fit the general picture drawn for Melanesia by Sahlins and Valentine. The patrisib structure is a common variety of segmentalized organization, and certainly there was nothing like a Polynesian royalty here, nor even a Trobriand type of paramount chief. Nonetheless, certain relatively unusual features moved the system somewhat off the center of the Melanesian type and toward the Polynesian. Specifically, they concerned the nature of Koriki political leadership. Much more than is usual for Melanesia, traditional Koriki leadership was an ascribed status. In this the similarities to Polynesia were more than superficial.

The ideological basis for ascription lay in the Purari concept of *imunu* and its influence on the role of the leader and, hence, on the nature of the man who had to fulfill the role. *Imunu,* a variant of the concept of *mana,* provides the Koriki's fundamental view of reality. Differences in kind and quantity of *imunu* are seen as the essential explanation of the variety of existence. Human *imunu* differs in quality from other *imunu,* such as that which may reside in pigs or sacred masks, and it exists in different quantities in different people. Cannibalism is a means of adding to one's *imunu* and also of placating important spirits which apparently have the ability to absorb all varieties of *imunu* but have a preference for the human. Herein lies the conceptual basis for cannibalism. In addition, sacred objects, such as masks, bullroarers, and the wicker spirit monsters are highly charged with *imunu,* particularly at certain times, and can be safely handled only by men who have learned some of the ritualized safety techniques and are, themselves, well supplied with *imunu.* A long and active career as a cannibal increased one's personal *imunu,* but since such food was shared fairly equally by the adult males of the village, the *imunu* strength of the community tended to rise or fall collectively as a result of cannibalism, rather than in such a way as to set one man off from another. Instead, differences occurred mainly through the quantity of *imunu* transmitted by one's family line. Some lines of descent carried more *imunu* than others, and it was from these that the men who led in war and ritual had to be chosen.

Ideally, the office passed from father to eldest son at the time of the leader's death or when he no longer felt sufficiently active for the role. Actually, the path of succession could be more complicated. Not infrequently a younger brother of the leader succeeded him, if none of his sons was of an appropriate age. The brother might eventually pass on the office to the former leader's son or divert it to his own. Such shifts were influenced greatly by family politics and by the relative age and vigor of the persons eligible when the position became available. In addition, personal competence was a factor, including some of the attributes of the "big man." A son who was of age but was regarded by the community as incompetent would almost inevitably be passed over in favor of a younger brother or a paternal uncle. Some public influence was regarded as essential, since, reflecting the ascribed nature of the status, once a leader was installed he was not easily removed. The threshold of endurable incompetency is difficult to define in the abstract. A community could languish for decades under uninspired leadership without being moved to the drastic solutions which were the only ones available to the Koriki. If the failure of leadership became impossible to bear, two paths were available. In one, the more frequent, the social unit broke up; individuals and families detached themselves and formed alliances elsewhere. Sometimes this involved a move to another village or village group, but often the shift was in social allegiance only. More rarely, a village might split in two or more fragments, each following a different leader. In the most extreme circumstances, when the leader was fully alienated from kin and community, and dissolution or fragmentation were unacceptable to the people, he could be executed. This, however, had to be done with the consent and, preferably, the participation of his close relatives.

In sum, while some of its features overlapped with "big man" leadership, the Koriki institution was different in that leadership status was essentially ascribed. A certain amount of competition might occur at the time of succession, but always within a markedly narrow range of the old leader's kin, and the eldest son, if he was mature and capable, could not ordinarily be prevented from following his father. Completely absent was the idea that, theoretically at least, anyone was a potential leader and could play the game of becoming a "big man." In contrast to other Melanesians, political succession was relatively predictable, and the Koriki were less likely to experience the political trauma which Sahlins has suggested is a frequent result of the death of a "big man" and the consequent collapse of his personally constructed political realm.

A second important feature of traditional Koriki leadership lay in its differentiation of role and the distribution of its separate statuses through the social structure. A fundamental distinction in role was found between leaders who were *mari* and those who were *amua*. There is a temptation at this point to say that the former dealt with the sacred realm and the latter with the secular. But experience with preliterate societies should tell us that such a distinction is situational and analytical at best and is more likely to distort than to clarify. The special sphere of the *mari* centered upon the men's house and the ceremonies which took place there, especially those which concerned the village as a whole, including those which involved cannibalism. The *mari* seldom participated physically in the ceremonies in the sense of singing special chants or firing the bow which killed the sacrificial pig. His role instead was to accept an ultimate responsibility that the ceremonies would be carried out and that they would be performed properly. In addition, his presence was apparently essential to the efficacy of the ceremonies and to the safe use of the sacred objects charged with *imunu*.

The *amua* also held forth mainly at the men's ceremonial house but with some difference in his concerns. While the *mari* might, through authority, persuasion, and harangue, move the population to a decision that a certain ceremony was overdue and should be carried out, after the decision was made the *amua* saw that the material and activity needs of the ceremony were accomplished. Frequently a raid on an enemy was required. In a society dedicated to war, the military aspects of leadership were often of overriding importance. In this the *amua* found one of his most important functions,[2] not as the warrior hero, but as the organizer and leader. If a raid was to be a significant one, that is, something more than a spur-of-the-moment foray by a few close relatives, the *amua* would take the primary responsibility in bringing together the raiding party, seeing that it was properly prepared and inspired, and furnishing the most authoritative voice on tactics and strategy. He would also see to it that a quantity of pigs, sago, coconuts, etc. would be forthcoming for an associated feast. Whether or not he would supply some of the items himself would depend upon his personal relation to the event. In the case of a boy's initiation, if none of the *amua*'s sons or nephews were involved, his material contribution would be rather slight. On the other hand, the raising of a new men's house in his own village would inevitably call for a large feast, all of which would be organized by the *amua,* and a substantial part would be his personal contribution. In each case his support as a leader was essential.

In addition, disputes within the village which could not be settled at the family or sib levels were referred to the *amua*. In all such cases, his

responsibility was to create an agreement between the disputants if possible and, if not, to render a judgment which was just according to
custom, and which, above all, would restore internal peace.

The roles of *mari* and *amua* can be seen as rather sharply distinct but
mutually reinforcing. In some respects they resemble Sahlins' generalized
type of the "big man." In particular, there are points of similarity with the
mumi in Oliver's excellent analysis of Siuai leadership. Both the *mari* and
the *amua* had to command considerable quantities of wealth to give
them the means to obligate people and make them responsive to their
influence. Wealth was mainly in shell ornaments, pigs, dogs, and chickens,
with the first two the most important. Both leaders had an initial advantage in the striving for wealth by virtue of the prerogatives of their
stations. Each received payment in pigs or ornaments for certain services.
A *mari* officiating at the ritual marking the raising of a new house could
expect to be paid a shell ornament. At larger and more important ceremonies he could receive a pig. The *amua,* depending on the nature of the
case, often received a share of the damages he awarded in a dispute. In
addition, since both *mari* and *amua* inherited their positions, ordinarily
they also inherited more than the average amount of wealth.

Besides inheritance and the special payments received by *mari* and
amua, men could add to their wealth by notable skills in carving, paint-
ing, or the decoration of canoes, weapons, or ceremonial plaques. These
activities ordinarily brought an ornament or two to the artist. The successful warrior, who had personally captured an enemy, was the ultimate
beneficiary of a ritual, the *dakea kavana* or "expedition payment," in
which other men could have sex relations with one of his wives for the
payment of a shell ornament. The expectable result of the *dakea kavana*
was a windfall of one to two dozen ornaments representing a substantial
increase in wealth. The cannibal raid had more than a few incentives.

However, the most important sources of wealth were associated with
marriage. More than anything else, bride wealth kept shell ornaments
moving throughout the community. The luck of a man in having an
excess of sisters and daughters over brothers and sons had an obvious
effect on his career as a manipulator of bride wealth. But beyond this, skill
played a great part in success or failure. Any particular presentation of
bride wealth was in most cases contributed to by a complex of relatives,
and a man's wealth at a given moment was not a matter of how many
ornaments he could show were in his house, but how he stood in the
number of ornaments owed him relative to those he owed to others. His
skill lay in being able to think in terms of large numbers of marriages
involving many relatives, occurring through a substantial dimension of
time. Most successful men made their moves within a mental perspective

of a generation or more. What one contributed today to the bride wealth which a paternal uncle was gathering for his third wife could be influenced by the expectation one had of outliving the uncle and thereby achieving a strong position to claim the lion's share of the bride wealth at the eventual marriage of the uncle's two-year-old daughter.

The aim of the activity was not to stockpile a hoard of bracelets or necklaces, but to develop and invest one's resources in such a way as to obligate as many people as possible. From this came political power. Another objective was to get sufficiently ahead of the game so that some proportion of these obligations could be translated into extra wives for oneself. For the ordinary man, an extra wife was desirable but not usually possible. For the *mari* or *amua,* however, polygyny was essential. Although men had their significant roles in the division of labor, women were the principal providers of foodstuffs (Maher 1961a: 85–86). Men cut sago logs, but women performed the long and arduous task of turning them into sago flour, and how much sago a household could produce was directly related to the number of its working women. In addition, women cared for the pigs and fowl and collected 90 per cent of the fish and crabs, the main sources of protein. They also prepared most of the food and cooked all of it.

A man's holdings in shell ornaments underlay much of his ability to influence his community, but if he were to have the influence appropriate to a *mari* or *amua,* he must also maintain an extensive network of relationships to individuals through regular gifts of food. No day went by without a gift to someone, and for an *amua* the need to give extended beyond his relatives, in-laws, and community to include a range of persons in other villages. By regular gifts he maintained effective relations with these individuals and emphasized his social presence.

In addition to such continuing, day-to-day generosity, the leader also had to provide substantial portions of food at various feasts. This too had to be carefully managed. Aside from pigs, Koriki foodstuffs do not keep and stockpile well. Instead, the *amua* or *mari* used the productive power of his polygynous household to accumulate obligations. He might, for example, have made a helpful contribution of sago and crabs to a man who was attempting to hold a feast to mark the raising of a house or his daughter's initiation. Neither was an event of the first rank, but all men faced these and other ceremonial requirements at one time or another, and the aid of an important man was often welcome. Later, when the *amua* or *mari* was faced with the expense of underwriting a large portion of a major feast, he would "cash in" the necessary quantity of such obligations. An important occasion sponsored by an *amua* could spring a whole village into a whirl of activity as people responded to the *amua*'s demand that now was the time for old obligations to be honored. The system was not only a means of making available on the call of authority the necessary perishable materials for events of public significance, but it was also a way in which the public itself was forced to be involved at the decision of a leader.

All men, important or not, were concerned to some degree as initiators in the complex activities of bride wealth and food gifts. The pattern was similar to those utilized elsewhere as roads to political power by Melanesian "big men." The difference in the Purari Delta was that the Koriki marked off their statuses at the top by another means. They made them ascribed statuses and, hence, not accessible through "big man" techniques of social climbing. On the other hand, to make the authority of his office come fully alive, the hereditary *amua* or *mari* had to become involved to a considerable extent in "big man" politics.

While the distinction between *mari* and *amua* was basic in Koriki leadership, the situation was complicated by the fact that there was more than one kind of *mari* or *amua*. Although Koriki social structure was essentially segmental, there was, in the system of patrisibs gathered in moiety groupings and all encapsulated within the boundaries of a village, a structural potential for hierarchical organization. The Koriki separation of leaders into different *amua* and different *mari* realized a part of this potential. Each village had three distinct *amua* statuses: *pa'iri amua, mekai amua,* and *iaki amua.* The *pa'iri amua* was the head *amua* of the village. Beneath him was an *amua* for each side of the dual division or *mekai,* and assisting him in special tasks was the *iaki amua* or "work" *amua.* The first two were hereditary positions and had the duties and prerogatives for their respective social spheres that have already been described. Without question the *pa'iri amua* was superior, a condition reinforced by the fact that the sides of the moiety seldom if ever engaged in independent activities, but co-operated as village subdivisions under his leadership. In some cases a *pa'iri amua* would also be the *amua* for his side of the dual division. The *iaki amua* was less well defined. The position was not hereditary, but was filled through appointment by a village or moiety *amua.* The appointed individual, acting with the authority of the *amua* who had chosen him, would be expected to give energetic direction to some project, such as a feast or the raising of a new ceremonial house, which was of particular concern to the appointing *amua.* He was, in a sense, an executive officer to the *amua.* Ordinarily he would be the kind of man who, in other Melanesian villages, might be expected to be a ranking "big man." He should be aggressive and ambitious and have a substantial network of obligated people under his influence, but he was, in turn, subject to the direction of the hereditary *amua.*

A similar hierarchy prevailed among the *mari,* but with some significant differences. Each village ceremonial house had a head *mari* and also one for each side of the dual division. More frequently than with the *amua,* one of the moiety *mari* would dominate and hold the head position as well. In addition, there were ceremonial specialists, such as the *aiau vake,* who manufactured the more significant of the ceremonial masks and were said to inherit the necessary quality to handle safely such sacred and powerful objects, and the *eria vake,* or croton men, whose duty it was to decorate the men's house with croton leaves for village ceremonies.

Unlike the *amua,* however, there was a *mari* who was regarded as the head *mari* for not one but all of the Koriki villages. Called *pa'iri pa'iri mari,* or *mari* of all the people, his status was hereditary, and his presence was sought at all important ceremonies. The same hierarchical circumstances held for the head of the "croton men," although his position was less powerful and prestigeful than that of the head *mari.*

For the *amua,* no such position of tribal, as opposed to village, leadership was formalized. Nonetheless, leadership of the *amua* sort was possible on a scale larger than the village, and an ambitious *amua* strove to enlarge his sphere of influence beyond the limits of his hereditary status through "big man" politics. The close physical association of villages presented constant possibilities. Village borders posed no necessary barriers to the construction of a network of persons obligated to an *amua* through the material aid he might furnish them. Obviously, the extent to which an *amua* might intrude in this fashion upon the loyalties of those in other villages depended directly upon the abilities of the local *amua* to counter his efforts. In this not all *amua* were equal. There is no clear evidence that any single leader of this type managed to dominate all the villages, but there were times when a skilled and aggressive man did achieve a superiority over the leadership of a number of villages beyond his own. The rewards were substantial. Although ceremonies and raids were matters of a particular village, an *amua* who had extended his power could tap the resources of other villages and turn them to local purposes. He could be responsible for feasts which were larger than his village could ordinarily support, and he could propose raids and other collective activities with a confidence that the necessary number of warriors or workers could be mustered. In sum, the *amua* who was adept at "big man" politics could effectively exploit the possibilities of the village-group settlement pattern and turn them to his own advantage.

Viewed against the nature of leadership as it is commonly found in Melanesia, and as it has been expressed in Sahlins' "big man" type, the traditional Koriki institution shows some clear departures in its ascrip-

tive and hierarchical characteristics. These were not accidental. Some of
the generalizations Udy (1959) has made from his cross-cultural analysis
of production organizations have an application, as Garland (1962) has
shown, to the explanation of political structures. In particular, the dense
and stable concentration of the Koriki population with its relatively high
and steady rate of social interaction might be expected to have produced a greater persistence and complexity to political actions than is
typical of most of Melanesia. Against this, the hierarchical division of
labor in leadership and the highly regularized means of recruitment
would be expectable in terms of Udy's findings, which indicate that
persistence and complexity in actions, particularly when four or more
activities must be co-ordinated at one time and for some time, tend to
develop a division of labor with hierarchical distinctions in governing
authority.

The Initial Control Phase: World War I to World War II

In the years between the two world wars, Australian control became firmly
established in the delta, and the Koriki were drawn into the complex and
sharply stratified colonial social system. The necessary conditions for membership, whether desired or not, had profound effects upon local political
leadership. The most obvious was the usurpation of ultimate authority by
the Australian magistrate and patrol officer. Their representative in the
village was the government-appointed village constable. The structure of
magistrate, patrol officer, and village constable was all of the colonial
hierarchy that the Koriki could see, and it was constructed without regard
for local political institutions. Ordinarily, perhaps always, the Administration attempted to appoint a traditional leader as constable. Although this
policy was often frustrated by the fact that the colonial authorities only
vaguely understood the local political structure, there was, in the earlier
years at least, a frequent coincidence between the post of constable and
the status of local leader. As the years went by, however, and as constables
died or retired, the Administration appointed successors without consideration for the hereditary nature of traditional leadership. In addition, a
number of the older constables fell afoul of European laws, particularly
those having to do with adultery, an old Koriki pastime, and were removed
and often imprisoned. The social visibility of the position vis-à-vis the
Administration, and its vulnerability to what the Koriki regarded as slight
offenses made it less and less attractive to the *amua* or *mari* who had their
own bases of power quite independent of the government. As a result, the
colonial and the Koriki hierarchies of political status remained distinct,
though by no means unconnected.

The other most significant price of membership in the colonial culture was the suppression of warfare. With it went cannibalism, an essential element in the important village ceremonies. These changes began at the most fundamental levels of Koriki culture and have not yet entirely run their course. Sporadic and poorly organized raiding as a means of vengeance still occurred in 1955, but as an activity which leaders and communities could reliably employ in serving the ceremonial system, war was interrupted at an early stage of European contact. Lacking its necessary cannibal victim, ceremonial activity was kept alive for a time by attempts to substitute pigs for men. In the end, however, the belief that the *imunu* of men and pigs were different and could not be interchanged made this a futile exercise. By World War II, ceremonial life was visibly running down.

The usurpation of ultimate political authority by the Australian Administration created an additional leadership hierarchy with which the traditional Koriki leaders had to contend. The suppression of warfare set in motion changes which eroded the roles of both *amua* and *mari*. The sequence of change first affected the purely military aspects of leadership and only later and more gradually the ceremonial aspects. In addition, the village constable intruded seriously upon the area of authority of the *amua* in the settlement of intra-village claims and disputes. Consequently, of the two main leadership statuses, it was the *amua* who was threatened most seriously by the initial events of Administration control. The role of the *mari* was affected more slowly as the ceremonial system began to falter under the failure of compromises thrust upon it by the suppression of cannibalism.

Given only these conditions, it would have been but a matter of time before the traditional institution of political leadership disappeared entirely, with a result described by Hogbin (1951) for Busama, in which all significant authority was absorbed by the colonial hierarchy. But with the Koriki, externally sanctioned authority, however it might challenge the role of local leadership, still could not duplicate the sources of that leadership. The hereditary nature of the *amua* or *mari* status did not allow it to be easily absorbed by a person from outside the lineage, no matter how strong his credentials of nontraditional authority. Furthermore, no one could wield a steady influence from within the village, whether he was a traditional *amua* or a modern constable, without developing an appropriately extensive network of individuals under obligation to him. Bride wealth and a large array of feasts were still vital parts of life. The blessings of the colonial Administration were no more sufficient to guarantee effective political power than was the birthright of the traditional leader. It acted similarly, however, in giving the appointed constable an advantage over ordinary men in the competition to bring others under his influence.

The presence in the villages of two hierarchies, the colonial and the traditional, created a number of organizational possibilities. To see how these developed, I gathered information in 1955 on the careers of twelve village constables and 26 *amua* and *mari,* both past and present. They include almost all of these ranks for six Koriki villages since World War I. In one possibility, the two hierarchies could be joined, but not made identical, if constable and village *amua* were the same. As mentioned previously, this was attempted in the early years of control, but in most cases conditions worked against the stability of the union. Although there were some notable exceptions, data on the succession of village *amua* and constable positions between the two World Wars clearly show a decreasing tendency for the same man to hold both positions. When two men held the positions, the possibilities for competition were obvious. What actually developed, however, in a particular village or group of villages depended upon a variety of conditions. The career of leadership became difficult to predict, and this itself was a profound change. The relationship between the two men before the constable received his appointment, the extent to which the *amua* could protect his authority in disputes from the constable's challenge, and their comparative success in acquiring and leading networks of indebted followers were some of the important influences upon the new relationship. How these inter-acted and developed determined to a great extent the structure of politi-cal leadership in the controlled villages. A constable who could not con-struct a local power base through the traditional means of dominating an extensive web of reciprocal obligations inevitably either lost his position or became a satellite of the *amua.* While this arrangement was most desirable from the latter's point of view and deplorable from the Adminis-tration's, my evidence shows that it was not nearly so common as some administrative officials seemed to believe. The other possible extreme was the total usurpation of authority by the constable. So far as I have been able to determine, such a complete collapse of an *amua*'s power was rare, but it did happen.

In most cases, neither constable nor *amua* could absorb the other, and village politics had to accommodate both. The new structure was conceptualized in traditional terms by categorizing the constable as an *iaki amua,* or work *amua.* Such neatness in taxonomy, however, failed to conceal the fact that changes had been made. The constable's exhorta-tions to the people that pig fences should be mended, walkways con-structed, and errant villagers brought to justice sounded much in style if not in content like those of an *iaki amua.* But, if so, there was a new and important question. Whose *iaki amua* was he, the village *amua*'s or the Government's? To this there was no single answer. The relationship between the two leaders varied in degree along axes of dominance-submission, friendship-hostility, and competition-co-operation according to the village situation. The ambiguity and transitoriness of "big man" leadership became increasingly a feature of Koriki political life.

By the beginning of World War II, the new political structure was still in the process of adjustment, but a number of its characteristics were apparent. Weak *amua* and constables had been shaken out of the system. For those who remained, the struggle between the two had in most villages become a stand-off in the sense that neither could completely reduce the other's position. An accommodation was reached through agreements in prerogatives and co-operation in village leadership. The arrangement was not necessarily between equals, but the new relationship came from the realization that neither could wholly draw the other into his circle of dependents. The consequence was a growing unity at the top through a new power elite which received some of its credentials from inherited status, some from the colonial hierarchy, and in both cases enlivened its influence by dominating a traditional network of reciprocal obligations. Government sponsored demagogues, such as Bumbu of Busama (Hogbin 1951), did not appear. The circumstances for traditional power remained too firm. On the other hand, the clear lines of authority and of succession which had characterized traditional political life were now ambiguous. The suppression of cannibalism gradually took the momentum out of ceremonial activities and brought a crisis in the careers of the *mari*. Some of the more ambitious and powerful of these responded to the constriction of their religious functions by attempting to take over authority which had traditionally been associated with the *amua*. The latter, beset by challenges from both constable and *mari* survived largely by "big man" politics. It was still true that only one born to the office could be a *mari* or an *amua*, but it was no longer certain that the village needed them. The result was an erosion of the finely drawn and rather complex lines of the traditional hierarchy. Although the process was by no means complete, the old structure of a well-defined division of labor in leadership had been made increasingly less relevant to the actions of contemporary politics as a result of the loss of functions in the conduct of war and ceremony. Developing in its place was an uneasy system of alliances between a reduced number of effective *amua* and the village constables. The traditional structure had simplified, but the whole had become more complex and unpredictable through the presence of the constable and the colonial authority he represented.

The Tommy Kabu Phase

The Second World War did not intrude physically on the Purari swamps, but it did draw off large numbers of young and middle-aged men for labor at Port Moresby and along the Kokoda trail. Wartime medical patrols reported the villages almost empty of active adult males. Their return in 1945 and 1946 marked the end of the already ailing ceremonial system, and with institutionalized tribal war already gone, the kin system of moiety and patrisib gave way to a bilateral structure (Maher 1961a, 1961b). Recurrent processes had given rise to directional processes (Vogt 1960), and the Purari revolution was under way.

Under the leadership of Tommy Kabu, a secular movement developed rapidly and by 1947 had effectively encompassed all of the Purari tribes and segments of neighboring tribes. Its principal objective was the achievement, mainly through economic modernization, of an imperfectly seen model of Western life. It also produced a clear effort toward political sovereignty, which was quickly and bloodlessly put down by the Australian Administration. The Movement continued, however, destroying ceremonial houses, moving villages to better ground, and establishing an economic enterprise called the Kompani which was to relate the tribal economies to the national and international markets.

Led with intelligence and riding a wave of rising expectations, the Movement received overwhelming support from the Koriki and other Purari tribes. In the first year or two of enthusiasm, a new political structure was built which incorporated the older power elite of *amua* and constable and went beyond it in a significant fashion. Essentially the new politics had to bring the previously separate tribes into an organization of economic cooperation and relate this to the colonial power which controlled the modern market. Village politics remained mainly in the hands of the *amua*-constable elite, which now was also the local arm of the Movement. However, arching over village and tribal boundaries was an organization of new leaders. These, headed by Tommy Kabu, were the "New Men" of the Movement. Mostly young and with substantial wartime experience with the wider world, it was their task to create an intertribal political structure which could command the loyalty of an array of separate and diverse villages, each with its own politics. Probably correctly, they never saw this as a problem separate from the Kompani. Political innovations were aimed at solving economic problems, at making the Kompani work. Consequently, the two structures were really one.

Rabia Camp, established near Port Moresby as a marketing center for the Kompani, also became the center of intertribal politics and the headquarters of the New Men, who thought of themselves as businessmen and not as politicians. It is likewise clear that the new political structure was not only intended to solve economic problems, but that its existence depended upon their solution. Its leaders, Tommy Kabu and the New Men, were cut off from either traditional or colonial sources of power. Neither *amua* nor constable, they were also uninvolved in the village networks of reciprocal obligations. Their power came specifically from the Kompani and its promise to deliver a new way of life and more generally from the people's perception of them as representatives of that new life. While the Kompani was in full operation, they had control over considerable village resources in the form of cash contributions for capital investment as well as quantities of sago and copra for marketing. In addition, they were strategically placed to influence the distribution of returns. It was at this time that the hierarchical nature of the new political structure was sharpest. All of the local *amua* and constables led their villages into the Movement. In the mood of the moment the people would have followed the New Men in any case, and some local leaders had to move very rapidly to appear to be in front. Under the circumstances there was nothing that the village power elite could do but deliver themselves to the authority of Tommy Kabu and his intertribal organization. For some village leaders this was clearly a sincere commitment, but for others it was an unfortunate necessity.

Within a year or two, however, the Kompani experienced difficulties in its operations which were impossible to ignore. Although well conceived in its general structure and purpose, the Kompani lacked the ordinary but essential technological skills which underlie record keeping, power boat operation, the packing of perishable commodities for shipment, and so forth. It also lacked effective support from the Colonial Administration. The major objectives seemed more and more out of reach, and, as this feeling spread throughout the villages, the power of the Kompani declined.

Even in times of closest co-operation between the villages and the Kompani, there had been points of stress and friction. The two sets of leaders were products of different experiences, drew power from different sources, and by no means had the identity of objectives which the initial enthusiasm for the Movement had implied. Specifically, the changes desired by the New Men went even further than those the people had accepted. In their attempt to destroy everything traditional the new leaders implicitly included inherited status, polygyny, and bride wealth. In addition, their initial desire for sovereignty had compromised the positions of the appointed constables. A complete development of the Movement's objectives would have destroyed the foundations of *amua* and constable authority. But these traditions, particularly bride wealth, were for the present too firm to be overturned, and the Kompani, under Tommy Kabu's ever-pragmatic leadership, used the existing elite.

Nevertheless, incidents occurred regularly which revealed a continuing antagonism between the two levels of leadership. Rabia Camp, the New Men's Port Moresby headquarters, became a haven for persons, particularly younger ones, who were evading the authority of the village leaders. Among them were people who had not paid damages judged against them by the *amua* or constable or who were escaping village responsibilities of other sorts. One of the most notable was the twentieth wife of the most powerful Koriki *amua*. She had run off to Port Moresby with a young man from a neighboring village. Although a year had gone by, the *amua,* unwilling to take the case to the Colonial Administration, was still not able to obtain real co-operation in the matter from the New Men. They professed to be powerless to act in the situation. In a physical sense this was not true, and what they were communicating was their lack of sympathy with polygyny and the complex of customs of which it was a part. Another message, which the local leaders could not miss, was that the Kompani was not to be trusted with the sources of local power.

While hopes ran high and the Kompani's activities excited people and held out promise for the future, the frictions between the local and the intertribal levels of the new political structure were resolved mainly in favor of the latter, but as difficulties emerged and expectations were not met, the situation changed. The power of the Kompani, based upon its promises to meet certain objectives, declined as it fell short of these objectives. By 1955 the hierarchical nature of the new political structure had become highly ambiguous. The New Men still moved across village and tribal lines and furnished leadership for parallel activities, although these were now on a smaller scale. The Kompani was still a vital force in Purari life, but its leaders now had to solicit cooperation from the village elites rather than demand it as they had before. Under these circumstances, some villages remained firmly behind the Movement and others withdrew entirely, but many were scenes of unsettled conflict between local leaders who differed among themselves on what their relation should be to the Kompani. In part, their differences were honestly held, but in part they masked new struggles for local power. Although it had not succeeded in destroying the foundations of village authority, the Movement had introduced enough new factors to disturb the balance of influence in some villages and to initiate a new competition for power among leaders and would-be leaders.

Of the various Purari tribes, the Koriki, particularly, found their village leaders in a new struggle for local authority. The situation can be illustrated by events in the Kinipo village group. Kinipo was established in

1947 near one of the mouths of the Purari River as a result of the dispersion of old Ukiaravi. It consists of four villages—Navara, Karara, Mira, and Akia—with a total population of almost 500. Since World War I, the Koriki have experienced rather sharp depopulation, and Kinipo represented more than a quarter of all Koriki as of 1955. In traditional terms the four villages would have presented twelve inherited *amua* statuses, eight *mari,* and one *eria vake,* together with a variable assortment of *aiau vake* and *iaki amua,* making a total of between 30 and 38 well-defined leadership statuses. In 1955 only nine men could still expect the title *amua,* and some of these were in fact hereditary *mari* rather than *amua.* Kinipo had two constables, one of whom was an hereditary *amua,* three government appointed counselors, who were minor figures in village politics, and several men without formal credentials who had gained entrance to the power elite through a combination of success in the system of obligations and leadership in market-oriented, local business enterprises.

Within the elite group of not much more than a dozen, five men had unquestioned prominence. Their distribution, two from Karara village and one from each of the other three villages, reflects the fact that the village continued to be the essential base of local power. One of these men, Kairi, was hereditary *amua* of Navara village. Although forceful and responsible in village matters, he systematically avoided issues which did not directly involve Navara. Another, Kaivira of Akia village, was both *pa'iri amua* and a government-appointed constable. Despite his double source of influence, he gave the impression of a man who was weary of the effort. Although his authority was substantial, he seemed to assert himself only in matters which involved his personal interest. Even in this he had lost vitality and was failing in some important obligations. He had, for example, gone far beyond the acceptable delay in giving a feast for a dead son, and one could hear children refer to him, although not to his face, as the "garbage man."[3]

Ove of Karara village was a new type of leader, a "businessman." Although he had no claim to authority from either traditional or colonial status, people referred to him as a man who talked sense in public affairs. In particular, he concerned himself with organizing small expeditions to such relatively nearby trading posts as Muru. There he and others with him sold crabs and sago for Australian currency, each man acting as agent for his own produce. Ove furnished leadership and the largest and most suitable canoe in Kinipo. The return was not great, but neither was the effort nor the risk, and the results were particularly satisfying to people who had encountered frustration with more ambitious projects. As might be expected, Ove also operated effectively within the traditional obligation system and had underpinned his reputation as a modern "business-man" with success in the older enterprises as well. In many respects his position was enviable. Unlike an *amua* or constable, he was not subject to criticism if he chose not to concern himself with the range of public problems in the village. Allowed to concentrate upon his own objectives, he had built a solid base of influence which included a new variety of obligations, those owed by the men who had benefited from his commercial leadership. On the other hand, the very fact that he had not interested himself in all of the problems identified as a leader's concern restricted his influence in village group politics. Just as Kairi had chosen to limit himself to Navara village affairs, so Ove had restricted his focus to matters of "doing business."

The remaining two men at the top of the power elite were not so inhibited. It was between them that the struggle in village group politics came to a focus. One, Evoi of Mira village, was frequently referred to as the *amua* of Kinipo, and whether accorded the title or not was generally regarded as the community's leading citizen. In proper traditional terms he was not an *amua* at all but the *pa'iri pa'iri mari* or *mari* of all the Koriki, a position he had inherited at his older brother's death before the war. At the time of his succession he was outside the Purari area, working as a contract laborer on a European plantation. With some difficulty and Administration assistance, he returned to the Koriki villages and took up the functions which were then regarded as essential. He also served for a time as a village constable, but was dismissed after a conviction for adultery. A jail sentence followed and with it an experience as a porter on patrols into uncontrolled territory. For Evoi and other Koriki the new dimensions to their lives included more than the Europeans. Shortly after his return, World War II, with its stirring of ideas and populations, brought an end to the ceremonial institutions and to his principal functions as a *mari*. An exceedingly able man, Evoi managed during those years to translate *mari* power into *amua* power and emerged as the political figure most identified with the Kinipo group as a whole. He was a dedicated Tommy Kabu supporter and by 1955 directed most of his leadership activities toward Movement objectives as they applied to Kinipo. He was without question the most respected man in the village group and had managed in a way which seemed natural to him to fill the roles of both the proper traditional *amua* and the forward-looking New Man. He was, to many, the embodiment of social responsibility in both its new and old forms.

The other leader, Ipai, was a constable of Karara village. Although without hereditary status in the political hierarchy, he had risen to power by combining an aggressive nature, his constable's appointment, and extreme good luck in the fortunes of birth and death within his extended family. In the latter, Ipai was indeed blessed. His father's two wives bore twelve children, seven girls and five boys, including Ipai who was the second son. The father and three of the brothers died, and in the meantime six of the girls married, bringing in bride wealth to Ipai and his remaining younger brother. The brother, however, had drifted off to Port Moresby and married a woman from the Central District. He had little leverage on the situation, and Ipai took to himself all but a small part of the considerable income in bride wealth. A classic nouveau riche, Ipai unrelentingly pursued power and higher status. He acquired six wives, two while I was his neighbor. Typically, he cut every corner in this as in other things. Most of his wives were bride-wealth bargains. Some were widows and one was partially crippled, all features which required a smaller distribution of bride wealth. Although ordinarily intelligent and politically astute, at times his drive for status pushed him to the point of public ridicule. At his sixth marriage, I asked to take a picture of him and his bride next to the display of bride wealth that was to go to her relatives. The bride was a childless widow who had lost the fingers of her right hand. The bride wealth involved was the smallest I recorded. As usual, Ipai was delighted to be photographed, but he led me and his bride to Akia village where another wedding was being celebrated and a much more substantial bride wealth was on display. Next to this he posed and the picture was taken. The public reaction was laughter and jeers. As he usually did when his ambition overreached him, Ipai disengaged himself by playing the fool and pretending it was all a joke. Although he lacked the style of either a traditional *amua* or a New Man, he nevertheless had authority and an aggressive will to use it. People seldom laughed at him long.

In his rise to the most influential position in Karara village, Ipai had pushed aside and now thoroughly dominated one of the most impressively titled of all the Koriki, a man named Kauoi. Kauoi had been both the village *amua* of Karara and *amua* of one side of the moiety division. He was also the *eria vake,* or "croton man," for all Koriki villages and was even regarded as an hereditary *amua* of one of the Navara village moieties. But sisters who had died before their marriages could bring bride wealth, wives who had died after their bride wealth had been given, and too many sons had greatly restricted his capacity to construct a power base through the reciprocity system. Changes in the culture had erased the office of croton man and made the position of an *amua* less certain. The combination of difficulties was not insurmountable, but the current was running against Kauoi at just the time of Ipai's good fortune. Still, Kauoi had inherited one of the most potent political foundations in the

Koriki area. Despite his troubles, which were not unique, he should have been able to muster the strength to overcome or at least blunt a challenge. Nevertheless, he did not. More than anyone else, Kauoi's credentials for leadership were from inherited statuses. Being the croton man for all Koriki villages was not only prestigious but it had also been a substantial source of income. Kauoi had needed "big man" politics less than any of the other traditional leaders, and now as the political emphasis shifted and men had increasingly to validate their positions in some way other than inheritance, Kauoi was neither prepared nor willing. Ipai, on the other hand, egocentric and aggressive, with everything to gain and little to lose, was perfectly suited to the adventures of "big man" politics. In a relatively short time he supplanted Kauoi as the important figure in Karara village. Kauoi made his alteration in status complete by withdrawing entirely from politics and even from the village itself. In 1955 he lived mostly at his isolated sago camp and appeared in the village only rarely.

Evoi, however, was quite otherwise. Within the traditional political structure or while the Tommy Kabu Movement was at full pace, it would have been inconceivable that Ipai could launch any challenge to Evoi's leadership. But with the old system eroded and simplified and the Movement in difficulties, Ipai's local influence and personal ambition made a struggle for power inevitable. Although foolish and vain in some things, Ipai knew his way in the now rather ambiguous pattern of local politics. As challenger he had the advantage of choosing the time and the issue. In this he was aided by Evoi's own actions. Since becoming dedicated to the Movement, Evoi had done a number of things which he saw as aligning his life more closely with the objectives of the New Men. For one, he gave most of his political attention to furthering the activities of the Movement. As a result, many of the village disputes and claims he would ordinarily have judged or arbitrated fell by default to Ipai and lesser leaders. For another, he had refused to acquire new wives when older ones had died. In 1955 he was down from six wives to three and lived with only one of these. As was necessary to an *amua*, he still maintained an extensive network of individuals to whom he made gifts, but the economic pressure on his reduced household had become more difficult to deal with.

Evoi's position was weakened further by his determination to make an early and advantageous marriage for his adolescent son. In this his motives seem to have been a mixture of paternal concern and a desire to simplify his life and make it more available to the Movement by putting as many of his family responsibilities behind him as possible. His choice for a daughter-in-law was an attractive girl several years older than his son and the obvious leader of her female age group in Kinipo. As it soon became clear that Evoi would settle for no one else, the bride-wealth demand of her relatives suited itself to the occasion and was the highest I have record of in Kinipo, almost triple the amount ordinarily regarded as appropriate for a good marriage. In order to gather it and to provide for the wedding feast, Evoi had to engage in a number of complicated transactions and "cash in" a significant portion of the credits he held in his reciprocity network.

Although his prestige was as high as ever, the number of persons directly obligated to him and hence receptive to his influence was at its lowest ebb in Evoi's mature life. This was the time for Ipai's challenge. All he lacked was an issue, and events had moved so as to make Evoi vulnerable on this score as well. Most people still desired the new life promised by Tommy Kabu, but the Movement with its inadequate technical machinery had failed too often. Each call to action took a greater amount of leadership and persuasion to move the villagers. Early in 1955, Tommy Kabu sent a message to Kinipo requesting a large shipment of sago for sale in Port Moresby. The request was well timed. Many of the Motu villages of the Central District were experiencing food shortages. The market would be good, and the request had at least informal Administration support. But these were not circumstances of which the Kinipo villagers had any clear awareness, and the request was received with ambivalence. Evoi's task was to move them to action, and it was on this issue that Ipai chose to make his open challenge to Evoi's status as number one.

To have simply opposed acting on Tommy Kabu's request, particularly in this time of less than sanguine feelings toward the Kompani, would not have been especially significant, but Ipai went beyond opposition and made a competitive proposal for collective activity. Typically, it was couched in terms of the public interest but would notably serve Ipai's purpose. His counter-proposal was an expedition to secure trees for new canoes. The advantages were several. A need for new canoes was perennial in any sizeable village, and at almost any time one could be sure of finding some householders who were feeling the need more or less strongly. Since appropriate logs were large and could only be obtained at inland forests behind the swamps, the enterprise required organization and a substantial number of workers. Consequently, it had a collective nature similar to the Tommy Kabu proposal, and this placed the two in direct opposition. The men could not cut sago palms and at the same time cut canoe trees. It had to be one or the other. Finally, Ipai needed a canoe; he was the only man of substance in Kinipo without a large, decorated men's canoe.

Confronted with the two proposals, a meeting of all the adult men was called to consider the matter and make a decision if possible. Some indication of the degree to which the village and the village group organizations were losing their relevance can be seen in the number of men who attended this presumably important conference. In the older days, or during the height of the Tommy Kabu Movement, nearly 100 men would have been present and involved, but on this day only 28 turned out. Many households now lived most of the time in small camps near their family sago grounds, and an increasing number of the younger men were leaving the tribal territory to sign on as laborers in Australian enterprises. The social actions which had focused in the village no longer seemed vital to them. In addition, the other principal leaders, Kairi, Ove, and Kaivira, all found reasons to busy themselves elsewhere. None saw any wisdom in becoming involved in the coming confrontation between Evoi and Ipai. As individuals they had held differing degrees of dedication to the Movement, but now they shared a general antipathy and preferred not to follow Evoi in meeting Tommy's order for sago. On the other hand, it is not likely that any of them was attracted to the idea of helping Ipai increase his authority. Unable to act in accordance with their own clear interest in the situation, they avoided it.

The meeting was conducted in an orderly fashion, and good relations held on the surface throughout the afternoon. Both Evoi and Ipai brought gifts of areca nut and tobacco to distribute amongst those present. Aside from this it would have been difficult to identify them as the principals. Most of the arguments were made by others in the form of long speeches. In each case praise was given to the merits of the opposition plan before rejecting it as less urgent. The tone of discussion was cautious so as not to injure feelings unnecessarily or cause an unbearable loss of face. There seemed to be a general recognition that the contest was dangerous and might easily get out of hand, causing more social damage than any were willing to sustain. Even Ipai, ordinarily a haranguer of the "big man" or *iaki amua* type, spoke softly and allowed others to press his case.

Through the first round of speeches, it seemed as though Evoi still held the necessary influence. But as the afternoon wore on, it became clear that the early speeches reflected deference to Evoi's traditional position rather than to his current influence. Men who could not, out of respect, oppose Evoi at the beginning of the hearing, gradually shifted the weight of their position toward Ipai's as time passed. In the end, neither leader had the necessary consensus, but Ipai, with the larger number of supporters, had clearly blocked Evoi's attempt to carry out Kompani activity. At this point, the constable proposed a compromise. They would first cut the canoe trees and build the canoes, then they would make sago. The timing was all wrong for Evoi's purposes, perhaps fatal to them, but it was calculated to strip him of the rest of his supporters, who now clearly saw themselves in a losing cause. He accepted, and Ipai had won.

Although it had a special significance, the one contest did not settle the struggle between Evoi and Ipai. The canoe expedition went and returned. Ipai, true to form, came back with not one but two logs, both of a soft wood which would be easy to work but which would not last very long. Some sago was made and sold in Port Moresby, although not on the scale originally envisaged. In the meantime, Evoi rebuilt some parts of his reciprocity network, obligating once more by aid and gifts those who had slipped from his influence because of the drain on his resources from his son's marriage. Several months later things were much as they had been. But the ambiguity and instability of the political system, and its vulnerability to outside influences, such as the fortunes of the Tommy Kabu Movement or colonial appointments of village constables, had clearly become persisting characteristics.

Summary and Conclusion

The original hierarchical structure of Koriki leadership, with its well-defined method of recruitment, can be seen as a special adaptation to the problems of a rather concentrated society. A high rate of social interaction in daily life and in the more widely spaced but recurrent activities of ceremony and war involving whole villages and village groups was associated with a division of labor which distributed the different functions of leadership among a variety of well-defined leadership statuses. The system also achieved an integrated hierarchy, through the possibilities implicit in the sib-moiety-village structure. Although some "big man" characteristics were essential to it, the system was distinguished by its ascriptive, hierarchical nature and the *imunu* ideology which underlay it. In these respects it had a Polynesian flavor.

Colonial control brought a loss of sovereignty and a "radical change in the way in which leaders are produced and particularly in the way they are removed from their privileged positions" (Barnes 1960: 227). Control eliminated important functions of the *amua* and *mari* in raiding and ceremony. By the same actions it weakened the village as the most important social unit for collective activities above the family level. The consequence was a gradual and then more rapid movement of individuals and families out of the villages to sago camps deep in the swamps or to European labor activities in the outside world. Only a few individuals were lost permanently, but by World War II the amount of social action in the village was markedly less than it had been in pre-control times. An important result was a simplification of the duties and authority of the traditional leaders, and with this came a simplification in the social structure of leadership. At the same time, colonial control complicated the total situation by introducing a new political hierarchy represented in the villages by the government-appointed constables. The tendency of local political development was toward an uneasy but relatively stable integration of the two sets of leaders into a new village power elite.

The situation, however, was further unsettled by World War II, out of which came the Tommy Kabu Movement, dedicated to directed change toward an imperfectly perceived model of Western life. Intertribal, incipiently nationalistic, and enjoying great popular support, the Movement created a new political structure which united the tribes in its objectives. At the top, directing intertribal activities, were Tommy Kabu and his New Men, but they related their decisions and actions to the villages through the existing power elite of *amua, mari,* and constables. For a relatively brief time, the local political hierarchies, although somewhat simplified from traditional times, became fused through the Movement into an extensive intertribal structure which had some of the appearance and ambitions of nationalism. The Movement's efforts, however, fell short of success, particularly in its crucial economic objectives. An inevitable consequence was the loss of its ability to hold together the intertribal political structure. The political focus returned to the villages, but circumstances had changed there also, and the future of any particular power elite had become, at least for the time, difficult to predict. The Movement persisted through the 1950s, as it does today, but without its old power. For a few years in the post-war era, however, it had shown the developmental potential of the local political structures in the Purari Delta.

NOTES

1. Notably Chalmers (1887), Holmes (1902, 1924), and Williams (1924). In addition, there is a scattering of significant but rather brief sources such as Haddon (1919) and of books which bear upon the subject rather indirectly such as Seligman (1910).

2. While I do not believe that Koriki war was "waged to prove and raise the status of a developing leader," as Bromley (1962: 22) feels is true for the Dani, it does seem to me that the war functions of leadership in pre-control Melanesia have often been slighted in studies based upon post-control data.

3. The term and its meaning seem to be parallel to one reported for Busama by Hogbin and translated by him as "rubbish man." We seem to have here different words but equivalent meanings in four cultures.

BIBLIOGRAPHY

Barnes, J. A. 1960. Indigenous Politics and Colonial Administration with Special Reference to Australia. Comparative Studies in Society and History 2: 133–149.

Bromley, M. 1962. The Function of Fighting in Grand Valley Dani Society. United Nations Temporary Executive Authority in West New Guinea-West Irian, Bureau of Native Affairs, Working Papers in Dani Ethnology 1: 22–25.

Chalmers, J. 1887. Pioneering in New Guinea. London.

Garland, W. 1962. The Nature and Determinants of the Political Community: An Inquiry into the Concepts and Hypotheses of Political Anthropology. Unpublished Ph.D. dissertation, University of Minnesota.

Groves, M. 1963. Western Motu Descent Groups. Ethnology 2: 15–30.

Haddon, A. C. 1919. The Kopiravi Cult of the Namau. Man 19: 177–179.

Hogbin, H., and C. H. Wedgewood. 1952–54. Local Groupings in Melanesia. Oceania 23: 241–276; 24: 58–76.

Holmes, J. H. 1902. Initiation Ceremonies of Natives of the Papuan Gulf. Journal of the Royal Anthropological Institute 32: 418–425.

———. 1924. In Primitive New Guinea. New York.

Maher, R. F. 1960. Social Structure and Cultural Change in Papua. American Anthropologist 62: 593–602.

———. 1961a. New Men of Papua: A Study in Culture Change. Madison.

———. 1961b. Varieties of Change in Koriki Culture. Southwestern Journal of Anthropology 17: 26–39.

Sahlins, M. D. 1963. Poor Man, Rich Man, Big Man, Chief: Political Types in Melanesia and Polynesia. Comparative Studies in Society and History 5: 285–303.

Seligman, C. G. 1910. The Melanesians of British New Guinea. Cambridge.

Williams, F. C. 1924. The Natives of the Purari Delta. Territory of Papua, Anthropology Report 5. Port Moresby.

Udy, S. H. Jr. 1959. Organization of Work: A Comparative Analysis of Production Among Non-Industrial Peoples. New Haven.

Valentine, C. A. 1963. Social Status, Political Power, and Native Responses to European Influence in Oceania. Anthropological Forum 1: 3–55.

Vogt, E. Z. 1960. On the Concepts of Structure and Process in Cultural Anthropology. American Anthropologist 62: 18–35.

Reciprocal Influence of Traditional and Democratic Leadership Roles on Ponape[1]

Daniel T. Hughes

In the emergence of a global village, societies are being bombarded with a new element of culture. One area of change is in the political systems. Hughes stresses leadership roles, one aspect of the political system. He notes how new leadership roles appear to be accepted and function more effectively if they are clearly differentiated from traditional roles. Roles with a traditional counterpart will be modified as they function within the societal context.

The normative roles of traditional leadership will change as the leaders' perspectives and actions on hierarchy reflect new regimes of state and class. New controversies such as voting, nationalism, parties, and judicialism will remind the reader that the formal adoption of democratic institutions leaves some key issues of the distribution of power and wealth open and unresolved.

THE RAPID RISE of new political systems throughout the world in the last few decades offers social scientists opportunities for study of both theoretical and practical significance. Many problems arising from this political transition can be profitably viewed from a role analysis framework. One incisive study using this general approach was the work of Force (1960: 120) on emerging leadership roles in Palau. Force found that new leadership roles with no traditional counterparts were productive of less leadership insecurity and contributed less to dysfunction than did leadership roles with traditional counterparts.

In an attempt to explain why this should be the case, I formulated and tested the following hypothesis (Hughes 1967). When a new political system is introduced into a society, people will apply introduced norms and principles of authority more quickly to new leadership roles with no traditional counterparts than to new leadership roles with traditional counterparts. It was reasoned that people tend to confuse the norms, behavior, and expectations of such new leadership roles with corresponding elements of their traditional counterparts. In support of this hypothesis I presented data on four new leadership roles on Ponape, two of which have traditional counterparts and two of which do not.

If my original hypothesis is valid, it should follow that, when a new political system is introduced into a society, any new leadership role with a traditional counterpart will be strongly influenced by the traditional system. The role recruitment, behavior, and expectations of such an introduced leadership role should be extensively modified by the traditional system. Conversely, any traditional leadership role with an introduced counterpart will be extensively modified by the introduced system. In the present essay I shall examine in detail one introduced leadership role of the contemporary Ponapean system (the Chief Magistrate) and its traditional counterpart (the Nanmwarki).

Traditional and Democratic System

The traditional political system, which still functions on the island of Ponape, is centered in the five kingdoms of Madolenihmw, Uh, Kiti, Net, and Sokehs (Riesenberg 1968: 4). Each of these kingdoms has traditionally been the realm of two rulers called the Nanmwarki and the Nahnken. The Nanmwarki is the primary ruler, with the Nahnken as his chief advisor and administrator. Beneath each of these two rulers in each of the five kingdoms there is a line of title holders. The first twelve title holders in both lines (including the Nanmwarki and Nahnken themselves) constitute a privileged, ruling, noble class. Those with lesser kingdom titles or with none constitute the commoner class.

The kingdoms are divided into a number of geographical sections (*kousapw*), which are ruled by section chiefs (*kaun*) appointed by the Nanmwarki. The section chief holds the first in a series of section titles, and in this respect he resembles the Nanmwarki (Riesenberg 1968: 21). The section itself is subdivided into farmsteads, which are generally clusters of two or three houses whose inhabitants work the surrounding landholdings.

In the democratic political system introduced by the American Administration there are six municipalities on Ponape, five of which are coextensive with the five traditional kingdoms. The sixth municipality was established a few years ago when the town of Kolonia, the base for foreign administrations since early Spanish times, separated from the kingdom and municipality of Net. The people of Kolonia thought that their interests would be better served by having their own municipality rather than by continuing as part of the Net Kingdom and municipality. Kolonia now has a population of about 5,700 inhabitants, many of whom are immigrants from the outer islands with no ties to the traditional Ponapean system.

Each of the six municipalities has an elected Chief Magistrate as its highest executive official and an elected Council as its legislative body. In addition to the Municipal Councils there are two other legislative bodies in the democratic system. The elected District Legislature has legislative authority over the entire Ponape District, which includes the islands of Ponape, Pingelap, Kusaie, Ngatik, Mokil, Nukuoro, and Kapingamarangi. Finally there is the Congress of Micronesia, which meets annually in Saipan with members elected from all six districts of the Trust Territory. Each district has as its chief executive a District Administrator appointed by the High Commissioner of the Trust Territory. The High Commissioner is appointed by the President of the United States and is responsible directly to the Secretary of the Interior.

The executive and legislative positions on the various levels of the Ponapean democratic political system are listed below. The four asterisked positions are elected, and the other two are appointed.

	Executive Position	Legislative Position
Territorial level	High Commissioner	*Micronesian Congressman
District level	District Administrator	*District Legislator
Municipal level	*Chief Magistrate	*Municipal Councilman

The traditional Ponapean political system extends only to the municipal or kingdom level. On this level the Chief Magistrate parallels the traditional Nanmwarki, while the Councilman parallels the section chief. The present report focuses on the positions of Chief Magistrate and Nanmwarki.

Role of Chief Magistrate

Role Recruitment

The Germans and Japanese made the Nanmwarkis their official administrators of the kingdoms and conducted all their business with the people through them. At first the American Administration continued this policy by appointing the Nanmwarkis as the Chief Magistrates of the kingdoms, which were now called "municipalities." Later the municipalities throughout the Trust Territory were encouraged to become chartered, and the election of the Chief Magistrates was incorporated in the charters granted to them. Consequently, the present mechanism for selecting a Chief Magistrate is a popular election, whereas the selection of a Nanmwarki is still largely on a hereditary basis.

Granted this difference in the mechanisms of recruitment, we may ask whether, in selecting their Chief Magistrates, the Ponapeans are influenced by the traditional assumption that a noble is more capable of ruling than a commoner. A random sample of 300 adult Ponapeans[2] were asked whether they would prefer a noble or a commoner as Chief Magistrate if both were equally qualified in all other regards. They responded as follows: noble preferred 26 per cent; commoner preferred 47 per cent; no preference 27 per cent. Despite this strong stated preference for a commoner, only three of the six Chief Magistrates in office at the time of this study were nobles: one Nanmwarki and two men holding lower titles in the Nanmwarki's line. Thus, in selecting Chief Magistrates by the introduced, democratic mechanism of popular elections, the Ponapeans in practice do seem to be influenced by the traditional assumption that a noble is more capable of ruling than a commoner.

At the time of the study only 17 per cent of the Congressmen and 13 per cent of the Legislators were nobles. The traditional assumption of the superiority of nobles seems, therefore, to affect the choice of Congressmen and Legislators far less than that of Chief Magistrates. I would suggest that the reason for this difference may lie in the fact that the role of Chief Magistrate has a traditional counterpart, whereas those of Legislator and Congressman do not. On the other hand, only 3 per cent of the Councilmen were nobles, even though this role also has a traditional counterpart, the section chief. The dearth of nobles in the ranks of the Councilmen can, however, be explained by other factors. Most nobles consider this position beneath their dignity and do not seek election to it. Also the traditional respectful behavior patterns still in vogue make it difficult for many people to have a noble in a position that they must deal with as often as the Councilmen.

Role Behavior

Communication between the Chief Magistrates and the people of their municipalities seems quite extensive. Sixty-one per cent of the random sample said they had heard their Chief Magistrate speak at public gatherings at least once during the preceding year, and 64 per cent said they had heard him speak on the radio at least once during the same period. However, only 19 per cent of the sample had personally gone to their Chief Magistrate to make any requests, inquiries, or complaints. When they did so, the issues most frequently discussed were taxes, schools, roads, bridges, and dispensaries. It is much more common for the Ponapeans to deal with their Chief Magistrates over matters like these through their Councilmen than to do so directly. Many people gave as a reason that their Councilmen, who usually reside in their own or a neighboring section, are more accessible. They also stated that they prefer to present a request, inquiry, or complaint to the Chief Magistrates in the traditional manner through a third party rather than directly.

The Chief Magistrate acts as chairman at the monthly Municipal Council meetings. These meetings are important because it is at them that municipal laws are passed and administrative policy is decided upon. An account of one Council meeting, in July at the municipal office in Kiti, will illustrate the type of problems taken up there. At this meeting each Councilman gave a report on the section he represented and informed his colleagues of the requests and complaints that had been brought to him during the past month. The Council then discussed the municipal budget for the following year, the possibility of extending the municipal hospital or building a new one, a report from the municipal Public Works Officer on road and bridge repair, and the possibilities of housing seven Peace Corps volunteers who were to be assigned to their municipality. As chairman, the Chief Magistrate directed the discussions and from time to time called for a vote on a particular issue.

At such a Council meeting the Chief Magistrate is fully absorbed in a vital process of the democratic system and thus might be expected to be dissociated from traditional values and patterns of behavior. But such was not the case. Whenever the Councilmen or other officials passed the Chief Magistrate during the meeting, they either bowed to bring their heads lower than his or made a motion toward doing so. Whenever anyone present gave the Chief Magistrate a paper or anything else, he presented it with his right hand crossed over his left wrist. These are traditional signs of respect which are now shown to the Chief Magistrate whether at a Council meeting or on any other occasion—more frequently in the municipalities that correspond to the traditional kingdoms than in the municipality of Kolonia, where the traditional social system has been weakened by prolonged contact with foreign administrators and with immigrants from other islands with different social systems.

Of the six Chief Magistrates in office at the time of the study those rated in the sample as the most effective were those of Madolenihmw (21 per cent) and of Net (13 per cent). Both men are forceful leaders, although the Chief Magistrate of Net is a Nanmwarki and the Chief Magistrate of Madolenihmw is a commoner. The reason most frequently given for rating these two officials so highly was their work for the common good of their municipalities. As examples, many people cited the work on roads and bridges accomplished under the administration of the Chief Magistrate of Madolenihmw and what he had done to raise the Ponapean standard of living by his work with the Madolenihmw Housing Co-operative, of which he was Vice President. Others stated that the Chief Magistrate of Net had helped the people by obtaining concessions from the American Administration regarding land that would be available for homesteading. Another reason frequently offered for the popularity of both leaders was their "fearlessness" in standing up to the Americans. Ponapeans are generally polite and deferential in dealing with each other and, if anything, even more so with foreigners. However, many Ponapeans think that their leaders have been too deferential toward American officials, and they have high praise for those who are not afraid openly to oppose the American Administration.

In evaluating their Chief Magistrates according to their contribution to the common good, Ponapeans are expressing a value stressed in the traditional system as well as in the new democratic system. The obligation of rulers to care for their followers and to work for their common welfare is a strong traditional Ponapean value (Fischer 1957: 175). "Fearlessness" is also a traditional value associated with all Ponapean men and has always been particularly expected of rulers.

Role Expectations

Official documents such as municipal charters describe the Chief Magistrate as the administrator of the municipality, but to refer to his position thus with no further explanation could be misleading. Such a statement could imply that the Chief Magistrate is the leader of the municipality, in contrast to the Nanmwarki who is the leader of the kingdom. Actually, the Ponapeans do not distinguish the roles of the Chief Magistrate and the Nanmwarki in this way. They use the same word, *wehi* to refer to both the kingdom and the municipality and seem to conceive of them as a single entity. They emphasize a distinction between the traditional (*pali en sapw*) and the nontraditional (*pali en opis*) and it would be a more accurate expression of their view to characterize the Nanmwarki as the leader of the kingdom or of the people in traditional affairs and the Chief Magistrate as their leader in nontraditional affairs.

The position of Chief Magistrate, like that of Nanmwarki, carries high prestige in contemporary Ponapean society. Ninety-six per cent of the sample rated the Chief Magistrate's job as "important" or "very important" for helping the people of the municipality, and 74 per cent rated their own Chief Magistrates as "diligent" or "very diligent" in performing their duties. The prestige a Chief Magistrate gains when people think he is doing a good job is a strong recompense for his work. The Ponapeans generally have a strong drive to be acknowledged as important persons. This drive supplied much of the necessary motivation for the traditional title-tribute system (Riesenberg 1968: 110), and it contributes toward making the position of Chief Magistrate a desired one.

The popular expectations associated with the role of Chief Magistrate as expressed by the people of our sample are outlined in Tables 1 to 3.[3] Table 1 indicates that the personal quality valued most highly for a Chief Magistrate is "love for the people." Actually this is a quality which has traditionally been valued in Ponapean leaders, and which is now expected of democratic leaders as well. Whether leadership status is attained by election in the democratic system or by hereditary prerogatives in the traditional system, any Ponapean leader today is expected to "love the people." Such love is manifested in kindness, gentleness, and approachability but also includes a determination to work for the common good. Other qualities are recognized as important but subordinate, and their lack may be excused, but when a Ponapean says of a particular leader that he "does not love the people" he is in effect saying that he is a leader in name only.

"Capability in administration" is deemed important for the Chief Magistrate because he is recognized as the chief executive official of the municipality, with the chief responsibility for such matters as the building of roads and the collection of taxes. This quality is rated more important for the Chief Magistrate than for the Nanmwarki (cf. Table 4). It is interesting to note that even for the Chief Magistrate the people rate the traditionally important quality of "ability to foster cooperation" more highly than the qualities of "education" and "intelligence."

Table 2 shows that the most highly rated duty of the Chief Magistrate is "to help the people of the municipality." This item is, of course, general enough to include such other duties as "explaining the laws to the people,"

TABLE 1
Qualities Valued Most Highly
in Chief Magistrate

Quality	No.	Percent
Love for people	194	65
Capability in administration	131	44
Ability to foster co-operation	115	38
Education	101	34
Intelligence	61	20

TABLE 2
Most Important Duties of Chief Magistrate

Duty	No.	Percent
Helping people	183	61
Representing people to the District Administration	163	54
Explaining laws	160	53
Guiding the Council	47	16
Assisting the District Administrator	44	15

but the Ponapeans do not speak in neatly contrasted and mutually exclusive categories. The items included under this and other questions are those that recurred again and again in an intensive pilot study. However vague and overlapping in some instances, these categories are the ones under which the Ponapeans discuss their leadership roles.

In explaining what they meant by "helping the people," it was evident that the Ponapeans expected the Chief Magistrate, like their traditional leaders, to work for the welfare of their followers both individually and collectively. "Representing the people to the District Administrator," i.e., discussing the needs of the people of his municipality with the District Administrator, is a means of helping the people which is quite specific to the Chief Magistrate, since he ordinarily meets with the District Administrator once a month for this purpose. "Explaining laws" to the people and "guiding the Council" in making good laws are also ways in which the Chief Magistrate is expected to help the people, but these tasks parallel the responsibilities of the traditional leaders to "teach the people." Ponapeans also expect the Chief Magistrate to "assist the District Administrator" by informing him of conditions in the municipality.

With respect to the ways in which a Chief Magistrate can best help the people of his municipality (Table 3), although great stress is again placed on his "representing the people to the District Administrator" and "explaining the laws to the people," another task is also given high priority, namely, that of "repairing roads." The "roads" in most Ponapean municipalities are in incredibly poor condition. Driving a jeep is impossible on most of them. In the few areas where the roads are maintained in good condition travel is obviously much easier. It was obvious from the pilot study that many Ponapeans were concerned about not losing Ponapean traditions in the change to a new political system, and the final item was included to determine whether the Ponapeans considered this to be solely a responsibility of traditional leaders and not at all of elected leaders like the Chief Magistrate.

TABLE 3
Ways Chief Magistrate Can Best Help People

Activities	No.	Percent
Representing people to the District Administrator	240	80
Repairing roads	164	55
Explaining laws	148	49
Assisting the District Administrator	37	12
Preserving traditions	9	03

Role of Nanmwarki

Role Recruitment

The same general norms apply to the choice of a Nanmwarki today as in traditional times. Ideally any vacancy in either noble line should be filled by the man holding the next lower title, but in practice it is still common for a man to skip one or more titles. Other factors are also considered, like the age of the person and his contributions to the common good (Riesenberg 1968: 34–39; Fischer 1957: 175). Normally the Nahnken and other high nobles of his line decide who will be the new Nanmwarki, and the Nahnken crowns him at a feast.

Role Behavior

I attended a feast given jointly by the five southernmost sections of Madolenihmw for their recently crowned Nanmwarki. A large crowd was standing around outside the feast house in the early afternoon when someone brought word that the Nanmwarki was coming. There was a great rush to get into position. One of the men gathered about fifty people together and began to lead them in songs as the Nanmwarki and his party came in sight along the path. About fifteen men, all walking in single file, accompanied the Nanmwarki and Nahnken. An air of excitement gripped the crowd and the singing increased in volume as the Nanmwarki drew nearer. Shouts of greeting and cheers for the new Nanmwarki filled the air and almost drowned out the singing as the Nanmwarki passed the group. Everyone joined in the procession and followed the Nanmwarki and his party into the feast house about thirty yards away.

Inside the feast house the high royalty sat on the platform facing the people. In front of each noble sat a servant in the traditional stylized position of respect. These are no longer permanent servants of the Nanmwarki and Nahnken but members of the group offering the feast.

They held their rigid, stylized position for hours, occasionally shifting a bit to talk or joke with each other or with some of the people on the ground level. Here men sat preparing kava (*sakau*) much as their ancestors had done in centuries past, but they now wore trousers instead of the traditional kilts. Yams, pigs, and kava were brought in, presented to the Nanmwarki, and then divided by the food distributor.

Although never considered divine, the Nanmwarki was traditionally so sacred that he was almost completely separated from contact with ordinary people by a series of complex patterns and taboos. No one could look directly at his face, and only the highest nobles and his servants could address him directly (Bascom 1965: 30), in which case they had to use the high language (Riesenberg and Garvin 1952: 205–206).[4] The way in which the people greeted the Nanmwarki as he approached the feast house in southern Madolenihmw showed how much the sacredness of the Nanmwarki had been mitigated since traditional times. The greeting was one more appropriate to a popular hero than to a sacred person. While this change is due largely to the increased contact between the Nanmwarki and the people which resulted from his role during the German and Japanese administrations as the official administrator of the kingdom (Bascom 1965: 25), it is probable that it has also been influenced by the egalitarian notions of the democratic system introduced by the Americans. This is not to say, however, that the Nanmwarki has now completely lost his unique position in Ponapean society. Quite the contrary. He is still held in great respect by the vast majority of Ponapeans and is still treated with many traditional signs of respect, involving tribute, kava, the royal language, deferential gestures, etc., especially in festive contexts.

During the feast in question the Nahnken announced that he and the Nanmwarki had decided to give *konot* titles (not in either royal line but carrying great prestige and the right to a large share of tribute at any feast the title-bearer attends) to the "chair" of the Municipal Chief Magistrate and the Judge of Madolenihmw, explaining that when these officials were replaced in office the titles would pass to their successors. This was the first time that titles had been awarded to a "chair," as the Nahnken put it, although they had often in the past been given to successful businessmen and government officials. The Nahnken later told me that he and the Nanmwarki had done so in order to show the people that the elected officials of the kingdom and the whole new system are important and that he and the Nanmwarki approved of and supported these officials and whoever might be elected to succeed them.

As in traditional times, only the Nanmwarki and Nahnken can distribute kingdom titles (Riesenberg 1968: 40). Several Nanmwarkis and

Nahnkens said that distributing titles is their most difficult task and that some people might hold life-long grudges against them if they did not receive the titles they felt they deserved.

The Nanmwarki and Nahnken still receive substantial tribute at feasts and first-fruits offerings. Today some of them, particularly the rulers of Kiti, return a large part of this tribute to the people making the offering. It has also become quite common today for the Nanmwarki to sell food given to him as tribute, especially yams, in which case he usually keeps the proceeds.

In return for the tribute given to him the Nanmwarki is expected to work for the good of the people. A number of informants recalled, for example, that Nanmwarki Moses of Madolenihmw and Nanmwarki Max of Net had instructed the residents of their kingdoms to plant yams and other crops immediately following World War II, planning and organizing this work through their section chiefs. When a typhoon later struck the island, the kingdoms of Madolenihmw and Net supplied food not only to their own people but also to those of other kingdoms. Even in traditional times the Nanmwarki seems to have helped his people through this sort of control of agriculture, although it was formerly usually exercised more through the Nahnken than directly.

The style of behavior of a Nanmwarki has changed considerably since traditional times. Perhaps the most notable difference is a marked decline in the awe at his sacredness, although it has by no means disappeared. The servants still sit in the same stylized position and avoid looking directly in the Nanmwarki's face. And they rebuke those who raise their heads above the Nanmwarki's or become too noisy—though today only with words and not the thrust of a spear.

As the aura of sacredness surrounding the Nanmwarki has diminished, his role has become more detached, i.e., he can more readily forego some expectations attached to his position. Several people reported that their Nanmwarki, upon seeing that they were embarrassed because they did not know the royal language, had told them not to bother trying to use it. A Nanmwarki can step out of his role even more easily in a nontraditional setting. On several occasions I have met Nanmwarkis in stores or on the streets of Kolonia, and have observed that in these situations their behavior was much like that of anyone else.

The traditional patterns of respect toward the Nanmwarki and the other nobles, however, are not set aside so readily, especially on such occasions as feasts. A number of young Ponapeans who have been away to school and then spent much of their time working in Kolonia have so little familiarity with the traditional patterns of respect that they feel too embarrassed to take part in feasts.

Role Expectations

Fifty-three per cent of the sample felt that the authority of the Nanmwarki is as strong today as it was before Chief Magistrates were elected, and 75 per cent said the Nanmwarki still has sufficient power to "help the people a lot." Tables 4 to 6 summarize the popular view of the Nanmwarki's role in contemporary Ponapean society.

The qualities selected as most desirable in a Nanmwarki (Table 5) reflect the importance of his tasks as father and teacher. The quality most stressed was "love for the people." The Ponapeans expect the Nanmwarki to look upon all the people of his kingdom as his own children, to treat them all equally like his children and to help all who are in need, both families and sections. Many said that he can demonstrate his "love for the people" by encouraging them to work and to care for their families. Some said that, when necessary, the Nanmwarki himself should plan and organize such work through his section chiefs.

As a loving father the Nanmwarki is also expected to be "patient" with his people's weaknesses and forgiving of their faults. When he does not live up to this ideal, the people are disturbed. Many Ponapeans explained that if the Nanmwarki is angry with them, either with an individual or with a group, they "feel very bad" and "cannot be happy." They consequently ranked "patience" as an important quality for the Nanmwarki.

"Capability in administration" and "intelligence" are also desirable qualities in a Nanmwarki but are certainly less important than "love for the people," "ability to foster co-operation," and "patience." "Education" as a possibly desirable quality for a Nanmwarki (or other traditional leaders) was completely rejected by all informants in the pilot study and was thus not included in the list of qualities from which the sample was asked to make a choice. Moreover, although the respondents were free to mention any quality they considered important, even though not in-

TABLE 4
Qualities Valued Most Highly
in a Nanmwarki

Quality	No.	Percent
Love of people	263	88
Ability to foster co-operation	148	49
Patience	111	37
Capability in administration	47	16
Intelligence	31	10

TABLE 5
Most Important Duties
of a Nanmwarki

Duty	No.	Percent
Father of people	197	66
Teacher of people	143	48
Giver of titles	90	30
Leader of people	84	28
Receiver of tribute	80	27

cluded on the list, none mentioned "education" as an important quality for a Nanmwarki.

The Ponapeans traditionally viewed the Nanmwarki as the successor of Isokelkel, the semi-historical founder of the Nanmwarki-Nahnken title system, and therefore as the "leader" or "ruler" of the people. Table 6 indicates that the Ponapeans still consider the Nanmwarki as the "leader of the people"—at least in traditional affairs such as feasts, tribute and titlegiving, but much greater stress is placed today on his role as "father of the people." This is now the key assumption regarding his relations with his people, and many values and norms associated with his role follow from this assumption. The task of ruling the people is now split between the Nanmwarki and the Chief Magistrate, so that the former is the ruler only "in traditional affairs."

As their father and as their leader the Ponapeans expect the Nanmwarki to be their teacher. Many say that he was traditionally the chief teacher of the people of the kingdom, although they may actually be confusing his role with the traditional role of the Nahnken, and they express a desire for him to fulfill this task vigorously. They expect him to tell them what is right and wrong, and to encourage them to work hard and to care for their families. They also expect him to tell them what is good in the new democratic system and to teach them how they can accept this system without losing the valuable elements of their traditional system. It is interesting that the Chief Magistrate is expected to explain the laws and regulations of the democratic system but that only the traditional leaders can show how the new and old systems can be linked together and how traditional values can be preserved.

The duty of the Nanmwarki rated third in importance is that of "giving titles." As in traditional times, only the Nanmwarki and Nahnken can distribute kingdom titles today. This exclusive right is perhaps the strongest support of their authority, for it would be difficult to exaggerate, even

TABLE 6
Ways a Nanmwarki Can Best Help His People

Activity	No.	Percent
Distribute tribute evenly	234	78
Help the municipal government	168	56
Join the traditional and modern systems	100	33
Preserve traditions	56	19
Distribute titles correctly	39	13

today, the importance of titles to the Ponapeans. Acquiring a high kingdom title is still a major goal for most Ponapeans. Several successful businessmen in Kolonia and the District Judge, when I interviewed them, proudly listed the titles they held in the various kingdoms of the island. Many Ponapeans still consider that the prestige from such titles outweighs the tribute they must pay for them.

The first item in Table 6 refers to the tribute given to the Nanmwarki by the people of his kingdom. Every section and every noble of a kingdom gives the Nanmwarki a feast of tribute once a year, either separately or in various combinations. In addition, the section chiefs bring offerings of first fruits to him throughout the year. Few Ponapeans question the Nanmwarki's right to receive tribute, but Table 6 indicates that a large proportion (78 per cent) of the sample state that the way a Nanmwarki can best help his people today is to distribute the tribute evenly. Many said he should either return most of the tribute to the person offering it or use it for the good of the people. Some people, who constitute a minority though a noticeable one, are quite bitter about this question and make statements such as: "The Nanmwarki does nothing today but receive tribute." Others extend their bitterness to include all the nobility, saying: "I have never seen a noble help the people."

It seems probable that the egalitarian principles of democracy have influenced the present Ponapean attitude toward the distribution of tribute. However, in explaining the people's present attitude toward tribute we must remember the history of such payments on Ponape in this century. The German administration, when they introduced taxes, greatly reduced the amount of tribute the Nanmwarki and Nahnken could receive, but under both the Japanese and the American administrations tribute was allowed to increase even though taxes continued (Bascom 1965: 59). This increase in traditional tribute, with the concomitant maintenance of the taxes originally proposed as a means of reducing tribute, is partially responsible for the present hostility toward both tribute and all forms of taxation.

Moreover, in traditional times there were institutionalized means by which the tribute to the rulers was used for the good of the people. In times of natural disaster, for example, the Nanmwarki and Nahnken broke out their stores of tribute to help the victims. In addition, such work for the kingdom as constructing channels in the lagoon was supported by supplies from the leaders' tribute. Nowadays, however, the people see no such return from their offerings to the kingdom leaders.

The next three expectations listed in Table 6 are all related to the roles of the Nanmwarki as "father" and "teacher" of the people. The Ponapeans want the Nanmwarki to "help the municipal government by supporting the Chief Magistrate and the Council because they realize that his support can still contribute as an important factor to the success of the municipal government. They also want him to help the people "join the traditional and the modern systems" and "preserve traditions" by teaching them what is good in the new system and show them how they can accept this without rejecting their traditional values. Their greater stress on the need to "join the traditional and modern systems" (33 per cent) than on the need to "preserve traditions" (19 per cent) indicates their awareness of the magnitude of the changes now occurring in Ponapean society.

Conclusion

At the beginning of this paper I stated that, when a new political system is introduced into a society, any new leadership role with a traditional counterpart will be strongly modified by the traditional system, and conversely that any traditional leadership role with an introduced counterpart will be strongly modified by the introduced system. I have offered supporting evidence for this principle by examining the manner and extent to which the introduced leadership role of Chief Magistrate on Ponape has been modified by the traditional system and the manner and extent to which its traditional counterpart, the role of Nanmwarki, has been modified by the new, democratic system. Comparison of this parallel pair of leadership roles has highlighted the reciprocal influence of the traditional and the introduced political systems in this situation of extensive socio-political change.

NOTES

1. Ponape, a fertile, mountainous island of 111 square miles with a population of about 13,000, is located in the Eastern Caroline Islands. This paper is based on field work conducted there from January to November, 1966.

2. A random sample of 300 respondents was selected from the slightly fewer than 6,000 Ponapeans who were 21 years of age or more. All tables in the present paper are based on data gathered from this random sample according to a precoded schedule drawn up after a pilot study of two and one-half months was conducted involving open-ended interviews with 67 Ponapeans from all social levels.

3. In obtaining the data summarized in each of the six tables, respondents were instructed to select two out of five possible responses.

4. The Ponapean language has many levels of complexity, each level being considered appropriate for a particular type of social situation. The major levels are: (1) the common language, (2) the polite or respectful language, and (3) the royal or high language. The common language is generally used with children or in informal situations with equals. The polite language is used in addressing superiors, or equals in formal situations; it includes humble words and forms referring to oneself and respectful words and forms referring to the addressee. The royal language, which includes further humble words and forms, is used in speaking to or in the presence of the nobility.

BIBLIOGRAPHY

Bascom, W. R. 1965. Ponape: A Pacific Economy in Transition. Anthropological Records 22: 1–149.

Fischer, J., and A. Fischer. 1957. The Eastern Carolines. New Haven.

Force, R. W. 1960. Leadership and Cultural Change in Palau. Fieldiana: Anthropology 50: 1–211.

Hughes, D. T. 1967. Democracy in a Traditional Society: A Role Analysis of the Political System of Ponape. Ann Arbor: University Microfilms.

Riesenberg, S. H. 1968. The Native Polity of Ponape. Washington.

Riesenberg, S. H., and P. Garvin. 1952. Respect Behavior on Ponape. American Anthropologist 54:201–220.

The Effects of Writing on the
Cuna Political System[1]

James Howe

The analysis of political change is the least developed area in current research. Social scientists can describe the change adequately, but it is still beyond their capabilities to predict and explain. Howe's essay helps us understand why. The factors that bring about change are limitless, they can include dramatic events such as war, migration, disease, or climatic change. Howe describes how the introduction of writing has an impact upon such areas as the increase of individual control and the emergence of specialized political units. Considering the fragility of a political structure, we should not be surprised by the turmoil in human societies. This case study of the Cuna suggests that: the political use of new techniques or technologies may impose new ideas and help shift power into already politically strong units; it may remove power holders from the consequences of their actions; and new technology may provide for new conceptions of human (that is, political) nature.

W RITING WOULD SEEM to be one of the great transformers in history. Generations of social theorists have asserted, or assumed a fundamental contrast between literate and preliterate cultures; and in describing and analyzing the evolution of society, they have assigned writing a place of honor alongside population growth, the neolithic revolution, irrigation, trade, warfare, plagues, and industrialism. Among such theorists, McLuhan has in recent decades gathered the most attention to himself, with his extreme and largely unsubstantiated claims for the power of various communication media to transform perception and thought. We also find, however, some very careful and solid social scien-

336

tists coming to similar, if somewhat less exaggerated, conclusions. Goody and Watt (1968) for instance, give writing credit for promoting the separation of myth and history, of "divine attributes from the natural world," and of symbolic classifications from social morphology, in other words, for putting an end to *la pensée sauvage*.

The problem with such generalizations is that we in fact know very little about what writing actually does, and in particular about what happens when a preliterate society first begins to use writing. We have only a handful of focused descriptions of the place of writing among contemporary non-industrial societies (most of them in Goody 1968), and materials from the ancient world tend to be fragmentary and one-dimensional. Researchers in the field of communications have analyzed the printed media in some depth, and others have investigated the economic and political effects of modern education and mass literacy (e.g., Cipolla 1969); but most empirical studies of writing itself have taken its social and cultural importance for granted, paying almost exclusive attention to the formal and logical characteristics of alphabets and other writing systems, the origin, spread, and evolution of such forms, and the deciphering of ancient writing (e.g., Diringer 1948; Gelb 1952; Ullman 1969). Thus, as Basso (1974) has forcefully argued, we badly need ethnographies of writing.

This paper describes the effects of writing on a traditional political system, one in which writing was adopted in the last few decades. It has often been noted that the organization of states and empires depends on writing (or on some substitute such as the Inca *quipu*), both for storing information and for maintaining communications over distance, and that the absence of writing seriously limits the ability of a polity to expand or maintain centralized control. How writing would affect a small-scale political system, one with a restricted territory, less pressing informational requirements, and a strong emphasis on face-to-face relations, is not so immediately apparent.

Ethnographic Background

The subjects of this paper are the San Blas Cuna, an indigenous population inhabiting the northeast coast of Panama. Except for nine small villages on the Caribbean shore, all of the roughly 25,000 Cuna inhabit some 39 villages situated on small coral islets close in along the shore, each of them within a few hundred yards of a mainland river. The Cuna gain their subsistence from slash-and-burn agriculture, fishing, and to a lesser extent from hunting, and as a cash crop they raise coconuts, all of them sold to boats from Colombia. They have their own reservation, la

Comarca de San Blas, under the general control of Panama, but within which they enjoy a considerable measure of local autonomy and self-government. Politically, San Blas villages are highly organized, with a hierarchy of chiefs and lesser leaders, nightly meetings, and a large number of governmental functions.

The Cuna embraced education and literacy only very recently. European and Euro-American historical sources from previous centuries indicate that some Cuna men learned to speak Spanish and English while away from home, and a few of them may have learned to read and write (Cullen 1853; Joyce 1934). Certainly by the end of the nineteenth century there was a very light sprinkling of men who had been schooled in Panama and elsewhere. The first schools appeared on a few acculturated islands in the early decades of the twentieth century (see Stout 1947; Holloman 1969). Some Cuna rejected education, at times violently, and a few highly conservative villages resisted schools until very recently; but surprisingly, a good many otherwise traditional Cuna accepted education very early in this century, seeing literacy as a useful tool and a weapon with which to defend Cuna sovereignty.

In 1970, the year of the most recent government census, 34 percent of the San Blas population over the age of ten was recorded as literate, with the literacy rate varying widely from island to island. The village that first accepted schools early in this century had in 1970 only 100 illiterates, undoubtedly concentrated among the oldest inhabitants, out of a total population of 647. At the other extreme, in several communities noted for their conservatism, the proportion of illiterates was 85 out of 96, 478 out of 500, 217 out of 230, and 39 out of 39.[2] It should be noted that, since an island needs only a handful of literate men to keep its records, the political uses of writing do not require a high literacy rate.

The Cuna have begun to use writing in several different areas of daily life. Ritualists have for some time been recording their chants and cures in a mnemonic picture-writing, and today those who are literate often write them out in Cuna, using a modified Spanish orthography. The Cuna occasionally obtain newspapers, books, and comics from the city, although the effects of the written mass media have so far been relatively slight. Schooling, on the other hand, has brought about drastic and rapid change by ending the traditional semi-seclusion of Cuna girls, interrupting the socialization into agriculture of Cuna boys, and modifying the world view of both sexes. In this paper, however, I discuss only the organizational changes in Cuna village government caused or facilitated by the political use of writing.

Cuna Secretaries

For several centuries the Cuna have been negotiating and bargaining with the outside world, and for this they have needed translators. Undoubtedly some of the earliest translators were bilingual but illiterate. By at least the turn of the present century, delegations sent to Panama or Colombia exploited the talents of the very few literate men then available to them. Some delegations would pick up literate men from their home communities and keep them on only for the duration of the mission, but the high chiefs who held sway over regional confederacies of islands in San Blas soon began to use them on a relatively permanent basis. Immediately after a brief but largely successful revolt against Panama in 1925, the famous inter-island chief Nele Kantule made a special point of recruiting young educated men as secretaries and bringing them to his home island of Ustuppu (Holloman 1969). The classic ethnographic compendium on the Cuna (Nordenskiold et al. 1938) consists in large part of documents recorded by Nele Kantule's secretaries and of information provided by one of those secretaries on a visit to Sweden in 1931.

In the 1920s some islands followed the lead of the high chiefs, establishing the post of *sikkwi* (bird) or *secretario* as a regular village office. Other villages, out of conservatism or lack of educated members, continued without secretaries; but over the years most of them eventually accepted this innovation, although some very traditional islands held out into the 1960s and early 1970s. Thus, during my first fieldwork in San Blas in 1970 and 1971, some villages had used writing for many years, some for shorter periods, and some still did without—a situation providing scope for internal comparison.

Although the Cuna apparently first began using secretaries to deal with the outside world, their skills were soon turned toward internal problems and needs. Today, in the majority of villages that have official secretaries, they handle any public business that involves writing or translation between Cuna and Spanish. At home they generally have their own table in the village meeting hall, at which they sit during nightly village meetings, and abroad they accompany village delegations. They work almost exclusively in Spanish, translating case records, depositions, and other records (see below) out of Cuna into Spanish to transcribe them. In terms of literacy and competence they cover a broad range, from graduates of secondary school or university to men with just a few years of primary schooling. The latter tend to write in an ungrammatical and misspelled shorthand version of Spanish, though even they usually perform adequately in the relatively simple tasks the village government requires of them.

The community I primarily studied tried to keep three ranked village secretaries at any one time, although the young men who filled the office tended to depart San Blas for migrant labor more often than other office-holders, frequently leaving the village shorthanded and forcing it to spend a good deal of time finding replacements. There were also a number of secretaries who acted only for specific functions (see below) rather than general village business. Thus, in a village with a moderate literacy rate (somewhat under 50 percent in the population over age ten) and a modest population (about 300), a significant proportion of the young literate men at home at any given moment could be coopted by the secretary's office. In other villages with very few literate men, most of them might be pressed into service. I use the word "co-opted" advisedly because the growing heterogeneity of the Cuna population and the resulting partial loss of consensus have put a strain on some village governments (Holloman 1969), especially on the largest islands, which cannot allow more than a small proportion of their men to hold office or even to speak in village meetings. In smaller and medium-sized islands, on the other hand, the secretary's office ties young men to village government, forces them to attend meetings, and affords them a standing there they would otherwise not achieve for some years. Nor are they just given a sop: secretaries speak more often and get a more respectful hearing than many of their own age, and in some villages they attain positions of considerable influence.

Many Cuna leaders resent being dependent on their secretaries, especially when they are travelling away from home, and feel distrustful toward them. Stories circulate of embezzled checks; misuse of village seals for private purposes, filching of village records, and deliberate mistranslation or deception of monolingual chiefs while on commissions to Panama.[3] Some chiefs are now bilingual or even literate, allowing them to dispense with interpreters away from home, and some delegations include literate men but not official secretaries.

Managing, Reinforcing, and Expanding Traditional Institutions

Cuna villages and their secretaries use a limited number of written forms—the letter, the list, the case record, and the deposition—but make extensive use of each one, fully exploiting its organizing potential. One of the ends to which they put lists is the defense of traditional institutions against the modern world.

Political life in San Blas centers on the *onmakket* (gathering) or *congreso,* of which there are two varieties, sacred and secular. In the secular gathering, the men of a village manage its affairs and adjudicate trouble cases. In the sacred variety, a village chief sings to the assembled men, women, and children for an hour or more, after which an *arkar* or *vocero* repeats and interprets the substance of the chief's chant in spoken Cuna. In most villages a gathering of one sort or another occurs almost every night of the week. The sacred gatherings play a key part in maintaining community integration and solidarity and in fostering a coherent world view, but at the same time they are long, slow-paced, repetitive, and after a full day's work, quite tiring. Community pressure has been the primary force encouraging attendance in the face of these inconveniences; but as villages have grown to several times their previous size and new diversions and acculturated attitudes compete with traditional culture, community pressure seems to have less effect. Many villages now feel the need to enforce attendance formally, by recording the names of absent members and applying sanctions against anyone who misses frequently.

The Cuna also hold such sacred meetings with participants from more than one island. Individual chiefs visit other islands to sing there, and leaders from neighboring villages come together from time to time for a few days of singing, speech-making, and feasting. Within the framework of a religious observance, the gatherings constitute a medium of alliance and communication between villages and a source of solidarity to the Cuna as a whole.

In the last two decades or so, the Cuna have been using writing to expand and formalize this arrangement. They record the names of delegates, schedule meetings on a regular basis, and send written invitations and reminders. During the meetings, they take attendance each night, march delegates off to meals according to their places on lists, and follow up with elaborate reports. Currently, delegates from all the 48 villages of San Blas hold a mass singing meeting several times a year, islands in three regional groupings come together every two or three weeks, and individual chiefly visits and informal reunions among neighboring islands continue as before. Clearly, out of the simple material of chiefly visiting, the Cuna have constructed a dominant institution in their regional politics, a development that could not have occurred without writing.

Other aspects of religion and ritual have been affected by writing, though in somewhat less spectacular ways than the singing gatherings. Many villages also take attendance at puberty ceremonies and menarche rituals, which occur several times a year on the average. Villages also sponsor elaborate eight-day exorcism rituals once every few years, as the need to put the spirit world in order arises (Howe 1976). Such rituals require an elaborate division of labor among a large number of men, both trained exorcists and volunteers, all of them recorded on a list, and they call for a great many medicines and materials, which must be collected in Colombia, the Darien interior, and other parts of San Blas as well as locally. The management of men and materials is done with the help of lists.

The Cuna also use writing to verify ritual competence. There are a great many ritual specialties, which take anywhere from two weeks to 30 years to learn. Esoteric learning provides one of the most important avenues to prestige; and since men often apprentice themselves away from their home villages, potential rivals, clients, and patients are eager to verify claims to knowledge and ritual mastery. Although most villages prefer that a teacher come testify in person to his pupil's "graduation," as a substitute they will accept a testimonial letter. Some villages, going one step further, require the letter in addition to the personal appearance, so as to provide a more enduring record.

Maintaining Village Boundaries

Native-born members make up the majority of the population of most Cuna islands. Inter-village visiting is very common, however; and nontraditional salaried jobs such as pastor, teacher, and agricultural laborer often take individuals to other islands, where they can fall in love or develop other attachments. Outsiders ask to immigrate and often to marry-in frequently enough to constitute a recurrent and time-consuming problem for village councils. Some villages actively discourage or even prohibit such immigration, and even those who are more accepting approach the subject with caution: petitioners may have left wives and children behind in their previous home; if they lack lands in their new village, they may be driven to theft; or they may turn out to be troublemakers of other sorts. Even if well-behaved, they may maintain divided loyalties between their new and old homes, eventually returning to their natal villages and taking their wives with them.

When two villages are immediate neighbors or occupy the same island, some of the difficulties of immigration (such as landlessness or limited information about a petitioner's past history) are lessened, but others are exacerbated. From the turn of the century to the 1960s, a number of Cuna communities fissioned, leaving two villages in the place of one, with the households pledged to each side thoroughly intermixed in most cases. Several other islands have only one village but lie within a few hundred yards of another that derives from the same parent population. In the mid-1970s most of the divided islands reunited, but until then the problems of village boundaries and autonomy were acute in such communities, notably when a man from one side wished to marry a woman from the other. For which village should he work? Which gathering should he and his wife attend? If household disputes arose, which village should adjudicate them? When two villages felt animosity toward each other, such cases had explosive potential.

Again, the Cuna often handled such problems with writing. Many villages established membership lists for adult members, clearly demarcating who did or did not belong. If an outsider from another village asked to immigrate and a village was favorably disposed, they sent a letter to the leaders of his home village, requesting a character reference and permission for him to switch allegiance. Whether from another island or the other side of a divided island, once accepted, a newcomer was in many cases immediately forced to sign the community rolls, while village leaders spelled out the (supposedly) irrevocable nature of this commitment. Some villages also charge a set fee to immigrants. The result of all these measures has been to do away almost completely with dual or ambiguous membership: one is either a member or one is not. They have also contributed to a process of individuation, a topic to which I return in the following section.

Expanding and Formalizing Communal Labor

In the past the Cuna handled a number of tasks through village communal labor. Each community built its own gathering house and *chicha* house, and it provided communally-built homes for its members. At the elaborate female puberty ceremonies and the somewhat simpler rituals that follow immediately after menarche, it contributed materials, labor, and the participation of all its members. For marriage it provided direction and a strong-arm crew to capture the groom, for whom marriage usually came as a surprise in those days. Some communities may have taken on other tasks as well. Cuna villages evidently attached considerable importance to these functions as signs of village solidarity as well as for their practical benefits, but they organized communal labor on a fairly informal basis. A village's primary chief, its policemen, and its notables provided whatever co-ordination was necessary, and formal sanctions to enforce participation were lacking.

Then, beginning in the 1920s, a number of Cuna villages began to expand and formalize communal labor, and over the years since then many others have followed suit. They added on new offices to manage specific tasks, including house chiefs, marriage chiefs, *chicha* chiefs, path chiefs (to supervise the clearing of trails in the forest), canoe chiefs (to oversee the hauling of canoe logs out of the forest), and cemetery chiefs. While continuing traditional kinds of construction, villages have added many new forms, building schools, churches, village-owned stores, wharfs, sea walls, drainage canals, maternity huts, health centers, and in some cases even airstrips. In the past, villages were concerned with finance to a very limited extent or not at all, but today they have acquired such sources of revenue as wharf taxes, fines, fees, lotteries, and special levies. Many villages have gone into business on a considerable scale by setting up coconut plantations, running launches up and down the coast, founding stores and bakeries—in all of which they compete with enterprises owned by individuals and co-operative societies. In short, an impressive array of communal objects and services, along with an administrative apparatus to manage them, have developed out of a relatively modest program of communal labor.

The development of this system has depended at almost every point on writing, in particular on lists, and most task managers have their own secretary or secretaries. Villages keep lists of their able-bodied workers, on which they enroll each male at a certain age or point in the life cycle. Other lists govern the order in which householders receive village services, such as communal housebuilding and support during puberty ceremonies. For house-building and public works, villages keep lists of the poles, thatch, stone, sand, and other materials owed by each worker.

Compliance is also enforced through writing. At work sessions secretaries take attendance and record the materials provided. Those who fail to work or meet their quota of materials are fined, often by amounts quite substantial relative to average cash income, and lists are maintained that record every man's indebtedness to the village. A great many Cuna men leave San Blas periodically for wage labor; while they are away, their villages continue recording their absence from work sessions and fining them. When they return they must pay off their accumulated debt before they will be allowed to leave again. One motive for levying these fines is to ensure that work parties turn out in sufficient numbers and that everyone pulls his share. Given the frequency of disputes and complaints about absenteeism, such measures seem justified. On the other hand, everyone is expected to miss occasionally, and no one blames the migrant laborers for the sessions they have missed. The fines are intended less as punishment than as compensation equivalent to the work done by other men. In effect, they convert a work tax into a monetary tax. (For a similar case, see Kobben 1973).

Keeping track of village finances and commercial ventures of course requires extensive use of writing. Receipts are given for taxes on trading boats and vendors who sell in the streets, as well as for fines and permit fees. Lotteries and special levies have their own lists, and village-owned enterprises record inventory, income, payments, and so forth. In this last area, however, my own experience and that of another ethnographer of the Cuna (Holloman 1969) indicate that bookkeeping procedures vary widely in efficiency and completeness. In most businesses, public and private, they tend to be very sketchy and crude. Typically, the most important protection against embezzlement is to divide the custody of a cash box and its key between two different men, rather than to keep careful accounts. This inefficiency in record-keeping hampers Cuna businesses, many of which have failed through gradual undetected embezzlement, mismanagement, or ignorance of how the business is faring.

It should be noted that the changes in communal labor have consisted of more than expansion and partial bureaucratization. They have also transformed the meaning of membership in a Cuna village, by making heavy demands on the time of villagers and by isolating the individual in his relations with the collectivity. In the past, communal labor depended on a diffuse ethic of mutual support, enforced only by informal pressures, and it consisted in large part of labor exchanges between members within the community. Today the Cuna sometimes persist in discussing communal labor in terms of this model, but the actual organization of that labor emphasizes mutual obligation between each individual and the village as a whole. As it now stands, task organization requires that a village keep track separately of each man (or for some tasks, each woman or household) in terms of his present and future obligations, his failures to meet past obligations, his accumulated debts to the village, and his requests for support. Thus communal labor reinforces the process of individuation already noted above, making village membership as much like citizenship in a modern nation or municipality as in a nineteenth century Cuna village.

My conclusion here, that writing promotes individuation, seems to echo that of several other writers (Carothers 1959; Riesman 1960; McLuhan 1964; Goody & Watt 1968). The Cuna case does not, however, lend any support to claims that writing necessarily encourages individualism or greater social concern for the uniqueness of each person. Having one's own place on a list of village workers, or, in the case of our own society, one's own file in the archives of a bureaucracy, does not make one stand out from the crowd—quite the opposite. The individuation here is administrative: it distinguishes people as units so that they can all be treated alike.

Keeping the Peace

The procedures by which Cuna villages resolve disputes and handle offenses have gone through changes comparable to those in communal labor, and again, writing has encouraged the solution of these procedures in particular directions. Here I focus on three key aspects of this process: the codification of law, the development of sanctions, and the recording of verdicts.

Written Law

Writing has served to systematize and formalize village law. In the present and remembered past each village has set its own consensus on proper conduct and procedures. While villages try to respect past precedents and keep within broad areas of agreement characteristic of the Cuna as a whole, they recognize that they have departed from the past and that each village must establish its own consensus. For instance, many or all Cuna villages used to consider divorce a private matter to be handled by a couple and the wife's father. Now many villages intercede in divorce cases, though some merely try to resolve the causes of a marital dispute, while others attempt (with only partial success) to forbid divorce altogether.

Many villages now write down their laws, and in some cases they have constructed elaborate codes covering a great many fields of conduct— the code for the largest village in San Blas contains more than 200 articles.[4] In formulating laws, it is clear that they had certain ends in mind. They praised and supported written laws in large part because the laws regularized procedures and encouraged equal treatment for all, thus, they hoped, transcending the weaknesses of individuals and limiting the discretionary powers of village leaders. In effect, they echoed a phrase often used in popular discussions of law and government in the United States— "the rule of laws, not of men."

It appears that by writing laws down, villages have turned general agreements and areas of consensus into something more precise and narrow. In place of an understanding that potential immigrants should be discouraged, for instance, they create a rule specifying when, how, and from where outsiders may be accepted. I cannot state with certainty just how far writing has changed customary law in this respect, because my informants were vague about the form of village regulations in the past; but to one extent or another writing does seem to have pushed them in the direction of precision and fixity. At the same time, it has reinforced the tradition of local autonomy and separatism, and it has encouraged villages to deal with new situations through legislation, as when several communities reacted to gasoline pollution of their rivers by closing them to outboard motors.

The idea of writing seems almost as important to the native conception of laws as the actuality. Speakers in village meetings often cite written laws or allude to the fact that a law has been recorded without consulting the document itself. In a couple of instances I observed when they did attempt to consult the code, it could not be located immediately or at all because a secretary had misplaced it, and in one embarrassing case it turned out that the regulation in question had not in fact been written down.

At least in the village that I know best and one or two others, the men meet occasionally in special legislative session specifically for the purpose of drafting and revising laws, and from time to time they modify individual regulations that seem out of step with current conditions. They experience difficulties, however, in thoroughly separating their legislative pose from administration and adjudication, and generally in keeping to the laws once they have established them, because the council consists of the same men regardless of the capacity in which they meet. They adjudicate disputes collectively, and a new consensus on an issue hammered out within an adjudication is binding and legal, even if it goes against a written law. Each judicial decision can be as much an examination of the law as of the particulars in the case at hand. The men appreciate this dilemma and worry about it, as the following excerpt from an adjudication indicates:

> When we gathered this law (*ikar*), all of us together, with the young men sitting here, we gathered this law. The elders all said, in complete agreement, "Let's not accept people from other places any more. Just us, only people from around here we'll accept. As far as Akkwapirmai in one direction and Namakkettup in the other"—thus we said. We deliberated, we did it, without any disagreement, we laid down the law, we did it. Our secretary worked too. He wrote it up right. . . . We didn't anticipate that later things would get fouled up. . . . We act this way. From time to time the law gets trampled on. The law that we ourselves made, later we take it apart.

Here the Cuna seem to be struggling to reconcile writing and the advantages they perceive in codified law with the flexibility of their decision-making and administrative procedures.

Punishment

According to my oldest informants, in the early years of this century the Cuna stressed the importance of public verbal admonishments in dealing with misconduct. In those years they inflicted only a few punishments, most notably the application of stinging nettles to an offender's body. In cases of homicide and wounding (which were and are rare), they sometimes left retribution to the victim's kinsmen. Today the emphasis on admonishing continues, and village elders frequently lecture those

guilty of misdemeanors without punishing them in any other way; but
self-help has all but disappeared, and the Cuna have brought together an
array of sanctions unknown in the past (Howe 1974; Holloman 1969).

Some villages have attempted to increase consistency and fairness by
fixing the penalties for each kind of offense, and even those that impose
punishments on a more flexible and ad hoc basis depend on writing to
record each sentence and keep track of implementing it. In the past, when
a village had an offender thrashed with stinging nettles or inflicted some
other kind of direct retribution, by necessity it acted soon after the offense
occurred. Today on the other hand, it may impose a certain number of
hours of sweeping the streets or a certain number of canoe loads of gravel
for its wharf demands that take at least several days to meet. In the same
way, it may levy a fine that exceeds the culprit's immediate cash resources,
forcing the village to collect in stages. Differences among the several field
sites studied by Holloman and myself indicate that the effectiveness and
degree of impartiality with which adjudicators apply sanctions vary somewhat (Holloman 1969); but clearly, however well or poorly this system
works in particular cases, to work at all it requires writing.

One important sanction, the exit permit, depends on writing to an
even greater extent than do fines and work punishments. According to
older informants, Cuna villages have for a long time been exerting some
control over their members' movements. When the Panamanian government began regulating the movement of Cuna in and out of the reservation and demanding documentation several decades ago, the villages
began to issue travel permits (cf. Holloman 1969). Except for brief visits
to neighboring islands, no Cuna may travel in San Blas or leave the
reserve without his village's written permission. Islands cooperate with
each other by demanding permits from visitors, and the government
collects permits from anyone leaving the reserve. Villages may deny permits as a primary sanction, or instance to discipline men and women who
fail to attend the sacred gatherings regularly. They may also use them as a
secondary reinforcement for fines and work punishments, by requiring
that anyone who wishes to leave clear all debts to the village first. Given
the large number of men who leave San Blas for wage labor, and the
pleasure Cuna take in visiting other islands, the permits provide an effective sanction.

Until recently, however, Cuna villages found it difficult to control
their members while they were outside San Blas. Information on a migrant worker's conduct might trickle back to the reserve, but only inter-
mittently and unreliably; and although a man who misbehaved in the city
or neglected the family he left behind might find himself confined to the
island for a long period upon his return, in the meanwhile he was more or

less out of reach. Since 1970, however, quite a few villages have set up community organizations in Panama City and Colón called *capítulos*. *Capítulos* and their villages exchange information about the misbehavior of migrant workers. Villages periodically send lists of the sums owed by absent members for the communal sessions they have missed, to be collected in the city. And when a man decides to return home, he must now obtain a reverse travel permit from his capitulo. Thus, unless a Cuna completely severs his ties with San Blas, his home community continues to influence his conduct.

Case Records and Depositions

In important trouble cases secretaries try to record not only the eventual decision and the penalty if any, but also the gist of what witnesses and adjudicants say. This is a largely hopeless task, given the speed with which the Cuna speak, and in my experience they usually end up taking down the essence of a few, presumably key statements in a very sketchy and muddled Spanish. If the men wish to refresh their memories concerning what was decided in a particular case, the secretary uses his record as a mnemonic aid, combining his notes with his recollections to reconstruct the case. Here again, writing seems to affect legal ideas as well as legal practice, because it reinforces the idea of the gathering committing itself to a clear-cut decision, one to which it can refer back if the same problem comes up again even if the members have forgotten just what they had decided.

In a seeming extension of case records, the Cuna use village books to record information and public commitments. The announcements and graduation letters for ritualists mentioned above are often recorded there. In the same vein, a number of other situations call for someone to make a public statement or commitment in the gathering and have it recorded. Couples who adopt children (as opposed to merely fostering them) announce their intentions; and if as is usual they intend to have the adopted child inherit land from them, they announce this as well. Any testamentary disposition of property, in fact, can be secured by announcing it ahead of time, so the heirs who would inherit in the absence of a special testament cannot subvert its intentions: a common example occurs when a childless person wishes to leave land to a helpful nephew instead of letting all of it pass to his siblings.

Such dispositions are not always voluntary: in one case witnessed, a village forced an elderly member who had an adopted daughter to affirm and formalize an old informal promise made when she was young to give her land, as he had been showing signs of wanting to leave it all to his sons. The gathering uses the same procedure to handle some complicated interpersonal situations, especially domestic problems; for the sake of consistency and order, they may force someone to stick to a certain course of action, even if the alternatives do not violate village laws. In divorce cases, for instance, when a couple has indicated a supposedly irrevocable desire to separate, the gathering sometimes extracts a promise from the wife's father not to accept his son-in-law back even if they want to reunite. The public promise, whether volunteered or coerced, sets a certain course of action, and the written record ensures that the commitment is preserved and honored. Here, as in other areas of social control, the Cuna are clearly concerned not only with composing problems that have already occurred, but also with forestalling reoccurrences of past problems and slowing down, putting the brakes, on the flux and disorder of village life.

Conclusion

This paper shares a defect with most historical studies that attempt to identify the causes of social change: a dependence on a relatively weak research paradigm called the "pretest-posttest," which compares the state of a dependent variable before and after the introduction of an independent variable without the benefit of a control group or random sampling (Campbell & Stanley 1963; Brim & Spain 1974). The flaw in the pretest-posttest paradigm is that it can seldom definitively separate the effects of one independent variable, such as writing, from those of other, extraneous variables, such as acculturation, population growth, or encapsulation in a nation state.[5] Some anthropologists have attempted to handle this difficulty by arguing that in particular cases, some feature of the change situation such as geographic isolation has delayed, minimized, or even eliminated influences on the subject population other than the one being investigated. Sharp's (1952) "Steel Axes for Stone Age Australians" is a classic example, and well known analyses by Murphy and Steward (1955) and Harner (1972) fit the same mold. However, in a great many cases, including that of the Cuna, the considerable number of influences working at the same time rule out this argument.

The case for writing is stronger than it might be, however, because many of the changes discussed in this paper concern attributes, i.e., the presence or absence of traits rather than the extent of their presence or rates of change, and because most of these changes depend on writing in a very direct way. Thus, I cannot eliminate other variables but at the same time I need not; because I am not arguing that writing effected these changes by itself, but rather that it was indispensable to them.

It is clear that, along with writing as a general mode of communication, the Cuna accepted specific written forms and the idea of applying writing to certain political tasks, such as the codification of laws. Concerning other applications of writing, such as taking attendance at rituals or requiring "diploma" letters from ritualists, I do not know whether the first Cuna to think of using writing in these ways borrowed the ideas from the surrounding hispanic cultures or conceived of them independently. It does not really matter, because the basic forms used in Cuna politics— the letter, the list, and the public record—are fundamental and universal rather than culturally contingent, and because the Cuna adapted these forms to ends that are peculiarly Cuna (Panamanians do not take attendance in church, for example).

It is, in fact, the distinctively Cuna nature of many of the changes encouraged by writing that argues most strongly against glossing them as acculturation. Contrary to the popular assumption that writing and schools immediately and invariably homogenize culture, many of the changes fostered by writing make the Cuna no more like Panama or Colombia than they were before. In the taking of attendance at rituals, the expansion of regional singing gatherings, and the regulation of ritual learning, writing has preserved or even increased differences with the national culture, just as many of the Cuna who first accepted writing hoped it would. This immediate turning of writing toward traditional ends seems to be one of the constants or near-constants of the sociology of writing. Thus the Mae-Enga of Highland New Guinea have their literate sons record the details of pig-exchanges (Meggitt 1968); the Somali draw up contracts for vengeance groups (Lewis 1968); Meso-American communities keep lists of candidates for their civil-religious hierarchies (Cancian 1965); and the Kwakiutl, to get around a Canadian law forbidding gift exchanges at large gatherings, at one point held "walking potlatches," in which the donor went from door to door giving gifts, with a secretary along to record his generosity (Drucker & Heizer 1967).

Clearly, the members of previously nonliterate cultures quickly perceive uses for writing. The absence of writing is a severe organizational restraint on many activities and institutions, in small-scale local communities as well as large chiefdoms and states, and the introduction of writing can free social systems to develop in directions previously denied them. Just as writing permitted the florescence of regional singing meetings among the Cuna, in Madagascar it encouraged men to compete for prestige through control of esoteric knowledge (Bloch 1968), and in Meso-America it made modification of some *cargo* systems possible (Cancian 1965). These changes should deter us from assuming that social systems as they are at any one moment reflect in any direct fashion the values and wishes of their members. In many cases, such systems may in effect be waiting for the opportunity to change, pushing against the restraints that currently bind them.

What is most striking about the effects of writing on Cuna political organization is the resemblance, not to Panama in particular, but to generic aspects of political evolution and organizational complexity. Traits that in this case turn up in small, quasi-tribal villages have been repeatedly identified as features of the rise of the state, the development of bureaucracies and other complex organizations, political "modernization," and general political evolution. Writing has, for instance, rendered Cuna political procedures more routine, specific, impersonal, unambiguous, and official—that is, they have become what has variously been called rational, secular, modern, bureaucratic (Blau 1956; Almond and Powell 1966; Peacock and Kirsch 1973). It has at the same time promoted individuation by making village membership and rights and duties vis-à-vis the village specific to individuals (cf. Durkheim 1964).

Most important, writing has facilitated the expansion of Cuna government and the differentiation of its parts into a more functionally specific division of labor, perhaps the most frequently noted attributes of social and political evolution (e.g., Spencer 1972; Durkheim 1964; Eisenstadt 1964; Almond and Powell 1966; Naroll 1970; Driver 1973; Carneiro 1973; Tatje and Naroll 1973). This process consists of the overall differentiation of village government from the rest of social organization and the separation of major governmental functions, as well as the more specific addition of new tasks and offices. Although in most Cuna villages the assembled men still deal communally with village matters of all sorts, they have begun to separate their legislative, judicial, and administrative poses more thoroughly than before, leaving behind the multiplex and multifunctional diffuseness often noted in traditional political roles and institutions (Easton 1959; Almond and Powell 1966; Fried 1967; Service 1975). Several progressive islands have even carried this differentiation one step further by establishing separate tribunals, legislative committees, and administrative boards. It can be expected that other communities will follow their lead in the next few years. The result of this process, even at the stage reached by the less innovative islands, is that each Cuna village has a government, not just a political organization.

I am not suggesting, however, that writing universally promotes these results, especially not in small indigenous communities. The examples discussed in the volume edited by Goody (1968), for instance, differ too much to allow such a generalization. The Cuna have been able to follow the course they set because, first, circumstances have allowed them some measure of autonomy and freedom in which changes could take place, since the traditional political system has neither been destroyed by outside forces nor ossified by an inflexible variety of indirect rule. Second, the Cuna have had a solid base on which to build—a tradition of local self-determination and strongly corporate villages, each with its own leadership and procedures for decision-making. Thus, it is not surprising that Cuna villages have gone through some of the changes characteristic of large-scale polities. The villages are not of course miniature states or bureaucracies, and writing has not done away with the essentially face-to-face nature of their politics; but they do share enough features with these more complex political organizations to develop in similar ways.

NOTES

1. This article is based on field research among the Cuna, from February, 1970 to February, 1971, September through November, 1971, June through August, 1975, and September, 1977 through May, 1978. I gratefully acknowledge financial support for this fieldwork from the National Institutes of Health, the National Endowment for the Humanities, and the Social Science Research Council. Preliminary versions of this paper were presented at a seminar sponsored by the Asociación Panameña de Antropología in July, 1976 and at the annual meetings of the American Anthropological Association in Houston, November, 1977. I received several helpful comments from the audiences at those presentations and from friends who read the article manuscript, notably from Francisco Herrera, Regina Holloman, Jean Jackson, Olga Linares, and Phillip Young.

2. These figures come from a preliminary data sheet from the 1970 census of Panama, which I was allowed to copy at the Panamanian national census bureau.

3. On the other hand, I have uncovered very little evidence of secretaries using writing in factional struggles, for instance by distorting or withholding village records, although secretaries sometimes play an active role in such struggles (cf. Frankenberg 1957).

4. Mac Chapin and Arnulfo Prestán provided me with copies of the laws from this village for two different years.

5. Moreover, like many other anthropologists studying social change, I have been forced to use a weakened version of this paradigm, one in which the state of the dependent variables before the introduction of writing is reconstructed from the memories of informants (Brim & Spain 1974). I would argue, however, that confidence in this reconstruction should be strengthened by agreement among informants on its essential points, and by information on the organization of villages which have begun using writing in government only very recently or have yet to do so. On the other hand, contemporary data do not provide much help in eliminating extraneous independent variables, since villages that delayed in accepting writing tend to be smaller, more isolated, and generally more conservative than those that began using writing some time ago.

354   JAMES HOWE

BIBLIOGRAPHY

Almond, G., and G. Powell. 1966. Comparative Politics. Boston.
Basso, K. 1974. The Ethnography of Writing. Explorations in the Ethnography of Speaking, eds. R. Bauman and J. Sherzer, pp. 433–452. Cambridge.
Blau, P. 1956. Bureaucracy in Modern Society. New York.
Bloch, M. 1968. Astrology and Writing in Madagascar. Literacy in Traditional Societies, ed. J. Goody, pp. 277–297. Cambridge.
Brim, J., and D. Spain. 1974. Research Design in Anthropology. New York.
Campbell, D., and J. Stanley. 1963. Experimental and Quasi-Experimental Designs for Research. Chicago.
Cancian, F. 1965. Economics and Prestige in a Maya Community. Stanford.
Carneiro, R. 1973. The Four Faces of Evolution: Unilinear, Universal, Multilinear, and Differential. Handbook of Social and Cultural Anthropology, ed. J. Honigmann, pp. 89–110. Chicago.
Carothers, J. 1959. Culture, Psychiatry, and the Written Word. Psychiatry 22: 307–320.
Cipolla, C. 1969. Literacy and Development in the West. Baltimore.
Cullen, E. 1853. Isthmus of Darien Ship Canal. London.
Diringer, D. 1948. The Alphabet: A Key to the History of Mankind. New York.
Driver, H. 1973. Cross-Cultural Studies. Handbook of Social and Cultural Anthropology, ed. J. Honigmann, pp. 327–368. Chicago.
Drucker, P., and R. Heizer, 1967. To Make My Name Good. Berkeley. Drukheim, E. 1964. The Division of Labor in Society. New York.
Easton, D. 1959. Political Anthropology. Biennial Review of Anthropology, pp. 210–262.
Eisenstadt, S. 1964. Social Change, Differentiation, and Evolution. American Sociological Review 29: 373–386.
Frankenberg, R. 1957. Village on the Border. London.
Fried, M. 1967. The Evolution of Political Society. New York.
Gelb, I. 1952. A Study of Writing: The Foundations of Grammatology. Chicago.
Goody, J., (ed.) 1968. Literacy in Traditional Societies. Cambridge.
Goody, J., and I. Watt. 1968. The Consequences of Literacy. Literacy in Traditional Societies, ed. J. Goody, pp. 27–68. Cambridge.
Harner, M. 1972. The Jivaro. Garden City, N.Y.
Holloman, R. 1969. Developmental Change in San Blas. Unpublished Ph.D. dissertation, Northwestern University.
Howe, J. 1974. Village Political Organization Among the San Blas Cuna. Unpublished Ph.D. dissertation, University of Pennsylvania.
———. 1976. Smoking out the Spirits: A Cuna Exorcism. Ritual and Symbolism in Native Central America, eds. P. Young and J. Howe, pp. 67–77. Eugene.
Joyce, L. 1934. Introduction. A New Voyage and Description of the Isthmus of America, by Lionel Wafer, ed. L. Joyce, pp. xi–lxvii. Oxford.
Kobben, A. 1973. Cause and Intention. A Handbook of Method in Cultural Anthropology, eds. R. Naroll and R. Cohen, pp. 89–98. New York.

Lewis, I. 1968. Literacy in a Nomadic Society: The Somali Case. Literacy in Traditional Societies, ed. J. Goody, pp. 265–276. Cambridge.

McLuhan, M. 1964. Understanding Media. New York.

Meggitt, M. 1968. The Uses of Literacy in New Guinea and Melanesia. Literacy in Traditional Societies, ed. J. Goody, pp. 298–310. Cambridge.

Murphy, R., and J. Steward. 1955. Tappers and Trappers: Parallel Processes in Acculturation. Economic Development and Culture Change 4: 335–355.

Naroll, R. 1970. What Have We Learned from Cross-Cultural Studies? American Anthropologist 72: 1227–1288.

Nordenskiold, E., with R. Perez Kantule. ed. S. H. Wassen. 1938. An Historical and Ethnological Survey of the Cuna Indians. Goteborg.

Peacock, J., and A. T. Kirsch. 1973. The Human Direction. New York.

Riesman, D. 1960. The Oral and Written Traditions. Explorations in Communication, eds. E. Carpenter and M. McLuhan, pp. 109–16. Boston.

Service, E. 1975. Origins of the State and Civilization. New York.

Sharp, R. L. 1952. Steel Axes for Stone Age Australians. Human Organization 11: 17–22.

Spencer, H. 1972. The Social Organism. Herbert Spencer on Social Evolution, Selected Writing, ed. J. Peel, pp. 53–70. Chicago.

Stout, D. 1947. San Blas Cuna Acculturation: An Introduction. New York.

Tatje, T., and R. Naroll. 1973. Two Measures of Societal Complexity: An Empirical Cross-Cultural Comparison. A Handbook of Method in Cultural Anthropology, eds. R. Naroll and R. Cohen, pp. 766–833. New York.

Ullman, B. 1969. Ancient Writing and Its Influence. Cambridge.

Bibliography

Please note that the following bibliography is by no means exhaustive of the rich ethnographic and theoretical published materials bearing on political anthropology. In addition to works cited in the introduction, the editors have listed books which they believe may be of benefit for the readers to explore in their own quests for understanding. Such a list is only suggestive.

Abrahams, R. and John Szwed. *After Africa*. New Haven, 1983.

Amin, Samir. *Unequal Development.* Paris, 1972.

Anderson, Perry. *Lineages of the Absolutist State*. London, 1974.

Asad, Talal. *Anthropology and the Colonial Encounter*. Ithaca, 1973.

Aston, T. H. and C. H. Pnilpin. *The Brenner Debate*. Cambridge, 1985.

Bailey, F. G. *Morality and Expediency*. Oxford, 1977.

————. *Stratagems and Spoils.*, New York, 1964.

Balandier, Georges. *Political Anthropology*. New York, 1970.

Banton, M. *Political Systems and the Distribution of Power*. London, 1965.

Barth, Frederick. *Political Leadership Among the Swat Pathans*. London, 1959.

Bloch, Maurice. *Marxism and Anthropology*. Oxford, 1983.

Bolland, O. Nigel. *Colonization and Resistance in Belize*. Belize, 1988.

Braudel, Fernand. *Capitalism and Material Life, 1400–1800*. New York, 1973.

Claessen, Henri and P. Skalnick. *The Early State*. The Hague, 1978.

Cohen, Abner. *The Politics of Elite Culture*. Berkeley and Los Angeles, 1981.

————. *Two-Dimensional Man.* London, 1974.

Cohen, R., and John Middleton. *Comparative Political Systems*. Austin, Texas, 1967.

Colson, Elizabeth. *Tradition and Contract.* Chicago, 1974.

Durkhein, Emile. *The Rules of Sociological Method*. Paris, 1895.

Donham, Donald. *History, Power, Ideology: Central Issues in Marxism and Anthropology.* Cambridge, 1990.

Engels, Frederick. *The Origins of the Family, Private Property, and the State*. New York, 1881.

Epstein, S. *Politics in an Urban African Community*. Manchester, 1956.

Evans-Pritchard, E. E. *The Nuer*. Oxford, 1940.

Fallers, Lloyd. *Bantu Bureaucracy*. London, 1963.

Fogelson, R. P., and R. Adams. *The Anthropology of Power.* New York, 1979.

Fortes, M. *The Dynamics of Clanship Among the Tallensi*. London, 1945.

Fortes, M., and E. E. Evans-Pritchard. *African Political Systems*. Oxford, 1940.

Frank, André G. *World Accumulation, 1441–1789*. New York, 1978.

Friedman, Jonathan. *System, Structuring, and Contradiction*. Copenhagen, 1979.

Gailey, C. W. *From Kinship to Kingship*. Austin, Texas, 1987.

Geertz, C. *Agricultural Involution*. Berkeley and Los Angeles, 1966.

Gledhill, J., B. Bender, and M. Larsen, eds. *State and Society*. London, 1988.

Gluckman, Max. *Order and Rebellion in Tribal Africa*. London, 1963.

———. *Political Law and Ritual in Tribal Society*. Oxford, 1965.

Godelier, M. *The Mental and the Material*. London, 1988.

———. *Perspectives in Marxist Anthropology*. Cambridge, 1977.

Hannerz, U. *Soulside*. New York, 1968.

Herskovitz, M. *The Myth of the Negro Past*. New York, 1940.

Hobsbawm, Eric. *The Age of Empire*. New York, 1989.

Kahn, J., and J. Llobera. *The Anthropology of Pre-Capitalist Societies*. Atlantic Highlands, N.J., 1981.

Kopytoff, Iyor. *The African Frontier*. Bloomington, IN, 1987.

Leach, Edmond. *Political Systems of Highland Burma*. Boston, 1954.

Leacock, E., and R. B. Lee. *Politics and History in Band Societies*. New York, 1982.

Lewellen, Ted. *Political Anthropology*. Boston, 1983.

Maine, Henry. *Ancient Law*. London, 1887.

Mann, Michael. *The Sources of Social Power*. Cambridge, 1986.

Meillasoux, Claude. *Maidens, Meal and Money*. Cambridge, 1981.

Mintz, S. *Caribbean Transformations*. New York, 1990.

Moore, Barrington. *The Social Origins of Dictatorship and Democracy*. Boston, 1966.

Morgan, Lewis Henry. *Ancient Society*. New York, 1877.

Morgen, Sandra. *Gender and Anthropology*. Washington, 1989.

Nash, J. *We Eat the Mines and the Mines Eat Us*. New York, 1979.

Patterson. T., and C. Gailey. *Power Relations and State Formation*. Washington, 1987.

Radcliffe-Brown, A. R. *Structure and Function in Primitive Society*. London, 1952.

Rey, P. P. *Les Alliances des Classes*. Paris, 1976.

Roseberry, William. *Anthropology and History*. New Brunswick, 1984.

Sahlins, Marshal. *Stone Age Economics*. Chicago, 1972.

Scott, James. *Domination and the Arts of Resistance*. New Haven, 1990.

Seaton, S. Lee, and H. Claessen. *Political Anthropology*. The Hague, 1979.

Skocpol, Theda. *State and Social Revolution*. Cambridge, 1979.

Smith, R. T. *Kinship and Class in the West Indies*. Cambridge, 1989.

Southall, Aiden. *Alur Society*. Cambridge, 1953.

Swartz, Marc, Victor Turner, and Arthur Tuden. *Political Anthropology*. Chicago, 1966.

Taussig, M. *The Devil and Commodity Fetishism in Latin America*. Chapel Hill, 1980.

Terray, E. *Marxism and Primitive Societies*. New York, 1971.

Turner, Victor. *Schism and Continuity in an African Society*. Manchester, 1957.

Upham, Steadman. *The Evolution of Political Systems.* Cambridge, 1990.

Van Velsen, J. *The Politics of Kinship.* Manchester, 1964.

Vincent, Joan. *Anthropology and Politics.* Tucson, 1990.

Wallerstein, Immanuel. *The Modern World System.* New York, 1974.

Whitten, N. and J. Szwed. *Afro-American Anthropology.* New York, 1970.

Williams, Raymond. *The Country and the City.* New York, 1973.

Wolf, Eric. *Europe and the People Without History.* Berkeley and Los Angeles, 1982.

―――. *Peasant Wars of the Twentieth Century.* New York, 1969.

Worsley, Peter. *The Trumpet Shall Sound.* London, 1957.